BEYOND THE PLEASURE PRINCIPLE

broadview editions
series editor: L.W. Conolly

BEYOND THE PLEASURE PRINCIPLE

Sigmund Freud

edited by Todd Dufresne
and translated by Gregory C. Richter

broadview editions

Library and Archives Canada Cataloguing in Publication

Freud, Sigmund, 1856-1939
[Jenseits des Lustprinzips. English]
    Beyond the pleasure principle / Sigmund Freud ; edited by Todd Dufresne
and translated by Gregory C. Richter.

(Broadview editions)
Includes bibliographical references and index.
ISBN 978-1-55111-994-6

    1. Psychoanalysis. 2. Pleasure principle (Psychology).
I. Dufresne, Todd, 1966- II. Richter, Gregory C. III. Title.
IV. Jenseits des Lustprinzips. English V. Series: Broadview
editions

BF173.F65 2011   150.19'52   C2011-900295-7

Broadview Editions
The Broadview Editions series represents the ever-changing canon of literature by
bringing together texts long regarded as classics with valuable lesser-known works.

Advisory editor for this volume: Juliet Sutcliffe

Broadview Press is an independent, international publishing house, incorporated in 1985.

We welcome comments and suggestions regarding any aspect of our
publications—please feel free to contact us at the addresses below or at
broadview@broadviewpress.com.

North America
PO Box 1243, Peterborough, Ontario, Canada K9J 7H5
2215 Kenmore Ave., Buffalo, New York, USA 14207
Tel: (705) 743-8990; Fax: (705) 743-8353
email: customerservice@broadviewpress.com

UK, Europe, Central Asia, Middle East, Africa, India, and Southeast Asia
Eurospan Group, 3 Henrietta St., London WC2E 8LU, United Kingdom
Tel: 44 (0) 1767 604972; Fax: 44 (0) 1767 601640
email: eurospan@turpin-distribution.com

Australia and New Zealand
NewSouth Books
c/o TL Distribution, 15-23 Helles Ave., Moorebank, NSW, Australia 2170
Tel: (02) 8778 9999; Fax: (02) 8778 9944
email: orders@tldistribution.com.au

www.broadviewpress.com

Broadview Press acknowledges the financial support of the Government of Canada
through the Canada Book Fund for our publishing activities.

This book is printed on paper containing 100% post-consumer fibre.

PRINTED IN CANADA

My part in this book I dedicate to MB-J and RG

—for time, freely given, and so taken.

TD

I gratefully dedicate my part in this book to my wife, Liyan.

GCR

Contents

Acknowledgements

Broadview editor Alex Sager championed this project and, with Greg Janzen, provided expert advice and guidance. Juliet Sutcliffe provided ideal editorial assistance: comprehensive, quick, and wise. Three blind reviews were useful and appreciated. I am also very pleased to acknowledge "Richter's Freud." Frankly, I would not have moved forward with this project without Greg Richter's new translations; translations that set a new standard for English readers of Freud. Beyond that, Greg's unfaltering good will, humor, and indulgence were invaluable. I thank Robert Kramer for pointing me in his direction.

I would also like to recognize the permissions departments that allowed the reproduction of their authors' work, always at fair rates. Without their cooperation, the book would be lesser—fewer pages, certainly, and less deep. A student researcher, Yuri Forbes-Petrovich, helped me get parts of this book in digital form, and helped with formatting. Chris Wood, a PhD candidate, helped me create some editorial notes, and prepared the entire index. An administrative assistant, Gail Fikis, also helped by typing a part of the manuscript. Thanks.

Parts of this book were funded by a grant supporting the Lakehead University Research Chair in Social & Cultural Theory, which I held between 2008 and 2010; and by a research grant from the Advanced Institute for Globalization & Culture (aig+c), also at Lakehead. I thank my colleagues in the Institute, as well as the VP of Research, Dr Rui Wang, for enabling my research activities during this period.

Finally, and as always, thanks to Dr Clara Sacchetti-Dufresne for indulging my interests, and to Chloe for being there.

"Shock and the Creative Process [1939]," from "On Some Motifs in Baudelaire," *Illuminations*, by Walter Benjamin, trans. Harry Zohn, New York: Schocken Books, 1969: 160-63. Excerpt from "On Some Motifs in Baudelaire" in *Illuminations* by Walter Benjamin, copyright 1955 by Suhrkamp Verlag, Frankfurt a.M., English translation by Harry Zohn copyright 1968 and renewed 1996 by Houghton Mifflin Harcourt Publishing Company, reprinted with permission of Houghton Mifflin Harcourt Publishing Company.

"Death, Desire, and Freud's Radical Turn [1954-55]," from *The Seminar of Jacques Lacan: Book II: The Ego in Freud's Theory and in the Technique of Psychoanalysis*, by Jacques Lacan, trans. Sylvia Tomaselli. Copyright 1978 by Les Editions du Seuil. English translation copyright 1988 by Cambridge University Press. Reprinted with permission of W.W. Norton & Company, Inc.

"On the Development of Mental Functioning [1958]," by Melanie Klein, from *Envy and Gratitude and Other Works, 1946-1963*, London: Hogarth Press, 1975: 236-46. Reprinted with permission of the Random House Group Ltd.

"Instinctual Dialectics against Instinctual Dualism" and "On Death, Time, and Eternity from Hegel to Freud [1959]," from *Life Against Death: The Psychoanalytical Meaning of History*, by Norman O. Brown, London Sphere Books, 1959: 79-82; 95-102.

"Superego and Culture: A Hermeneutic Interpretation" and "Open Questions: On Negation, Pleasure, Reality [1965]," by Paul Ricoeur, from *Freud and Philosophy: An Essay on Interpretation*, New Haven: Yale University Press, 1970: 293-338. Reprinted with permission of Yale University Press.

"Sadism, Masochism, and the Death Instinct [1967]," from "Coldness and Cruelty" by Gilles Deleuze in *Masochism* by Gilles Deleuze and Leopold von Sacher-Masoch, New York: Zone Books, 1991: 111-21. Reprinted with permission of Zone Books.

"The Mystic Writing Pad [1967]," from "Freud and the Scene of Writing," *Writing and Difference*, by Jacques Derrida, trans.

Alan Bass, Chicago: University of Chicago Press, 1978: 226-29. Reprinted with permission of University of Chicago Press.

"'A Decisive Correction': Non-Repressive Progress and Freud's Instinct Theory [1970]," from "Progress and Freud's Instinct Theory" in *Five Lectures: Psychoanalysis, Politics, and Utopia* by Herbert Marcuse, trans. Jeremy J. Shapiro and Shierry M. Weber, Boston: Beacon Press, 1970: 32-43.

"Economic Paradox of the Death Drive [1970]," from "Why the Death Drive?," *Life and Death in Psychoanalysis*, by Jean Laplanche, trans. Jeffrey Mehlman, Baltimore: Johns Hopkins University Press, 1976: 106-07, 110, 122-24. Reprinted with permission of Johns Hopkins University Press.

"First Positive Task of Schizoanalysis [1972]," translated by Helen Lane, Mark Seem, and Robert Hurley, from *Anti-Oedipus* by Gilles Deleuze and Felix Guattari, translated by Helen Lane, Mark Seem, and Robert Hurley, copyright 1977 by Viking Penguin Inc., English language translation. Pages 329-37. Reprinted with permission of Viking Penguin, a division of Penguin Group (USA) Inc.

"A Humanist Response to the Death Instinct Theory [1973]," from "The Power and Limits of the Death Instinct" in *The Anatomy of Human Destructiveness*, by Erich Fromm, New York: Holt, Rinehart and Winston, 1973: 463-69; 471.

"Scientific Discourse in Light of Metapsychological Speculation [1974]," from "The Witch Metapsychology" by Rodolphe Gasché in *Returns of the "French Freud": Freud, Lacan, and Beyond*, ed. Todd Dufresne, New York: Routledge, 1997.

"The Metaphor of the Death Drive and Its Counter-Finality [1976]," from "The Death Drive" in *Symbolic Exchange and Death*, by Jean Baudrillard, trans. Iain Hamilton Grant, London: Sage Publications, 1993.

"The Work of Death [1976]," from "On Death-Work" in *Frontiers in Psychoanalysis: Between Dream and Psychic Pain* by J.-B. Pontalis, trans. Catherine Cullen and Philip Cullen, London: Hogarth Press, 1981: 190-91.

"Freud, Aristophanes, and the Phantastic Hypothesis [1979]," from "Speculation: The Way to Utter Difference" in *The Legend of Freud* by Samuel Weber, Minneapolis: University of Minneapolis Press, 1982: 149-63. Copyright waived by Walter Verlag and provided by University of Minnesota Press.

"'A Kind of Discourse on Method': Freud's Performative Writing [1980]," from "To Speculate—On 'Freud'," *The Post Card: From Socrates to Freud and Beyond*, by Jacques Derrida, trans. Alan Bass, Chicago: University of Chicago Press, 1987: 273-74; 283-85; 298-304; 320-21; 322-23; 344-45; 358-59; 369-75; 377; 383-84; 385; 391; 405-06; 408. Reprinted with permission of University of Chicago Press.

"The Pleasures of Repetition: A Phenomenological Perspective [1987]," by Judith Butler, from *Pleasure Beyond the Pleasure Principle*, ed. Robert A. Glik and Stanley Bone, New Haven: Yale University Press, 1990: 260-61; 267-70; 271-73; 274-75. Reprinted with permission of Yale University Press.

"'The Possibility of Happiness': Absolute Narcissism and the Problem of Sociality [2000]," from "Sociality and the Absolute Narcissist," *Tales From the Freudian Crypt: The Death Drive in Text and Context*, by Todd Dufresne, Stanford: Stanford University Press, 2000: 158-64. Reprinted with permission of Stanford University Press.

"Paradox of the Freudian Death Drive [2006]," from *The Parallax View* by Slavoj Žižek, Cambridge, MA: The MIT Press, 2006: 62-63. Reprinted with permission of The MIT Press.

Introduction

Todd Dufresne

Beyond the Pleasure Principle (*BPP*) of 1920 is a key work in Sigmund Freud's oeuvre, the culmination of the "metapsychology" of the middle period and the foundation for all of his late cultural works—including the best-known work of his career, *Civilization and Its Discontents* (1930). Arguably Freud's most difficult work, *BPP* is often characterized as his most philosophical. In it Freud speculates, not just about the theory of psychoanalysis, but about eternal questions of life and death, pleasure and pain, even as he makes direct and indirect reference to philosophers such as Empedocles, Plato, Kant, Schopenhauer, and Nietzsche.

BPP has been of the greatest interest to Continental thinkers, and for at least four reasons: first, because Freud's discussion of the repetition compulsion, *Wiederholungszwang*, plugs into contemporary interests in repetition, sameness, and difference; second, because Freud's theory of trauma, characterized as the overflowing of energy into the delicate interior of the psyche, has proven to be widely influential among theorists generally; third, because *BPP* is not just difficult, and thus intriguing, but is at times bewilderingly so—a work of seemingly unrestrained speculation; fourth and finally, because Freud in *BPP* exhibits his characteristic hostility toward philosophy, which he dismisses and subtly disparages. While the last two hallmarks, admittedly perverse as reasons for interest, would normally sink a work's reputation, Continental thought has instead found in Freud a fellow-traveler who, like Nietzsche before him and Heidegger after, is considered a trailblazer posing deep, fundamental, and truly upsetting questions. Certainly Continental thought has been just as keen to push the bounds of intelligibility, to think through, for example, the unavoidable limitations of figurative language and representation, even as it undermines traditional disciplinary boundaries. That this lattermost quality necessarily implicates the boundaries that define what it means to be a philosopher and to do philosophy is so much the better. After all, the critique of philosophy is one of the most enduring features of twentieth-century Continental thought.

As a consequence, *BPP* has become a potent site for philosophic reflection, or, put otherwise, a test case for establishing and then debating sometimes very different intellectual projects among theorists. So, for example, *BPP* has provoked Marxist, phenomenological, hermeneutic, broadly post-structural, and explicitly deconstructive interpretations from thinkers as different as Herbert Marcuse (see Appendix B14), Jacques Lacan (see Appendix B6), Paul Ricoeur (see Appendices B10 and B11), Gilles Deleuze (see Appendix B12), Jacques Derrida (see Appendix B13 and B22), and Judith Butler (see Appendix B23).

One cannot help being impressed by the collective effort, as evidenced by the caliber of thinkers collected in this book—however irreconcilable the myriad results. The overall impression is not unlike a Rorschach test, where every Freudian speculation is an inkblot provoking distinctive responses among major philosophers. One fortunate consequence: readers are left with exemplary snapshots of interpretive orientation or, depending on one's own commitments, evidence of another's interpretive monomania.

Such is the heuristic value of collecting together these works, along with *BPP* and contemporaneous works from Freud, in one convenient package. That Gregory C. Richter has contributed thoughtful, contemporary translations of Freud's German—as well as recording in the Translator's Note his valuable impressions—only clinches the long-term significance of this book. Beginner and advanced students are encouraged to follow the works in chronological order or simply select points of entry that suit them best. The idea in either case is to think through the canon of contemporary Continental thought as reflected against the foil of an important and influential work of Freud's, *Beyond the Pleasure Principle*.

The Death Drive Theory

Of course, psychoanalysts have also wrestled with *Beyond the Pleasure Principle*, often accepting, at least superficially, the theory of repetition compulsion as well as the *fort-da* [gone-there] story about the deep meaning of a child's play. But psychoanalysts have mostly dismissed or downplayed Freud's most controversial and famous speculation from *BPP*: *Todestriebe*, the death drive theory.

Two famous exceptions are Melanie Klein, the analyst who hailed from Hungary, ultimately settling in England in

1926, and Jacques Lacan, the controversial French analyst most responsible for bringing psychoanalysis to post-war France. Klein made the death drive theory a centerpiece of her involved interpretations of unconscious "phantasy" at work even in the pre-linguistic period of early childhood. Lacan made it a part of his elaborate and always-evolving revaluation of Freudian theory in light of Alexandre Kojève's interpretation of Marx's early Hegelianism. Lacan's basic claim: the death drive is really a "symbol" of Freud's attempt to return psychoanalysis to the depth model of the early, brooding, supposedly more radical work on the unconscious—sometimes called the id psychology. Selections from their works, as well as the dissenting viewpoint of neo-Freudian (and one-time Frankfurt School member) Erich Fromm, are included here to help represent psychoanalysis after Freud (see Appendix B). For, in addition to being a form of psychotherapy, professional practice, and socio-political movement, institutional psychoanalysis has also been a significant incubator of theoretical ideas. In the case of Lacan, it would be hard to underestimate his influence on French philosophy—first among structuralists, then among (what anglophone readers call) post-structuralists. One major impact is that a significant number of scholars influenced by the "French Freud" have inherited an almost complete disregard, if not disdain, for any discussion of the outdated biologism that informs *BPP*.

Freud's attempt to think "beyond" the pleasure principle—*jenseits*, the noun form of which means "the hereafter"—certainly betrays the heady thrust of his thinking. In the investigation Freud tries to think outside the dictates and principles of life, beyond what can be known according to the norms of society or culture. Freud thereby commits himself, and in turn commits his readers, to following a path that is decidedly "meta": meta-psychological, as he calls it, and meta-physical, a word he carefully avoids. That this may be a fool's errand, not least of all for a trained neurologist and self-described scientist, only makes the attempt more poignant. After all, what would it mean to follow Freud—as a reader but also, more urgently perhaps, as an adherent or follower—when he seeks out a place, or non-place, as silent as death, where he himself could not possibly go? Or, put differently, how could one follow Freud to a place whence there is no possible return? With Hegel, we all know that death is the outer limit of reason. Quite rightly, then, most psychoanalysts have refused to follow Freud into the speculative "hereafter," instead remaining loyal to the Freud of the pleasure principle.

Why "quite rightly"? Because when Freud proposes to think "beyond the pleasure principle," he is simultaneously flirting with a beyond of science or, more exactly, a beyond of the science of the pleasure principle. To follow the Freud of *BPP* is to follow him, in short, beyond psychoanalysis proper. Life itself is at stake in this question of proper and improper, appropriate and inappropriate speculation—yours and mine, but also that of the psychoanalytic "Cause," *die Sache*. What psychoanalysts have understood better than anyone, and to their credit, is that Freud in *BPP* threatens the very foundations of what it means to practice psychoanalysis; that the radical metapsychology of the hereafter undercuts the merely prosaic psychotherapy of everyday life. To Freud's credit, at least arguably, he ignores this danger. Psychoanalysis was his creation, and unlike his followers he was free to imperil its practice in the suspense of a speculative metapsychology without guaranteed returns. As Derrida playfully argues, Freud held in his hands all the "strings/sons, *fils*," and so dictated the shape of his legacy. The pleasure principle, a.k.a. psychoanalysis, was his plaything, his pleasure, which in 1920 he cast about, *fort!*, like the primitive yo-yo he describes in *BPP*, and pulled in again, *da!*, according to his own incalculable interests. Such is the "auto-bio-thanato-hetero-graphical scene of writing" that so delights Derrida (1987: 336), and which has inspired reflection by other deconstructionists such as Rodolphe Gasché and Samuel Weber.

And yet if *BPP* qualifies as a "masterpiece" of "transcendental" thinking along Kantian lines, as Gilles Deleuze (111, and in Appendix B12) claims, it is not because it breaks decisively and irrevocably from scientific discourse. On the contrary: *BPP* represents a remarkable return of some of Freud's oldest "pre-psychoanalytic" preoccupations. Many of the central ideas of *BPP* are in fact the uncanny repetition of ideas first floated, during his cocaine phase, in the "Project for a Scientific Psychology" of 1895—an ambitious and at times grandiose attempt to bridge the distance between psychology and neurology or, more broadly, between psychology and biology. That Freud abandoned the "Project" doesn't mean he forgot its many ideas. In fact, Freud's biologism informs nearly all of his work. As the English psychoanalyst and Freud translator James Strachey understood perfectly well, "The 'Project,' or rather its invisible ghost, haunts the whole series of Freud's theoretical writings to the very end" (Strachey 290).

The continuities between *BPP* and the "Project," new and old, psychoanalytic and pre-psychoanalytic, include four notable features: the so-called "economic" perspective, according to which one attends to quantities of energy that flow through the psyche; the pleasure principle, *das Lustprinzip*, which dominates psychic life; the importance of repetition; and the theory of constancy, influenced by popular ideas about energy conservation, entropy, and thermodynamics but first applied to psychology by Gustav von Fechner, which states that all psychic energy seeks the lowest, most stable state (see Ellenberger 218).

The historian of science Frank Sulloway was the first to systematically demonstrate, and decisively so, that Freud's early commitments to nineteenth-century theories of biology—the "metabiology"—inform nearly all theory innovation in the history of psychoanalysis. But this fact was already documented in the literature, including in Ernest Jones's official biography of Freud (Jones 310–13). A key feature of Freud's metabiology is his unwavering belief in Jean-Baptiste Lamarck's theory that evolution is fueled by the inheritance of acquired characteristics, a claim that perfectly complements the theory of recapitulation championed by Ernst Haeckel. According to Haeckel's once-popular view, individuals in the present ontogenetically repeat the (phylogenetic) history of the species. As Freud translates in a letter of July 1915 to his close friend Sándor Ferenczi, "What are now neuroses were once phases of the human condition" (*Freud-Ferenczi* 66). Or, as he states very plainly in chapter 5 of *BPP*, and just before his famous speculation about a conservative drive: "ultimately it must be the developmental history of our earth and of its relation to the sun that has left its mark on the evolution of organisms" (*BPP* 79). This subject was far from being a side issue: Freud and Ferenczi contemplated writing a joint work on "Lamarck and Psychoanalysis" in the years immediately preceding the writing of *BPP*. In a way, *BPP* is that book.

It was with the metabiology in mind that Freud thought psychoanalysis, on the analogy of archaeology, could penetrate history to its collective prehistorical roots—as in the fantasies of *Totem and Taboo* (1913) and *Moses and Monotheism* (1939)—and identify what romantic philosophers called *Urphänomene*. For example, one could correlate what Freud calls "the hard school of the glacial age" (*Freud-Ferenczi* 66; Freud *Phylogenetic* 13-14) with the period of "cold indifference" that characterizes adolescent attitudes toward members of the opposite sex (Ferenczi *Stages* 201-02; and Freud *Phylogenetic* 13-14).

While insufficiently appreciated in the secondary literature, Freud's influential theory of repetition compulsion is similarly a late flowering of these old and, after the rediscovery of Gregor Mendel's work on genetics in 1900, already discredited ideas. For example, Freud in *BPP* links the repetition compulsion to the biological imperative that regulates spawning habits of some fish, migratory patterns of birds, and above all the "facts of embryology"—the latter being conclusive proof, according to Freud, of "the organic repetition compulsion" (*BPP* 76).

Most psychoanalysts regret Freud's unsupportable commitments. In private letters Ernest Jones, for one, urged him to excise his Lamarckian views (Jones 313). But Freud held steadfast to the old metabiology, which in any case he could hardly jettison. In *Moses and Monotheism*, one of his last works, Freud admits: "My position, no doubt, is made more difficult by the present attitude of biological science, which refuses to hear of the inheritance of acquired characteristics by succeeding generations. I must, however, in all modesty confess that nevertheless I cannot do without this factor in biological evolution" (*Standard* 23: 100).

If psychoanalysts have had trouble accepting and even comprehending that Freud in 1920 had explicitly reinvested psychoanalytic theory in the failed, pre-psychoanalytic, biologistic and mechanistic ideas of the "Project," it has been no less troubling for philosophers. For example, although defined by their laudable interest in close textual reading, many structuralists and post-structuralists share an almost willful disinterest in the intellectual history of psychoanalysis—including most especially the fact of Freud's unwavering biologism. The result is an at times stunning ahistoricism that is nearly as troubling as the motivated whitewashing that characterizes so much of the scholarship conducted by psychoanalysts.

On the other hand, Continental philosophers, unlike most psychoanalysts, are in principle and by job description interested in the problems of interpretation that attend a work like *BPP*. Moreover, philosophers share with the Freud of *BPP* a boundless curiosity about ultimate questions and are far more open to uncertain theoretical speculation than are therapists. Philosophers grant Freud the utility of a thought experiment, and agree to follow an interesting train of thought on the grounds that Freud himself gives, namely, as "an *advocatus diaboli* who does not, for all that, sign a pact with the devil" (*BPP* 95). What philosophers also share with Freud, no doubt ironically, is an ambiguous relationship to therapy and treatment. Philosophers do not (typically) seek to cure the soul, but to understand something about it; or, even more often nowadays, to engage the discourses of the soul without doctrinal commitments one way or another. The efficacy of psychoanalytic therapy is therefore often ignored by philosophers, swept under the rug along with the ethics of psychoanalytic practice.

Therapists, by contrast, ignore the nuts-and-bolts issue of efficacy at their own peril. When Freud announced the death drive theory, his colleagues had good reason to worry: the new, highly abstract theory undermined the fairly well established theory of sexuality. Worse, the death drive theory countenanced a disturbing form of therapeutic nihilism. For if noisy life really is set asunder by the silent forces of death, and these forces are the genetic inheritance of our phylogenetic past, then there is, in the final analysis, very little any therapy can do to assuage the roots of human suffering.

Freud's "new" ideas of *BPP* couldn't have been any darker. It is not just that one is left, in 1920, with the choice of dying in one's own way. Or even, as Freud clarifies in 1930, that one is left with two tragic, radically anti-social choices in life: destroy others or destroy one's self, sadism or masochism. It is also, as Freud concludes in "Analysis Terminable and Interminable" of 1937, that the practice of psychoanalysis is thereby rendered interminable. The life Freud describes is given over to endless struggle—with the demons of one's own phylogenetic past, and with the pasts of other people similarly stricken. Contentment with civilization therefore lies not in the psychoanalytic present, but in what Freud in *The Future of an Illusion* (1927) calls "geological" time; to wit, the distant future where the totality of miniscule (ontogenetic) advances, not of decades or even centuries but of millennia, finally add up to something discernibly better for human beings, both individually and collectively. The upshot: Freud evinced none of the *furor therapeuticus* that distinguishes well-intending but over-zealous physicians. Far from it. As Ferenczi reports, Freud in 1932 actually admitted that "neurotics are a rabble, good only to support us financially and to allow us to learn from their cases: psychoanalysis as a therapy may be worthless" (*Clinical* 185-86).

Although an eager partner in Freud's wild biological speculations, Ferenczi finally recoiled from the dark, tragically over-determined ends of the new metapsychology. He came to believe that therapy trumped theory, and in this regard led the way for later generations of "Freudians." In fact, Ferenczi was one of the first neo-Freudians out to save the practice of psychoanalysis from the extremes of its own theory—from Freud.

Not all philosophers have ignored the therapeutic dimension of psychoanalytic practice. But it was Norman O. Brown, an American classicist, who did the most to grapple intellectually and theoretically with it. Inspired by contact with Herbert Marcuse, best known for his "Freudo-Marxism" of the 1950s, Brown agreed that Freud's late dualism of life and death drives was untenable. While his book *Life Against Death* (1959) includes wild speculations of its own, his guiding prescription is perfectly sober: with help from Marx and Hegel, we must translate the dualistic despair of Freud into the dialectics of hope. In Brown's work, as in Marcuse's, Eros is given a fighting chance against a death drive that in Freud, despite appearances, seems almost omnipotent (see Marcuse 28; Deleuze and Guattari 331; Dufresne 23). Brown, in fact, is one of the few thinkers to recognize that Freud's new dualism, in part created to stave off a Jungian-styled monism of sexuality, quickly resolved into another kind of monism, that of death.[1]

Philosophers have tended to be more interested in the intel-lectual puzzle of *BPP* than in its possibly monstrous ethical implications. Even Marcuse was wholly unsympathetic to the practical, therapeutic issues of Fromm and other neo-Freudians; issues that were tarred as conformist and, with the chauvinism present in some European thought, "American." But intellectual puzzlement is only one reason for philosophy's decades of interest in *BPP*. Another reason concerns disciplinary turf. If *BPP* seems like a bizarrely scientistic rendering of some suspiciously familiar

---

1   Taking a step back, it is only the pairing of Jung/Freud that can save the dualism of life or sex and death—a conclusion that would have infuriated Freud.

metaphysics, that's because it is. "We have unwittingly sailed," Freud says in chapter six of *BPP*, "into the harbor of Schopenhauer's philosophy" (*BPP* 87). To Schopenhauer's declaration in *The World as Will and Representation* that "death is the real aim of life," Freud adds that life is a detour on the path of death. Freud, always ready to downplay his retrograde attraction to Schopenhauer, later defends himself in the *New Introductory Lectures*:

> You may shrug your shoulders and say: 'That isn't natural science, it's Schopenhauer's philosophy!' But, Ladies and Gentlemen, why should not a bold thinker have guessed something that is afterwards confirmed by sober and painstaking detailed research? Moreover, there is nothing that has not been said already, and similar things had been said by many people before Schopenhauer. (*Standard* 22: 107)

Freud's rhetoric is characteristic: he accepts and rejects his debt to philosophy in nearly the same breath. Indeed, a similar double operation opens *BPP*, where Freud's debt is immediately recognized, *da!*, only to be sent far away, *fort!* In a delightfully facetious passage in his "Autobiographical Study" of 1925, Freud chortles: "Even when I have moved away from observation, I have carefully avoided any contact with philosophy proper. This avoidance has been greatly facilitated by constitutional incapacity" (20: 59).

Privately, however, Freud could strike a different tone altogether. In a letter of 1 August 1919, Freud tells his friend and analytic colleague (also Nietzsche's would-be love interest), Lou Andreas-Salomé: "For my old age I have chosen the theme of death; I have stumbled on a remarkable notion based on my theory of the instincts [*Triebe*, drives], and now I must read all kinds of things relevant to it, e.g., Schopenhauer, for the first time" (Freud and Andreas-Salomé 99). Official recognition of a kind followed in a 1935 postscript to the "Autobiographical Study," where Freud finally concedes that the theories of *BPP* returned him not just to his oldest ideas about mental life, but to his earliest interest in philosophy. He writes: "Threads which in the course of my development had become inter-tangled have now begun to separate; interests which I acquired in the later part of life have receded, while the older and original ones become prominent once more" (*Standard* 20: 71). And again: "My interests, after making a lifelong *détour* through the natural sciences, medicine, and psychotherapy, returned to the cultural problems which had fascinated me long before" (72). How long before? To his fiancée, Martha Bernays, Freud had in August 1882 admitted his illicit attraction to cultural problems and to philosophy. "Philosophy," the twenty-five year old writes, "which I have always pictured as my goal and refuge in my old age, gains every day in attraction" (in Jones 41).

Freud's theory: Every organism, having repeated all the historically acquired conditions that made it possible, having completed the many practical detours required of the reality principle (reflecting law, society, the horde), merely wishes to "die in its own way," to at last achieve the pleasure of nonexistence. Freud's translation of theory into autobiography: His late return to philosophy is evidence of a drive to end things on his own terms, to be done with the detour called life (and its psychoanalysis), and to finally become the inorganic nothing from whence he came. As he put it in a letter to Andreas-Salomé in May 1925: "A crust of indifference is slowly creeping up around me; a fact I state without complaining. It is a natural development, a way of beginning to grow inorganic" (Freud and Andreas-Salomé 154). Of course, such philosophy has an ancient pedigree: namely, philosophy as preparation for dying.

The truth is, the botched metabiology that Freud in *BPP* lifts, holus-bolus, from the "Project," and before that from Fechner and others, is of a piece with the unbridled philosophical speculation of his youth. Despite Freud's many protestations to the contrary, we know that he took formal classes in philosophy with Franz Brentano at the University of Vienna, where they discussed the unconscious; corresponded and passionately debated philosophy with his friend, Eduard Silberstein; in a letter expressed interest in completing a PhD in philosophy and zoology; read works by Plato, Aristotle, David Hume, Kant, Schopenhauer, Eduard von Hartmann, Ludwig Feuerbach, Nietzsche, Franz Brentano, Theodor Gomperz, and Henry Thomas Buckle; translated into German (for Gomperz) an essay on women by John Stuart Mill; was almost certainly aware of and likely influenced by a work on Aristotle and catharsis written by his wife's uncle, Jakob Bernays; and was obviously influenced, not just by Schopenhauer's thoughts on death, but by Nietzsche's ideas, such as the "id" (*das Es*), the "will to power," and by the "eternal return of the same," the last appearing (unattributed) in quotation marks in passages about repetition compulsion in *BPP* and elsewhere.

Those in Freud's inner circle were aware of his interests, if not his debts, and were not always shy about saying so. Freud's friend and fellow analyst, Arnold Zweig, gushed the following compliment to Freud in a letter of late 1930:

> To me it seems that you have achieved everything that Nietzsche intuitively felt to be his task, without his really being able to achieve it with his poetic idealism and brilliant inspirations. He tried to explain the birth of tragedy; you have done it in *Totem and Taboo*. He longed for a world beyond Good and Evil; by means of analysis you have discovered a world to which this phrase actually applies. Analysis has reversed all values, it has conquered Christianity, disclosed the true Antichrist, and liberated the spirit of resurgent life from the ascetic ideal. (Freud-Zweig 23)

Similar sentiments are recorded in the *Minutes of the Vienna Psychoanalytic Society* in April 1908. Paul Federn, who would later co-edit the *Minutes*, is claimed to have remarked: "Nietzsche has come so close to our views that we can ask only, 'Where has he not come close?' He intuitively knew a number of Freud's discoveries; he was the first to discover the significance of abreaction [acting out], of repression, of flights into illness, of the instincts—the normal as well as the sadistic" (Nunberg and Federn I: 359). Of course, Nietzsche's name was a double-edged one. Years after his falling-out with Freud, analyst Otto Rank sent a gift on Freud's 70th birthday that apparently wasn't appreciated: the complete leather-bound works of Nietzsche (Roazen 1997).

The thematic coupling of death and doubling—of being mistaken for or haunted by another, of split personalities, and so on—was a standard feature of the Romanticism that also made psychoanalysis possible, from Robert Louis Stevenson's novel about Dr. Jekyll and Mr. Hyde and E.T.A. Hoffmann's short story "The Sandman" to Friedrich von Schiller's poetry. And, of course, the famous doubling of conscious/unconscious was a staple of Romanticism that had a profound influence on Freud, one that begins with the magnetism of Franz Anton Mesmer and culminates with medical hypnosis as legitimized by James Braid and practiced by contemporaries such as French hypnotherapist Hippolyte Bernheim (whose work Freud translated into

German). It cannot be surprising to learn, therefore, that the themes of death, doubling, and the uncanny pervade the thinking of Freud's everyday life. Decades before he died, Freud had been haunted by his own impending death; had in fact long been superstitious about numerological portents of that sort; collected antiquities, most especially Egyptian and Greek burial urns; and was at times compelled to tell departing guests, "Goodbye; you may never see me again" (in Jones 279).

Of course, if one can point to biographical fragments to rationalize Freud's morbid and "Romantic" character, then one can also use them to rationalize away everything about *BPP*. Much of the psychoanalytic literature, perhaps not surprisingly, has done just that. We are variously told that *BPP* is the unfortunate result of poorly analyzed pessimism and misanthropy; internecine politics of the psychoanalytic movement, including defections from once-close friends such as Alfred Adler (1911) and Carl Jung (1912); decline and the prospect of old age (Freud was 64 in 1920); the interwar period in general, when worry about death dominated everyday life; realistic anxiety felt for his two sons, Martin and Ernst, who fought in World War One; the deaths of his analytic colleague Viktor Tausk (July 1919), his friend and benefactor Anton von Freund (January 1920), and above all his favorite daughter, Sophie Freud Halberstadt (January 1920); and the cancer of his jaw, a sickness to which Freud ultimately succumbed in 1939 after relocating to Hampstead in North London. That these biographical rationales include even the cancer he didn't know he had until 1923 says something about their ingenuity—and also their desperation.

On the other hand, it's too easy to cry foul or complain haughtily about supposedly ad hominem or reductionist explanations culled from Freud's biography. After all, psychoanalysis is supposed to have been derived in large measure from Freud's interpretations of his own hidden, subjective, irrational motives. Psychoanalysis is the science of the subject's repressed unconscious, and it is Freud who opened this Pandora's box in *The Interpretation of Dreams* (1900), perhaps earlier, and not his critics, biographers, and psycho-historians. And so in a way it is perfectly reasonable, or at least consistent, to ask why Freud devised the death drive theory in 1920 and not, say, in 1910; and to this end recall some of the biographical rationales for the existence of the death drive theory. In 1909 Freud had certainly balked at

Alfred Adler's theory of a drive for power, loosely derived from Nietzsche's "will to power"; had ignored Wilhelm Stekel's work on "Thanatos" in that same year;[1] and was skeptical about Sabina Spielrein's presentation about a destructive instinct in 1911 at a meeting of the Vienna Psychoanalytic Society. Freud rejected it all. As he admits in *Civilization and Its Discontents*, "I recall my own resistance when the idea of the destructive drive first arose in psychoanalytic literature, and how long it took before I became receptive to it" (*CD* 132–33).

In *BPP*, the death drive theory is carefully put forward as one hypothesis among others. As he says in chapter four: "The following is speculation, often far-fetched speculation, which each person will appreciate or disregard according to his or her particular interests" (*BPP* 65). And again in chapter six: "It would be reasonable to ask me whether and to what extent I am convinced of the hypotheses developed here. My answer would be the following: neither am I convinced myself, nor do I seek to convince others to believe in them" (*BPP* 95). But the cool dispassion of the devil's advocate quickly gave way to abiding faith in his own theory—perhaps already in *BPP*, where Freud's own rhetoric of nonchalance must not be accepted at face value (without selling us to the devil of depth analysis). Freud is more forthcoming elsewhere. "I can no longer think in any other way," Freud writes in 1930, and then adds a few lines of characteristic derision aimed at critics: "'For little children do not like to hear it' when mention is made of the inborn human inclination to 'evil', to aggression and destructiveness, and thus to cruelty as well. God made them in the image of His own perfection, and no one wants to be told how hard it is to reconcile the existence of evil ... with His omnipotence or His all-goodness" (*CD* 132-33). Simply put, the death drive theory became the dominant theory of psychoanalysis in the late period precisely because Freud came to believe it. And because he believed it, he also came to believe in the existence of "primary masochism" and the "negative therapeutic reaction"—the latter being Freud's

---

1   Freud only used the word "Thanatos" in conversation, never in print, although it is commonly used in the secondary literature (Jones 1957: 273). Paul Roazen claims that Freud's refusal to write of Thanatos can be traced to a priority issue with Stekel, who wrote of Thanatos, god of death, in 1909 (*Followers* 218).

translation, in "The Economic Problem of Masochism," of resistance to psychoanalytic treatment as an unconscious need for punishment.

The new beliefs were of course made possible by other beliefs—lifted from literature, philosophy, medicine, and biology, and imbibed through everyday culture—that predate the birth of psychoanalysis. In this respect it is only convenience that has us speak of a pre-psychoanalytic period, or even of early, middle, and late periods, since the various stages of theory-building clearly inform and blur into each other. Indeed, a major aspect of Freud's attraction lies in just this propensity to transgress again and again accepted disciplinary boundaries, an admirable reflection, obviously not of plagiarism, but of genuine creativity and originality. Hence the fundamental challenge of what I call Critical Freud Studies: always playing catch-up with Freud's own broad interests and considerable talents.

Critical Directions

All of which leads me to a provocation: without a proper appreciation of *Beyond the Pleasure Principle*, most especially the biologic of the death drive theory, one does not understand anything about the late period of Freud's work. In this respect, and to stretch it just a little, *BPP* is the Rosetta Stone of Freudian theory—the key that unlocks the psychological theories of the late works precisely because it provides a translation of the biological theories of the earliest. As for the third side of the stone, to continue the analogy, that would have to be the partially legible script in *BPP* devoted to Schopenhauer, Nietzsche, and the suppressed history of philosophy.

In this context, three kinds of misunderstanding of Freud's *BPP* are worth noting. The first kind is highly motivated or willful, which in the best case signifies an authentic *critical* reckoning. A fair portion of the Continental interpretation of *BPP* fits into this camp. For example, Marcuse repairs and remakes Freudian theory in his own Freudo-Marxist image, and is to that extent perfectly justified—despite the uselessness of his works as a faithful commentary on Freud's own claims and arguments. The second kind of misunderstanding is driven by ideology. The resulting scholarship often appears sound, as judged, for instance, by the number of references cited, but that is a pleasant illusion. At best this work represents an authentic *political* reckoning, the references themselves just more ideology parading as scholarship. Let's return to this issue in a moment, because it's important. The third basic kind of misunderstanding is neither critical nor political. It is merely the result of ignorance—the accumulation and regurgitation of sausage-insights produced by almost a century of moonlighting by amateur scholars, chief among them psychoanalysts and their former patients.[1]

The misunderstandings of *BPP*, which are often alloyed with each other, have in turn generated misperceptions about the essential meaning of the cultural works and the epistemological status of ego psychology. With the exceptions of Brown and Paul Ricoeur, almost no one has attended carefully to the connection between *BPP* and Freud's late analysis of *Kultur*. This is unfortunate, since the reasoning of *BPP* dictates that the so-called "cultural" works are really asocial if not anti-cultural in orientation; elaborate refutations of the relevance that culture has vis-à-vis Freud's biologically driven, and therefore irrefutable, psychology. If psychoanalysis has anything to say about culture, it is that it always plays second fiddle to the radical depths of a tragic metapsychology as elaborated in these late works (see Dufresne 145–83, and Appendix B24).

The second misperception fails to address the connection between the metapsychology of *BPP* and the ego psychology that follows. Either the logical and intellectual coherence of the metapsychology is downplayed, as in Fromm, or its singular radicality is overplayed, as in Lacan. But to the chagrin of both Fromm and Lacan—and by extension to the chagrin of American and French traditions of psychoanalysis—works such as *Group Psychology and the Analysis of the Ego* of 1921 and *The Ego and the Id* of 1923 are in fact continuous with *BPP*, reflections of the metapsychology and not exemplars of a paradigm shift toward ego psychology. *Group Psychology*, partly composed at the same time as *BPP* and with a foot in both camps (ego psychology and cultural works), provides

---

1   It really is a scandal. No other field, least of all one paying lip service to the principles of science, is as thoroughly compromised by a history of dubious authorship circulated by vanity and in-house publishing. For this we can thank Freud, who laundered most of his own works and the work of the psychoanalytic "Cause" through venues he and his benefactors (such as Anton von Freund) created and funded.

the logical flipside of Freud's analysis of the death drive: namely, an analysis of group love and Eros. Similarly, Freud explicitly conceived of *The Ego and the Id*, the work most closely associated with the advent of ego psychology, as a continuation of ideas begun in *BPP*. "I am occupied with something speculative," the vacationing Freud tells Ferenczi in July 1922, "which is a continuation of 'Beyond', and will either become a small book or nothing" (*Freud-Ferenczi* 3: 84). He repeats the claim in *The Ego and the Id*.

The majority of analysts were right, however, to complain that metapsychology subverts psychoanalysis. On this score the political reckoning with Freud can't be ignored. For institutional psychoanalysis after *BPP* is nothing if not the exorcism of this unwanted metapsychology, whether by theorizing the conformist ego of a presentist and pragmatic psychology or by theorizing the non-conformist id of a utopic and aspirational psychology. In effect, institutional psychoanalysis after Freud perfectly reflects a crisis that begins with *BPP* and never ends—the battle between idealized versions of American and French psychoanalysis merely echoing, critically *and* politically, the eternal battle of life and death that Freud left them with. Ironically, in other words, even when psychoanalysts rejected *BPP* (by minimizing it or transforming metabiology into a symbol of something else) they ended up perpetuating it—compulsively, of course, as though driven by the death drive that Freud injected into psychoanalysis. If so, they are themselves the overall shape of the death drive that Freud had trouble proving, the concrete and very noisy examples he himself created even as he stumbled, in *BPP*, to find instances of it at work in the everyday world of mechanical trauma and child's play.

The unavoidable conclusion: *BPP* is itself the name of the trauma Freud inflicted on psychoanalysis, playfully or otherwise, from a position inside psychoanalysis. The history of this trauma's reception—interpretation after interpretation, book after book—is therefore the history of its compulsive drive, not for mastery, as Freud insists, but for nothingness.

This new edition of *Beyond the Pleasure Principle* is a call for deeper thinking—about psychoanalysis as a cross-discipline, about the "theory of psychoanalysis," about its complex relationship with philosophy, and about the irreconcilable yet totally fascinating efforts of Continental thinkers to find their own interpretive legs between the lines of Freud's theory. If ever there was a forum for debating what literary critic Harold Bloom calls "strong reading" or, less generously, "misreading,"[1] then this is it. How we fit ourselves into this debate about interpretation reveals a lot, possibly everything, about what we think of philosophy today. As always, the thinking about limits, our own and that of the field's best thinkers, is a potent way of sharpening and justifying beliefs—and to that extent renewing the task of philosophy, no matter what we might think about the life and death of psychoanalysis.

★★★

By 1920 Freud had returned to the philosophical reflection of his youth, and to that extent made psychoanalysis answer to metapsychology—to wit, to the theory of psychoanalysis and to the suppressed history of Romantic thought and metaphysics that made it all possible. This homecoming was Freud's gift, his pleasure, first of all to himself, no doubt because he thought his own time was short, and second of all to philosophy.

In this respect, to speak of the "death of psychoanalysis" is just another way of saying that Freud is finally where he belongs: beyond psychoanalysis, in philosophy. Sometimes in death one gets exactly what one deserves out of life.

Freud's hereafter is now our pleasure.

1 Harold Bloom, *A Map of Misreading*. New York: Oxford UP, 1975.

Sigmund Freud: A Brief Chronology

6 May 1856	"Sigismund" Freud is born in Moravia, the present-day Czech Republic.
1860	The Freud family relocates to Vienna, Austria.
1873	Freud enters University of Vienna as medical student.
1874-75	Takes extra credit in Philosophy with Franz Brentano.
1875	Under direction of Carl Claus at Institute of Comparative Anatomy, Freud dissects testes of four hundred eels.
1876-82	Works as researcher under Ernst Brücke at Institute of Physiology, where he examines nerve cells of crayfish and the nervous system of the fresh-water crab. Meets well-known Viennese physician, Josef Breuer, at Institute.
1880	Translates John Stuart Mill for Theodor Gomperz.
1881	Having extended his studies, Freud finally graduates as Doctor of Medicine.
1882	Becomes engaged to Martha Bernays.
1882-85	Residency at Vienna General Hospital. Freud is a reluctant physician, preferring university life as a researcher. Anti-Semitism is a factor in career choice.
1884-87	Cocaine research, including publications. Freud advocates its usage professionally and personally. A friend, encouraged by Freud to use cocaine, dies of an overdose.
1885-86	Four months study with Jean-Martin Charcot at the Salpêtrière Hospital in Paris. Increased interest in hypnosis and hysteria.
1886	Marries Martha Bernays and establishes private practice as a neurologist or "nerve doctor." Translates Charcot's two latest lectures into German.
1887-1902	Meets, befriends, and then corresponds with Wilhelm Fliess, a Berlin ear, nose, and throat specialist. Wild metabiological/

	metaphysical ideas exchanged, including Fliess's ideas of periodicity and human bisexuality. Friendship ends in 1902.
1887	Freud begins using hypnotic suggestion in clinical practice.
1887-95	Birth of six children, Anna being the youngest.
1893	Freud and Breuer publish "Preliminary Communication." Theoretical claim: "hysterics suffer from reminiscences."
1895	Publishes with Josef Breuer *Studies on Hysteria*. Case studies claim that hysterical suffering is cured by cathartic talk. Includes ur-case of "Anna O." Freud later invokes and/or maligns Breuer as their views diverge over the next ten years. Breuer distances himself formally from Freud in a separate preface to the 1908 edition of the *Studies*.
1895	Freud attempts to bridge psychology and physiology in the never completed "Project for a Scientific Psychology."
1896	First mention of the word "psychoanalysis."
1896-97	Freud's father Jacob, a wool merchant, dies in 1896. "Seduction theory" is proposed: trauma is caused by repressed childhood sexual abuse.
1897	To Fliess, Freud privately questions the "seduction" etiology that he has already publicly championed in essays. Freud, however, keeps his change of heart from the public for another eight years.
1897-1900	Period of "self-analysis" culminates with *The Interpretation of Dreams*. Dreams are "the royal road to an understanding of the unconscious."
1901	Publishes *The Psychopathology of Everyday Life*. As in the Dream Book, Freud examines mild pathology under conditions of outward normality, e.g., "parapraxes," or faulty acts, such as slips of the tongue.
1902	Granted the title of Professor Extraordinarius at the University of Vienna. Although it is not

a paid chair position, Freud comes to be known as "the Professor."

1902-06	"Wednesday Evening Meetings" at Freud's home; gatherings of disparate people loyal to Freud's ideas. After breaks with Breuer and then Fliess, the group is used as sounding board for Freud's ideas.
1905	Publishes *Three Essays on the Theory of Sexuality*. Psychosexual stages of development. Psychoanalysis as the investigation of sexual fantasy (not "seduction") finally gets public currency—although without declaring that a shift had indeed occurred. Also publishes *Jokes and Their Relation to the Unconscious*.
1906-15	Founding of the Vienna Psychoanalytic Society, and with it the greater institutionalization of Freud's ideas.
1908	First International Psychoanalytic Congress in Salzburg.
1909	Freud and Carl Jung are invited to lecture at Clark University in Worcester, Massachusetts, and receive honorary doctorates.
1911	Nine of 35 members of the Vienna Society, led by Alfred Adler, break with Freud and found the Society for Free Psychoanalysis.
1911-15	Freud, many years after publishing "findings" of psychoanalysis, finally publishes papers on the technique of psychoanalysis.
1912	Wilhelm Stekel leaves Vienna Society.
1913	Publishes *Totem and Taboo*, at least in part in reaction to Jung's status as heir apparent. Basic claim: society begins with parricide.
1914	Jung "defects." Freud writes "A History of the Psychoanalytic Movement," which polemicizes against Adler and Jung.
1914	Freud publishes important essay "On Narcissism."
1914	Writes his last significant case study, "From the History of an Infantile Neurosis," a.k.a. the case of the "Wolf Man," published in 1918. None of his published cases, as Freud admits at the time or as we now know, are

	successful cures. Failure propels his examinations, not just of unconscious fantasy, but of "resistance," "transference," and the "negative therapeutic reaction."
1915-20	Freud develops his "metapsychology," or theory of psychoanalysis. An explicit return to "energy" themes from 1893-95. Many essays are lost. One important exception is *A Phylogenetic Fantasy: Overview of the Transference Neuroses*, published in 1987 (posthumously).
1916-17	Publishes *Introductory Lectures on Psychoanalysis*.
1919	International Psychoanalytic Press is founded in Vienna and England.
1920	Publishes *Beyond the Pleasure Principle*. This culmination of the metapsychology writings re-establishes a dualistic ontology and introduces the "repetition compulsion" and "death drive" theories. Basic claim: aim of life is non-existence.
1921	Publishes *Group Psychology and the Analysis of the Ego*, the flipside of his discussion of the death drive.
1923	Publishes *The Ego and the Id*. Moves from conscious/unconscious structure of mind toward id/ego/superego "topography." Origin of "ego psychology."
1923	Learns of cancer of the jaw and undergoes first operation of thirty-one in total. Eventually, pain and the lack of parts of the palate hinder speech.
1924	Otto Rank, once a close friend, adherent, and collaborator, breaks with Freud.
1925	Freud publishes "An Autobiographical Study."
1926	Publishes "The Question of Lay Analysis." Major debate, legal and intellectual, about the status of non-medical analysts. Quackery charges against Theodor Reik in Austria. Freud sides with "lay" analysts like Reik, but institutional forces are against him, especially in America.

1927	Publishes *The Future of an Illusion*. Basic claim: religion is an infantile attachment to Daddy. Beginning of the so-called "cultural" works of Freud's late years.
1930	Hungarian analyst Sándor Ferenczi, Freud's oldest close friend and collaborator, is increasingly estranged from Freud and psychoanalysis.
1930	Publishes *Civilization and Its Discontents* and draws the conclusions of the death drive theory. Probably his best known work.
1930	Wins Frankfurt city's Goethe Prize for "creative impact."
1933	Hitler elected in Germany. Freud's books publicly burned in Berlin.
1934-38	Writes *Moses and Monotheism*.
1937	Publishes "Analysis Terminable and Interminable." Freud's own skepticism about analytic practice is made explicit.
1938	Hitler invades Austria; Freud and immediate family leave for London, England. They settle in Hampstead, north of the center.
23 September 1939	Freud, suffering badly, requests and is administered lethal doses of morphine by his friend, the analyst-physician Max Schur.

Translator's Note

Gregory C. Richter

Freud began work on *Jenseits des Lustprinzips* early in 1919. He first mentions the book in a letter to Sándor Ferenczi, 31 March 1919: "In it [*Beyond the Pleasure Principle*] I am saying many things that are quite unclear, out of which the reader has to make the right thing. Sometimes one can't do otherwise" (Dufresne 14). On 27 May 1920 Freud wrote to Max Eitingon: "I am now correcting and completing *Beyond*, that is, the pleasure principle, and am once again in a productive phase. *Fractus si illabatur orbis impavidum ferient ruinae*" (Kiell 442). The Latin quotation, from Horace's third *Ode*, certainly contributes to the impression that Freud was feeling positive about the book: "If the sky falls, broken, its ruins will strike an undaunted man." The work was published in December 1920 by Internationaler Psychoanalytischer Verlag, and subsequently reissued in German several times, including in 1940, in Volume 13 of *Gesammelte Werke*. .

C.J.M. Hubback's English translation, *Beyond the Pleasure Principle*, appeared in 1922. The preface, though, is by the editor, Ernest Jones, and it is not always clear which portions of the translation are Hubback's and which are revisions by Jones. He writes: "I have revised this translation, so carefully made by Miss Hubback, several times," and then goes on to explain his renditions of various German expressions. In the current translation, I have occasionally adopted technical terms from the Hubback/Jones version when they seem particularly serviceable.

The best known English version is by James Strachey (1887-1967), first published in 1950 by Hogarth Press. For the 1955 edition, in Volume 18 of *The Standard Edition of the Complete Psychological Works of Sigmund Freud*, Strachey produced numerous new footnotes and sometimes provided detailed comments on Freud's own. In producing the current translation, I have often consulted his version. Indeed, it would be impossible now to produce a version completely independent of Strachey, who, with his wife, Alix, dedicated his life to translating Freud. Here, I have adopted the choices he made for the translation of several German terms. It must be emphasized, though, that I have not retained his style. Throughout the *Standard Edition*, Strachey maintained a nearly unchanging, consistently elevated style far removed from the varied but often direct and unadorned style of Freud. This generalization certainly applies for *Beyond the Pleasure Principle*: Freud's German is often simple and straight-forward, allowing him to express complex meanings through ordinary words, while Strachey's English vocabulary emphasizes terms derived from Latin and Greek. Clearly, Strachey assigned to the classical languages greater scientific value than he did to the basic Germanic vocabulary of English, and accordingly much of the flavor of the original work is lost. This includes Strachey's use of *the ego* to render Freud's *das Ich*, though this decision had actually been made years before by Ernest Jones, who rejected Strachey's arguments that the English term should be *the I*. In sum, *Beyond the Pleasure Principle,* comprising Freud's often tentative, speculative, even fanciful cogitations on the nature of consciousness, sounds much more definitive and authoritative in Strachey's version than it does in the original. Holder remarks: "I think that one of the apparent merits of Strachey's transla-tion is its presentation of a streamlined Freud—Freud shorn of the polyphony of his style, of the ambiguities, uncertainties, and imaginative ponderings that are so characteristic of the original. This may make for more coherence and ease of understanding, but it presses Freud into a peculiar scientific framework" (Holder 85). All of this is not to condemn Strachey's translation. The lan-guage is rich, and the basic meaning of Freud's German is clearly conveyed. Strachey's translation provides a common ground to which other renditions can be compared. One can think of it as an undiminished monumental achievement. Yet it is a translation for its own time. Referring to Strachey's entire opus, Ornston (Ornston "Obstacles": 222) puts it succinctly: "The *Standard Edition* is a deliberately elegant period piece." Such observations have been made by other writers as well, including Mahony, who calls for research into "the ideology behind Strachey's staid Victorian prose," and remarks upon "its cleaning up of Viennese colloquialisms [and] its reliance on Greek and Latin to render the familiar in German" (Mahony 159). Thus new renditions of Freud's works, especially those striving to suggest Freud's German style, certainly have their place.

Key technical terms I have adopted from Strachey include the following. With Strachey, I translate *Seelenleben* as *mind* or occasionally *mental life*; I translate both *seelisch* and *psychisch* as *mental* (though I have eschewed his frequently invoked alternative, *psychical*, which now seems archaic). Similarly, I translate *Regung* as *impulse*, *Erregung* as *excitation*, *Reiz* as *stimulus*, and *Übertragung* as *transference*. With Strachey, I translate *Unlust* as *unpleasure*. Although *Unlust* in Freud's sense is a normal German antonym of *Lust* (pleasure), the English word *unpleasure* is rare. It occasionally appeared in the late eighteenth and early nineteenth centuries meaning "displeasure," first appearing in a psychoanalytic sense in 1919 (*Oxford English Dictionary*). Indeed, it does seem desirable, where possible, to select a single English word as the equivalent of a single word in German, and *unpleasure* is certainly more practical than Jones's *"pain"*—always in quotes to distinguish it from *pain*, Hubback's translation of *Schmerz*.

In other cases, my technical terminology differs from Strachey's. As an equivalent for *Wiederholungszwang*, I have adopted Hubback's *repetition compulsion*—a more direct translation than Strachey's *compulsion to repeat*. The German term *Abfuhr* also presents difficulties: as an equivalent I have adopted *discharge*, as did both Strachey and Hubback, but the English term is not ideal. *Discharge* is the appropriate translation in the context of electricity, but the other English senses do not overlap well with the German ones. The English term may bring to mind the idea of shooting, or even of bodily fluids, but in German these connotations are absent. The German term is more passive than the English one, and conveys the idea of unloading or of conveying away. Still, given the electricity metaphor that permeates the book, *discharge* remains the best choice.

Other difficult cases remain. Consider Freud's term *Besetzung*, which has basic senses of "occupation" or "investment," and which in *Beyond the Pleasure Principle* Freud invokes in the context of mental energy. He probably did not intend the word in a highly technical sense, but Strachey clearly sought to imbue it with special significance. Ornston discusses the translation of this word at some length, referring to "Strachey's earnest ... concoction of the concept he called 'cathexis'" (Ornston "Improving": 14). He continues: "*Cathexis* signifies something different from the vague imagery implied in Freud's ... everyday words about psychological organization based on the common word stem *-setz-* ("set").... Be-*setz*-en is a colorless term that is usually defined by its context." (The German context is very often a military one.) Strachey's *cathexis*, by contrast, is based on the

Greek *kata* (down) plus *echein* (hold). He first introduced the term in *Group Psychology and the Analysis of the Ego,* his 1922 translation of Freud's *Massenpsychologie und Ich-Analyse* (Freud 1921). In *Beyond the Pleasure Principle,* he first uses the word in its adjectival form, referring to "cathectic energy in the elements of the psychical systems," and soon proceeds to use the plural noun as well: "Cathectic energy is summoned from all sides to provide sufficiently high cathexes of energy in the environs of the breach" (*Standard* 18: 27, 30). A few lines below, he introduces a participial form, referring to "a system which is itself highly cathected" (30). Holder remarks that "*cathexis* is one of the more extreme examples of ... 'classical nomenclature' and could be replaced, as could the word *instinct,* without major problems. This might make it possible to approximate Freud's German more closely" (Holder 92). Indeed, in his preface to Hubback's translation, Jones writes: "The word *Besetzung* (literally: state of being occupied) ... has been rendered by the words 'investment' or 'charge,' the latter being taken from the analogy of electricity" (Jones 1922). In the current translation, the term *charge* is used throughout: it seems desirable to select a consistent English equivalent for a German term appearing so often in the text, and given the pervasive "analogy of electricity" Jones refers to, this choice seems justified. Further justification is provided in that *charge* functions as an antonym to *discharge.* The terms work in tandem: *charge* gradually accumulates in the system, and when the amount of energy becomes excessive, there must be *discharge.*

Almost as an anecdote, one might add that Strachey eventually had his way: Freud did use the English term *cathexis* once—and only once. In the German version of his 1926 article on psychoanalysis for *Encyclopaedia Britannica,* he writes: "... dass die psychischen Vertretungen der Triebe mit bestimmten Quantitäten Energie besetzt sind (Cathexis)" (Freud 1934: 302), which Strachey translates as: "... the mental representatives of the instincts have a charge (*cathexis*) of definite quantities of energy" (*Standard* 20: 265-66). Here, for once, Strachey is forced to translate *besetzt sind* as *have a charge* since the term *cathexis* itself must be reserved to render Freud's *Cathexis.* He then adds a humble footnote: "... This seems to be the only instance in which Freud himself used this English equivalent of the German *Besetzung*" (266). Roazen, however, reports that Strachey may have felt more gleeful about Freud's use (or at least quotation) of the term than the seemingly objective footnote reveals: "Strachey proudly told me that although Freud at first had been somewhat doubtful about the choice of 'cathexis,' he had by the end of his life incorporated that term in one of his texts" (Roazen 100).

Another key term that produces difficulties is Freud's *Trieb*. Throughout, I have translated *Trieb* as *drive*, though it might be argued that *instinct* is more appropriate in non-human contexts, e.g., in the discussion of evolution (Chapter 5), and that *drive*, as a distinct term, is appropriate in the human context. Strachey, by contrast, always translates *Trieb* as *instinct*, even in the context of humans, yet this would seem the less desirable choice for a unitary term in English, given that the German term *Instinkt* does not appear in *Beyond the Pleasure Principle*; Holder indicates that where it does occasionally appear in other works, this is always in the context of animals (Holder 93). Although Freud did on occasion distinguish processes in animals from those in humans, he used a single term, *Trieb*, in *Beyond the Pleasure Principle*, suggesting that a biological reading is still appropriate: processes in humans are biologically connected with those in animals. Indeed, Dufresne comments that Freud "never bothered to reserve a special word for a nonbiological, metaphorical force" (Dufresne 189)—that biology is "the original detour, the master trope which structures the logic of *Beyond the Pleasure Principle*" (143). In any case, the consistent translation of *Trieb* as *drive* provides the most direct rendering. A connected difficulty arises in the translation of *Geschlechtstrieb*, which I have rendered as *sex drive*—a two-noun sequence as in the original German. Although this term has acquired unfortunate slangy connotations in English, it does provide symmetry with less problematical terms designating types of drives, e.g., *ego drive*, *death drive*, and *life drive*.

For stylistic comparison, it may be helpful to adduce sample excerpts from the current translation with the corresponding passages from Strachey. The current translation, for example, reads: "The phenomena of transference clearly serve the resistance exercised by the ego, which insists on repression" (Chapter 3), while Strachey's version reads: "The phenomena of transference are obviously exploited by the resistance which the ego maintains in its pertinacious insistence upon repression" (*Standard* 18: 23). The current version is a nearly word for word rendering of the original, while Strachey's seems quite different in style, and as is often the case, inserts extra words: no word in the original corresponds to Strachey's *pertinacious*. Similarly, in the discussion of trauma-neurotics (Chapter 4), the current version reads: "wish fulfillment ... is brought about by dreams," while Strachey has: "The fulfilment of wishes is, as we know, brought about ... by dreams" (*Standard* 18: 32). Nothing in the original corresponds to Strachey's *as we know*; these words lend the English text a finality not found in the original. Consider also Freud's discussion of the repetition compulsion (Chapter 5). Freud at one point has *demonischen Zwanges* (Freud 1940: *Jenseits des Lustprinzips*: 37), which I translate as "demonic compulsion," but which Strachey translates as "compulsion with its hint of possession by some 'daemonic' power" (*Standard* 18: 36). Strachey, apparently assuming readers will be unable to process figurative language, does his utmost to ensure that they will not think Freud believed in demons!

On other occasions it could be said that the issue is merely one of wordiness. The current version reads: "The processes ... give us a prototype for how this apparent 'drive toward perfection' could have arisen" (Chapter 5), while Strachey translates: "The processes ... present us with a model of the manner of origin of this supposititious 'instinct towards perfection'" (*Standard* 18: 42). Occasionally, though, the opposite problem arises: a word may be omitted. Thus, the current translation has the literal rendering "libidinal self-preservation drives" (Chapter 6), while Strachey (*Standard* 18: 53) declines to translate Freud's *libidinös* (Freud 1940: *Jenseits des Lustprinzips*: 57). On other occasions, it is likely that Strachey simply will not be understood. Thus, wherever *Lage* clearly signifies "location," Strachey renders it as *situation*. The current translation reads: "Perhaps we shall be more successful in explaining such a location for our system" (Chapter 4), while Strachey writes: "Perhaps *we* shall be more successful in accounting for this situation in the case of our system" (*Standard* 18: 24). Similarly, where *Keim* (Chapter 5) clearly signifies "embryo," Strachey has *germ*.

One might also adduce other minor issues in Strachey's rendition. Freud often used quotation marks to suggest a non-literal or loose sense, yet Strachey often omits them, cf. "[O]ne of the ... most important functions of the mental apparatus is to bind the instinctual impulses" (*Standard* 18: 62), where in the corresponding passage of the original and in several others, Freud places the German *binden* in quotes. Similarly, where Strachey uses italics, this may merely indicate his own desire to emphasize the words so marked: often there is no such emphasis in the original. Conversely, passages Freud placed in g e s p e r r t type (equivalent to italics) are often not italicized in Strachey's version. Finally, Strachey freely introduces parentheses and new paragraph divisions where these are absent in the original—e.g., in the very first paragraph of *Beyond the Pleasure Principle*.

Occasionally there are outright errors of various types in Strachey's translation. In the discussion of children's play (Chapter 2), Freud addresses "*die affektive Einschätzung dieses Spieles*" (Freud 1940: *Jenseits des Lustprinzips*: 13), which I translate as "the affective evaluation of this game," while Strachey has: "the effective nature of the game" (*Standard* 18: 15). In the discussion of Wilhelm Fliess's theoretical work (Chapter 6), Freud, perhaps with a light-hearted touch of sarcasm, describes it as *grossartig*—marvelous, grandiose, fantastic, grand—but Strachey simply renders the term as *large*. The translation is simply incorrect, and all the humor is lost. (With Hubback, I select *grandiose*.) In the immediately ensuing discussion of biology, I translate *Tierchen* as *microorganisms*, while Strachey invents the pseudo-Latin *animalculae*, with a grammatically incorrect nominative plural feminine suffix on a neuter stem. In the same discussion, though, other difficulties are created by Freud himself: Freud uses the terms *Protista* and *Protozoa* to mean exactly the same thing—apparently for variety—and I have retained the distinction even though this may create some initial confusion.

On occasion, the nuances of Freud's German simply cannot be adequately conveyed. One such example occurs in Chapter 2, where Freud presents a discussion of a child he has been observing at play. In paragraph after paragraph, with great scientific detachment, Freud refers to the child as *es*, the third person neuter pronoun corresponding to the neuter noun *Kind* (child). Yet in the last sentence of the discussion he can no longer restrain himself: he imbues the child—his grandson Ernst, in fact—with full humanity, suddenly switching to the pronoun *er* (he) in his final reference to the child. This is such an abrupt change that it is at first difficult to identify the referent, but a similar switch in pronouns is impossible in English.

At this point, a few words on John Reddick's 2003 translation will be appropriate. Laudable for its careful attention to detail,

Reddick's translation, like Strachey's, adopts a style that can be characterized as eloquent, erudite, and literary, whereas in preparing the current translation a conscious decision was made to retain Freud's often straightforward style, selecting terms from the same register as Freud's often quite ordinary vocabulary. Thus, the current version and Reddick's are strikingly different. Often, Reddick retains Strachey's terminology, e.g., *cathexis*, *cathectic*, *psyche*, *psychic*, and *animalcule*, while the current choices are *charge*, *charged*, *mind*, *mental*, and *microorganism*. On some occasions all three versions differ. Thus Strachey has *situation*, Reddick has *locus*, and the current version has *location*. Occasionally, though, the current translation overlaps with Strachey's, while Reddick's differs, e.g., in lieu of Strachey's *bound energy*, *preconscious residues*, and *vital differences*, Reddick selects *annexed energy*, *preconscious residua*, and *vital differentiae*.

Six briefer translations of works from the period 1919-37, all thematically related to *Beyond the Pleasure Principle*, are included in the current volume. First is a new rendition of portions of Chapter 2 from Freud's 1919 essay "Das Unheimliche" ["The Uncanny"]. (The current translation renders pages 233-38 from the 1947 edition.) There are three English translations of the entire work: those by Alix Strachey (1925), James Strachey (1955), and David McLintock (2003). In the introduction to his 1955 version (*Standard Edition*), Strachey explains that he adopted portions of the 1925 version, but that the two are substantially different. He continues: "Nothing is known as to when it [the essay] was originally written or how much it was changed, though the footnote quoted from *Totem and Taboo* shows that the subject was present in [Freud's] mind as early as 1913. The passages dealing with the 'compulsion to repeat' must in any case have formed part of the revision. They include a summary of much of the contents of *Beyond the Pleasure Principle*" (*Standard* 17: 218).

Included as well is a new rendition of portions of Freud's 1923 volume *Das Ich und das Es* [*The Ego and the Id*]. (The current translation includes the beginning of the preface, all of Chapter 4, and the second half of Chapter 5.) There are three English versions of the entire work: those by Joan Riviere (1927), James Strachey (1961), and John Reddick (2003). Of special interest here, from the standpoint of terminology and translation, is Freud's introduction of the term *das Es*, paralleling *das Ich*, and translated by Strachey in Latin as "the id," paralleling "the ego." Freud borrowed the term *das Es* from Georg Groddeck; earlier, it had also been used by Nietzsche to refer to impersonal components of the mind. In his introduction (*Standard Edition*), Strachey remarks on the difficulties in translation: "There was to begin with a good deal of discussion over the choice of an English equivalent. 'The id' was eventually decided upon in preference to 'the it,' so as to be parallel with the long established 'ego'" (*Standard* 19: 7). However, in a personal letter to Alix Strachey, he provides a more candid account of the discussion that actually occurred: "They [Jones and Riviere] want to call 'das Es' 'the id.' I said I thought everyone would say 'the Yidd.' So Jones said there was no such word in English. ... 'Pardon me, doctor. "Yidd" is a current slang word for a Jew.' 'Ah! A slang expression. It cannot be in very widespread use then'" (Ornston "Alternatives": 108). Strachey obviously acquiesced, and now, for better or worse, the Latin version has entered the English language.

Another difficult term in *The Ego and the Id* is *Angst*. Ideally, the German term would always be translated as *anxiety*, but in certain contexts in English this is impossible. Thus *Kastrationsangst* can be rendered directly as *castration anxiety*, but *conscience anxiety* for *Gewissensangst* is stylistically problematic. In the current rendition, the English term *fear of conscience* has been adopted, but this creates a differentiation in English (*anxiety/fear*) where none exists in the original language. (Reddick translates the German term as *consciential fear*, declaring in a footnote that he makes no apology for his use of the term!) On some occasions, in fact, Strachey uses a third English term, *dread*. This issue is also connected with a hilarious typographical error. In the conclusion to the discussion of castration anxiety, Strachey's version reads: "It is this dread that persists as the *ear* of conscience" (*Standard* 19: 57).

"The Economic Problem of Masochism" is a new rendition of Freud's 1924 essay "Das ökonomische Problem des Masochismus." This work too was previously translated twice—first in 1924 by Joan Riviere, and then by James Strachey (*Standard* 19: 159). Here, Freud develops ideas on masochism and the pleasure principle first presented in Chapter 6 of *Beyond the Pleasure Principle*. In the concluding portions of the discussion, Freud expresses his support for ideas on "Reason and Necessity" espoused by the Dutch philosopher and author Multatuli (Eduard Douwes Dekker). Although Freud does not specify the relevant work, the current edition clarifies that it is volume I of Multatuli's seven-volume philosophical magnum opus *Ideën* [*Ideas*] (1862-77). Indeed, the Dutch writer was among Freud's favorites. King writes that in 1907, "Freud was one of thirty-two distinguished people asked by the publisher Hugo Heller to name 'ten good books'" (King 75). Multatuli appeared on Freud's list, but so favorable was his general impression that he declined to name any specific work. (The list goes on to mention Twain's *Sketches* and Kipling's *The Jungle Book*.) Freud's use of the term *imago* is also of interest. Strachey's note clarifies that Freud himself attributed the term to Jung, who "partly chose the word from the title of a novel of the same name by the Swiss writer, Carl Spitteler [1906]" (*Standard* 19: 168). Strachey also indicates that Hanns Sachs and Otto Rank, who founded the journal *Imago* in 1912, took that name from the same source.

"A Note about the 'Mystic Writing Pad'" is a new rendition of Freud's 1926 article "Notiz über den Wunderblock." In the introduction to his translation (*Standard* 19: 227-32), Strachey indicates that the article was probably written in the autumn of 1924: in a letter to Karl Abraham of that year, Freud mentions his work on revising it. The work includes reflections on *Beyond the Pleasure Principle* centering on the idea that the "inexplicable phenomenon of consciousness" arose in the perceptual system in lieu of lasting memory traces, which are housed instead in deeper-lying "memory systems."

The current volume also includes a new rendition of the concluding portions of Chapter 6 from *Das Unbehagen in der Kultur* [*Civilization and Its Discontents*] (1930). There are three English versions of the entire work: those by Joan Riviere (1930), James Strachey (1961), and David McLintock (2002). Strachey notes that his version is based on Riviere's, and that he adopted her rendition of the title as well. Indeed, translating the German terms *Unbehagen* and *Kultur* in the context of the title is challenging, and Riviere's solution is persuasive. Given that human cultures are based on suppression of drives, the themes of Chapter 6 are both social and psychological. In passages filled with sarcasm, ironic humor, and indictments of religion, an obviously pessimistic Freud reiterates his belief in the death or destructive drive, arguing that it is the "greatest impediment to civilization." In discussing the "undeniable" existence of evil, Freud adduces appropriate passages from Goethe's *Faust*. Although Riviere and

Strachey selected Bayard Taylor's English renderings (1870), which sacrifice meaning at the altar of rhyme, the current volume provides literal translations of Goethe's poetry.

As a final contribution from Freud, the current volume includes a new rendition of portions of Section 6 from Freud's late essay "Die endliche und unendliche Analyse" (1937). I have retained Strachey's very apt English title— "Analysis Terminable and Interminable"—as well as his translation of the technical term *Ichverschiedenheit*, "distinguishing characteristics of the ego." Strachey (*Standard* 23: 212) comments that the essay expresses a "cool attitude toward therapeutic ambitions," but it is noteworthy that in 1937, just two years before his death, Freud was still deeply occupied with such themes as the struggle of Eros and the death drive. Although Strachey's translation is generally serviceable, it contains at least one error worthy of comment: in the discussion of Empedocles, Freud comments that his theory differs from that of the Greek philosopher in that Freud's is *biopsychisch*—a term I have rendered as "biopsychic"—while Strachey's "biophysical" is surely inaccurate.

In these six works, Strachey's style is sometimes wordy, e.g., in "The Uncanny" he writes: "... it is only this factor of involuntary repetition which surrounds what would otherwise be innocent enough with an uncanny atmosphere" (*Standard* 17: 237) while the current version translates directly: "... it is only the factor of unintended repetition that makes the otherwise unremarkable uncanny." One also notices the many incomplete sentences in Freud's German—especially the lengthy noun phrases and prepositional phrases exemplifying a previously introduced concept. Strachey, striving for grammatical correctness, typically adds extra material to render them complete, but in the current version few such adjustments are made. It is hoped that the current version, while conveying the intellectual content, will suggest something of Freud's style as well. No two languages ever overlap completely. No translation will ever replace Freud's original German, yet each translation has an important role, supplying a new interpretation and allowing readers to see Freud's work in a new light.

BEYOND THE PLEASURE PRINCIPLE

I

In psychoanalytic theory we immediately assume that the course of mental events is automatically regulated by the pleasure principle. That is, we believe that the course of mental events is in every case given its impetus by an unpleasurable tension, and that it then goes in a direction such that its final state coincides with a reduction of this tension, i.e., with the avoidance of unpleasure or the production of pleasure. If we consider this course while regarding the mental processes we have studied, we will be introducing an economic[1] point of view into our work. I believe a depiction which, beside the topographic and the dynamic forces, also attempts to address this economic force is the most comprehensive one we can now imagine, and that such a depiction deserves to be specially designated as *metapsychological.*

In establishing the pleasure principle, it will be of no interest to investigate the degree to which we have approached or adopted any particular historically established philosophical system. We arrive at such speculative hypotheses in an attempt to describe and account for the facts of daily observation in our field. Priority and originality are not among the aims set for psychoanalytic research; the impressions underlying the establishment of the pleasure principle are so obvious that it is hardly possible to overlook them. On the other hand, we would gladly express our appreciation to a philosophical or psychological theory able to tell us the meanings of the sensations of pleasure and unpleasure, which have such imperative force for us. Unfortunately, nothing useful is offered us here. This is the darkest and most inaccessible region of the mind, and if it is impossible to avoid dealing with it, I believe the loosest hypotheses will be the best. We have decided to associate pleasure and unpleasure with the quantity of excitation present in the mind but not bound in any way, and

---

1 Freud conceived of the psyche in four ways, beginning roughly in 1900: as topographic, dynamic, economic, and structural. By topographic Freud meant the division of the mind into conscious, pre-conscious, and unconscious systems. By dynamic Freud meant the push and pull of conflicting forces at work in the psyche. By economic he meant the quantity of energy that flowed within the psyche. Metapsychology is almost exclusively concerned with this feature. And by structural he meant, in his last phase, the division of mind into ego/id/superego.

to do this such that unpleasure corresponds to an increase in this quantity and pleasure to a decrease. Here, we are not thinking of a simple correspondence between the strength of the feelings and the changes they are associated with; least of all, given all the experience of psychophysiology, are we thinking of a directly proportional relation. The size of the decrease or increase within a period of time is probably what determines the feeling. This might conceivably be accessible to experimentation, but for us analysts further penetration into these problems is inadvisable until we can be led by completely definite observations.

Yet we cannot be indifferent on finding that a researcher of such deep vision as Gustav Fechner[1] expressed a conception of pleasure and unpleasure basically coinciding with the one psychoanalytic work compels us to adopt. Fechner's statement is contained in his small work *Einige Ideen zur Schöpfungs- und Entwicklungsgeschichte der Organismen* [Some Ideas on the History of the Creation and Development of Organisms (1873)]:

> In so far as conscious impulses always relate to pleasure or unpleasure, pleasure or unpleasure can also be conceived as psychophysically related to states of stability and instability. On this basis is founded a hypothesis I shall develop in more detail elsewhere—the hypothesis that every psychophysical motion surmounting the threshold of consciousness is linked with pleasure to the degree that, beyond a certain limit, it approaches total stability, and that it is linked with unpleasure to the degree that, beyond a certain limit, it deviates from total stability; between the two limits, which can be designated as qualitative thresholds of pleasure and unpleasure, there exists a certain area of perceptual indifference. (Fechner 94)

The facts that have made us believe in the dominance of the pleasure principle in the mind are also expressed in the hypothesis that the mental apparatus strives to keep the quantity of excitation within it as low as possible, or at least constant. This is the same thing expressed in a different way, for if the work of the mental apparatus aims to keep the quantity of excitation

---

1 Gustav Theodor Fechner (1801-87), 'psycho-physicist,' known for wild speculation about psychology and nature, and founder of experimental psychology.

low, then everything likely to increase the quantity of excitation will be deemed detrimental to function, i.e., as unpleasurable. The pleasure principle is derived from the constancy principle. More precisely, the constancy principle was deduced from the facts compelling us to assume the pleasure principle. Through a deeper discussion we will also find that this aim we have ascribed to the mental apparatus can be classified as a special case of Fechner's principle of the tendency toward stability, to which he relates feelings of pleasure and unpleasure.

But now we must say that it is actually wrong to speak of the dominance of the pleasure principle in the course of mental processes. If there were such a dominance, the vast majority of our mental processes would be accompanied by pleasure or lead to pleasure, but ordinary experience strongly contradicts this conclusion. Thus it must merely be the case that a strong tendency toward the pleasure principle exists in the mind, but that certain other forces or relations oppose the pleasure principle such that the result cannot always accord with the tendency toward pleasure. We may compare Fechner's comment on a similar point: "... that the tendency toward an aim still does not mean the aim is reached; the aim can be reached only in approximations ..." (90). If we turn now to the question of what circumstances can block the imposition of the pleasure principle, we are once again in safe and familiar territory, and can abundantly adduce our analytic experience in providing an answer.

The first example of such an inhibition of the pleasure principle is familiar as a regularly occurring one. We know that the pleasure principle characterizes a primary modus operandi of the mental apparatus, and that for the survival of the organism in the difficulties of the physical world, from the very start, it is useless and indeed extremely dangerous. Under the influence of the ego's drives for self-preservation, the pleasure principle is supplanted by the *reality principle*, which, without renouncing the intention to gain pleasure in the end, nevertheless demands and effects the postponement of gratification, the suspension of various possibilities for gaining gratification, and the temporary toleration of unpleasure on the detour leading to pleasure. For a long time, though, the pleasure principle remains the modus operandi of the sex drives, which are harder to "educate"; often, starting from those drives or in the ego itself, it overpowers the reality principle and harms the organism as a whole.

Yet there is no doubt that the replacement of the pleasure principle by the reality principle is responsible only for a small portion of the unpleasurable experiences, and not for the most intense ones. Another equally regular source for the discharge of unpleasure originates in the conflicts and splits in the mental apparatus during the ego's development toward more coordinated structures. Almost all the energy filling the apparatus arises from the accompanying drive impulses, but these are not all permitted to develop equally. In the course of events, individual drives or components of drives constantly prove incompatible in aims or demands with the other drives that can join into the comprehensive unity of the ego. These individual drives are then split off from that unity through the process of repression; they are retained at lower levels of mental development and are temporarily cut off from the possibility of gratification. If they then succeed—as can easily occur with repressed sex drives—in fighting their way through, via detours, to direct or substitute gratification, this success, which would otherwise have been an opportunity for pleasure, is felt by the ego as unpleasure. Due to the old conflict resulting in repression, the pleasure principle once again breaks through just when certain drives, following the principle, were on their way to gaining new pleasure. The details of the process by which repression transforms a possibility of pleasure into a source of unpleasure are not yet well understood or cannot be clearly portrayed, but all neurotic unpleasure is surely of this type—pleasure that cannot be felt as pleasure.[1]

The two sources of unpleasure mentioned here certainly do not explain the majority of our unpleasurable experiences, but we can argue with at least some justification that the presence of the other sources does not contradict the dominance of the pleasure principle. Most of the unpleasure we experience is of course perceptual unpleasure—either the perception of urges from ungratified drives, or external perception. Either the perception is distressing in itself or it arouses unpleasurable expectations in the mental apparatus and is recognized by it as a "danger." The reaction to these demands from drives and these threats of danger, a reaction in which the actual

---

1 The important thing is that pleasure and unpleasure, being conscious sensations, are bound to the ego. [Freud's note]

activity of the mental apparatus expresses itself, can then be correctly directed by the pleasure principle or by the reality principle, which modifies the pleasure principle. Here it does not seem necessary to recognize any significant limitation of the pleasure principle, but specifically the investigation of the mental reaction to the external danger can provide us with new material and raise new questions concerning the problem discussed here.

II

After severe mechanical accidents, railway crashes, and other life-threatening incidents, there arises a condition that has long been designated as "traumatic neurosis." The terrible war [World War One] that has just ended has produced many cases of this illness, and has at least ended the temptation to attribute it to organic injury of the nervous system through mechanical force (cf. Freud et al. 1919). The symptomatology of traumatic neurosis approaches that of hysteria in the abundance of similar motor symptoms, but usually surpasses it in its strongly developed indications of subjective suffering, as in hypochondria or melancholia, and in evincing a far more comprehensive general weakening and disturbance in mental abilities. No full understanding has yet been achieved of the war neuroses, nor of the traumatic neuroses of peace. With the war neuroses, it was both enlightening and confusing that the same symptoms arose from time to time in the absence of any gross mechanical violence. In ordinary traumatic neurosis two prominent traits have been noted. First, the weightiest element in their causation seemed to be the factor of surprise, of fright; and secondly, a wound or injury received at the same time usually counteracted the development of a neurosis. The terms *fright* [Schreck], *fear* [Furcht], and *anxiety* [Angst] are incorrectly used as synonyms; they can be clearly distinguished in their relation to danger. *Anxiety* denotes a certain state of expecting danger and preparing for it, even for an unknown danger. *Fear* requires a definite object to be feared. *Fright*, though, designates the state of a person who encounters danger unprepared; it emphasizes the factor of surprise. I do not believe that anxiety can produce a traumatic neurosis. In anxiety there is something that protects one from fright and thus from fright-neurosis. We will return to this later.

We may consider the study of dreams the most reliable way to investigate deep processes in the mind. The dreams experienced in traumatic neurosis are characterized by their reintroducing the patient again and again into the situation of his accident, a situation from which he awakens with renewed fright. This should really surprise people much more than it has. The fact that the traumatic experience repeatedly imposes itself on the patient even in sleep is taken as proof of the strength of the impression made by that experience. The patient is mentally fixated to the trauma, as it were. Such fixations to the experience that provoked the illness have long been familiar to us in hysteria. Breuer and Freud claimed "Hysterics suffer mainly from reminiscences" (Breuer and Freud 1893). For the war neuroses, too, observers like Ferenczi and Simmel have been able to explain several motor symptoms by adducing fixation to the moment of the trauma.

Yet as far as I know, patients suffering from traumatic neurosis do not occupy themselves much, while awake, with memories of their accident. Perhaps, rather, they strive not to think about it. If one accepts at face value the claim that their nightly dreams place them back into the pathogenic situation, one has misunderstood the nature of dreams. It would better accord with their nature to present the patient with images from the time when he was healthy, or of the desired cure. To prevent the dreams of traumatic neurotics from raising doubts about the wish-fulfilling tendency of dreams, one might still argue that in this condition the dream function, like so much else, has been shaken and diverted from its aims, or one might contemplate the mysterious masochistic tendencies of the ego.

Now I propose to leave the dark and gloomy subject of traumatic neurosis and study the modus operandi of the mental apparatus in one of its earliest normal activities: children's play.

The various theories of children's play have just recently been brought together and evaluated in terms of psychoanalysis by Sigmund Pfeifer, to whose article I would refer the reader (Pfeifer). These theories strive to discern the motives of children's play without emphasizing the economic point of view—consideration of the gain in pleasure. Without wishing to cover all these phenomena, I have taken advantage of an opportunity that presented itself to me to explain the first game invented by a boy one and a half years old. It was more than a fleeting observation: for several weeks I lived under one roof with the child and his parents,[1] and it took some time before the curious and constantly repeated performance revealed itself to my understanding.

In his intellectual development, the child was by no means precocious. At age one and a half he could say only a few comprehensible words, also including in his repertoire several meaningful sounds understood by the household. But he had a good relationship with his parents and the servant-girl, and was praised for his "good" behavior. He did not disturb his parents at night, he conscientiously obeyed rules against touching certain objects or entering certain rooms, and most notably, he never cried when his mother left him for several hours. Yet he was very attached to his mother, who had not only nourished him herself, but had also cared for him without assistance. Yet this good boy had the sometimes irritating habit of taking all the small objects he could find and throwing them far away into the corner of a room, under the bed, and so on, so that gathering his toys was often no easy chore. While thus engaged, and with an expression of interest and satisfaction, he would produce a loud, extended "o-o-o-o" which his mother and I agreed was no interjection, but signified the word *fort* [gone]. I finally noticed that it was a game, and that he used his toys for no other purpose than to play "gone" with them. One day I noticed something that confirmed my interpretation. The child had a wooden spool with a piece of string tied around it. It never occurred to him to drag it along the floor behind him and pretend it was a carriage, for example. Instead, he very skillfully threw the spool, attached to the string, over the edge of his little curtained bed so that it disappeared therein, all the while uttering his meaningful "o-o-o-o." Then, using the string, he pulled the spool out of the bed again and greeted its appearance with a joyful *da* [there]. So this was the whole game—disappearance and return—of which it was usually

1   In September 1915 Freud visited his daughter Sophie's home in Hamburg and had occasion to observe his grandson Ernst. See Jones 1957: 267. Sophie was Freud's favorite, who died of influenza pneumonia in January 1920, while Freud was still composing *BPP*.

possible to see only the first act, tirelessly repeated as a game in its own right, though the greater pleasure was no doubt associated with the second act.[1]

The interpretation of the game was then clear. It was connected with the child's great cultural achievement: by renouncing his drives (renunciation of drive gratification) he allowed his mother to leave without protest. He compensated for this, so to speak, by enacting the same sort of disappearance and return of the objects in his reach. For the affective evaluation of this game, of course, it does not matter whether the child invented it himself or adopted it in response to a suggestion from elsewhere. We are interested in another point. The mother's departure could not possibly have been pleasant for the child, nor can he have felt indifferent about it. But how does his repetition of this unpleasant experience as a game accord with the pleasure principle? Perhaps it will be replied that the departure had to be enacted as a precondition for the joyful reappearance—that the true intent of the game lay in the latter. But this would be contradicted by the observation that the first act, the departure, was staged as a game in its own right, and indeed much more often than the whole sequence with a pleasurable ending.

The analysis of a single case like this one can yield us no sure decision. If one keeps an open mind, one gains the impression that the child turned the experience into a game for another reason. At first, he was passive, overcome by the experience, but then he took on an active role: he repeated it, though it was unpleasurable, as a game. One might ascribe these efforts to a drive for mastery acting independently of the pleasurable or unpleasurable nature of the memory. Yet one might still attempt a different interpretation. Throwing the object away from oneself to make it "gone" could be the gratification of an impulse for revenge on the mother in response to her going away—an impulse repressed in real life. It would have the defiant meaning: "Well, then, go

---

1 This interpretation was later fully confirmed by a further observation. One day when the mother had been away for many hours, she was greeted upon her return with the utterance "Baby o-o-o-o!", which at first was not understood. It soon turned out, though, that during the long time alone the child had found a way of making himself disappear. He had discovered his reflection in a full-length mirror that almost reached the floor, and had then crouched down so that his reflection was "gone." [Freud's note]

away! I don't need you. I'll send you away myself." A year later, the same child I had observed at age one and a half playing his first game would often take a toy he was irritated with and throw it on the floor, saying: "Go in war!" At that time he had been told that his absent father was "in the war"; he did not miss his father at all, but made it very clear that he did not wish to be disturbed in his sole possession of his mother.[1] We know that other children behave in the same way—that they can express similar hostile impulses by throwing objects away from themselves as substitutes for people (cf. Freud 1917). Thus doubts arise as to whether the urge to mentally process whatever has made a great impression—to master it completely—can express itself in a primary sense, independent of the pleasure principle. In the case discussed here, it is possible that the child was able to repeat an unpleasant experience in play due only to the fact that a different type of gain in pleasure, but a direct one, is connected with such repetition.

Further consideration of children's play will not help us choose between these two conceptions. It can be seen that in play children repeat everything that has made a great impression on them in life, and that here they are abreacting the strength of that impression—mastering the situation, as it were. But on the other hand it is quite clear that all their play occurs under the influence of the wish that dominates them at this time—the wish to be grown up and to be able to do the things adults do. One may also observe that the unpleasurable nature of an experience does not always render it unusable in play. If the doctor has examined a child's throat or performed a small operation on him, this frightening experience will certainly be taken up in the next game, yet the gain in pleasure from another source should not be overlooked. As children switch from the passivity of the experience to the activity of play, they impose on a playmate the unpleasant experience they have undergone, thus taking their revenge on this substitute.

In any case, it is clear from these discussions that we need not assume a special imitative drive as a cause for play. Let

---

1 When the child was five years and nine months old, his mother died. Now that she was really "gone" ("o-o-o"), the boy showed no grief over her. Indeed, a second child had been born in the meantime and had awakened in him the strongest jealousy. [Freud's note]

us also emphasize that the artistic play and imitation carried out by adults—aimed, unlike the activities of children, at an audience—does not spare that audience, for example in tragedy, from the most painful impressions, and yet is felt to be highly enjoyable. We are thus convinced that even under the dominance of the pleasure principle, there are enough ways and means of transforming the unpleasurable into an object remembered and mentally processed. We can leave these cases and situations that end up with a gain in pleasure to be considered by an economically oriented aesthetic system. They are useless for our purposes, for they assume the existence and dominance of the pleasure principle and give no evidence for the operation of tendencies beyond the pleasure principle—tendencies more primal than the pleasure principle, and independent of it.

III

Today, after twenty-five years of intense work, the primary aims of psychoanalytic technique are completely different than they were at the outset. Then, the analyzing physician could only aim to guess the unconscious content hidden from the patient, to assemble it, and, at the appropriate time, to communicate it. Psychoanalysis was mainly an interpretive art. Since the therapeutic task could not be solved in this way, another aim immediately arose: to compel the patient to confirm the analyst's construction through his own memory. In this effort the main emphasis was on the resistances of the patient: now the art focused on uncovering them as soon as possible, on presenting them to the patient, and, through human influence, on bringing him to give them up. (This was the locus of suggestion, operating as "transference.")

But it became ever clearer that the established aim of making the unconscious conscious is not fully achievable in this way either. The patient cannot remember everything repressed in him—maybe not even the most important thing—and thus gets no convincing evidence that the construction communicated to him is accurate. Indeed, he is compelled to *repeat* the repressed content as current experience instead of *remembering* it, as the physician would prefer, as part of the past (Freud 1914:

"Erinnern"). This reproduction, arising with such undesired accuracy, always contains something of infantile sexual life—of the Oedipus complex and its derivatives—and regularly plays out in the domain of transference, in the relation to the physician. At this stage, one can say that the earlier neurosis has now been replaced by a fresh transference neurosis. The physician attempts to limit the extent of this transference neurosis as much as possible, to push as much material as possible into the memory, and to admit as little as possible into the domain of repetition. The relation between the remembered and the reproduced is unique to each case. As a rule, the physician cannot spare the patient under analysis this phase of the treatment. He must make him re-experience a certain portion of his forgotten life, but must ensure that some degree of detachment is preserved. Through this detachment, apparent reality will constantly be recognized as the reflection of a forgotten past. If this succeeds, the patient can be convinced, and the associated therapeutic success can be achieved.

To better grasp this "repetition compulsion," expressed during the psychoanalytic treatment of neurotics, we must avoid the mistake of believing that in fighting resistances we are dealing with resistance by the "unconscious." The unconscious—the "repressed"—does not resist the efforts of the treatment at all. Indeed, it strives only to break through the pressure weighing it down so as to emerge into the conscious or be discharged through a real act. Resistance during treatment arises from the same higher layers and systems of the mind that earlier caused repression. But since the motives of resistances and even the resistances themselves, in our experience, are initially unconscious during treatment, we are well advised to correct an inadequacy in our terminology. In the interest of clarity, we should contrast not the conscious and the unconscious, but the coherent *ego* and the *repressed* content. Much of the ego itself is surely unconscious—specifically what may be called its core. We shall designate only a small portion thereof as the preconscious. Having replaced purely descriptive terms with systematic or dynamic ones, we can say that the resistance of patients under analysis arises from their ego. Then we shall immediately understand that the repetition compulsion must be attributed to the unconscious repressed content. It probably could not express itself until the work of the treatment had gone part way toward loosening the repression.[1]

There is no doubt that the resistance exercised by the conscious and the preconscious ego serves the pleasure principle in that it desires to obviate the unpleasure that would be excited by the release of the repressed content, but we are attempting to bring about the acceptance of that unpleasure by appealing to the reality principle. Yet what relation to the pleasure principle characterizes the repetition compulsion, this expression of the power of the repressed content? It is clear that most of what is re-experienced under the repetition compulsion must bring the ego unpleasure, for it reveals activities of repressed drive impulses. That, however, is unpleasure we have already addressed, and which does not contradict the pleasure principle; it is unpleasure for one system and, at the same time, gratification for the other. But the new and remarkable fact we must now describe is that the repetition compulsion also reproduces past experiences that include no possibility of pleasure, and which at no time can have been gratifications even of subsequently repressed drive impulses.

The early flowering of infantile sexuality is destined to extinction since the wishes of that period are incompatible with reality and since the child's stage of development is inadequate. This flowering perishes in highly distressing circumstances and amidst deeply painful feelings. Loss of love and the experience of failure leave behind a lasting reduction in self-regard—a narcissistic scar, which in my experience and also in Marcinowski's opinion is the strongest contributor to the "feeling of inferiority" often observed in neurotics (Marcinowski). Sexual investigations, limited by the child's stage of physical development, give him no satisfactory answer. This leads to the later complaint: "I can't accomplish anything; I can never succeed." Tender affection, usually toward the parent of the opposite sex, succumbs to disappointment, to vain expectation of gratification, or to jealousy at the birth of a new baby,

---

1 I have argued elsewhere [1923] that it is the "suggestive effect" of the treatment that now comes to the aid of the repetition compulsion, i.e., submissiveness to the physician, deeply based in the unconscious parental complex. [Freud's note added in 1923] Reference: Freud, Sigmund. "Remarks on the Theory and Practice of Dream-Interpretation," *Standard* 19: 109-21.

which unambiguously proves the infidelity of the beloved. The child's own attempt to produce such a baby himself, undertaken with tragic seriousness, is a humiliating failure. The reduction in the affection expressed toward the child, the increased demands of education, harsh words, and the occasional punishment finally reveal the full extent of the *scorn* that is his lot. These are a few of the regularly recurring ways the typical love experience of this period of childhood is brought to an end.

The neurotic repeats all of these undesired circumstances and painful affective states in the transference, reanimating them with the greatest ingenuity. They strive for the cessation of the treatment in mid-course. They know how to recreate for themselves the sensation of scorn, and how to make the physician utter harsh words and treat them coldly. They find suitable objects for their jealousy. They replace the intensely desired baby of earlier times with the plan or promise of a great gift—which usually turns out to be just as unreal as the baby. None of this can have been pleasurable in the past. One would suppose that all this would produce less unpleasure today if it appeared as a memory or in dreams, rather than shaping itself as new experience. We are of course dealing with the action of drives intended to lead to gratification, but past experience has borne no fruit; previously, too, those drives brought only unpleasure in place of gratification. Nevertheless, past experience is repeated: a compulsion requires it.

What psychoanalysis reveals in the transference phenomena of neurotics appears also in the life of certain normal persons. With such persons, one has the impression of a persecuting fate or of something demonic in their experience, and from the outset psychoanalysis has considered such a fate to be mainly self-imposed by the individual and determined by early infantile influences. The compulsion expressing itself here differs not at all from the repetition compulsion of neurotics, though these persons have never shown signs of a neurotic conflict dealt with through the production of symptoms. Everyone knows people whose human relationships all end up in the same way. This includes benefactors who are eventually deserted in resentment by every one of their protégés—as much as these protégés may otherwise differ from one another, and who thus seem fated to taste to the dregs all the bitterness of ingratitude. This includes men whose friendships all end in the same way: betrayal. This includes others who during their life, time and time again, repeatedly raise another person into a position of great authority in the private or public sphere, only to overthrow this authority figure after a certain time and replace him with someone else. This includes lovers whose love affairs with women all go through the same phases and come to the same end. This "eternal return of the same" does not surprise us when it is an active behavior of the person involved, and when we can discover in his being the unchanging character trait that must express itself in the repetition of the same experiences. We are much more strongly affected by those cases in which a person seems to experience passively something over which he has no influence, while constantly experiencing the repetition of the same fate. For example, we might think of the story of the woman who married three men in a row, each of whom soon thereafter became terminally ill and had to be nursed by her until death.[1] The most moving poetic representation of such a fate is that of Tasso in the romantic epic *Gerusalemme Liberata*. The hero Tancred has unwittingly killed his beloved, Clorinda, while she was doing battle with him in the armor of an enemy knight. After her burial he makes his way into an eerie enchanted forest that terrifies the army of the Crusaders. There he slashes a tall tree with his sword, but from the wound in the tree blood streams forth and the voice of Clorinda, whose soul was held captive in the tree, accuses him of harming his beloved again.

Given such observations relating to behavior in the transference and relating to human fate, we will be so courageous as to assume that in the mind there really is a repetition compulsion which supersedes the pleasure principle. We will now also be inclined to relate to this compulsion the dreams of the trauma-neurotic and the child's impulse to play.

We must nevertheless remind ourselves that only in rare cases can we perceive the effects of the repetition compulsion pure and unaided by other motives. In children's play we have already emphasized the other interpretations its emergence permits. The repetition compulsion and the direct pleasurable gratification of drives seem to converge here in an intimate commonality. The phenomena of transference clearly serve the resistance exercised by the ego, which insists on repression. The

---

1 Cf. C.G. Jung's apt remarks about this (Jung). [Freud's note]

repetition compulsion, which the treatment wished to utilize, is drawn as it were by the ego to its own side: the ego seeks to cling to the pleasure principle. Much of what could be called the compulsion of fate seems comprehensible through rational consideration: we feel no need to set up a new and mysterious motive. Dreams of accidents are perhaps the least suspicious case, but after closer consideration it must be admitted that in the other examples as well, the situation is not explained through any accomplishment of the motives known to us. There is enough left over to justify the hypothesis of a repetition compulsion—and this compulsion seems more primal, more elementary, more drive-oriented than the pleasure principle, which it pushes aside. But if such a repetition compulsion exists in the mind, we would like to know something about it— what function it corresponds to, under what conditions it can emerge, and in what relation it stands to the pleasure principle, which earlier we certainly believed capable of ruling over the course of the processes of excitation in the mind.

IV

The following is speculation, often far-fetched speculation, which each person will appreciate or disregard according to his or her particular interests. It is furthermore an attempt to follow an idea consistently, out of curiosity, to see where this will lead.

Psychoanalytic speculation begins with the impression, gained from the investigation of unconscious processes, that consciousness may not be the most general characteristic of mental processes, but only a special function thereof. Metapsychologically, it declares that consciousness is the activity of a particular system that it designates as C [Consciousness]. Since consciousness mainly delivers perceptions of excitations from the external world and of feelings of pleasure and unpleasure that can only arise from within the mental apparatus, the system P-C [Perception-Consciousness] can be assigned a spatial position. It must lie on the border of outside and inside. It must be turned toward the external world and must house the other mental systems. We will observe that with these hypotheses we have proposed nothing new, but have only followed localistic brain anatomy, which places the "seat" of consciousness in the cerebral cortex—the outermost, encapsulating layer of the central organ. Brain anatomy need not concern itself with why, anatomically speaking, consciousness is housed on the surface of the brain, rather than residing well protected somewhere in the deepest interior thereof. Perhaps we shall be more successful in explaining such a location for our system P-C.

Consciousness is not the only unique feature we attribute to the processes in this system. Supported by our impressions from psychoanalytic experience, we assume that all excitatory processes in the other systems leave lasting traces as the basis of memory—memory traces having nothing to do with becoming conscious. They are often the most powerful and the most durable when the process that left them behind never comes to consciousness. But we find it hard to believe that these lasting traces of excitation also occur in the system P-C. If they always remained conscious, they would very soon limit the ability of the system to receive fresh excitations.[1] However, if they were unconscious, we would have to explain the existence of unconscious processes in a system whose function is otherwise accompanied by the phenomenon of consciousness. With our hypothesis that becoming conscious is assigned to a special system, we would, as it were, have changed nothing and gained nothing. While this is not an absolutely binding consideration, it may still lead us to suspect that becoming conscious and leaving behind a memory trace are incompatible within the same system. Thus we could say that in the system C the excitatory process becomes conscious but leaves no lasting trace; all those traces of the excitatory process that form the basis of memory would arise in the adjacent inner systems when the excitation is transmitted to them. The schema I included in the speculative section of my *Interpretation of Dreams* also adopts this hypothesis. If one considers how little we know, from other sources, about the origin of consciousness, the claim that *consciousness arises instead of a memory trace* should at least be acknowledged as a rather explicit proposal.

The system C would thus be characterized by the peculiarity that in it the excitatory process does not leave behind any lasting change in its elements, as it does in all other mental systems, but fizzles out, as it were, in the phenomenon of becoming

---

1 All of this is based on Breuer's discussions in the theoretical section of Breuer and Freud 1895.

conscious. Such an exception to the general rule calls for an explanation through a causal factor applying only in this one system, and this factor, not claimed by the other systems, could easily be the exposed location of the system C—its immediate connection with the external world.

Let us imagine a living organism in its most simplified form as an undifferentiated vesicle of substance able to receive stimuli. Then its surface, turned toward the external world, is differentiated by its very location and will serve as an organ for receiving stimuli. As a recapitulation of evolutionary history, embryology also demonstrates, in fact, that the central nervous system originates from the ectoderm, and that the grey matter of the cerebral cortex is merely a descendant of the primitive surface and could have taken on some of its essential properties through inheritance. It would then be easy to imagine that through the unrelenting impact of external stimuli on the surface of the vesicle, its substance was permanently altered down to a certain depth, so that its excitatory process proceeds differently than in the deeper layers. Thus a crust formed, which eventually became so burned through with stimulation that it presented the most favorable conditions for the reception of stimuli and was no longer capable of modification. With reference to the system C, this would mean that its elements can no longer undergo permanent alteration as excitation passes through, for they are already totally modified in terms of this function. Now, though, they have become capable of producing consciousness. Concerning the nature of this modification of the substance and of the excitatory process, one can imagine various proposals, but these cannot be verified at this time. One can assume that in passing from one element to another, an excitation would have to overcome a resistance, and that this reduction of the resistance would lay down the lasting trace of the excitation (clearing a pathway). In the system C there would no longer exist any such resistance to passage from one element to another. To this conception one can relate Breuer's distinction between resting (bound) and free charged energy in the elements of the mental systems (Breuer and Freud 1895). The elements of the system C would then conduct no bound energy, but only freely dischargeable energy. But I believe that for the time being it would be preferable to express oneself as tentatively as possible on these points. With this speculation, in any case, we would to some degree be associating the origin of consciousness with the location of the system C and the characteristics that must be ascribed to it in connection with the excitatory process.

There is more to say about the living vesicle with its cortical layer for the reception of stimuli. This particle of living substance hovers in the midst of an external world charged with the strongest energies, and would be killed by the stimuli coming from these energies if it were not provided with a *shield against stimuli*. It acquires this shield as follows: its outermost surface gives up the structure of living matter, becomes to an extent inorganic, and functions as a special capsule or membrane resisting stimuli. Accordingly, the energies of the external world now pass with only a fraction of their intensity into the closest still-living layers. Behind the shield, these layers can now devote themselves to the reception of the quantities of stimuli allowed to pass through. By dying, however, the outer layer has saved all the deeper ones from this fate—provided, at least, that no stimuli of such strength arrive that they break through the shield. For the living organism, defense against stimuli is almost a more important task than reception. The shield is provided with its own supply of energy, and must above all strive to preserve the special forms of transformation of energy operating within it against the equalizing and thus destructive influence of the monumental energies operating outside. The receptive function serves mainly to determine the direction and nature of the external stimuli, and for this purpose it must suffice to take small samples from the external world—to taste it in small quantities. In highly developed organisms the cortical layer that the earlier vesicle dedicated to the reception of stimuli withdrew long ago into the depths of the interior of the body, but portions remain on the surface, immediately below the general shield against stimuli. These are the sense organs, which basically contain structures for the reception of specific stimulatory effects, but also contain devices for renewed protection against excessively large quantities of stimuli and for blocking inappropriate types of stimuli. It is characteristic of them that they process only minimal quantities of external stimuli, and merely perform random sampling of the external world. Perhaps they can be compared to feelers that emerge timidly into the external world and then withdraw from it.

At this point I shall briefly address a topic that deserves extremely thorough treatment. Today, due to certain psychoanalytic discoveries, Kant's pronouncement that time and space are necessary categories of the mind can be brought to discussion. We have discovered that the unconscious mental processes are in themselves "timeless." That is to say, first of all, that they are not ordered chronologically, that time changes nothing in them, and that one cannot apply to them the concept of time. These are negative characteristics that can only be clarified through comparison with the conscious mental processes. Our abstract concept of time, by contrast, seems to be completely derived from the modus operandi of the system P-C and to correspond to a self-perception by that modus operandi. This mode of function in the system might possibly be another way of providing a shield against stimuli. These comments will surely sound very obscure, but I must restrict myself to such hints.

We have discussed how the living vesicle is provided with a shield against stimuli from the external world. Earlier, we showed that the next cortical layer must be differentiated as an organ for reception of external stimuli. But this sensitive cortical layer, the future system C, also receives excitations from within. The location of the system, between outside and inside, and the variance in the conditions for influence from the two sides, respectively, become the defining factors for the functioning of the system and of the entire mental apparatus. Toward the outside there is a shield against stimuli, and the arriving quantities of excitation will have only a reduced effect. Toward the inside such a shield against stimuli is impossible, and the excitations from the deeper layers are transmitted to the system directly and undiminished, while certain characteristics of their path generate feelings from the gamut that ranges from pleasure to unpleasure. In any case, in their intensity and in other qualitative characteristics (perhaps including amplitude), the excitations coming from within will accord better with the modus operandi of the system than do the stimuli streaming in from the external world. But two things are decisively determined through these conditions: first, the dominance of feelings of pleasure and unpleasure—indices of processes in the interior of the apparatus—over all external stimuli; and second, a manner of proceeding against those internal excitations that produce an excessive increase in unpleasure. This will result in the tendency to treat them as though they were exercising their influence not from within, but from outside. Thus, it will be possible to use against them the defensive means of the shield against stimuli. This is the origin of *projection*, assigned such a large role in the causation of pathological processes.

I have the impression that through these last considerations we are better able to understand the dominance of the pleasure principle, but we still have no explanation for those cases that oppose the pleasure principle. Let us therefore go one step further. We shall designate as *traumatic* those excitations from outside strong enough to break through the shield against stimuli. I believe the concept of trauma requires this characterization with respect to an otherwise effective barrier to stimuli. An event like an external trauma certainly produces a huge disturbance in the energy operations of the organism and sets in motion all means of defense. Simultaneously, though, the pleasure principle is incapacitated for the time being. There is no longer any defense against the flooding of the mental apparatus by great quantities of stimuli. Instead, another challenge arises—that of overpowering the stimuli and mentally binding the quantities of stimuli that have broken in, so that they can then be discharged.

The specific unpleasure of bodily pain probably arises because the shield against stimuli has been breached in a limited region. Then, from this site on the periphery, excitations continuously stream to the central mental apparatus in a manner normally possible only for excitations coming from the interior of the apparatus (Freud 1915). And what can we anticipate as the reaction of the mind to this invasion? From all sides, charged energy is summoned to create correspondingly large charges of energy in the region of the invasion. An immense "opposite charge" is produced, in whose interest all other mental systems are impoverished, resulting in an extensive crippling or reduction of other mental functions. From such examples we wish to learn how to use this type of evidence in support of our metapsychological speculations. From this situation, we conclude that a system that is itself highly charged is capable of receiving new streams of energy and transforming it into resting charge—mentally "binding" it. The higher the resting charge of the system itself, the greater will be its binding force; conversely, the lower its charge, the less it will be capable of receiving new streams of energy and the more violent will be the consequences of such a breach of the shield against stimuli. It would not be correct to object that the increase in charge around the breached site can be explained much more simply as a direct consequence of the arriving quantities of excitation. If that were so, the mental apparatus would only experience an increase in its charges of energy; the crippling character of pain and the impoverishment of all other systems would still be unexplained. Nor is our explanation negated by the very violent discharging effects of pain, for these are reflex reactions, i.e., they occur without the involvement of the mental apparatus. The indefiniteness of all our discussions that we have designated as metapsychological of course arises from the fact that we know nothing of the nature of the process of excitation in the elements of the mental system, and do not feel justified in making any hypotheses about this. Thus we are always operating with a large X, which we must carry over into every new formula. The claim that this process occurs with quantitatively varying energies can be easily accepted; the claim that it has more than one quality (e.g., in amplitude) may also seem probable. As a new consideration we have adduced Breuer's proposal that there are two charges energy may take, so that in the mental systems (or their elements) one must distinguish between free-flowing charge, pressing toward discharge, and resting charge. We may suspect that the "binding" of the energy streaming into the mental apparatus consists in its conversion from the free-flowing state to the resting state.

I believe we can attempt to conceptualize the common traumatic neurosis as the result of an extensive breach of the shield against stimuli. This would corroborate the old, naive theory of shock, which apparently contradicts a later and psychologically more ambitious one attributing etiological significance not to the mechanical force and its effects, but to fright and the threat to life. But these opposites are not irreconcilable, and the psychoanalytic view of the traumatic neurosis is not identical to the most simplistic form of the shock theory. While the latter attributes the essence of shock to direct damage to the molecular structure, or even to the histological structure of the elements of the nervous system, we are seeking to understand its effects in the context of the breach of the shield against stimuli for the mental organ, and in the context of the resulting challenges. For us as well, fright retains its significance. Its necessary condition is the absence of preparedness for anxiety, including super-charge of the systems that immediately receive the stimulus. Due to this low charge, the systems are not in a good position to bind the inflowing quantities of excitation, and the consequences of the breach of the shield against stimuli fall all the more easily into place. Thus we find that preparedness for anxiety, with super-charge of the receptive systems, constitutes the last line of defense for the shield against stimuli. For numerous traumas, the difference between the unprepared systems and those that are prepared through super-charge may be the deciding factor for the outcome; for a trauma beyond a certain strength, this factor will presumably cease to be relevant. While the dreams of trauma-neurotics so regularly lead them back to the situation of the accident, they certainly do not serve wish fulfillment, which nevertheless, in a hallucinatory manner, is brought about by dreams: under the dominance of the pleasure principle, this has become their function. However, we may assume that here they serve another purpose, which must be achieved before the pleasure principle can begin to exercise its dominance. After the fact, these dreams seek to master the stimulus by developing anxiety, the lack of which was the cause of the traumatic neurosis. They thus afford us a view into a function of the mental apparatus; without contradicting the pleasure principle, this function is nevertheless independent of it and seems to be more primal than the goal of gaining pleasure and avoiding unpleasure.

Here it would be appropriate first of all to admit an exception to the principle that dreams constitute wish fulfillment. Anxiety dreams, as I have shown repeatedly and in detail, are not among the exceptions. Nor are "punishment dreams," for these merely replace the rejected wish fulfillment with the corresponding punishment, and thus are the wish fulfillment of the guilty conscience reacting to the repudiated drive. But the aforementioned dreams of trauma-neurotics cannot be considered wish fulfillments, and the same holds for the dreams that occur during psychoanalyses, bringing back memories of the mental traumas of childhood: they obey the repetition compulsion, which is admittedly supported in analysis by the wish—a wish encouraged by "suggestion"—to conjure up the forgotten and the repressed. Thus the function of dreams to remove motives for the interruption of sleep by fulfilling the wishes of the disturbing impulses is apparently not their original function. Dreams could take on this function only after the whole of mental experience had accepted the dominance of the pleasure principle. If there is a "beyond the pleasure principle," it is only logical to admit a time before the wish-fulfilling tendency of dreams. This is not to contradict their later function. But once the general rule has been broken, a further question arises concerning those dreams which, in the interest of mentally binding traumatic impressions, obey the repetition compulsion: can such dreams occur outside of analysis as well? The answer is certainly "yes."

Concerning the "war neuroses" (to the extent that this designation refers to more than the causation of the illness) I have argued elsewhere that they could very well be traumatic neuroses that have been caused by an ego conflict (See Freud 1919, introduction). The previously mentioned fact—the fact that a simultaneous gross physical injury brought about by the trauma lessens the chance that a neurosis will develop—is no longer incomprehensible if one recalls two facts emphasized by psychoanalytic research. First, mechanical agitation must be recognized as one of the sources of sexual excitation (cf. the comments on the effect of swinging and of railway travel, Freud 1905). Second, during its entire course, painful and fever-producing illness has a powerful effect on the distribution of the libido. Thus, the mechanical violence of the trauma would free up a quantity of sexual excitation which, given the lack of preparation for anxiety, has a traumatic effect, but the simultaneous physical injury would bind the surplus of excitation by demanding a narcissistic super-charge of the ailing organ (Freud 1914: "Einführung"). It is also well known, though insufficiently utilized in the libido theory, that such serious disturbances in the distribution of libido as that produced by melancholia are temporarily suspended by an intervening organic illness; indeed, under the same conditions, even fully developed dementia praecox [schizophrenia] can temporarily go into remission.

V

The fact that the cortical layer receiving stimuli lacks a shield against excitations from within must have the consequence that these transmissions of stimuli have the greater economic significance and often produce economic disturbances that can be equated with traumatic neuroses. The most abundant sources of this excitation within are the so-called drives of the organism, the representatives of all the effective forces that arise within the body and are transferred to the mental apparatus—itself the most important yet the most obscure element of psychological research.

Perhaps it will not seem too bold to assume that the impulses emanating from the drives are not in the category of bound neurological processes, but in that of freely moving neurological processes pressing toward discharge. The best portion of what we know of these processes stems from the study of dream work. There we found that the processes in the unconscious systems are thoroughly different from those in the (pre)conscious systems. We found that in the unconscious, charges can easily be transferred, shifted, and condensed in their totality, which could only lead to faulty results if this occurred with preconscious material, and which also leads to the well-known peculiarities of the manifest dream after the preconscious residues of the day have been processed according to the laws of the unconscious. I called this type of process in the unconscious the "primary mental process," in contrast to the "secondary process" applying in our normal waking life. Since all drive impulses impinge on the unconscious systems, it is certainly nothing new to say that they obey the primary process; on the other hand, it is not difficult to identify the primary mental process with freely moving charge, and the secondary process with the changes in the bound or tonic charge—both as in Breuer's theory (cf. Freud 1900, Chapter 7: The Psychology of Dream Processes). Then it would be the task of the higher layers of the mental apparatus to bind the excitation of the drives as this excitation reaches the primary process. Unsuccessful binding would produce a disturbance analogous to a traumatic neurosis; only after successful binding could the dominance of the pleasure principle (and of its modification as the reality principle) assert itself. Until then, however, the other task of the mental apparatus, to master or bind excitation, would be dominant—not in opposition to the pleasure principle, but independent of it, and to some degree without regard to it.

The phenomena presented by a repetition compulsion, phenomena we have described in the early activities of the child's mental life and among the experiences of psychoanalytic treatment, strongly show a drive-based character and, when opposing the pleasure principle, a demonic character. In the case of children's play, it seems clear that children also repeat an unpleasurable experience because they can, through their activity, achieve a far more solid mastery of the powerful impression than was possible through mere passive experience. Each new repetition seems to improve the mastery the child is striving for, and in the case of pleasurable experiences too, children can never get enough of these repetitions, and will inexorably insist that the impression be identical each time. This character trait subsequently disappears. A joke heard for the second time will remain nearly without effect. A theatrical production will never again recreate the impression it made the first time. Indeed, it would be hard to convince an adult immediately to reread a book he has greatly enjoyed. Novelty is always the condition of enjoyment. But children never tire of asking an adult to repeat a game shown to them or played with them—until the adult refuses, exhausted. And if a child has been told a nice story, he always wants to hear this same story again and again, rather than a new one, inexorably insisting that the repetitions be identical, and correcting every modification the narrator is guilty of producing, though such modifications may have been made with the desire to please the child anew. Yet these facts do not contradict the pleasure principle; it makes sense that repetition, the re-encountering of identity, is itself a source of pleasure. With a patient under analysis, though, the compulsion to repeat in the transference the events of childhood clearly supersedes the pleasure principle in *every* way. The patient behaves in a completely childish manner, thus showing us that the repressed memory traces of his earliest experiences are not present in the bound state, and indeed are to a degree incapable of obeying the secondary process. Furthermore, this unbound state also accounts for their ability to create—by clinging to the residues of the day—a wish fantasy to be presented in a dream. The same repetition compulsion frequently presents itself to us as a therapeutic obstacle when, at the end of the treatment, we want to effect total detachment from the physician; it can be assumed that the obscure anxiety of persons unfamiliar with analysis, who hesitate to awaken something they believe should be left asleep, is fundamentally a fear of the appearance of this demonic compulsion.

But how is the realm of drives related to the repetition compulsion? Here the idea is forced upon us that we are now on the track of a universal characteristic of drives, and perhaps of all organic life—a characteristic previously unrecognized or at least not explicitly stressed. In this view, *a drive is an urge inherent in living organic matter for the restoration of an earlier state* — one that a living being has had to give up under the influence of external disturbing forces; it is a kind of organic elasticity, or, in a manner of speaking, the expression of the inertia in organic life.[1]

This conception of drives sounds strange because we have become used to seeing in the drive the factor pressing toward change and development, but now are expected to recognize in it the complete opposite—the expression of the *conservative* nature of living matter. On the other hand, we will soon recall those examples from animal life that seem to confirm the historically determined nature of drives. Certain fish undertake arduous migrations at spawning time to spawn in particular waters far removed from their normal habitat. According to the interpretation of many biologists, they are merely seeking the earlier habitat of their species, which in the course of time they have exchanged for another. The same is thought to apply to the migrations of migratory birds, but we are soon relieved of our search for further examples by recalling that it is in the phenomena of heredity and in the facts of embryology that we have the greatest proofs of the organic repetition compulsion. We see that in the course of its development the embryo of a living animal must necessarily recapitulate—even if only briefly and in an abbreviated way—the structures of all the life forms from which the animal descends, rather than quickly taking the shortest path toward its definitive shape. Only a very small portion of this behavior can be explained mechanically; the historical explanation cannot be disregarded. Similarly, the regenerative capability that allows replacement of a lost organ with a completely identical one reaches far up into the animal kingdom.

We certainly must not leave unconsidered the naturally arising objection that in addition to the conservative drives pressing toward repetition, there may be others pressing toward new forms, toward progress. This idea will later on be included in our considerations. But for now it is tempting to follow to its final conclusion the hypothesis that all drives aim to restore an earlier state. The emerging discussion may seem like "false profundity" or mysticism, but we know we have not striven for any such thing. We are seeking the unadorned

---

1 I do not doubt that similar suppositions on the nature of "drives" have already been expressed many times. [Freud's note]

results of research, or of reflection based on it, and we wish to lend these results nothing but the character of certainty.[1]

Accordingly, if all organic drives are conservative, historically acquired, and oriented toward regression—toward restoration of an earlier state—we must attribute the successes of organic evolution to external disturbing and diverting influences. From the beginning, given constant conditions, the elementary living being would have no desire to change itself, and would always repeat the same course of life. But ultimately it must be the developmental history of our earth and of its relation to the sun that has left its mark on the evolution of organisms. The conservative organic drives have taken on each one of these imposed modifications of the course of life and preserved them for repetition. Thus, these drives must give us the false impression that they are forces striving for change and progress, whereas they merely aim to reach an old goal in ways old or new. This final goal of all organic striving can be identified as well. It would contradict the conservative nature of drives if the goal of life were a state never previously achieved. Rather, it must be an old state, an original state that the living being has left at some time, and toward which it strives to return through all the detours of evolution. If we may accept as an observation without exception that every living being dies for *internal* reasons, returning to the inorganic, then we can only say that *the goal of all life is death*, and, looking backwards, that *the nonliving existed before the living.*

At some time, and through the influence of a completely inconceivable force, the characteristics of life were awakened in nonliving matter. Perhaps this was a process similar in type to that other process which later brought about the emergence of consciousness in a particular layer of the living matter. The tension then arising in the previously inanimate substance strove toward equilibrium. Thus arose the first drive: the drive to return to the nonliving. For the substance living at that time, dying was still easy; there was probably only a brief course of life to be run through, whose direction was determined by the chemical structure of the young life. For a long time, then, living substance may have been created again and again, and may have

---

1 It should be kept in mind that the following develops an extreme line of thought that will subsequently be limited and corrected when sex drives are taken into consideration. [Freud's note]

died easily, until there was a change in definitive external influences, forcing the still surviving substance toward greater and greater deviations from its original path of life and toward more and more complex detours before reaching its goal: death. These detours to death, faithfully retained by the conservative drives, would offer us today the image of the phenomena of life. If one insists on the exclusively conservative nature of drives, no other suppositions on the origin and goal of life are possible.

The implications for the great groups of drives we have placed behind the phenomena of life in organisms sound just as strange as the previous cogitations. The idea of self-preservation drives, which we have assigned to every living being, stands in marked opposition to the hypothesis that the whole of drive function serves to bring about death. Seen in this light, the theoretical significance of the drives for self-preservation, for power, and for dominance is reduced. These are component drives for securing the organism's own path toward death and for keeping away all possibilities of return to the inorganic other than the immanent ones, but the organism's peculiar determination to assert itself against all opposition—impossible to integrate into any context—now disappears. The conclusion is that the organism seeks to die only in its own way; these guardians of life, too, were originally the bodyguards of death. This gives rise to the paradox that the living organism struggles with maximal energies against effects (dangers) which could help it reach its life's goal in the shortest way (by short circuit, as it were), but this behavior characterizes purely drive-based efforts, as opposed to intelligent ones.

But let us carefully consider: this cannot be so. The sex drives, for which the theory of the neuroses claims a special place, now appear under a very different light. Not all organisms have succumbed to the external pressure driving them toward more and more extensive evolution. Many have succeeded in remaining at their low level up to the present; it is clear that many, though not all, living beings resembling the early stages of the higher animals and plants are still living today. Similarly, not all the elementary organisms comprising the complex body of a higher organism follow the developmental path all the way to natural death. Some of them, the gametes, probably preserve the original structure of living substance and, laden with all their inherited and newly gained drive-inclinations, separate themselves from the main organism after a certain time. Perhaps it is precisely these two characteristics that make their independent existence possible. Given favorable conditions, they begin to develop, i.e., to repeat the game to which they owe their origin, and ultimately a portion of their substance once again goes through development to the end, while another portion, as a new residual gamete, again falls back on the beginning of development. Thus these gametes work against the death of the living substance and manage to win for it what must strike us as potential immortality, though this perhaps means only a lengthening of the path toward death. It is of the utmost significance for us that the gamete is strengthened—even made capable—for this function through merging with another gamete, similar yet different from it.

Those drives which attend to the destinies of these elementary organisms that survive the individual, which preserve them safely as long as they are without defense against the stimuli of the external world, which bring about their meeting with other gametes, and so on, form the group of the sex drives. They are conservative in the same sense as the other drives in that they re-establish earlier states of the living substance, but they are even more conservative in that they prove especially resistant to external effects, and also in that they preserve life itself for a longer time.[1] They are the actual life drives. Since they work against the intent of the other drives—an intent functionally leading to death—an opposition is evinced between them and the others; the theory of neurosis early on recognized this opposition as significant. This is like a wavering rhythm in the life of organisms: one group of drives storms forward to reach the final goal of life as soon as possible, but the other group shoots back to a certain location on the path to retrace it from a given point, thus prolonging the journey. Although sexuality and the distinction between the sexes certainly did not exist when life began, it is still possible that those drives that would later be designated as sexual came into operation at the very start; it may not be the case that they took on their opposition to the play of the "ego drives" only later.[2]

---

1 And yet they are the only drives to which we can attribute an internal tendency toward "progress" and higher development! [Freud's note]

2 In this context, it should be understood that "ego drives" is here intended as a temporary designation connected with the earliest terminology of psychoanalysis. [Freud's note]

Let us now look back for once to ask if it might not be the case that all of these speculations are unfounded. *Beside the sex drives,* are there really no other drives as such seeking to re-establish an earlier state? Are there no others striving toward a state never previously achieved? I know of no sure example in the organic world that would contradict our proposed characterization. It is certainly not possible to identify any universal drive toward higher development in the animal or plant kingdom, though it is actually uncontroversial that this has been the direction of evolution. But on the one hand it is often merely a subjective judgment if we declare one stage of development higher than another; on the other hand biology demonstrates that higher development in one aspect very often occurs at the cost of decline in another aspect, or that the decline balances the advance. There are also many animals whose juvenile forms allow us to see that their evolution has in fact gone back toward more primitive levels. Both higher development and decline could be the result of external forces demanding adaptation; and in both cases the role of drives might be limited to retaining the imposed modification as an internal source of pleasure.[1]

For many of us, it may also be hard to renounce the belief that there dwells in human beings a drive toward perfection which has brought them to their present heights of intellectual achievement and ethical sublimation, and which can be expected to provide for their development into supermen. But I believe in no such inner drive, and see no way of maintaining this agreeable illusion. It seems to me that human evolution up to its present state needs no other explanation than that applying to animals. What is observed in a small number of individuals as an untiring urge toward further perfection can easily be understood as a consequence of the repression of drives; it is on this repression that the most valuable achievements of human culture are founded. The repressed drive never gives up striving for complete gratification, which would be found in the repetition of a primary experience of

---

1 Following another path, Ferenczi has reached the possibility of the same conception: "If this train of thought is taken to its logical conclusion, it will be necessary to acquaint oneself with the idea of a tendency for persistence or regression dominating organic life as well, while the tendency for further development, adaptation, and so forth, is activated only due to external stimuli" (Ferenczi 137). [Freud's note]

gratification. All substitute or reaction formations and all subli- mations will be insufficient to eliminate the continuing tension of the repressed drive, and from the difference in quantity between the pleasure of gratification which is found and that which is demanded arises the driving factor that permits no pause in any of the situations produced, but, in Goethe's words "*ungebändigt immer vorwärts dringt*" [always presses forward unsubdued] (Mephistopheles in Faust's laboratory, *Faust*, Part 1). The path leading backward, toward complete gratification, is generally obstructed by the resistances that support the repressions, and thus there is no other choice but to advance in the remaining, still available direction of development, though without the prospect of being able to complete the process or reach the goal. The processes in the formation of a neurotic phobia, which is of course only an attempt to flee from the gratification of a drive, give us a prototype for how this apparent "drive toward perfec- tion" could have arisen, but which cannot possibly be ascribed to all individuals. The necessary dynamic conditions are no doubt universally present, but the economic situation seems to support this phenomenon only in rare cases.

A word will suffice to suggest the probability that the strivings of Eros to combine the organic into larger and larger unities provide a substitute for this indemonstrable "drive toward perfection." In combination with the effects of repression these strivings of Eros could account for the phenomena ascribed to the supposed drive.

VI

Our result thus far, which makes a sharp distinction between the "ego drives" and the sex drives, and has the former pressing toward death and the latter pressing toward the continuation of life, will certainly remain unsatisfactory in many respects, even to us. Furthermore, it is actually only for the first group that we can claim a conservative or indeed regressive drive character corresponding to a repetition compulsion. For we are assuming that the ego drives arise from the animation of inanimate matter and seek to re-establish inanimacy. As for the sex drives, on the other hand, it is obvious that they reproduce primitive states of the organism, but the goal for which they strive with all their means is the merging of two gametes differentiated in a specific manner. If this union does not occur, the gametes die just like all the other elements of the multicellular organism. Only under the condition of merging can the sexual function prolong life and lend life the appearance of immortality. But which important event in the evolutionary path of living substance is repeated in sexual reproduction, or in its forerunner, the conjugation of two protista? We do not know, and would therefore be relieved if the entire theoretical framework turned out to be erroneous. The opposition between the ego (or death) drives and the sexual (or life) drives would then be obviated, and the repetition compulsion would lose the significance ascribed to it.

Let us therefore return to a hypothesis we have previously woven into our discussion, expecting to be able to refute it with an exact proof. We have based further conclusions on the premise that all living matter must die from internal causes. We made this hypothesis so casually since, in fact, it does not strike us as a mere hypothesis. We are used to thinking in terms of this hypothesis; in doing so, we are supported by our authors and poets. Perhaps we do so with such conviction because there is comfort in this belief. If we ourselves must die—after losing our loved ones through death—we prefer submission to an inexorable law of nature, the sublime *Anánke* [Necessity], rather than to a chance event which could conceivably have been avoided. But maybe this belief in the internal necessity of dying is only one of the illusions we have created for ourselves *um die Schwere des Daseins zu ertragen* [to bear the weight of existence] (Schiller, *Die Braut von Messina* [*The Bride of Messina*], I, 8). This belief was certainly not primordial, and the concept of "natural death" is unknown among primitive peoples: they attribute every death among them to the influence of an enemy or an evil spirit. Thus, in examining this belief, we must not neglect to turn to biology.

In doing so, we may be amazed how little agreement there is among biologists on natural death, and indeed that the entire notion of death melts away in their hands. The fact that there is a fixed average length of life in higher animals, at least, certainly provides evidence for death from internal causes. But this impression is eliminated by the fact that certain large animals and gigantic trees reach a very great age, which at present cannot be estimated. According to the grandiose conception of Wilhelm

Fliess,[1] all the phenomena of life in organisms—certainly including death as well—are bound up with the completion of fixed periods; these express the dependence of two living substances (one male and one female) on the solar year (Fliess). But when we see how easily and extensively the influence of external forces is able to modify chronologically the phases of the life cycle, especially in the plant world—to advance or delay them—such observations bristle against the rigidity of Fliess's formulas and at least raise doubts about whether the laws he has established are the only ones in effect.

The greatest interest for us is connected with the treatment of the duration of life and the death of organisms in the works of August Weismann (Weismann 1882, 1884, 1892). It was he who proposed a distinction in living substance between mortal and immortal halves. The mortal half is the body in the narrower sense, the soma, which alone is subject to natural death. The gametes, by contrast, are potentially immortal: under certain favorable conditions they can develop into a new individual, or, in other words, surround themselves with a new soma (Weismann 1884).

The fascinating thing here is the unexpected analogy with our own view, which took such a different path of development. Weismann views living substance morphologically and sees in it one component fated to die—the soma, the body as distinct from the substance associated with sex and heredity—and an immortal component, the germ-plasm, promoting the survival of the species and for reproduction. We have not been examining the living substance itself, but rather the forces acting within it, and have been led to distinguish two types of drives: those that seek to lead life toward death, and the others, the sex drives, which continuously strive for and in fact achieve the renewal of life. This sounds like a dynamic corollary to Weismann's morphological theory.

But the appearance of a significant correspondence quickly fades when we learn of Weismann's approach to the problem

1   Wilhelm Fliess (1858-1928), a Berlin ear, nose, and throat specialist, was a close friend with whom Freud shared his earliest theories, including the seduction theory. Among much else, Fliess also originated the idea of human bisexuality and was convinced that life was governed by periodicity in both sexes. See Sulloway 1977, 2007. Freud's side of the correspondence survives, and is the best entrée into the controversial "pre-history" of psychoanalysis.

of death. He claims a distinction between the mortal soma and immortal germ-plasm only for multicellular organisms: in unicellular organisms the individual and the reproductive cell are still one and the same (Weismann 1882: 38). Thus he declares the unicellular organisms potentially immortal; death first appears in the metazoa, the multicellular organisms. This death in higher life forms is a natural one to be sure, a death from internal causes, but is based on no primal characteristic of living substance (Weismann 1884: 67), and cannot be conceived as an absolute necessity based on the nature of life (Weismann 1882: 33). Death is more of an expedient, an expression of adaptation to the external conditions of life: once the cells of the body have been distinguished as soma and germ-plasm, the unlimited duration of life in the individual would be a completely useless luxury. With the advent of this differentiation in multicellular organisms, death became possible and expedient. Since then, the soma of the higher life forms has died off for internal reasons and at fixed times, but the protista have remained immortal. Yet it is not the case that reproduction arose simultaneously with death. Rather, it is a primal characteristic of living matter, like growth—from which it arose—and since its first beginnings on earth, life has remained continuous (Weismann 1884, conclusion).

It is easy to see that admitting a natural death in higher organisms is of little help to our cause. If death is a late acquisition of life forms, then there can be no death drives that originated with the beginning of life on earth. Multicellular organisms may nevertheless die for internal reasons—inadequacies in their differentiation or imperfections in their metabolism—but this is not relevant for the problem concerning us. Such a conception of death, and such a view of its origins, surely accord much more closely with customary ways of thinking than does the strange hypothesis of "death drives."

The discussion that arose in response to Weismann's proposals has, in my judgment, produced nothing conclusive in any direction (cf. Hartmann, Lipschütz, Doflein). Some writers have returned to the framework of Goette, who saw death as a direct consequence of reproduction (Goette). Hartmann characterizes death not with the presence of a dead body—a dead portion of the living substance—but defines it as the "termination of individual development" (Hartmann 29). In this sense the protozoans are also mortal, for with them death always coincides with reproduction, yet death is partially obscured by reproduction since the entire substance of the parent animal can be transferred directly into the young individuals of the next generation (29).

Research interests soon turned to experimentation with unicellular organisms so as to test the hypothesized immortality of living substance. The American biologist Lorande Woodruff produced multiple generations of a ciliate infusorian, the "slipper-shaped" infusorian, which reproduces by dividing into two individuals. He continued until the 3029th generation, when he broke off the experiment; each time, he isolated one of the component products, placing it in fresh water. This late descendent of the first slipper-shaped infusorian was just as lively as its ancestor, and showed no signs of aging or degeneration. Thus, if such figures prove anything, the immortality of the protista seemed to have been experimentally demonstrated (for this and what follows, cf. Lipschütz 26, 52).

Other experimenters arrived at other results. Maupas, Calkins, and others, contrasting with Woodruff, found that after a certain number of divisions these infusorians also became weaker, diminished in size, lost a portion of their structure, and ultimately died unless they were provided certain restorative factors. It would thus appear that after a phase of aging, protozoans die exactly like the higher animals—in direct contradiction to the claims of Weismann, who sees death as a late acquisition of living organisms.

From the totality of these investigations we shall emphasize two facts that seem to offer us firm ground. First: if the microorganisms are able to merge as a pair before showing any modification due to aging, i.e., if they are able to "conjugate"—upon which they again separate after a certain time—they are spared from aging; they are "rejuvenated." Conjugation is presumably the precursor of sexual reproduction in higher forms; it still has no relation to propagation, and is limited to the mixing of the substances of the two individuals (Weismann's "amphimixis"). The restorative effect of conjugation, however, can be replaced by certain types of stimulation, changes in the composition of the nutrient fluid provided, an increase in temperature, or shaking. This brings to mind Jacques Loeb's famous experiment in which, through certain chemical stimuli, he induced the process of cell division in sea urchin eggs, which otherwise occurs only after fertilization.

Secondly: it is certainly probable that the vital processes of infusorians lead to their natural death, for the contradiction between Woodruff's findings and those of others arises because he introduced each new generation into fresh nutrient fluid. When he did not do so, over the generations he observed the same modifications due to aging as the other researchers. He concluded that microorganisms are harmed by the metabolic products they excrete into the surrounding fluid. He was then able to demonstrate convincingly that it is only the products of its *own* metabolism that lead to death in a certain generation in a given species. For in a solution over-saturated with the waste products of a more distantly related species, those same microorganisms thrived very well that had consistently perished when amassed in their own nutrient fluid. Left to itself, then, an infusorian dies a natural death due to imperfect elimination of its own metabolic products. But perhaps the cause of death in all the higher animals too is essentially this same inability.

We may now wonder whether it was useful at all to seek an answer to the problem of natural death in the study of protozoans. The primitive organization of these life forms may obscure important factors present in them, but recognizable only in higher animals, where they are morphologically expressed. If we abandon the morphological point of view and adopt the dynamic one, it becomes completely unimportant for us whether or not natural death can be demonstrated in protozoans. In them, the substance later recognized as immortal has not yet been separated from the mortal one in any manner. The drive forces seeking to lead life into death may also be active in them from the beginning, but their effects may be concealed by those of the life-preserving forces such that it becomes very difficult to demonstrate them directly. Indeed, we have learned that the observations of biologists allow us to assume for protista as well such internal processes leading to death. But even if the protista prove immortal in Weismann's sense, his assertion that death is a late acquisition applies only for the manifest expressions of death, and does not render impossible any hypothesis about the processes pressing toward death. Our expectation that biology would deftly eliminate all evidence for the recognition of the death drives has not been fulfilled. Thus, given further justification, we can occupy ourselves further with the possibility of their existence. The striking similarity between Weismann's distinction of soma and germ-plasm and our separation of death drives and life drives remains, regaining its significance.

Let us briefly consider this exquisitely dualistic conception of drive function. According to Hering's theory of the processes in living substance, there are two types of processes constantly working in opposition—some constructive or assimilatory, and the others destructive or dissimilatory. Shall we be so bold as to recognize in these two directions of the vital processes the activation of our two drive impulses, the life drives and the death drives? There is, furthermore, something else we cannot ignore: we have unwittingly sailed into the harbor of Schopenhauer's philosophy. For him death is "the actual result" and to that extent the purpose of life, whereas the sex drive is the embodiment of the will to live (Schopenhauer).

Let us boldly attempt to advance one step further. There is general consensus that the union of numerous cells into a vital association, as in multicellular organisms, has become a means for extending their life. One cell helps to preserve the life of the others, and the confederation of cells can live on even if individual cells must die. We have already heard that conjugation, too, the temporary merging of two unicellular organisms, affects them both in a life-preserving and rejuvenating manner. Thus one might attempt to extend the libido theory, gained through psychoanalysis, to the relation of cells to one another, imagining that it is the life drives or sex drives active in each cell that take the other cells as their objects, partially neutralizing the death drives in those cells—i.e., the processes incited by them—and thus preserving their life. Simultaneously, other cells do the same for *them*, and still others sacrifice themselves in carrying out this libidinal function. In this view, even the gametes would behave in an absolutely "narcissistic" manner—the customary designation in the theory of the neuroses when an entire individual retains the libido in the ego, spending none of it on object charges. The gametes need their libido, the activity of their life drives, for themselves, as a reserve for their later, immensely constructive activity. Perhaps we can also describe the cells of malignant growths that destroy the organism as narcissistic in the same sense. Pathology is ready to consider their germ cells innate and to grant them embryonic attributes. Thus the libido of our sex drives would coincide with the Eros of the poets and philosophers, which holds together all forms of life.

Here it is appropriate to review the gradual development of our libido theory. The analysis of the transference neuroses compelled us to adopt the opposition between "sex drives," directed toward their object, and other drives, of which we had only very insufficient knowledge and which we provisionally described as "ego drives." Among these, it was necessary to recognize first the drives promoting the self-preservation of the individual. It was impossible to say what other distinctions would be required. In founding an actual psychology, no information would have been more important than approximate insights into the common nature and possible unique aspects of the drives. But in no area of psychology was there more groping in the dark. Each researcher proposed as many drives or "basic drives" as he wished, busying himself with them like the ancient Greek natural philosophers with their four elements—earth, air, fire, and water. Psychoanalysis, which could not avoid making some hypothesis about the drives, adhered at first to the popular distinction of drives collapsed in the phrase "hunger and love." This, at least, was no arbitrary act. Accordingly, the analysis of the psychoneuroses made a great step forward. Indeed, the concept of "sexuality," and therefore of the sex drive, had to be extended until it included much that could not be classified within the reproductive function, causing quite a stir in the strict, respectable or merely hypocritical world.

The next step occurred when psychoanalysis was able to grope its way closer to the psychological ego, which had at first made itself known only as a repressive, censoring authority capable of constructing protective structures and reactive formations. Indeed, critical and far-seeing minds had long ago objected to restricting the concept of libido to the energy of the sex drives directed toward an object. But they neglected to explain where they had come by their better insights; they were unable to derive from it anything useful for analysis. Proceeding at a more measured pace, psychoanalytic observation showed how regularly libido is taken from the object and directed onto the ego (introversion). By studying the development of the libido in children in its earliest phases, psychoanalysis came to the realization that the ego is the actual and original reservoir of the libido, and that it is only from there that it is extended onto an object. The ego was classified among the sexual objects and was immediately recognized as the most distinguished among them. When the libido was thus housed in the ego, it was described as "narcissistic" (cf. Freud 1914: "Einführung"). This narcissistic libido was of course also the expression of the force of sex drives in the analytical sense; these had to be identified with the "self-preservation drives" recognized from the beginning. Thus the original opposition between the ego drives and sex drives had become inadequate. A portion of the ego drives was recognized as libidinal; sex drives too were claimed to be active in the ego—probably alongside others—but we are justified in saying that the old claim that psychoneurosis is based on a conflict between ego drives and sex drives contains nothing requiring rejection today. The distinction between the two types of drives, which was originally intended as somehow qualitative, must now be characterized in a different way—as *topographic*. Crucially, the transference neuroses, the actual object of psychoanalytic study, remain the result of a conflict between the ego and the libidinal charge of objects.

We must now emphasize all the more the libidinal character of the self-preservation drives, for we shall now be bold enough to take the further step of recognizing the sex drive as all-preserving Eros, and of deriving the narcissistic libido of the ego from the contributions of libido the somatic cells use in clinging to one another. But now we suddenly face another question: if the self-preservation drives too are of a libidinal nature, do there now remain no non-libidinal drives? In any case, none can be seen. But then we will have to agree with those critics who suspected from the beginning that psychoanalysis explains *everything* through sexuality, or with innovators like Jung who, deciding over-hastily, have used the word *libido* for "drive force" in general. Is this not the case?

It was not our intention, however, to produce such a result. Rather, we began with a sharp distinction between ego drives (= death drives) and sex drives (= life drives). Indeed, we were ready to count the supposed self-preservation drives of the ego among the death drives, though we subsequently corrected ourselves and withdrew the proposal. From the beginning, our conception has been *dualistic*, and is today even more dualistic than before, now that we no longer describe the opposition as existing between ego drives and sex drives, but as existing between life drives and death drives. Jung's libido theory, however, is a monistic one; the fact that he named his only drive force "libido" did cause confusion, but will no longer affect us. We suspect that in addition to the libidinal self-preservation drives there are other drives active in the ego; we should be able to point them out. Regrettably, the analysis of the ego has made such little progress that it is extremely difficult for us to do so. Yet the libidinal drives of the ego may be connected in a special way with the other, still unfamiliar ego drives. Even before narcissism had been clearly recognized, the suspicion already existed within psychoanalysis that the "ego drives" had drawn libidinal components toward themselves. But these are very uncertain possibilities that our opponents will hardly notice. It remains unfortunate that analysis has thus far enabled us to demonstrate libidinal drives only. However, this should not lead us to conclude that others do not exist.

Given the present obscurity in the theory of drives, it would be inadvisable to reject any idea that promises to enlighten. We began with the great opposition between life drives and death drives. Object love itself shows us a second such polarity— between love (affection) and hate (aggression). If only we could relate these two polarities to each other and derive the one from the other! From the very beginning we have recognized a sadistic component in the sex drive (beginning with *Three Essays on the Theory of Sexuality*, 1st edition). As we know, it can make itself independent and, as a perversion, dominate all the sexual strivings of the individual. It also arises as the dominant component drive in one of the "pregenital organizations," as I have called them. But how shall we derive the sadistic drive— which aims to harm the object—from life-preserving Eros? Can we not now suppose that this sadism is actually a death drive which, through the influence of the narcissistic libido, was forced away from the ego such that it only appears in the context of an object? It now enters the service of the sexual function. In the oral stage of organization in the libido, gaining an object for love still coincides with the destruction of that object. Later the sadistic drive splits off and, for the purpose of reproduction, in the stage of genital primacy ultimately takes on the function of overpowering the sexual object to the extent required to carry out the sexual act. Indeed, one could say that the sadism expelled from the ego has shown the way for the libidinal components of the sex drive; later, these follow along to the object. Wherever the original sadism experiences no moderation or admixture, the well-known ambivalence of love and hate in love life is restored.

If such a hypothesis may be permitted, we have now satisfied the demand for the demonstration of a death drive, albeit a displaced one. Yet this view is far from being easily comprehensible, and makes a perfectly mystical impression. We now come under suspicion of having tried to find an escape from a great embarrassment at any price. We can defend ourselves with the fact that such a hypothesis is not new—that we already made one before there was any talk of embarrassment. Clinical observations previously compelled us to adopt the view that masochism, the component drive complementary to sadism, is to be understood as a recoil of sadism back upon the individual ego (Freud 1905, 1915). But the turning of the drive from an object to the ego is essentially equivalent to its turning from the ego to an object—the latter case being the new topic in question. Masochism, the drive's turning against the individual ego, would then actually be a return to an earlier phase of the drive—a regression. In one point the depiction of masochism presented at that time must be corrected as too exclusive: it might be possible to look at it as primary masochism—a proposal I wanted to argue against in the works just cited.[1]

Let us return now to the life-preserving sex drives. From research with protista we have already learned that conjugation—the merging of two individuals, which then soon separate without subsequent cell-division in either—has a strengthening and rejuvenating effect on both (cf. Lipschütz). In later generations they show no degeneration and seem able to withstand for a longer period the harmful effects of their own metabolism. I believe this single observation can be taken as typical for the effect of sexual union as well. But how does the merging of two minimally different cells bring about this renewal of life? The experiment

---

1 In a rich and thoughtful article, though one that is unfortunately not fully clear to me, Sabina Spielrein anticipated a significant part of this speculation (Spielrein). She characterizes the sadistic components of the sex drive as "destructive." In another manner, August Stärcke has attempted to identify the concept of the libido itself with the theoretically justified biological concept of a *drive toward death* (Stärcke). See also Rank (Rank). All these considerations, like those in my text above, evince the demand for a still awaited clarification in the theory of drives. [Freud's note]

replacing the conjugation of protozoans with the application of chemical and even mechanical stimuli (cf. Lipschütz) certainly allows one to give a conclusive answer: this occurs through the introduction of new quantities of stimuli. This accords well with the hypothesis that the life process of the individual leads for internal reasons to an equilibrium of chemical tensions, i.e., to death, whereas union with the living substance of a distinct individual increases these tensions and introduces new *vital differences*, as it were, which must then be lived out. For this variability there must of course be one or more optimum conditions. We recognized a striving—as expressed in the pleasure principle—to reduce, keep constant, or eliminate internal tension due to stimuli as the dominant tendency of mental life and perhaps of nervous life in general (the *nirvana principle*, as Barbara Low calls it), and this recognition is one of our strongest reasons for believing in the existence of death drives (Low 73).[1]

But there is a sensitive issue we still perceive as a disturbance to our line of thinking: it is precisely for the sex drive that we are unable to demonstrate the characteristic of a repetition compulsion—the very characteristic that first led us to seek the death drives. The realm of embryonic developmental processes is certainly very rich in such repetition phenomena; the two gametes in sexual reproduction and their life history are themselves only repetitions of the beginnings of organic life. But the essential thing in the processes sexual life aims for is indeed the merging of two cell bodies. It is only through this fact that the immortality of the living substance is secured in higher organisms.

In other words, we must acquire more information on the origin of sexual reproduction and on the source of the sex drives in general—a task outsiders will shrink back from, and which even specialists have thus far been unable to accomplish. Therefore, in a very brief summary, among all the conflicting facts and opinions let us emphasize those that allow a connection with our train of thought.

---

1 Barbara Low (1877-1955), early British psychoanalyst. Freud cites Low, but a similar idea is found in Fechner, and before him in Buddhist teachings. Others would add the Third Law of Thermodynamics (entropy) to this list of possible influences on this idea.

One of these views eliminates the mysterious fascination of the question of reproduction by presenting it as a partial manifestation of growth (propagation by division, sprouting, or budding). The origin of reproduction by sexually differentiated gametes may be imagined in terms of a sober Darwinian mode of thought by supposing that the advantage of amphimixis—the result, at one time, of the chance conjugation of two protista—was retained and further exploited in subsequent evolution.[1] In this view, "sex" would not be very old, and the extremely intense drives seeking to bring about sexual union would be repeating something that once occurred by chance and has since established itself as advantageous.

As with the issue of death, the question arises whether we should ascribe to protista only what they exhibit, or whether we can assume that forces and processes which first become visible in higher life forms also originated in the protista. For our purposes, the aforementioned view of sexuality is of little use. It might be objected that it presupposes the existence of life drives already active in the simplest life form, for otherwise conjugation, which resists the course of life and renders the task of dying more difficult, would not have been retained and developed, but would have been avoided. Accordingly, if we do not desire to abandon our hypothesis of death drives, we must associate them from the very beginning with life drives. But it must be admitted that in that case we are working on an equation with two unknowns. Science provides so little additional information on the origin of sexuality that this problem can be compared to a darkness into which not one ray of a hypothesis has penetrated. In quite a different place, though, we do come across such a hypothesis, but it is of such a fantastical kind—more a myth than a scientific explanation—that I would not presume to present it here if it did not fulfill precisely the condition for whose fulfillment we are striving. Specifically, it derives a drive from *the need to restore an earlier state.*

I am of course referring to the theory which Plato has

---

1   Although Weismann denies this advantage as well: "In no case does fertilization correspond to a rejuvenescence or renewal of life, nor is its occurrence necessary in order that life may endure: it is merely an arrangement *which renders possible the intermingling of two different hereditary tendencies*" (Weismann 1893: 231). Yet he regards an increase in the variability of organisms as the effect of such an intermingling. [Freud's note]

Aristophanes develop in the *Symposium*,[1] and which involves not only the origin of the sex drive but also that of its most important variation in relation to its object.

"[O]ur nature as it was, once upon a time, was not the same as it is now, but of a different kind. In the first place, human beings were divided into three kinds, not two as they are now, male and female: in addition to these there was also a third in which both of these had a share..." All the body parts of these beings were double: accordingly they had four hands and four feet, two faces, two sex organs, and so on. Then Zeus was persuaded to cut each of these beings in two, "like people who cut up sorb-apples before they preserve them. Because their natural form had been cut in two, each half longed for what belonged to it and tried to engage with it; throwing their arms around each other and locking themselves together, because of their desire to grow back together..." (Plato 51).[2]

---

1   See Appendix B2
2   I am indebted to Professor Heinrich Gomperz of Vienna for the following suggestive comments on the origin of the Platonic myth, which I repeat partly in his words. I would like to point out that essentially the same theory is already found also in the *Upanishads*. In the *Brhadāranyaka-upanishad* 1, 4, 3, where the origin of the world from the *ātman* (the self or ego) is depicted, we read:
    "But he felt no delight. Therefore a man who is lonely feels no delight. He wished for a second. He was so large as man and wife together. He then made this his Self to fall in two, and then arose husband and wife. Therefore Yagñavalkya said: 'We two are thus (each of us) like half a shell.' Therefore the void which was there, is filled by the wife" (Müller 2: 85).
    The *Brhadāranyaka-upanishad* is the most ancient of all the Upanishads, and is not dated later than about 800 BC by any competent scholar. Contrasting with prevailing opinion, I would not want to deny absolutely the possibility that Plato could have depended at least indirectly on these Indian cogitations, for it is probable that such a possibility cannot be directly rejected either for the doctrine of transmigration. Such an indirect dependence, initially through Pythagoreans, would by no means detract from the coincidence in thought, for Plato would not have adopted such a story somehow conveyed to him through eastern tradition—not to mention granting it such a significant place—had it not seemed to him that it bore a resemblance to the truth.
    In an essay by Ziegler that systematically examines this uncertain idea before the time of Plato, it is traced back to Babylonian conceptions (Ziegler). [Freud's note]

Following the hint of the poet-philosopher, shall we be so bold as to assume that when living substance was animated, it was torn into small particles which have been striving ever since, through the sex drives, for reunification? And that these drives, in which the chemical affinity of inanimate matter was perpetuated, gradually overcame (during their evolution in the kingdom of the protista) the difficulties the environment imposed against this striving—an environment which was charged with deadly stimuli and which compelled them to form a protective crust? And that these scattered particles of living substance thus attained a multicellular structure and ultimately transferred the drive for reunification, in highly concentrated form, to the gametes? Here, I think, we can break off this discussion.

But not without adding a few words of critical reflection. It would be reasonable to ask me whether and to what extent I am convinced of the hypotheses developed here. My answer would be the following: neither am I convinced myself, nor do I seek to convince others to believe in them. More precisely: I do not know how far I believe in them. It seems to me that the affective factor of being convinced need not come into consideration at all here. One can surely dedicate oneself to a train of thought and follow it as far as it leads—out of mere scientific curiosity, or, if one prefers, as an *advocatus diaboli* who does not, for all that, sign a pact with the devil. I am fully aware that the third step in the theory of the drives, which I am taking here, cannot claim the same level of certainty as the two earlier ones—the expansion of the concept of sexuality and the proposal of narcissism. These innovations were direct translations of observation into theory, and were no more tainted by sources of error than is inevitable in all such cases. However, the claim that the character of drives is *regressive* also rests upon observed material—namely on the facts of the repetition compulsion. Perhaps, though, I have overestimated their significance. Yet one cannot pursue this idea without repeatedly combining the factual with the speculative, thus greatly distancing oneself from observation. Clearly, the more often this is done in developing a theory, the more unreliable the result will be, yet the degree of uncertainty cannot be calculated. One may have made a lucky guess, or may have gone terribly astray. In this type of research I do not attribute much to so called "intuition"; what I have seen of it seems more like the result of intellectual impartiality. Unfortunately, though, one is seldom impartial when dealing with the ultimate questions—the great problems of science and life. I believe that here each person is dominated by deep-rooted internal prejudices, into whose hands his speculations unwittingly play. With such good grounds for distrust, nothing but cool benevolence toward the results of one's own intellectual effort remains possible. I would only hasten to add that such self-criticism does not oblige one to any special tolerance for dissenting opinions. One may inexorably reject theories contradicted by the very first steps in analyzing observation, knowing all the while that the validity of the theories one espouses can be only provisional. In judging our speculation about the life and death drives, we would not be much disturbed by the fact that so many strange and unclear processes occur in them, e.g., one drive may be driven out by others, or may turn from the ego to the object, and so on. This is merely a result of the fact that we are obliged to work with scientific terminology, i.e., with our own figurative language, that of psychology (or more correctly: depth psychology). Otherwise, we would be completely unable to describe the processes in question; indeed, we would not even have noticed them. The deficiencies of our description would probably disappear, were we already able to invoke physiological or chemical terms in lieu of psychological ones. Admittedly, those terms too belong merely to a figurative language—but one long familiar to us and perhaps simpler as well.

Yet we should understand clearly that the uncertainty of our speculation was greatly increased by the need to borrow from the science of biology. Biology is truly a realm of unlimited possibilities. We may expect from it the most surprising revelations, and cannot guess what answers it may provide in a few decades to the questions we have posed—answers, perhaps, of such a kind as to blow apart our entire artificial structure of hypotheses. If that is the case, one might ask why such tasks as the one presented in this section should be taken on at all, and why they have been shared with readers. Here, I cannot deny that some of the analogies, connections, and relations in this section seemed to me to be worthy of consideration.[1]

VII

If seeking to restore an earlier state is such a universal characteristic of drives, we should not be surprised that there are so many processes in mental life that take place independently of the pleasure principle. This characteristic would be conveyed to each component drive and would in each case seek to regain a particular stage on the path of development. But all of this, over

---

1 In conclusion, a few words to clarify our terminology, which in the course of these discussions has undergone a certain development. We understood the "sex drives" from their relation to the sexes and to the function of reproduction. We then retained this name even when we were compelled by the findings of psychoanalysis to loosen their connection with reproduction. With the hypothesis of the narcissistic libido and the extension of the concept of the libido to the individual cells, the sex drive transformed itself for us into Eros, which seeks to push together and hold together the parts of living substance; those drives generally called sex drives appear as the portion of this Eros directed toward objects. These speculations then have Eros operating from the beginning of life and acting as a "life drive" in contrast to the "death drive," which arose through the animation of the inorganic. These speculations. seek to solve the riddle of life by assuming these two drives struggling with each other from the very beginning. It may be harder to gain a view of the transformations undergone by the concept of the "ego drives." Initially we used this term to designate all the drive orientations unknown to us in greater detail, but distinguishable from the sex drives directed toward an object; we opposed the ego drives to the sex drives, whose expression is the libido. Later we approached the analysis of the ego and recognized that a portion of the "ego drives" too is of libidinal nature, having taken the subject's own ego as its object. These narcissistic drives for self-preservation then had to be included among the libidinal sex drives. The opposition between ego drives and sex drives was transformed into that between ego drives and object drives, both of a libidinal nature. But in its place arose a new opposition between libidinal drives (ego drives and object drives) and others; these must be located in the ego and may perhaps be noted among the destructive drives. These speculations transform the opposition into that between life drives (Eros) and death drives. [Freud's note]

which the pleasure principle has not yet gained any control, need not therefore stand in opposition to it, and we still have not solved the problem of determining the relation of the drive processes of repetition to the dominance of the pleasure principle.

We recognized as one of the earliest and most important functions of the mental apparatus that of "binding" the arriving drive impulses, of replacing the primary process reigning in them with the secondary process, and of transforming their freely moving charged energy into mainly resting (tonic) charge. During this transformation no attention can be given to the development of unpleasure, but this does not suspend the pleasure principle. Rather, the transformation occurs in the service of the pleasure principle; the binding is a preparatory act introducing and securing the dominance of the pleasure principle.

Let us separate function and tendency more sharply than we have previously done. The pleasure principle, then, is a tendency serving a function whose task is to render the mental apparatus completely free of excitation, or to keep the amount of excitation in it constant or as low as possible. We cannot yet decide with certainty on any of these versions, but we observe that the function identified in this way would take part in the universal striving of all living things to return to the peace of the inorganic world. We have all experienced that the greatest pleasure we can attain, that of the sex act, is associated with the momentary extinction of a greatly heightened excitation. But the binding of the drive impulse would be a preliminary function to prepare the excitation for its final release in the pleasurable discharge of energies.

In the same context there arises the question of whether the feelings of pleasure and unpleasure can be produced in the same way from the bound and the unbound processes of excitation. Here, there seems to be no doubt whatsoever that the unbound processes—the primary processes—produce far more intense feelings in both directions than the bound processes, those of the secondary process. Furthermore, the primary processes are the earlier ones chronologically. At the beginning of mental life there are no others, and we may conclude that if the pleasure principle were not already active in them, it could not establish itself for the later processes. Thus we arrive at what is essentially not a simple result—that the striving for pleasure at the beginning of mental life expresses itself far more intensely than later, but not in such an unrestricted way: it has to tolerate frequent breaches. In more mature individuals, the dominance of the pleasure principle is far more secure, but it can no more escape being brought under control than any of the other drives. In any case, whichever aspect of the process of excitation produces feelings of pleasure and unpleasure must be present in the secondary process just as in the primary process.

This is the place to start further studies. From within, our consciousness conveys to us feelings not only of pleasure and unpleasure, but also of a peculiar tension which itself can be pleasurable or unpleasurable. Is it the bound and the unbound processes of energy that we should distinguish by means of these feelings? Or shall we relate the feeling of tension to the absolute quantity, or perhaps the level, of charge, while the series of feelings of pleasure and unpleasure points to a change in the quantity of the charge per unit of time? We will also notice that the life drives have so much more to do with our internal perception since they act as disturbers of the peace and continually bring along tensions whose release is felt as pleasure, while the death drives seem to do their work inconspicuously. The pleasure principle seems to serve the death drives directly. It does guard against external stimuli, considered dangers by both types of drives, but guards especially against increases in internal stimuli aiming to make the task of living more difficult. Connected with this are innumerable other questions that cannot at present be answered. We must be patient and await further means and opportunities for research—and be prepared as well to leave a path we have followed for a while if it seems to lead to no good result. Only those believers who demand in science a substitute for the catechism they have renounced will take it amiss if a researcher develops or even transforms his views. Concerning the slow advances of our scientific knowledge we are also comforted by the words of a poet [final lines of "Die beiden Gulden" ("The Two coins"), Friedrich Rückert's rendition of the third of the *Maqamat* (Assemblies), ca. 1100, by al-Hariri of Basra]:

Was man nicht erfliegen kann, muss man erhinken.
...
Die Schrift sagt, es ist keine Sünde zu hinken.
[What one cannot fly to one must limp to. ... The Scripture says that limping is no sin.]

Appendix A: Other Works by Sigmund Freud

[The significance of *Beyond the Pleasure Principle* can be readily measured by its reception and amendment by thinkers as different as Marcuse, Klein, Baudrillard, and Derrida. But it can also be measured as it works across Freud's own corpus, some examples of which are included in this Appendix.

Beyond the Pleasure Principle is best known for two innovations, the repetition compulsion and the death drive theory. Both were foreshadowed in earlier works, most especially in those we call "pre-psychoanalytic," but also quite explicitly in some contemporaneous works. For example, in "The Uncanny" of 1919 Freud links the Romantic theme of doubles and doubling with death. Doubling, in this respect, is just another way of discussing repetition and the uncanny impression Freud claims it makes.

The death drive theory makes an important appearance in *The Ego and The Id*, written a few years after *BPP*. In it Freud states that his new examination of ego psychology is conceived against the backdrop of the death drive theory–an inconvenient reminder for later ego psychologists who often downplay *BPP* as a relic of outdated biologism and unchecked philosophizing.

In "A Note about the 'Mystic Writing Pad'" (1926) Freud didn't hesitate to extend the metaphors of "beyond" to an imaginative rendering of primary and secondary processes, repression, and the unconscious. That these metaphors link the unconscious to a kind of writing is a useful heuristic image. But after Derrida it can also be understood as another instance of a metaphysics that eschews, even as it invokes, the materiality of writing.

"The Economic Problem of Masochism" draws out an implication Freud avoids in *BPP*, namely the theory of "primary masochism." Similarly, *Civilization and Its Discontents* of 1930 teases out the implications that the metabiological *BPP* has for our understanding of *Kultur*—the world of everyday life. His much-misunderstood conclusion: psychoanalysis is concerned with everyday life, but metapsychology points to a beyond that is of another order, that of death. In short, the metapsychology is radically anti-social and anti-cultural. In this way Freud already sets up the conditions for the dark conclusions of "Analysis Terminable and Interminable" (1937). In this nearly final statement, Freud delivers a verdict on clinical practice that is stunningly pessimistic. For the first time Freud links the death drive theory to the ancient theory of Empedocles: life as strife.

All works, in part or in whole, have been newly translated by Gregory C. Richter.]

1. From "The Uncanny" (1919)

E.T.A. Hoffmann[1] is the unparalleled master of the uncanny in literature. His novel *Die Elixire des Teufels* [*The Devil's Elixirs*] shows numerous themes to which one might wish to ascribe the uncanny effect of the narrative. The content of the novel is too rich and complex to attempt a summary. At the end of the book, when the background details of the plot previously withheld from the reader are finally revealed, the result is not the enlightenment of the reader, but total bewilderment. The author has piled up too much material of the same kind. The impression of the whole does not suffer from this, but one's understanding is certainly reduced. One must be content to emphasize the most prominent among those uncanny themes in order to investigate whether they too can be derived from infantile sources. These are the themes of the double in all its grades and developments. This includes the presence of characters who because of their identical appearance must be considered identical; the intensification of this relation in that the mental processes of one character spring into the other—what we would call telepathy—so that the one shares the knowledge, feeling, and experience of the other; identification with another person so that a character is not sure which ego is his own, or replaces his own ego with that of another—doubling, dividing, and exchanging of the ego; and finally the constant return of the same, the repetition of the same facial features, personality

---

1   Ernst Theodor Wilhelm (Amadeus) Hoffmann (1776-1822), a German romantic author and composer best known by his nom de plume of E.T.A. Hoffmann, the last name. Freud was greatly influenced by nineteenth-century Romanticism, of which Hoffmann was a major figure.

traits, experiences, criminal acts, and even names over several consecutive generations.

The theme of the double has been discussed in detail in an article of the same name by Otto Rank (Rank 1914).[1] The article investigates the connections of the double with reflections, shadows, guardian spirits, the doctrine of the soul, and the fear of death; the surprising developmental history of this theme is also shown in a clear light. Indeed, the double was originally an insurance against the demise of the ego, an "energetic denial of the power of death"; the "immortal" soul was probably the first double of the body (Rank 1914). The creation of such doubling as a defense against destruction has its counterpart in a feature of dream language, which is fond of expressing castration through doubling or multiplication of the genital symbol; in the culture of the ancient Egyptians this defense became a stimulus for the art of making the image of the dead in lasting material. But these ideas have arisen on the foundation of unrestricted self-love, of the primary narcissism dominating the mental life of the child and of primitives, and when this phase is surmounted the omen of the double changes: at first the insurer of immortality, it becomes the uncanny harbinger of death.

The idea of the double does not necessarily disappear with this primal narcissism, for it can gain new content from the later developmental stages of the ego. In the ego a special agency slowly develops which can remain distinct from the rest of the ego; this agency serves for self-observation and self-criticism and performs mental censorship, and is known to our conscious mind as the "conscience." In the pathological case of delusions of being observed, this agency becomes isolated, split from the ego, and noticeable to the physician. The fact that such an agency exists, capable of treating the rest of the ego as an object—the fact, then, that humans are capable of self-observation—makes it possible to fill the old idea of the double with new content and to ascribe to this idea various things—especially those things that

---

1 Otto Rank (1884-1939), a lay analyst, was a central figure in Freud's inner circle of adherents (ca. 1905-25). For years Rank was Freud's favorite colleague, and they worked very closely intellectually and institutionally until Rank's own work drifted from Freud's.

seem to self-criticism to belong to the old surmounted narcissism of primeval times.[1]

But it is not only this content, offensive to criticism of the ego, that can be incorporated in the double, but also all the unfulfilled possibilities of fate that fantasy still wants to cling to, all the ego-strivings incapable of asserting themselves due to unfavorable external circumstances, and all the suppressed decisions of the will that have produced the illusion of free will.[2]

But after having thus observed the manifest motivation of the figure of the double, we must say that none of this renders comprehensible the extraordinarily high degree of uncanniness that pervades that figure; and given our knowledge of pathological mental processes we can add that none of this content could explain the striving for defense that projects this content out from the ego as something foreign. The quality of uncanniness can only derive from the fact that the double is a creation belonging to surmounted primeval times in mental life, and which in any case had a friendlier sense then. The double has become an image of terror, just as gods, after the collapse of their religion, become demons (Heine, *Die Götter im Exil* [*The Gods in Exile*]).

The other ego-disturbances utilized by Hoffmann can easily be evaluated according to the pattern of the theme of the double. They reach back to particular phases in the developmental history of ego-feeling—a regression to times when the ego had not yet sharply delineated itself from the external world and from others. I believe these themes are partially responsible for the

---

1 I believe that when poets complain that two souls dwell in the human breast, and when popular psychologists talk of the splitting of the ego, they are thinking of this division, belonging to ego-psychology, between the critical agency and the rest of the ego, and not of the antithetical relation discovered by psychoanalysis between the ego and the unconscious repressed content. In any case, the distinction is blurred by the fact that in the material rejected by ego-criticism derivatives of the repressed content are prominent. [Freud's note]

2 In Hanns Ewers's *Der Student von Prag* [The Student of Prague], with which Rank's study on the double begins, the hero has promised his beloved not to kill his dueling opponent, but on the way to the place of the duel he meets his double, who has already killed his rival. [Freud's note]

impression of uncanniness, though it is not easy to deduce their distinct share in that impression.

The factor of repetition of the same, perhaps, will not be appreciated by everyone as a source of the uncanny feeling. According to my observations, under certain conditions and combined with certain circumstances this repetition undoubtedly calls forth such a feeling, which, furthermore, resembles the helplessness felt in some dream states. As I was walking, one hot summer afternoon, through the unfamiliar, deserted streets of an Italian provincial town, I ended up in a district about whose character I could not long remain in doubt. At the windows of the small houses only painted women were to be seen, and I hurried to leave the narrow street at the next turn. But after I had wandered about for a while without any guide, I suddenly found myself in the same street again, where my presence was now beginning to be noticed; my swift departure resulted only in my ending up in the very same place, through a different detour, for the third time. But then I was overcome by a feeling I can only describe as uncanny; declining further voyages of discovery, I was glad to find myself back at the piazza I had recently left. Other situations which, like that just described, involve the unintended return of the same, but which profoundly differ from it in other respects, also produce the same feeling of helplessness and uncanniness. For example, when one has lost one's way in a mountain forest, perhaps having been overtaken by a sudden fog, and then despite all attempts to find a marked or familiar path repeatedly ends up in the same place, identified by some particular feature. Or when one wanders about in a dark, unfamiliar room, looking for the door or the light switch, and bumps into the same piece of furniture for the umpteenth time—a situation that Mark Twain transformed into an irresistibly comical one through grotesque exaggeration (Twain 107).

Examining another set of experiences, we easily recognize that it is only the factor of unintended repetition that makes the otherwise unremarkable uncanny, forcing upon us the idea of the fateful and inescapable when we would otherwise have spoken only of "chance." For example, receiving a ticket with a certain number, let us say 62, for a coat turned in at the cloakroom is certainly an unremarkable experience, as is finding that the cabin assigned one on a ship bears that number. But this impression changes if both unremarkable events occur close together so that the number 62 shows up numerous times on the same day, or if one notices that everything bearing a number—addresses, hotel rooms, train compartments, etc.—continually reproduces the same number, at least as a component. One finds this "uncanny," and anyone who is not thoroughly impervious to the temptations of superstition will be inclined to ascribe a secret meaning to this obstinate return of the same number, perhaps as an indication of the age to which one is fated to live. Or if one has just been engaged in studying the works of the great physiologist, Ewald Hering [1834-1918], and then within the next few days receives letters from two people bearing that name, from different countries, though one has never before had any contact with anyone called Hering. A brilliant researcher recently attempted to reduce events of this type to certain laws, which would eliminate the impression of the uncanny (Kammerer). I will not presume to decide whether he has succeeded.

Here, I can only hint at how the uncanny in the return of the same can be derived from infantile mental life; for a full account, I must refer the reader to a detailed presentation, in another context, now lying ready (Freud 1920). Indeed, in the unconscious mind we recognize the dominance of a *compulsion to repeat* proceeding from the drive impulses—a compulsion that probably depends on the very nature of the drives themselves, is strong enough to override the pleasure principle, lends a demonic character to certain aspects of mental life, still expresses itself very clearly in the strivings of small children, and governs a portion of the course taken by the analysis of neurotics. Through all these considerations, we are prepared to recognize that whatever is reminiscent of this inner "compulsion to repeat" will be perceived as uncanny.

2. From *The Ego and the Id* (1923)

The following discussions continue trains of thought begun in *Beyond the Pleasure Principle* (Freud 1920), and which, as mentioned there, I regarded with a sort of benevolent curiosity. The discussions take up these thoughts, link them with various facts of analytic observation, and seek to derive new conclusions from this union, but undertake no fresh loans from biology and therefore stand closer to psychoanalysis than does *Beyond the Pleasure Principle*. They have more the character of a synthesis than of a speculation, and seem to have aimed for a high goal. Yet I know they provide only the roughest sketch—a limitation I am very willing to accept. [...]

IV: The Two Types of Drives

We already said that if our differentiation of the mental realm into an id, an ego, and a super-ego provides an advance in our understanding, it should also serve as a means for achieving a deeper understanding and a better description of the dynamic relations within the mind. It is already clear to us as well that the ego stands under the special influence of perception, and that one can say, roughly, that perceptions have the same significance for the ego as drives have for the id. Simultaneously, the ego is also subject to the influence of the drives, as is the id, of which it is indeed only a specially modified component.

Concerning the drives, I developed a view recently (*Beyond the Pleasure Principle*) which I will maintain here and which I provide as a basis for further discussions: the view that one must distinguish two types of drives, one of which, the *sex drives* or *Eros*, is by far the more conspicuous and easier to examine. It comprises not only the actual uninhibited sex drive and the goal-inhibited and sublimated drive impulses derived from it, but also the self-preservation drive, which we must ascribe to the ego and which at the beginning of the analytic work we contrasted with the sexual object-drives—and with good reason. Demonstrating the second type of drives proved difficult for us; ultimately, we found a solution in recognizing sadism as its representative. Based on theoretical considerations supported by biology, we hypothesized a *death drive*, assigned the task of leading organic life back into the lifeless state, while Eros pursues the goal of complicating life by combining in a more and more complex manner the living substance dispersed in particles—and of course of preserving it in so doing. Here, strictly speaking, both drives behave conservatively in that they aim for the re-establishment of a state destroyed by the emergence of life. The emergence of life would thus be the cause of further life and simultaneously of the striving toward death, and life itself would be a struggle and a compromise between these two strivings. The question as to the origin of life would remain a cosmological one, and the question as to the purpose and intention of life would be answered *dualistically*.

With each of these two types of drives would be associated a particular physiological process (synthesis or disintegration), and in every particle of living substance both types of drives would be active, but in unequal proportions, so that one substance could take on a role as principal representative of Eros.

It would still be impossible to imagine how the drives of the two types combine, mix, and alloy with each other, but that this occurs regularly and on a large scale is an assumption we cannot reject in this context. As a result of the combination of unicellular elementary organisms into multicellular life forms, it would be possible to successfully neutralize the death drive of the single cell and divert the destructive impulses to the external world through the involvement of a special organ. This organ would be the musculature, and the death drive would now express itself—though probably only in part—as a *destructive drive* toward the external world and other life forms.

Once we have assumed the idea of an admixture of the two types of drives, the possibility of a—more or less complete—*separation* of those drives also imposes itself upon us. In the sadistic component of the sex drive we would be presented with a classic example of an efficient admixture of drives, and in the *sadism* that has become independent as a perversion we would have the example of a separation, though one not carried to extremes. Then we are afforded a view into a great realm of facts not yet observed in this light. We recognize that the destructive drive is regularly placed, for purposes of discharge, in the service of Eros; we suspect that the epileptic fit is a product and an indication of a separation of drives, and that among the effects of some severe neuroses—for instance, the obsessional neuroses—drive separation and the primacy of the death drive deserve particular consideration. As a swift generalization, we might suspect that a regression of libido, for example from the genital to the sadistic-anal phase, is essentially based on a separation of drives, just as, conversely, the advance from the earlier phase to the definitive genital phase has as its condition a contribution of erotic components. The question also arises whether regular *ambivalence*, which we so often find intensified in the constitutional disposition to neurosis, cannot be conceived as the result of a separation of drives; but ambivalence is so primal that it must on the contrary be considered an incomplete admixture of drives.

Our interests naturally turn to the question of whether revealing connections can be discovered between the hypothesized structures—the ego, the super-ego, and the id, on the one hand, and the two types of drives on the other; and further, whether we can ascribe to the pleasure principle, which dominates mental processes, a constant relation to the two types of drives and to mental differentiations. But before entering into this discussion, we must remove a doubt that arises concerning the very statement of the problem. Indeed, while there is no doubt about the pleasure principle, and the differentiation of the ego has clinical justification, the distinction between the two types of drives does not seem sufficiently assured, and facts of clinical analysis might eliminate such a claim.

There does seem to be one such fact. For the opposition between the two types of drives we may adduce the polarity of love and hate. Finding a representative of Eros is not difficult for us, but we are very satisfied that in the destructive drive, to which hate shows the way, we can point to a representative of the elusive death drive. Now clinical observation teaches us not only that hate accompanies love with unexpected regularity (ambivalence), and not only that hate is often the precursor of love in human relations, but also that in situations of various types hate is transformed into love and love into hate. If this transformation is more than mere temporal succession, but is a true replacement, then clearly the foundation is removed for such a fundamental distinction as that between erotic drives and death instincts—a distinction that presupposes physiological processes running in opposite directions.

Now the case in which someone first loves and then hates the same person (or the reverse) when the person has given cause for this is not relevant to our problem. Nor is the other case, in which a not yet manifest feeling of being in love first expresses itself in hostility and an aggressive tendency, for here the destructive component in the object-charge could have rushed forward, whereas the erotic component could join it later. But we are familiar with several cases in the psychology of the neuroses in which the assumption of a transformation seems more reasonable. In *paranoia persecutoria* the patient resists an excessively strong homosexual attachment to a particular person in a particular way, and the result is that this most beloved person becomes a persecutor, against whom the often dangerous aggression of the patient is directed. We have the right to claim that a previous phase had transformed love into hate. In the origin of homosexuality, but also of desexualized social feelings, analytic investigation has only recently introduced us to the existence of violent feelings of rivalry that lead to an aggressive inclination; only after these are surmounted does the previously hated object become the beloved object or the object of an identification. The question arises whether in these cases a direct conversion of hate into love is to be assumed. This, of course, involves purely internal changes in which a change of behavior in the object plays no part.

Analytical investigation of the process of change in paranoia, however, introduces us to the possibility of another mechanism. From the beginning an ambivalent attitude is present, and the transformation occurs through a reactive displacement of charge in that the energy is withdrawn from the erotic impulse and added to the hostile energy.

Not this, but something similar occurs when hostile rivalry is overcome, leading to homosexuality. The hostile attitude has no prospect of gratification and therefore—for economic reasons—is replaced by a loving attitude, one which offers better prospects for gratification, i.e., for the possibility of discharge. Thus for neither of these cases must we assume a direct transformation of hate into love; this would be incompatible with the qualitative difference between the two types of drives.

But we notice that in adopting this other mechanism of changing love into hate, we have tacitly made another assumption—one which deserves to be stated. We have operated as though there were in the mind—whether in the ego or in the id is undetermined—a displaceable energy, which, neutral in itself, can join with a qualitatively differentiated erotic or destructive impulse and increase its total charge. Without assuming such a displaceable energy we cannot manage at all. One can only ask where it comes from, who it belongs to, and what it signifies.

The problem of the quality of drive impulses and of their preservation through the various fortunes of the drives is still very obscure and has as yet hardly been addressed. In the component drives of the sexual realm, which are especially accessible to observation, one can identify a few processes belonging to this same category, e.g., we see that the component drives communicate with each other to some degree; that a drive from one particular erotogenic source can transmit its intensity to reinforce another component drive from another source; that the gratification of one drive substitutes for the gratification of another; and other similar facts, all of which must give us the courage to presume assumptions of a certain type.

Indeed, in the present discussion, I have only a hypothesis to offer, but no proof. It seems plausible that this displaceable and neutral energy, probably active in the ego and in the id, derives from the narcissistic store of libido, and is thus desexualized Eros. The erotic drives, after all, certainly appear to be more plastic, more deflectable, and more displaceable than the destructive drives. Then one can continue unconstrained and assume that this displaceable libido functions in the service of the pleasure principle to prevent damming up and to facilitate discharge. Here, we cannot fail to notice a certain indifference as to how the discharge occurs, so long as it occurs somehow. We know this trait as characteristic for the processes of charge in the id. It is found in erotic charges, where a special indifference regarding the object is developed, and especially in transferences during analysis—transferences that must be carried out regardless of the person involved. Recently Rank adduced some good examples of how neurotic acts of revenge are directed against the wrong people (Rank 1913). Noting this behavior by the unconscious, one recalls the comical anecdote in which one of the three village tailors is to be hanged because the single village blacksmith has committed a capital crime. Punishment there must be, even if it does not fall upon the guilty one. In the displacements effected by the primary process in the dream-work we first noted this type of looseness. While in the dream-work it is the objects that are of only secondary importance, in the case that concerns us here it is the paths of the discharge reaction. It would be typical of the ego to insist on greater exactitude in choosing an object and a path of discharge.

If this displaceable energy is desexualized libido, it may also be termed *sublimated*, for it would still cling to the main purpose of Eros, to unite and to bind; it would serve for the establishment of that unity—or that striving for unity—that characterizes the ego. If, among these displacements, we include thought processes in the wider sense, then the activity of thought is also provided through the sublimation of erotic drive-forces.

Here again we encounter the previously addressed possibility that sublimation regularly occurs through the mediation of the ego. We recall the other case, in which the ego deals with the first and certainly also the subsequent object-charges of the id by taking over their libido into itself and binding it to the alteration of the ego brought about by identification. This transformation into ego-libido is of course connected with a giving up of the sexual goals—a desexualization. In any case this provides us with insights into an important function of the ego in its relation to Eros. By seizing the libido of the object-charges in this way, putting itself forward as the sole love-object, and desexualizing or sublimating the libido of the id, the ego works against the intentions of Eros and places itself in the service of the opposing drive impulses. Yet it must accept another portion of the object-charges of the id—participate in them, so to speak. Later we will have an opportunity to discuss another possible result of this activity by the ego.

An important amplification in the theory of narcissism would now be in order. At the very beginning, all the libido is accumulated in the id, while the ego is still forming or is still feeble. The id sends a portion of this libido out onto erotic object-charges, whereupon the strengthened ego seeks to seize this object-libido and force itself on the id as a love-object. The narcissism of the ego is thus a secondary one, extracted from objects.

Again and again we find that the drive impulses we can follow reveal themselves to be derivatives of Eros. Without the considerations presented in *Beyond the Pleasure Principle* and, ultimately, without the sadistic contributions to Eros, we would find it difficult to maintain our underlying dualistic conception. But since we are obliged to adopt this conception, we gain the impression that the death drives are essentially mute and that the commotion of life emanates mainly from Eros.[1]

And from the struggle against Eros! One cannot reject the view that the pleasure principle serves the id as a compass in the struggle against the libido—the introducer of disturbances into the course of life. If Fechner's constancy principle[2] rules life, which would then be a gliding into death, it is the claims of Eros, of the sex drives, which, as drive-needs, prevent the sinking of the level and introduce new tensions. Led by the pleasure principle, i.e., by the perception of unpleasure, the id

---

1 Indeed, in our view, the destructive drives directed outward have been diverted from the self through the mediation of Eros. [Freud's note]

2 See note 1, page 52 and Freud's discussion pages 52-53.

resists these tensions in various ways. It does so first of all by complying as swiftly as possible with the demands of the non-desexualized libido—that is, by struggling for gratification of the directly sexual strivings. And also in a far more elaborated manner with respect to one of these gratifications, where all component demands converge: by release of the sexual substances, which are, so to speak, saturated carriers of the erotic tensions. The ejection of the sexual substances in the sexual act corresponds in some degree to the separation of soma and germ-plasm. This accounts for how similar the state following complete sexual gratification is to dying, and for the fact that in lower animals death and the procreative act coincide. These life forms die in reproducing since after the elimination of Eros through gratification, the death drive has a free hand for effecting its intentions. Finally, as we have heard, the ego makes the id's task of achieving mastery easier by sublimating some of the libido for itself and its purposes.

V: The Dependent Relations of the Ego
[...]
How is it that the super-ego expresses itself essentially as a feeling of guilt (or more accurately, as criticism: the feeling of guilt is the perception in the ego corresponding to this criticism) and in so doing displays such extraordinary harshness and severity toward the ego? If we turn first to melancholia, we find that the super-strong super-ego, which has gained control of consciousness, rages against the ego with merciless vehemence, as if it had taken over all the sadism available in the individual. Given our view of sadism, we would say that the destructive component has deposited itself in the super-ego and turned against the ego. What now reigns in the super-ego is like a pure culture of the death drive, and often enough it really is successful in driving the ego into death if the ego does not resist its tyrant in time through a change into mania.

The reproaches of conscience in certain forms of obsessional neurosis are similarly painful and tormenting, but here the situation is less transparent. In contrast to melancholia, it is notable that the obsessional neurotic never actually takes the step of self-destruction; he is immune, as it were, to the danger of suicide, and much better protected from it than the hysteric. We understand that it is the retention of the object that guarantees the safety of the ego. In obsessional neurosis it has become possible, through a regression to the pregenital organization, for the love impulses to transform themselves into aggressive impulses against the object. The destructive drive has again become free and seeks to destroy the object, or it at least gives the appearance that this intention exists. The ego has not taken up these tendencies, and it resists them with reaction formations and precautions; these tendencies remain in the id. But the super-ego behaves as if the ego were responsible for them, and simultaneously shows, through the seriousness with which it persecutes these destructive intentions, that this is not an impression produced by the regression, but is a true replacement of love by hate. Helpless on both sides, the ego defends itself in vain against the impositions of the murderous id and against the reproaches of the punishing conscience. It is successful in holding off at least the coarsest actions of both; at first, the result is endless self-torment; in later development it is a systematic torturing of the object, if accessible.

The dangerous death drives are handled in the individual in various ways—in part being rendered harmless through admixture with erotic components, and in part being diverted outward as aggression—but indeed, to a great extent, they continue their internal work unhindered. How is it, then, that in melancholia the super-ego can become a sort of accumulation site for the death drives?

From the point of view of drive restriction, of morality, one can say that the id is completely amoral, that the ego strives to be moral, and that the super-ego can become hyper-moral—and then as cruel as only the id can be. It is remarkable that the more a person restricts his outwardly aimed aggression, the more severe—the more aggressive—he becomes in his ego-ideal. To the normal view this appears the other way around: in the demand of the ego-ideal the normal view sees the motive for the suppression of aggression. But the fact remains as we have stated it: the more a person masters his aggression, the more the aggressive inclination of his ideal toward his ego increases. This resembles a displacement, a turning against his own ego. Even ordinary, normal morality has the character of something harshly restricting and cruelly prohibiting. From this, indeed, arises the conception of an inexorably punishing higher being.

I cannot further explicate these circumstances without introducing a new hypothesis. The super-ego certainly arose through an identification with the father as a model. Every such identification has the character of a desexualization or even of a sublimation. It now seems that with such a change, a separation of drives also occurs. After sublimation, the erotic component no longer has the power to bind all the added destructiveness, and this becomes free as an aggressive and destructive inclination. From this separation would arise the entire ideal of the harsh, cruel trait of imperious Obligation.

Another brief consideration of obsessional neurosis. Here, the circumstances are different. The separation changing love to aggression did not arise through any function of the ego, but is the consequence of a regression that has occurred in the id. But this process has extended from the id to the super-ego, which now intensifies its severity toward the innocent ego. In both cases, though, the ego, which has overcome the libido through identification, would suffer punishment for this through the aggression of the super-ego mixed with the libido.

Our ideas on the ego are beginning to make themselves clear, and its various relationships are becoming distinct. We now see the ego in its strength and in its weaknesses. It is entrusted with important functions. Given its relation to the perceptual system it establishes the temporal ordering of mental processes and submits these to reality testing. Through the intervention of thought processes, it achieves a postponement of motor discharges and governs access to motility. This last governing function is certainly more formal than factual; in its relation to action, the ego has something like the position of a constitutional monarch, without whose sanction nothing can become law, but who considers the matter in great depth before vetoing a proposal of the parliament. The ego is enriched through all life experiences from without, but the id is its other exterior world, which it strives to subject to itself. It extracts libido from the id and converts the object-charges of the id into ego-structures. With the help of the super-ego, in a manner still obscure to us, it draws upon the prehistoric experiences accumulated in the id.

There are two paths along which the content of the id can penetrate into the ego. One is direct, while the other leads via the ego-ideal, and for some mental activities it may be decisive on which of the two paths they occur. The ego at first perceives drives, but later controls them; at first it obeys drives, but later inhibits them. In this achievement a significant role is played by the ego-ideal, which in part is certainly a reaction formation against the drive processes of the id. Psychoanalysis is a tool intended to make possible a progressive conquest of the id by the ego.

But on the other hand we see the same ego as a poor unfortunate, in three types of service and therefore threatened by three types of danger: from the external world, from the libido of the id, and from the severity of the super-ego. Three types of anxiety correspond to these three dangers, for anxiety is the expression of a retreat from danger. As an entity on the border of two regions, the ego seeks to mediate between the world and the id, to make the id submissive to the world and, through its muscular actions, to make the world comply with the wishes of the id. It actually behaves like the physician during an analytic treatment: with its consideration of the real world, the ego offers itself to the id as a libido object and seeks to direct the libido of the id toward the ego itself. It is not only the helper of the id, but also its submissive servant, soliciting its master's love. Where possible, it seeks to remain in concord with the id; it covers the id's *unconscious* commands with its *preconscious* rationalizations; it falsely claims that the id obeys the admonitions of reality, even when the id has remained stiff and unyielding; it makes a secret of the id's conflicts with reality and, where possible, of its conflicts with the super-ego as well. In its intermediate position between the id and reality, it only too often succumbs to the temptation to become sycophantic, opportunistic, and deceitful—like a politician who sees the actual state of affairs but wants to maintain his good standing in public opinion.

Toward the two types of drives, the ego does not behave in an unbiased manner. Through its work of identification and sublimation it supports the death drives of the id in overpowering the libido, but in so doing finds itself in danger of becoming the object of the death drives and in danger of perishing. In order to provide assistance, it has had to fill itself with libido; thus the ego itself becomes the representative of Eros and now wants to live and be loved.

But since the ego's work of sublimation has as its consequence a separation of drives and a liberation of the aggressive drives in the super-ego, it exposes itself in its struggle against the libido to the danger of maltreatment and death. If the ego suffers under the aggression of the super-ego or even succumbs, its fate is parallel to that of the protista, which perish from the products of decomposition they themselves have created. In the economic sense, the morality at work in the super-ego seems to us to be such a product of decomposition.

Among the dependent relations of the ego, the relation to the super-ego is probably the most interesting.

Indeed, the ego is the actual seat of anxiety. Threatened by three types of dangers, the ego develops the flight reflex by withdrawing its own charge from the threatening perception or from the similarly evaluated process in the id and emitting this charge as anxiety. This primitive reaction is later replaced by the enactment of protective charges (the mechanism of the phobias). What the ego fears from the external danger and from the libidinal danger in the id cannot be stated; we know that the ego fears being overpowered or destroyed, but which of these cannot be determined analytically. The ego simply heeds the warning of the pleasure principle. On the other hand, it is possible to state what is concealed behind the ego's anxiety regarding the super-ego, i.e., behind the fear of conscience. At one time, the higher being that became the ego-ideal threatened castration, and this castration anxiety is probably the core around which the subsequent fear of conscience accumulates; it is this anxiety that persists as the fear of conscience.

The eloquent phrase, "every fear is actually the fear of death," conveys hardly any meaning, and in any case cannot be justified. Rather, it seems to me perfectly correct to distinguish the fear of death from object anxiety (real anxiety) and from neurotic libido anxiety. The fear of death presents psychoanalysis with a difficult problem, for death is an abstract concept with negative content for which no corresponding unconscious material can be found. The mechanism of the fear of death can only be that the ego relinquishes its narcissistic libidinal charge on an expansive scale, thus giving itself up, just as it normally gives up another object in the case of anxiety. I believe that the fear of death is played out between the ego and the super-ego.

We are familiar with the appearance of the fear of death under two conditions (entirely analogous, furthermore, to those of anxiety development in other cases): as a reaction to an external danger and as an internal process, for example in melancholia. The case of neurosis may once again aid us in understanding the real case.

The fear of death in melancholia permits only one explanation: that the ego gives itself up because it feels itself hated and persecuted, rather than loved, by the super-ego. For the ego, then, living is synonymous with being loved—being loved by the super-ego, which here too appears as the representative of the id. The super-ego carries out the same protecting and saving function as did the father formerly, and later Providence or Fate. But the ego must also come to the same conclusion when it finds itself in extremely great real danger it believes it cannot overcome on its own. It sees itself abandoned by all protecting forces and lets itself die. This is, furthermore, still the same situation underlying the first great anxiety-state of birth and the infantile anxiety of longing—that of separation from the protecting mother.

Based on these explanations, the fear of death, like the fear of conscience, can be conceived as an extension of castration anxiety. Given the great significance of the feeling of guilt for the neuroses, we cannot reject the idea that common neurotic anxiety in severe cases undergoes an intensification through the development of anxiety between the ego and the super-ego (castration anxiety, fear of conscience, fear of death).

The id, to which we finally redirect our attention, has no means of demonstrating love or hate to the ego. The id cannot say what it wants; it has not produced a unified will. Eros and the death drive struggle within it; we have heard with what means the one group of drives defends itself against the others. We could depict the situation as if the id stood under the control of the mute but powerful death drives, which desire peace and, taking the hint from the pleasure principle, want to put Eros, the trouble-maker, to rest—but here we would hope to avoid underestimating the role of Eros.

3. From "The Economic Problem of Masochism" (1924)

One is justified in characterizing the existence of a masochistic striving in human drive function as mysterious in an economic sense. For if the pleasure principle dominates mental processes such that avoiding unpleasure and gaining pleasure become their primary aim, then masochism is incomprehensible. If pain and unpleasure can cease to function as warnings and be goals themselves, the pleasure principle is paralyzed: the watchman over our mental life is anesthetized, as it were.

Masochism, then, appears to us in the light of a great danger, which in no way applies to its counterpart, sadism. We are tempted to call the pleasure principle the watchman over our life—and not merely the watchman over our mental life. But then the task arises of investigating the relation of the pleasure principle to the two types of drives we have distinguished—the death drives and the erotic (libidinal) life drives. In our consideration of the problem of masochism, we can proceed no further until we have heeded this call.

As will be recalled, we have considered the principle governing all mental processes as a special case of Fechner's *tendency for stability* (Freud 1920, Chapter 1). In so doing, we have ascribed to the mental apparatus the intention of eliminating, or at least keeping as low as possible, the sum of excitation flowing to it. For this supposed aim, Barbara Low has proposed the name of *nirvana principle*, and we accept this designation. But we have blithely identified the pleasure-unpleasure principle with this nirvana principle. Every unpleasure would thus have to coincide with an increase, and every pleasure with a decrease, of stimulus-tension in the mind; the nirvana principle (and the pleasure principle supposedly identical to it) would stand completely in the service of the death drives, whose aim is to lead unsettled life into the stability of the inorganic state, and it would serve to warn about the claims of the life drives—those of the libido—which seek to disturb the course of life aspired to. But this conception cannot be correct. It seems that we feel directly in the series of sensations of tension an increase or decrease in the quantities of stimulus, and there are undoubtedly pleasurable tensions and unpleasurable relaxations. The state of sexual excitation is the most commanding example of such a pleasurable increase in stimulus, but certainly not the only one. Pleasure and unpleasure, then, cannot be related to an increase or decrease in the quantity we call *stimulus-tension*, although they clearly have much to do with this factor. It seems that they do not depend on this quantitative factor, but on a characteristic thereof which we can only designate as qualitative. We would be much more advanced in psychology were we able to identify this qualitative characteristic. Perhaps it is the rhythm—the temporal course of the changes, rises, and falls in the quantity of stimulus. We do not know the answer.

In any case, we must realize that the nirvana principle, belonging to the death drive, has undergone a modification in the living organism—a modification through which it has become the pleasure principle; from now on we shall avoid considering the two principles one. If there is any desire to pursue this, it will not be hard to guess from what power this modification emanated. It can only be the life drive, the libido, which has in this way, beside the death drive, won its share in the regulation of the processes of life. Thus we gain a small but interesting series of relations: the *nirvana* principle expresses the tendency of the death drive, the *pleasure* principle represents the claims of the libido, and finally the modification of that principle, the *reality* principle, represents the influence of the external world.

None of these three principles is actually inactivated by another. They can normally tolerate one another, although conflicts will be provoked from time to time given that in one case a quantitative reduction of the load of stimulus has been set as a goal, while in another case the goal is a qualitative characteristic of the load of stimulus, and in the last case the goal is a delay in discharging the stimulus and a temporary allowance of the unpleasure produced by tension. The conclusion derived from these considerations is that the designation of the pleasure principle as the watchman over our life cannot be rejected.

Let us return to masochism. It appears to us in three forms: as a condition imposed on sexual excitation, as an expression of feminine nature, and as a norm of behavior. Thus one can distinguish an *erotogenic*, a *feminine*, and a *moral* masochism. The first masochism, erotogenic, or pleasure in pain—underlies both other forms as well; it is based in biology and constitution, and remains incomprehensible unless one adopts certain assumptions about circumstances that are quite obscure. The third, and in some respects most important form of masochism has just recently been recognized by psychoanalysis as a mainly unconscious feeling of guilt, but can already be completely explained and incorporated into our other knowledge. Feminine masochism, however, is the most accessible to our observation and the least mysterious; it can be surveyed in all its relations. Our discussion can begin with this form.

We are sufficiently familiar with this type of masochism in men (to whom, based on my material, I limit my comments here) from the fantasies of masochistic (and therefore often impotent) patients, which either terminate in an onanistic act or represent sexual gratification in themselves. The real performances of mas- ochistic perverts coincide perfectly with these fantasies, whether the performances are carried out as an end in themselves or for the production of potency, leading to the sexual act. In both cases— the performances are of course only the playful enactment of the fantasies—the manifest content comprises being gagged, bound, painfully beaten, whipped, mistreated in some manner, forced into unconditional obedience, dirtied, and debased. Much more rarely, and only with great restrictions, are mutilations included in this content. The obvious and easily reached interpretation is that the masochist wants to be treated like a small, helpless, and dependent child—but especially like a naughty child. It is unnecessary to adduce cases: the material is highly uniform, and accessible to any observer, including the non-analyst. But if one has an opportunity to study cases in which masochistic fantasies have undergone especially rich processing, one easily discovers that they place the person concerned in a situation characterized by feminine features—and thus signify being castrated, being copulated with, or giving birth. I have therefore called this form of masochism, *a potiori* as it were [based on the most powerful exam- ple], the feminine form, although so many of its elements point to infantile life. Later, this layering of the infantile and the feminine will find a simple explanation. Castration—or blinding, which represents it—has often left behind its negative trace in fantasies: the condition that it is precisely to the genitals or the eyes that no injury is permitted. (Masochistic tortures, incidentally, rarely make such a serious impression as the cruelties of sadism, fanta- sized or enacted.) In the manifest content of masochistic fantasies, a sense of guilt is also expressed in the assumption that the person concerned has committed some crime (left indefinite) which is to be expiated through all the painful and torturous procedures. This looks like a superficial rationalization of the masochistic contents, but a connection with infantile masturbation lies just behind. On the other hand, this factor of guilt leads over to the third, moral, form of masochism.

Feminine masochism, which we have described, is based entirely on primary, erotogenic masochism—on pleasure in pain; this pleasure in pain cannot be explained without considerations reaching very far back.

In *Three Essays on the Theory of Sexuality*, in the section on the sources of infantile sexuality, I proposed that sexual excitation arises as an associated effect in a large set of internal processes as soon as the intensity of these processes has exceeded certain quantitative limits [Freud 1905]. I even adduced the possibility that nothing of great importance occurs in the organism without making its contribution to the excitation of the sex drive. Accordingly, the excitation of pain and unpleasure must also have this result. This libidinal component of excitation in the case of tension from pain and unpleasure would be an infantile physiological mechanism that later ceases to function. In various sexual constitutions it would undergo varying degrees of development, but would in any case provide the physiological foundation then built on in the mind in the form of erotogenic masochism.

The inadequacy of this explanation, however, is seen in the fact that no light is cast on the regular and intimate relations of masochism with its counterpart in drive function, sadism. If one goes a bit further back, to the hypothesis of the two types of drives we believe are active in the organism, one arrives at another derivation, which, however, does not contradict the one above. In (multicellular) organisms the libido meets the death drive or destructive drive, dominant in them, which seeks to tear apart the cellular organism and lead each of its elementary organisms into a state of inorganic stability (though this may be only relative). The libido has the task of rendering this destructive drive harmless, and accomplishes this—soon with the help of a special organ system, the musculature—by diverting the drive mainly outward and directing it toward the objects in the external world. The drive might be called the destructive drive, the drive for mastery, or the will to power. A portion of this drive is placed directly in the service of sexual function, where it has an important task. This is actual sadism. Another portion does not share in this displacement outward, but remains in the organism and, with the help of the associated sexual excitation already mentioned, is libidinally bound there. In this portion we must recognize the original, erotogenic masochism.

We lack any physiological understanding of the ways and means by which this taming of the death drive by the libido may occur. In the psychoanalytic realm, we can only assume that a very extensive admixture and combining of the two types of drives takes place, variable in its proportions, so that we should never expect pure life drives or pure death drives, but only various blends of the two. Corresponding to the admixture of drives, under certain influences a separation of these drives may occur. The portion of the death drives that escape this taming—this being bound to additional libidinal components—cannot presently be surmised.

If one is willing to overlook a certain imprecision, one can say that the death drive at work in the organism—primal sadism—is identical with masochism. After its main portion has been transferred outward onto objects, the actual erotogenic masochism remains within as its residue; on the one hand it has become a component of the libido, while on the other hand it still has the self as its object. This masochism would thus be an attestation to, and a remainder of, that developmental phase in which the alloying of the death drive and Eros occurred—a process so important for life. We will not be surprised to hear that under certain circumstances the sadism, or destructive drive, that has been turned outward, projected, can again be introjected, turned inward, and in this way regress to its earlier situation. Then it produces a secondary masochism, which adds itself to the original masochism.

Erotogenic masochism shares all the developmental stages of the libido and takes from them its psychologically shifting coverings. Anxiety about being devoured by the totem animal (the father) stems from the primitive oral organization; the wish to be beaten by the father comes from the subsequent sadistic-anal phase; as a precipitate of the phallic stage of organization, castration, although later disavowed, enters the content of masochistic fantasies; and from the final, genital organization are of course derived the situations of being copulated with and of giving birth, characteristic of the feminine (Freud 1923: "Die infantile"). Also the role of the buttocks in masochism, disregarding its obvious justification in the real world, is easy to understand. The buttocks are the erotogenically preferred body part in the sadistic-anal phase, as is the breast in the oral phase and the penis in the genital phase.

The third form of masochism, moral masochism, is remarkable mainly in that it has loosened its relation to what we recognize as sexuality. All other masochistic sufferings have the condition that they must proceed from the beloved person and are endured at the behest of that person, but this restriction is dropped in moral masochism. The suffering itself is the important thing; it does not matter whether it is imposed by a beloved person or by an indifferent one. Even if the suffering is caused by impersonal powers or circumstances, the true masochist always turns his cheek whenever he has the prospect of receiving a blow. In explaining this behavior, one is greatly tempted to leave the libido aside and restrict oneself to the hypothesis that here the destructive drive has been turned inward again and now rages against the self, but there must be some reason that language use has not given up the relation between this norm of behavior and the erotic, and also refers to these self-injurers as masochists.

Keeping to our technical habit, let us address first the extreme and undoubtedly pathological form of this masochism. I have explained elsewhere how in analytic treatment we encounter patients whose behavior against that treatment compels us to ascribe to them an "unconscious" feeling of guilt (Freud *Das Ich un das E*s: 49). I indicated there the factor by which one can recognize such persons (the "negative therapeutic reaction"), and I did not conceal the fact that the strength of such an impulse is one of the gravest resistances, and the greatest danger for the success of our medical or educational goals. The gratification of this unconscious feeling of guilt is perhaps the most powerful station in the generally compound gain from illness—in the sum of energies that struggle against recovery and refuse to give up the illness. The suffering brought by neurosis is precisely the factor through which it becomes valuable to the masochistic tendency. It is also instructive to discover that contrary to all theory and expectation a neurosis that has defied all therapeutic efforts can disappear if the affected person lands in the misery of an unhappy marriage, loses all his money, or contracts a dangerous organic disease. Then one form of suffering has been replaced by another, and we see that the only thing that mattered was being able to hold fast to a certain amount of suffering.

The unconscious sense of guilt is not easily believed in by patients when they hear of it from us. They know only too well the torments—the remorse of conscience—in which a conscious feeling of guilt, a consciousness of guilt, expresses itself, and therefore cannot admit that they harbor within themselves quite analogous impulses of which they feel absolutely nothing. I think that to some degree we may acknowledge their objection if we give up the term "unconscious feeling of guilt," psychologically incorrect in any case, and say instead "need for punishment," which covers the observed state of affairs just as concisely. We cannot, however, restrain ourselves from judging and localizing this unconscious feeling of guilt in the same way we do a conscious one.

We have ascribed the function of conscience to the super-ego, and in the consciousness of guilt we have recognized the expression of a tension between the ego and the super-ego. The ego reacts with feelings of anxiety (anxiety of conscience) to the perception that it has failed to meet the demands of its ideal, the super-ego. Now we want to know how the super-ego has acquired this demanding role, and why the ego, in the case of a difference with its ideal, must be afraid.

We have said that the ego functions to unite the claims of the three agencies it serves—to reconcile them; we may add that here, in the super-ego, it also has a model it can strive after. Indeed, this super-ego is as much the representative of the id as of the external world. It arose when the first objects of the libidinal impulses of the id—the parents—were introjected into the ego. When this occurred, the relation to the parents was desexualized, deflected from the direct sexual goals. Only in this way could the Oedipus complex be surmounted. The super-ego retained essential characteristics of the introjected persons—their strength, their severity, their inclination to supervise and punish. As I have said elsewhere, it can be easily conceived that through the separation of drives that occurred with this intro-duction into the ego, the severity was increased (Freud 1923: *Das Ich und das Es*). The super-ego—the conscience at work in the ego—can now become hard, cruel, and inexorable toward the ego it watches over. Kant's categorical imperative is thus the direct heir of the Oedipus complex.

But the same persons who go on functioning in the super-ego as an agency of conscience, even after they have ceased to be objects of the libidinal impulses of the id, do also belong to the real exter-nal world. It is from the external world that they were taken; their power, behind which all the influences of the past and of tradition hide, was one of the most easily felt expressions of reality. Thanks to this coincidence, the super-ego, the substitute for the Oedipus complex, also becomes a representative of the real external world and thus a model for the strivings of the ego.

Thus, as already historically surmised, the Oedipus complex proves to be the source of our individual ethical sense (morality) (Freud 1913, Section 4). In the course of childhood development, which leads to increasing detachment from the parents, their personal significance for the super-ego recedes. To the imagos they render superfluous are then linked the influences of teachers, authorities, models chosen by the individual, and publicly recognized heroes, whose persons no longer need be introjected by the now more resistant ego. The last figure in this series beginning with the parents is the dark power of fate, which only the fewest of us manage to conceive as impersonal. When the Dutch writer Multatuli replaces the *Moira* [Fate] of the Greeks with the divine pair *Lógos kai Anánke* [Reason and Necessity], there can be little objection; but all who transfer control over events in the world to Providence, God, or God and Nature, arouse the suspicion that they still perceive these ultimate and furthest powers as a parental pair—mythologically—and believe themselves linked to those powers through libidinal bonds (Multatuli).[1] In *The Ego and the Id* I attempted to derive humankind's real fear of death, too, from such a parental conception of fate. It seems very hard to free oneself from this conception.

After these preliminary discussions we can return to our consideration of moral masochism. We said that the individuals concerned, through their behavior in treatment and in life, create an impression of excessive moral inhibition, as if they were dominated by an especially sensitive conscience, although they are not conscious of any such super-morality. On closer inspection we will presumably notice the difference that distinguishes such an unconscious extension of morality from moral masochism. In the former, the accent falls on the increased sadism of the super-ego, to which the ego submits, but in the latter, it falls on the ego's own masochism, which seeks punishment, be it from the super-ego or from the parental powers beyond. Our initial confusion of the two may be forgiven, for in both cases we are dealing with a relation between the ego and the super-ego or powers equivalent to it; in both cases the essential thing is a need satisfied by punishment and suffering. Thus it is no irrelevant detail that the sadism of the super-ego usually becomes glaringly conscious, while the masochistic striving of the ego normally remains hidden from the person concerned and must be deduced from his behavior.

---

1   Eduard Douwes Dekker (1820-87), better known by his nom du plume Multatuli, was a Dutch satirist and philosopher much admired by Freud.

The fact that moral masochism is unconscious leads us to an obvious hint. We were able to translate the expression "unconscious feeling of guilt" as a need for punishment by a parental power. We now know that the wish to be beaten by the father, so common in fantasies, stands very close to the other wish—to enter into a passive (feminine) sexual relation to him—and is only a regressive distortion of it. If we insert this explanation into the content of moral masochism, its hidden significance is revealed to us. Conscience and morality arose through overcoming and desexualizing the Oedipus complex; through moral masochism morality is resexualized, the Oedipus complex is revived, and a path is opened for a regression from morality to the Oedipus complex. This occurs to the advantage neither of morality nor of the person concerned. The individual may, it is true, have preserved all or some measure of his ethical sense beside his masochism, but a large part of his conscience may have been lost to masochism. Yet masochism creates the temptation to commit "sinful" acts, which then must be expiated through the reproaches of the sadistic conscience (as in so many Russian character-types) or through chastisement by the great parental power of Fate. In order to provoke punishment by this last representative of the parents, the masochist must do the inexpedient—act against his own interests, destroy the prospects that open up for him in the real world, and perhaps destroy his own real existence.

The turning back of sadism against the self regularly occurs under the *cultural suppression of drives*, which holds back a large part of the person's destructive drive components from application in life. One can suppose that this withdrawn portion of the destructive drive appears in the ego as an intensification of masochism. But the phenomena of conscience allow one to suspect that the destructiveness returning from the external world is also taken up by the super-ego without such a transformation, increasing its sadism against the ego. The sadism of the super-ego and the masochism of the ego supplement one another and unite to produce the same results. I think it is only in this way that one can understand how—frequently or quite generally—a feeling of guilt arises from the suppression of drives, and how the conscience becomes more severe and more sensitive the more the person restrains himself from aggression against others. One might expect that an individual who knows he habitually avoids culturally undesirable acts therefore has a good conscience and watches over his ego less suspiciously. This is usually presented as if the ethical demand were primary and the renunciation of drives were its consequence. Thus the origin of the ethical sense remains unexplained. In reality, it seems to be the other way around: the first renunciation of drives is forced upon the individual by external powers, and it is this renunciation that creates the ethical sense, expressed in the conscience and demanding further renunciation of drives.

Thus moral masochism becomes a classical instance of the existence of the admixture of drives. Its danger lies in the fact that it derives from the death drive and corresponds to the portion of that drive that escaped being turned outward as a destructive drive. But since, on the other hand, it has the significance of an erotic component, even the self-destruction of the person concerned cannot occur without libidinal gratification.

4. From "A Note about the 'Mystic Writing Pad'" (1926)

If I distrust my memory—neurotics, as is well known, do so to a conspicuous degree, but normal persons, too, have every reason to do so—I can extend and insure its function by writing myself a note. Then the surface that preserves this note, the pad or sheet of paper, is, as it were, a materialized portion of the apparatus of memory—an apparatus I otherwise carry within myself invisibly. Merely by noticing the place where this now fixed "memory" is stored, I can "reproduce" it at any time, whenever I wish, always sure that it has remained unchanged—that it has escaped the distortions it might have undergone in my memory.

If I want to make extensive use of this technique for improving my memory function, I notice that two distinct methods are available to me. First, I can choose a writing surface that will preserve the note entrusted to it intact for an indefinitely long period of time—for example, a sheet of paper I write on with ink. Then I have a "lasting memory-trace." The disadvantage of this method is that the receptive capacity of the writing surface is soon exhausted. The sheet of paper is full of writing and has no room for new notations; I am forced to begin using another sheet that has not yet been written on. The advantage of this method, which provides a "lasting trace," can also lose its value for me—specifically if my interest in the note is extinguished after a time and I no longer want to "retain it in memory." The other process is free of both deficiencies. If, for example, I write on a slate with chalk, I have a receptive surface that remains receptive for an unlimited period of time; I can immediately destroy the notations on it when they no longer interest me, without needing to discard the writing surface itself. The disadvantage here is that I cannot preserve a lasting trace. If I want to make new notations on the slate, I must erase the ones already covering it. Unlimited receptive capacity and the preservation of lasting traces thus seem to be mutually exclusive in the types of apparatus we substitute for our memory: either the receptive surface must be renewed or the notation must be destroyed.

The aids we have invented to improve or intensify our sensory functions are constructed like the corresponding sense organs themselves, or portions thereof (glasses, cameras, ear trumpets, etc.). Measured by this standard, these aids to our memory seem particularly deficient, for our mental apparatus achieves precisely what they cannot: it has unlimited receptive capacity for constantly new perceptions, and yet does create lasting, though not immutable, memory-traces of them. In *The Interpretation of Dreams* I already expressed the suspicion that this unusual capacity was to be distributed to the achievements of two different systems (organs of the mental apparatus) (Freud 1900). It can be claimed that we possess a system P-C [Perception-Consciousness], which receives perceptions but preserves no lasting trace of them, so that toward every new perception it can behave like a clean sheet of paper. Thus the lasting traces of the excitations received would arise in "memory systems" lying behind it. Later, in *Beyond the Pleasure Principle*, I added the remark that the inexplicable phenomenon of consciousness would thus arise in the perceptual system *in lieu of* the lasting traces (Freud 1920).

Recently a small apparatus appeared on the market under the name of the *Mystic Writing-Pad* [*Wunderblock*], promising to do more than a sheet of paper or a slate. It presents itself merely as a writing tablet from which one can remove the notations with a convenient motion. But if one examines it more closely, one will find in its construction a remarkable correspondence with the structure of our perceptual apparatus as I have conceived it, and will be convinced that it can really deliver both components: an always ready receptive surface and lasting traces of the notations made.

The Mystic Writing-Pad is a tablet of dark-brownish resin or wax held in a paper frame; over the tablet a thin, transparent sheet has been laid, firmly attached to the wax tablet at the upper end, but freely lying upon it at the lower end. This sheet is the more interesting part of the small apparatus. It itself consists of two layers, which can be separated from each other except at the two sides. The upper layer is a transparent celluloid sheet, the lower one a thin and thus translucent sheet of waxed paper. When the apparatus is not being used, the lower surface of the waxed paper adheres lightly to the upper surface of the wax tablet.

One uses this Mystic Writing-Pad by writing on the celluloid surface of the sheet covering the wax tablet. For this purpose, no pencil or chalk is needed, for the writing does not depend on material being deposited on the receptive surface. This is a return to the way ancient peoples wrote on small tablets of clay or wax. A pointed stylus scratches the surface; the depressions therein convey the "writing." With the Mystic Writing-Pad this scratching occurs not directly, but indirectly via the cover sheet that lies above. At the places it touches, the stylus presses the lower surface of the waxed paper onto the wax tablet, and on the otherwise smooth whitish-gray surface of the celluloid these furrows become visible as dark writing. If one wishes to destroy the writing, it is sufficient to lift the compound cover sheet from the wax tablet, grasping it lightly and starting from its free lower edge. The close contact between the waxed paper and the wax tablet where it has been scratched—the contact through which the writing becomes visible—is thus suspended; nor is it restored when the two surfaces once again touch. The Mystic Writing-Pad is now free of writing and ready to take up new notations.

The small imperfections of the apparatus, of course, are of no interest for us since we only want to pursue its approximation to the structure of the perceptual apparatus of the mind.

If one carefully lifts the celluloid sheet from the waxed paper while the Mystic Writing-Pad has writing on it, one will see the writing just as clearly on the surface of the latter, and may ask why the celluloid surface of the cover sheet is necessary at all. Experiment will then show that the thin waxed paper could very easily be wrinkled or ripped if one wrote directly on it with the stylus. The celluloid sheet is thus a protective covering for the waxed paper, responsible for deterring harmful external effects. The celluloid is a "shield against stimuli"; the layer actually receiving stimuli is the waxed paper. Here I might point out that in *Beyond the Pleasure Principle* I claimed that the perceptual apparatus of our mind consists of two layers—an external shield against stimuli, responsible for decreasing the quantity of the arriving excitations, and the surface behind it that receives stimuli, the system P-C.

This analogy would be of no great value could it not be further pursued. If one lifts the entire cover sheet—celluloid and waxed paper—from the wax tablet, the writing disappears and, as mentioned, is not restored. The surface of the Mystic Writing-Pad is free of writing and once again receptive. But it can easily be determined that the lasting trace of the writing is preserved on the wax tablet itself and is legible under suitable illumination. Thus the pad delivers not only a continuously reusable receptive surface, as does a slate, but also lasting traces of the writing, as does an ordinary pad of paper: it solves the problem of uniting the two functions by *distributing them within two separate but mutually connected components—systems*. But according to my hypothesis mentioned above, this is exactly how our mental apparatus carries out its perceptual function. The layer receiving stimuli—the system P-C—forms no lasting traces, and the foundations of memory arise in other, adjacent systems.

It need not disturb us that in the Mystic Writing-Pad the lasting traces of the received notations are not utilized; it is enough that they exist. Indeed, the analogy between such an auxiliary apparatus and the organ serving as prototype must end somewhere. Nor can the Mystic Writing-Pad "reproduce" writing from within, once it has been erased. It would truly be a mystic writing-pad, if, like our memory, it could achieve that. However, it does not strike me as too far-fetched to equate the celluloid and waxed paper cover with the system P-C and its shield against stimuli, the wax tablet with the unconscious lying behind that system, and the appearance and disappearance of the writing with the flaring up and subsiding of consciousness during perception. Indeed, I must admit that I am inclined to take the comparison even further.

With the Mystic Writing-Pad the writing always disappears if one breaks the close contact between the paper receiving the stimulus and the wax tablet preserving the impression. This accords with a conceptualization I long ago formed about the modus operandi of the perceptual apparatus of our mind, but which I have thus far kept to myself. I hypothesized that charged innervations are sent out and withdrawn again, in rapid periodic impulses, from within into the completely permeable system

P-C. As long as that system is charged in such a way, it receives perceptions that are accompanied by consciousness and directs the excitation into the unconscious memory systems. As soon as the charge is withdrawn, consciousness is extinguished and the function of the system comes to a halt. It is as if the unconscious, mediated by the system P-C, were sending out feelers toward the external world and hastily withdrawing them after they have sampled its excitations. Thus I hypothesized that the interruptions, which in the Mystic Writing-Pad are of external origin, arise through the discontinuity in the current of innervation; in lieu of a real cessation of contact, I posited the periodically occurring unexcitability of the perceptual system. I further suspected that this discontinuous modus operandi of the system P-C underlies the emergence of the concept of time.

If one imagines one hand writing on the surface of the Mystic Writing-Pad while another hand periodically lifts the cover sheet from the wax tablet, this will provide an image of how I wanted to imagine the function of the perceptual apparatus of our mind.

5. From *Civilization and Its Discontents* (1930)

The assumption of the death or destruction drive has encountered resistance even in analytic circles; I know that there is often an inclination to ascribe everything found to be dangerous and hostile in love to an original bipolarity in its own nature. Initially, I had only tentatively proposed the conceptions developed here, but in the course of time they have taken hold of me so strongly that I can no longer think in any other way. I believe that they are far more useful in theoretical work than all other possible conceptions; they produce that simplification which neither disregards nor does violence to the facts—a simplification we strive for in scientific work. I recognize that in sadism and masochism we have always seen before us the expressions, strongly alloyed with eroticism, of the destructive drive directed both outward and inward, but I can no longer understand how we could have overlooked the ubiquity of non-erotic aggression and destructiveness, neglecting to give it its due place in the interpretation of life. (Indeed, unless it is erotically colored, the desire for destructiveness directed inward mostly escapes our perception.) I recall my own resistance when the idea of the destructive drive first arose in psychoanalytic literature, and how long it took before I became receptive to it. The fact that others showed, and still show, the same resistance surprises me less. "For little children do not like to hear it" [Goethe: "Ballade vom vertriebenen und heimgekehrten Grafen" ("Ballad of the Banished and Returned Count")] when mention is made of the inborn human inclination to "evil," to aggression and destructiveness, and thus to cruelty as well. God made them in the image of His own perfection, and no one wants to be told how hard it is to reconcile the existence of evil—undeniable despite the protestations of Christian Science—with His omnipotence or His all-goodness. As an alibi for God, the devil would be the best way out; he would thus take on the same economically discharging role as the Jew in the world of the Aryan ideal. But even then, one can of course hold God accountable for the existence of the devil and of the evil he personifies. Given these difficulties, it would be advisable for everyone, in an appropriate place, to make a low bow to the deeply moral nature of humankind; this will help one become generally popular, and much will be forgiven for it.[1]

---

1 In Goethe's Mephistopheles, the identification of the principle of evil with the destructive drive is especially convincing:

>   Denn alles, was entsteht,
>   Ist wert, dass es zu Grunde geht.
>   ...
>   So ist dann alles, was Ihr Sünde,
>   Zerstörung, kurz das Böse nennt,
>   Mein eigentliches Element.

[For all that arises deserves to perish.... Thus all that you call sin, destruction—evil, in brief—is my proper element.]
The devil himself names as his opponent not the holy and the good, but nature's power to create and multiply life, i.e., Eros:

>   Der Luft, dem Wasser, wie der Erden
>   Entwinden tausend Keime sich,
>   Im Trocknen, Feuchten, Warmen, Kalten!
>   Hätt' ich mir nicht die Flamme vorbehalten,
>   Ich hätte nichts Aparts für mich.

[From air, water, and earth a thousand germs free themselves, in dry, wet, warm, and cold! Had I not reserved flame, I would have nothing special for myself.] [Freud's note]

The name "libido" can again be used for the powerful expressions of Eros to distinguish them from the energy of the death drive.[1] Admittedly, it is much more difficult for us to grasp the death drive, and we suspect it only as a reserve behind Eros, so to speak; admittedly, it recedes from us wherever it is not revealed by being alloyed with Eros. In sadism, where the death drive bends the erotic aim in its own sense, yet fully satisfies the erotic striving, we succeed in gaining the clearest insight into its nature and its relation to Eros. But even where it appears without sexual intent, e.g., in the blindest destructive rage, it is obvious that the satisfaction of the drive is associated with extremely great narcissistic pleasure as this satisfaction shows the ego the fulfillment of the latter's old wishes for omnipotence. Moderated and tamed, inhibited in its aim, as it were, the destructive drive must, when directed toward objects, provide the ego with the satisfaction of its vital needs and with control over nature. Since the assumption of the drive is based mainly on theoretical grounds, one must admit that this assumption is not entirely secure from theoretical objections. But this is how things appear to us just now, in the present state of our insights; future research and reflection will surely bring decisive clarity.

In all further discussions, therefore, I take the standpoint that the aggressive tendency is an original, independent drive-disposition in humankind, and I reiterate that it is the greatest impediment to civilization. At some point in the course of this investigation the view imposed itself upon us that civilization is a special process played out in humankind; we still espouse that idea. We would add that civilization is a process in the service of Eros—a process that seeks to combine individual humans, then families, ethnic groups, peoples, and nations, into one great unity—humanity. Why this must happen, we do not know; we would claim that this is precisely the work of Eros. These sets of human beings are to be libidinally bound to one another. Necessity alone, and the advantages of collective labor, will not hold them together. But the natural aggressive drive in humankind, the hostility of one against all

---

1 Our present conception can be roughly expressed in the statement that libido is involved in every expression of a drive, but that not everything in such an expression is libido. [Freud's note]

and all against one, opposes this program of civilization. This aggressive drive is the derivative and main representative of the death drive, which we have found beside Eros, and which shares world dominion with it. And now, I think, the meaning of the development of civilization is no longer obscure to us. It must show us the struggle between Eros and Death, between the life drive and the destructive drive, as it plays out in the human species. This struggle is the essential content of all life, and therefore the development of civilization can simply be characterized as the struggle for life of the human species.[1] And it is this battle of the giants that our nursemaids seek to appease with their "lullaby about Heaven" [Heine: "Deutschland" ("Germany")]!

6. From "Analysis Terminable and Interminable" (1937)

[...] The distinguishing characteristics of the ego that are at fault in another group of cases—namely, as sources of resistance against analytic treatment and as impediments to therapeutic success – may be different and may have deeper roots. Here we are dealing with the ultimate things psychological research can recognize: the behavior of the two primal drives, their distribution, fusion, and separation—things which cannot be conceived as being limited to a single province of the mental apparatus, the id, the ego, or the super-ego. There is no stronger impression of the resistances during analytical work than that presented by a force which resists recovery with all possible means and absolutely wants to hold on to illness and suffering. We have recognized one portion of this force, doubtless correctly, as the sense of guilt and the need for punishment, and have localized it in the ego's relation to the super-ego. But this is only the portion that is, so to speak, mentally bound by the super-ego and in this way becomes recognizable; other quantities of the same force, in bound or free form, may be at work in unspecified locations. If one considers the total picture constituted by the phenomena of the immanent masochism of so many persons, the phenomena of the negative therapeutic reaction, and those of neurotics' sense of guilt, it will

---

1 We can probably say more precisely: how this struggle had to be conducted after a certain, still to be determined event. [Freud's note]

no longer be possible to adhere to the belief that mental events are exclusively dominated by a striving for pleasure. These phenomena are unmistakable indications of the presence of a power in mental life which, according to its goals, we call the aggressive or destructive drive, and which we derive from the original death drive of living matter. There is no possibility of an opposition between an optimistic and a pessimistic theory of life. Only the cooperation or mutually opposing workings of the two primal drives—Eros and the death instinct—explain the rich variety of the phenomena of life; one of them alone can never do so.

***

[...] But the theory of Empedocles that deserves our interest is the one that comes so close to psychoanalytic drive theory that one would be tempted to claim the two are identical if it were not for the difference that the Greek philosopher's theory is a cosmic fantasy, while ours restricts itself to the claim of biological validity. Yet the fact that Empedocles ascribes to the universe the same animate nature as to the individual organism removes much of the significance of this difference.

The philosopher teaches that there are two principles in the events of physical and mental life, and that these two principles are engaged in eternal war with each other. He calls them *philia* (love) and *neikos* (strife). One of these forces—which for him are basically "natural forces operating like drives, and by no means consciously purposeful intelligences" (Capelle 186)—strives to compress the elementary particles of the four elements into a single unity; the other, by contrast, wants to undo all these fusions and separate the elementary particles of the elements from one another. Empedocles thinks of the process of the universe as a continuous, never-ceasing alternation of periods, in which the one or the other of the two basic forces is victorious, so that at one time love and the next time strife fully imposes its intention and dominates the universe, whereupon the other, defeated, portion asserts itself and in turn beats down its partner.

The two basic principles of Empedocles—*philia* and *neikos*—are, both in name and function, the same as our two primal drives, Eros and destruction—one dedicated to combining what exists into ever greater unities, the other to dissolving these unions and destroying the structures which have arisen through them. But we will not be surprised that this theory, having reemerged after two and a half millennia, has been altered in several aspects. Apart from the restriction to the biopsychic realm imposed on us, our basic substances are no longer the four elements of Empedocles; living matter has sharply differentiated itself from the inanimate, and we no longer think of the fusion and separation of particles of substance, but of the soldering and differentiation of drive components. We have given some biological support to the principle of "strife" by deriving our destructive drive from the death drive, from the urge of living matter to return to a lifeless state. This is not to deny that an analogous drive already existed before, nor, of course, to assert that such a drive only arose with the emergence of life. And no one can foresee in what guise the grain of truth in Empedocles' theory will present itself to later insights.

Appendix B: Antecedents and Continental Responses to Beyond the Pleasure Principle

[No selection of readings, even one organized around a single key text, is ever complete. I urge readers to consult the original versions of abridged texts included here; the contexts in which readings first appeared; their place within a larger oeuvre, especially in the case of major figures like Lacan (1901-81) and Derrida (1930-2004); and the bibliographic sources that inspire and inform each of the readings collected in this edition of *Beyond the Pleasure Principle*.

I have not included any of the relevant psychoanalytic literature that informs Freud's *Beyond the Pleasure Principle*, or much that was informed by it after 1920. The theoretical works of Freud's collaborator, the Hungarian analyst Sándor Ferenczi (1873-1933), are very important to the genesis of Freud's thinking in this period. Three works in particular are worth consulting: "Stages in the Development of the Sense of Reality" of 1913; *Thalassa: A Theory of Genitality*, a book of wild metabiological speculation inspired by their jointly held beliefs, published in 1924; and "The Unwelcome Child and the Death Instinct" of 1929. See also the correspondence between the two men. The work of three other analysts is also of some relevance to Freud's ideas, although just how much is debated: Sabina Spielrein (1884-1942), Wilhelm Stekel (1868-1940), and Alfred Adler (1870-1937). Interested readers should consult the vast secondary literature to get an idea of where to start. To this end, begin with Ronald Clark's biography of Freud, John Kerr's book on Spielrein and Jung, and Richard Webster's critical analysis of Freud's legacy; then see Frank Sulloway's intellectual history and my own analysis of the death drive theory and its context—a sampling of which I include here.

As for psychoanalysts who took up the death drive theory, either as supporters or detractors, see Wilhelm Reich's (1897-1957) work (which begins critical but, in the late absurd phase, is supportive); all of Klein's (1882-1960) work, which is a pure expression of the Hungarian school of psychoanalysis led by Ferenczi (and faithful to the most speculative side of Freud); aspects of Erich Fromm's (1900-80) work, most especially his public battle with Marcuse in the mid-1950s in the pages of *Dissent*; and Max Schur's book on Freud, which provides a sceptical analysis of the death drive theory and much else.

I have included the work of four psychoanalysts: Lacan, Klein, Laplanche, and Pontalis. All four are important figures in the "Continental" response to *Beyond the Pleasure Principle*, and have certainly influenced how philosophers think. In addition to the samples included here, I urge readers to consult Laplanche and Pontalis's well-known *The Language of Psychoanalysis*, in which they provide detailed discussions of key terms in psychoanalysis— such as the death drive and the repetition compulsion.

I have also included some other thinkers who are not technically "philosophers," but who have advanced our philosophical and theoretical understanding of *Beyond the Pleasure Principle* in important ways. Among this group I have included one short selection from social critic and sometime-member of the Frankfurt School, Walter Benjamin (1892-1940), two selections from the American classicist Norman O. Brown (1913-2002), and one from the deconstructive literary critic Samuel Weber. These works are not just fundamental, but fill in a gap in the secondary literature and have provided ample inspiration to thinkers from across disciplines.

Much of the remaining readings are key texts by key philosophers that capture the spirit of dominant theoretical movements in twentieth-century Continental thought. Frankfurt School philosopher Herbert Marcuse (1898-1979) is an example of Freudo-Marxist reinterpretation of Freud; Paul Ricoeur (1913-2005) is an example of hermeneutics; Gilles Deleuze (1925-95) is an example of late 1960s French post-structuralism and, with Félix Guattari (1930-92), of their unique brand of "schizoanalysis"; Jacques Derrida, Rodolphe Gasché, and Weber are each quite different examples of that strain of post-structuralism called deconstruction; French sociologist-philosopher Jean Baudrillard (1929-2007) represents yet another strain of post-structuralism, although he is most often cast under the (almost meaningless) banner of "postmodern" philosophy; and American feminist philosopher Judith Butler (1956-) provides an example, in the late 1980s, of a continuing interest in phenomenology.

I have also selected a few antecedents to Freud's ideas, limiting myself to those texts that are alluded to by Freud himself—in *Beyond the Pleasure Principle* and in later texts discussing its ideas, such as "Analysis Terminable and Interminable." Please note that Gregory Richter has provided new translations for samples from Schopenhauer (1788-1860) and Nietzsche (1844-1900).

Obviously there is no decisive way of approaching this literature, which is vast and intimidating even in its abridged and/or selected form. I have organized the secondary responses to Freud chronologically, according to when they were published (or, in some cases, when they were written), but do not assume that readers should follow this format. Best to begin wherever it suits you best—for example, by starting with an orientation, such as Marcuse's Freudo-Marxist reinterpretation of Freud or Fromm's humanist criticism of the death drive theory. Or it may be simpler yet to start with a discussion of Plato's *Symposium* as found in Weber's fairly detailed discussion. Please note that I have also included two readings each from Brown and Ricoeur precisely because they are very useful for readers less familiar with Freud: Brown because he covers some classic territory with informed discussion of Hegelian dialectics and Nietzschean *jouissance*; Ricoeur because he provides a disinterested *explication de texte* that covers a fantastic amount of territory in Freud's work, including the much-ignored cultural dimension of Freud's theorizing.

Another way to access these readings would be to begin with the classical antecedents included in Appendix B—namely, Empedocles, Plato, Schopenhauer, and Nietzsche—and only then turn to Freud's *Beyond the Pleasure Principle*. From there one might continue with the other selections of Freud's works or, if you prefer, begin with the secondary responses and work backward to these other selections from Freud. Either way, it makes good sense to pair up works, for example, Freud's essay on the "mystic writing pad" with Derrida's discussion of it included in the book; Freud's essay on masochism with Deleuze's discussion of the death instinct; Plato's *Symposium* with Weber's selection on Freud and Aristophanes; and so on.

A few closing remarks: I have retained whatever English translations of Freud that these thinkers have referred to; and I have left the spelling in its published form, whether American or British. I have also, in many cases, adjusted or invented entirely new titles for the selections collected here. For example, Benjamin never wrote anything called "Shock and the Creative Process"; that selection is actually a small part of his "On Some Motifs in Baudelaire." I have also, in a few cases, removed subheadings when abridged material no longer does justice to the original heading. This is especially true in the selection by Derrida that I have called "'A Kind of Discourse on Method': Freud's Performative Writing." No such title exists in Derrida's long essay "To Speculate—On 'Freud'," although the quoted part of the title is taken from the work and the rest of the title is faithful to his analysis—albeit at the expense of being more descriptive than Derrida usually is. But all of his subheadings have been removed. Finally, I have occasionally removed author notes. Readers are again urged to consult the original texts, ideally in their original language, to get a better sense of any given author's presumed intent.]

1. *Love and Strife* (ca. 420 BCE)[1]
Empedocles

66. And these [elements] never cease changing place continually, now being all united by Love into one, now each borne apart by the hatred engendered of Strife, until they are brought together in the unity of the all, and become subject to it. Thus inasmuch as one has been wont to arise out of many and again with the separation of the one the many arise, so things are continually coming into being and there is no fixed age for them; and farther inasmuch as they [the elements] never cease changing place continually, so they always exist within an immovable circle.

74. But come, hear my words, for truly learning causes the mind to grow. For as I said before in declaring the ends of my words: Twofold is the truth I shall speak; for at one time there grew to be the one alone out of many, and at another time it separated so that there were many out of the one; fire and water and earth and boundless height of air, and baneful Strife apart from these, balancing each of them, and Love among them, their equal in length and breadth.

96. But come, gaze on the things that bear farther witness to my former words, if in what was said before there be anything defective in form. Behold the sun, warm and bright on all sides,

---

1 From *Fragments* (494-434 BCE).

and whatever is immortal and is bathed in its bright ray, and behold the rain-cloud, dark and cold on all sides; from the earth there proceed the foundations of things and solid bodies. In Strife all things are, endued with form and separate from each other, but they come together in Love and are desired by each other.

110. For they two (Love and Strife) were before and shall be, nor yet, I think, will there ever be an unutterably long time without them both.

169. But now I shall go back over the course of my verses, which I set out in order before, drawing my present discourse from that discourse. When Strife reached the lowest depth of the eddy and Love comes to be in the midst of the whirl, then all these things come together at this point so as to be one alone, yet not immediately, but joining together at their pleasure, one from one place, another from another. And as they were joining together Strife departed to the utmost boundary. But many things remained unmixed, alternating with those that were mixed, even as many as Strife, remaining aloft, still retained; for not yet had it entirely departed to the utmost boundaries of the circle, but some of its members were remaining within, and others had gone outside.

186. For all things are united, themselves with parts of themselves—the beaming sun and earth and sky and sea—whatever things are friendly but have separated in mortal things. And so, in the same way, whatever things are the more adapted for mixing, these are loved by each other and made alike by Aphrodite. But whatever things are hostile are separated as far as possible from each other, both in their origin and in their mixing and in the forms impressed on them, absolutely unwonted to unite and very baneful, at the suggestion of Strife, since it has wrought their birth.

247. This is indeed remarkable in the mass of human members; at one time all the limbs which form the body, united into one by Love, grow vigorously in the prime of life; but yet at another time, separated by evil Strife, they wander each in different directions along the breakers of the sea of life. Just so it is with plants and with fishes dwelling in watery halls, and beasts whose lair is in the mountains, and birds borne on wings.

333. For it is by earth that we see earth, and by water water, and by air glorious air; so, too, by fire we see destroying fire, and love by love, and strife by baneful strife. For out of these

[elements] all things are fitted together and their form is fixed, and by these men think and feel both pleasure and pain.

369. There is an utterance of Necessity, an ancient decree of the gods, eternal, sealed fast with broad oaths: whenever any one defiles his body sinfully with bloody gore or perjures himself in regard to wrong-doing, one of those spirits who are heir to long life, thrice ten thousand seasons shall he wander apart from the blessed, being born meantime in all sorts of mortal forms, changing one bitter path of life for another. For mighty Air pursues him Seaward, and Sea spews him forth on the threshold of Earth, and Earth casts him into the rays of the unwearying Sun, and Sun into the eddies of Air; one receives him from the other, and all hate him. One of these now am I too, a fugitive from the gods and a wanderer, at the mercy of raging Strife.

2. *Aristophanes' Discourse on Love* (ca. 385 BCE)[1]
Plato

Aristophanes professed to open another vein of discourse; he had a mind to praise Love in another way, unlike that of either Pausanias or Eryximachus. Mankind, he said, judging by their neglect of him, have never, as I think, at all understood the power of Love. For if they had understood him they would surely have built noble temples and altars, and offered solemn sacrifices in his honour; but this is not done, and most certainly ought to be done: since of all the gods he is the best friend of men, the helper and the healer of the ills which are the great impediment to the happiness of the race. I will try to describe his power to you, and you shall teach the rest of the world what I am teaching you. In the first place, let me treat of the nature of man and what has happened to it. The original human nature was not like the present, but different. The sexes were not two as they are now, but originally three in number; there was man, woman, and the union of the two, of which the name survives but nothing else. Once it was a distinct kind, with a bodily shape and a name of its own, constituted by the union of the male and the female: but now only the word 'androgynous' is preserved, and that as

---

1 From "The Symposium." *The Dialogues of Plato* (ca. 385 BCE). Trans. Benjamin Jowett. Toronto: William Benton (*Encyclopaedia Britannica*), 1952. 157-59.

a term of reproach. In the second place, the primeval man was round, his back and sides forming a circle; and he had four hands and the same number of feet, one head with two faces, looking opposite ways, set on a round neck and precisely alike; also four ears, two privy members, and the remainder to correspond. He could walk upright as men now do, backwards or forwards as he pleased, and he could also roll over and over at a great pace, turning on his four hands and four feet, eight in all, like tumblers going over and over with their legs in the air; this was when he wanted to run fast. Now the sexes were three, and such as I have described them; because the sun, moon, and earth are three; and the man was originally the child of the sun, the woman of the earth, and the man-woman of the moon, which is made up of sun and earth, and they were all round and moved round and round because they resembled their parents. Terrible was their might and strength, and the thoughts of their hearts were great, and they made an attack upon the gods; of them is told the tale of Otys and Ephialtes who, as Homer says, attempted to scale heaven, and would have laid hands upon the gods. Doubt reigned in the celestial councils. Should they kill them and annihilate the race with thunderbolts, as they had done the giants, then there would be an end of the sacrifices and worship which men offered to them; but, on the other hand, the gods could not suffer their insolence to be unrestrained.

At last, after a good deal of reflection, Zeus discovered a way. He said: "Methinks I have a plan which will enfeeble their strength and so extinguish their turbulence; men shall continue to exist, but I will cut them in two and then they will be diminished in strength and increased in numbers; this will have the advantage of making them more profitable to us. They shall walk upright on two legs, and if they continue insolent and will not be quiet, I will split them again and they shall hop about on a single leg." He spoke and cut men in two, like a sorb-apple which is halved for pickling, or as you might divide an egg with a hair; and as he cut them one after another, he bade Apollo give the face and the half of the neck a turn in order that man might contemplate the section of himself: he would thus learn a lesson of humility. Apollo was also bidden to heal their wounds and compose their forms. So he gave a turn to the face and pulled the skin from the sides all over that which in our language is called the belly, like the purses which draw tight, and he made one mouth at the centre, which he fastened in a knot (the same which is called the navel); he also moulded the breast and took out most of the wrinkles, much as a shoemaker might smooth leather upon a last; he left a few, however, in the region of the belly and navel, as a memorial of the primeval state. After the division the two parts of man, each desiring his other half, came together, and throwing their arms about one another, entwined in mutual embraces, longing to grow into one, they began to die from hunger and self-neglect, because they did not like to do anything apart; and when one of the halves died and the other survived, the survivor sought another mate, man or woman as we call them—being the sections of entire men or women—and clung to that. Thus they were being destroyed, when Zeus in pity invented a new plan: he turned the parts of generation round to the front, for this had not been always their position, and they sowed the seed no longer as hitherto like grasshoppers in the ground, but in one another; and after the transposition the male generated in the female in order that by the mutual embraces of man and woman they might breed, and the race might continue; or if man came to man they might be satisfied, and rest, and go their ways to the business of life. So ancient is the desire of one another which is implanted in us, reuniting our original nature, seeking to make one of two, and to heal the state of man.

Each of us when separated, having one side only, like a flat fish, is but the tally-half of a man, and he is always looking for his other half. Men who are a section of that double nature which was once called androgynous are lovers of women; adulterers are generally of this breed, and also adulterous women who lust after men. The women who are a section of the woman do not care for men, but have female attachments; the female companions are of this sort. But they who are a section of the male follow the male, and while they are young, being slices of the original man, they have affection for men and embrace them, and these are the best of boys and youths, because they have the most manly nature. Some indeed assert that they are shameless, but this is not true; for they do not act thus from any want of shame, but because they are valiant and manly, and have a manly countenance, and they embrace that which is like them. And these when they grow up become our statesmen, and these only, which is a great proof of the truth of what I am saying. When they reach manhood they are lovers of youth, and are not naturally inclined to marry or beget children—if at all, they do so only in obedience to custom; but they are satisfied if they may be allowed to live with one another unwedded; and such a nature is prone to love and ready to return love, always embracing that which is akin to him. And when one of them meets with his other half, the actual half of himself, whether he be a lover of youth or a lover of another sort, the pair are lost in an amazement of love and friendship and intimacy, and one will not be out of the other's sight, as I may say, even for a moment: these are the people who pass their whole lives together, and yet they could not explain what they desire of one another. For the intense yearning which each of them has towards the other does not appear to be the desire of lover's intercourse, but of something else which the soul of either evidently desires and cannot tell, and of which she has only a dark and doubtful presentiment. Suppose Hephaestus, with his instruments, to come to the pair who are lying side by side and to say to them, "What do you mortals want of one another?" They would be unable to explain. And suppose further, that when he saw their perplexity he said: "Do you desire to be wholly one; always day and night in one another's company? for if this is what you desire, I am ready to melt and fuse you together, so that being two you shall become one, and while you live a common life as if you were a single man, and after your death in the world below still be one departed soul, instead of two—I ask whether this is what you lovingly desire and whether you are satisfied to attain this?"—There is not a man of them who when he heard the proposal would deny or would not acknowledge that this meeting and melting into one another, this becoming one instead of two, was the very expression of his ancient need. And the reason is that human nature was originally one and we were a whole, and the desire and pursuit of the whole is called love. There was a time, I say, when we were one, but now because of the wickedness of mankind God has dispersed us, as the Arcadians were dispersed into villages by the Lacedaemonians. And if we are not obedient to the gods, there is a danger that we shall be split up again and go about in basso-relievo, like the profile figures showing only one half the nose which are sculptured on monuments, and that we shall be like tallies.

Wherefore let us exhort all men to piety in all things, that we may avoid evil and obtain the good, taking Love for our leader and commander. Let no one oppose him—he is the enemy of the gods who opposes him. For if we are friends of God and at peace with him we shall find our own true loves, which rarely happens in this world at present. I am serious, and therefore I must beg Eryximachus not to make fun or to find any allusion in what I am saying to Pausanias and Agathon, who, as I suspect, are both of the manly nature, and belong to the class which I have been describing. But my words have a wider application—they include men and women everywhere; and I believe that if our loves were perfectly accomplished, and each one returning to his primeval nature had his original true love, then our race would be happy. And if this would be best of all, the best in the next degree must in present circumstances be the nearest approach to such a union; and that will be the attainment of a congenial love. Wherefore, if we would praise him who has given to us the benefit, we must praise the god Love, who is our greatest benefactor, both leading us in this life back to our own nature, and giving us high hopes for the future, for he promises that if we are pious, he will restore us to our original state, and heal us and make us happy and blessed. This, Eryximachus, is my discourse of love, which, although different to yours, I must beg you to leave unassailed by the shafts of your ridicule, in order that each may have his turn; each, or rather either, for Agathon and Socrates are the only ones left.

3. *Death is the Résumé of Life* (1892)[1]
Arthur Schopenhauer

Procreation and Death

That procreation and death must be regarded as something belonging to life, and essential to this phenomenon of the will, also follows from the fact that they both show themselves to us merely as the more highly energized expressions of that which all other life also consists of. Indeed, this is absolutely nothing but a continuous change of matter in the context of an unchanging form; and this also characterizes the transitoriness of individuals in the context of the permanence of the species. Constant nourishment and regeneration differs from procreation only in degree; constant excretion differs from death only in degree. The former shows itself most simply and clearly in the plant. The plant is absolutely nothing but the constant repetition of the same drive, that of its simplest fiber, which groups

---

1 From *Die Welt als Wille und Vorstellung* (1892, The world as will and representation). Leipzig: Reclam. Translation by Gregory C. Richter.

itself into leaf and twig; it is a systematic aggregate of plants of the same kind, all supporting one another, whose constant regeneration is its only drive. For the complete satisfaction of this drive, utilizing the stepladder of metamorphosis, it finally achieves blossom and fruit, that compendium of its existence and striving in which it now attains, on a shorter path, what is its only goal—now producing at one stroke a thousandfold what it previously produced within the individual: the repetition of itself. Its development toward the fruit is related to that fruit as writing is to the printing of books. It is clearly the same with animals. The process of nourishment is a constant regeneration, and the process of procreation is a more highly energized form of nourishment; the pleasure associated with procreation is the more highly energized pleasantness of the feeling of life. On the other hand, excretion, the constant exhalation and discarding of matter, is of the same essence as death, which has increased power and is the opposite of reproduction. Just as here we are always content to retain the same form without mourning the discarded matter, we must behave in the same way when, in death, the same thing happens—with increased power, and completely— that occurs in the individual daily and hourly with excretion: just as we are indifferent to excretion, we should not recoil at death. From this point of view, then, it seems just as wrong to desire the continuance of one's individuality, which is replaced by other individuals, as to desire the permanence of the matter of our body, which is continuously replaced by new matter. It seems just as foolish to embalm corpses as it would be to carefully preserve our waste. As for the individual consciousness bound to the individual body, it is completely interrupted every day by sleep. Deep sleep, for its duration, is not at all different from death, into which it passes quite continuously, e.g., in freezing to death; it differs from death only with respect to the future, in terms of awakening. Death is a sleep in which individuality is forgotten; everything else awakens again, or rather has remained awake.

Achieving Salvation

Thus, if suffering has such a sanctifying power, to an even higher degree this will be the case with death, feared more than any suffering. Correspondingly, in the presence of every deceased person, we feel a sort of awe related to the awe that great suffering produces in us; indeed, every case of death presents itself to some extent as a kind of apotheosis or canonization. Therefore we do not regard the corpse of even the most insignificant person without awe, and indeed, as strange as the remark may sound here, in the presence of every corpse the guard arms itself. For dying should be considered the actual purpose of life; at the moment of dying everything is decided which, through the whole course of life, was only prepared and introduced. Death is the result, the résumé, of life, or the total sum that pronounces at *one* time all the instruction that life has given in separate portions, piece by piece—the teaching that the whole striving, the phenomenon of which is life, was a futile, vain, and self-contradictory one, to have returned from which is a redemption. Just as the entire slow vegetation of the plant is related to the fruit that at *one* stroke now achieves a hundredfold what the plant achieved gradually, piece by piece, life, with its obstacles, disappointed hopes, thwarted plans, and continuous suffering is related to death, which at *one* stroke destroys everything, everything that the person has willed, and thus crowns the instruction life has given that person. The completed course of life, which one looks back on while dying, has an effect on the whole will objectifying itself in this perishing individuality; this effect is analogous to that exercised by a motive on a person's actions. Specifically, the completed course of life gives those actions a new direction, which is thus the moral and essential result of life. Precisely because a *sudden* death makes this retrospection impossible, the Church regards such a death as a misfortune, and one prays that it may be averted. Since both this retrospection and the clear foreknowledge of death, being conditioned by reason, are possible only in humans, and not in animals, and since it is therefore only humans who actually drain the cup of death, humanity is the only stage at which the will can negate itself and completely turn from life. To the will that does not negate itself, every birth grants a new and different intellect—until it has recognized the true nature of life, and consequently no longer wills it.

4. *Repetition, Pleasure, and Pain* (1882, 1886, posthumous)
Friedrich Nietzsche

The heaviest burden (no. 341 *GS*)[1]
What if some day or night a demon stealthily pursued you into your loneliest loneliness and said to you: "This life as you now

---

1 From *Die Fröhliche Wissenschaft* (1882, *The gay science*). *Nietzsches Werke*, v.5. Leipzig: Kröner, 1922. Translated by Gregory C. Richter.

live it and have lived it you will have to live once again and countless times again; and there will be nothing new therein, but every
pain and every pleasure and every thought and sigh and everything inexpressibly small or great in your life must come back to
you, and all in the same order and sequence—and even this spi-
der and this moonlight between the trees, and even this moment
and I myself. The eternal hourglass of existence is turned over
again and again—and you with it, you speck of dust!" Would
you not throw yourself down and gnash your teeth and curse
the demon who said these things? Or have you ever experienced
a tremendous moment when you would answer him: "You are a
god; I have never heard anything more divine." If that thought
took hold of you, it would transform you and perhaps crush you,
as you are; the question in everything and in each thing—"Do
you want this once again and countless times again?"—would lie
as the heaviest burden on your actions! Or how much would you
have to accept of yourself and of life so as *to yearn* for nothing
more than for this last eternal endorsement and seal?

God is a Vicious Circle? (no. 56 BGE)[1]
Whoever, like me, due to some mysterious desire, has long striv-
en to think about pessimism in great depth and to free it from
the half-Christian, half-German narrowness and stupidity with
which it has finally presented itself to this century, namely, in
the form of Schopenhauer's philosophy; whoever has really ever
looked with an Asiatic and super-Asiatic eye inside and under
the most world-renouncing of all possible modes of thought-
beyond good and evil, and no longer, like Buddha and Schopenhauer, under the spell and delusion of morality—precisely
in doing so, he has perhaps inadvertently opened his eyes to the
opposite ideal: to the ideal of the most high-spirited, energetic,
and world-approving person, who has not only found peace
with and learned to accept that which was and is, but wants to
have it again for all eternity, *as it was and is*, insatiably calling
out *da capo*, not only to himself, but to the entire play; and not
only to a play, but essentially to Him who actually needs this
play—and makes it necessary, for he needs himself again and
again—and makes himself necessary.—What? And this doesn't

---

1 From *Jenseits von Gut und Böse* (1886, *Beyond good and evil*). *Nietzsches
Werke*, v.7. Leipzig: Kröner, 1922. Translated by Gregory C. Richter.

show it: *circulus vitiosus deus*? [God is a vicious circle / a vicious circle as God?]

Pleasure and Pain[1]
No. 695 *WP* (March-June 1888)
If *pleasure* and *displeasure* relate to the feeling of power, then life must represent an increase in power, such that the difference associated with this increase would enter consciousness. A given level of power being maintained, pleasure would only need to measure itself in terms of decreases in the level: states of displeasure—*not* states of pleasure. The will for more is in the essence of pleasure: that power increases, that the difference enters consciousness.

From a certain point onward, in decadence, the *opposite difference*—the decrease—enters consciousness: the memory of former strong moments depresses the present feelings of pleasure: the comparison now *weakens* pleasure.

No. 697 *WP* (November 1887-March 1888)
The normal dissatisfaction of our drives—e.g., hunger, the sexual drive, the drive for movement—still holds within itself absolutely nothing depressing; rather, it works to agitate the feeling of life, just as every rhythm of small, painful stimuli *strengthens* it, regardless of how the pessimists may lecture us: this dissatisfaction, rather than causing disgust toward life, is the great *stimulation* of life.

One could perhaps characterize pleasure in general as a rhythm of small, unpleasurable stimuli.

No. 698 *WP* (Summer-Fall 1883)
Kant said: "I subscribe with complete conviction to these sentences of Count Verri (Sull'indole del piacere e del dolore [On the nature of pleasure and of pain]: 1781): 'Il solo principio motore dell' uomo è il dolore. Il dolore precede ogni piacere. Il piacere non è un essere positivo' [The only motor principle of man is pain. Pain precedes every pleasure. Pleasure is not a positive entity]."

---

1 From *Der Wille zur Macht* (posthumous, *The will to power*). Leipzig: Kröner, 1930. Translated by Gregory C. Richter.

Pain is something different from pleasure—I mean it is *not* its opposite. If the essence of pleasure has been accurately characterized as a feeling of *increase in power* (and thus as a feeling of difference that presupposes comparison), the essence of displeasure is still not defined.

The false opposites that the people and *consequently* language believes in have always been dangerous roadblocks to the progress of truth. There are even cases in which a kind of pleasure is conditioned by a certain *rhythmic progression* of small, unpleasurable stimuli: thus a very rapid increase is achieved in the feeling of power, in the feeling of pleasure. For example, this is the case with tickling, and with the sexual tickling in the act of coitus: thus we see displeasure active as an ingredient of pleasure. A small hindrance that is surmounted and immediately followed by another small hindrance that is overcome in turn—it seems this game of resistance and victory is what most strongly excites the comprehensive feeling of extra, surplus power, which is the essence of pleasure. The reverse, an increase in the sensation of pain through small, interposed pleasurable stimuli, is lacking, for pleasure and pain are not opposites.

Pain is an intellectual process in which a judgment has definitely been expressed—the judgment "harmful," in which long experience has been summed up. There is no pain as such. It is *not* the injury that hurts; it is the experience of what bad consequences an injury can have for the total organism—an experience that speaks in the form of that profound shock called displeasure. (In the context of harmful influences unknown to earlier humanity, e.g., from newly combined poisonous chemicals, the pronouncement of pain is lacking—and we are lost.)

In pain, the truly specific thing is always the long-lasting shock, the lingering vibrations of a terrifying shock in the cerebral center of the nervous system: one does *not* actually suffer from the cause of pain (some injury, for example), but from the long-lasting disturbance of equilibrium that occurs due to that shock. Pain is an illness of the cerebral nerve centers; pleasure is certainly not an illness.

That pain is the cause of reflex actions is supported by the appearance of things and even by the prejudice of philosophers; but in cases of sudden pain, if one observes precisely, the reflex comes noticeably earlier than the sensation of pain. I would be in a bad way if, when I stumbled, I had to wait until that fact rang the bell of consciousness and a hint about what to do was telegraphed back. Rather, I perceive as clearly as can be that the reflex of my foot to prevent the fall occurs first, and that later, within a measurable distance in time, a sort of painful wave can suddenly be felt in the anterior part of the head. Thus one does *not* react to pain. Pain is subsequently projected into the wounded place—but the essence of this local pain is nevertheless not the expression of the type of the local injury; it is a mere sign of location whose strength and pitch corresponds to the injury the nerve centers have received from it. The fact that due to this shock the muscular strength of the organism measurably declines does not provide any support for seeking the *essence* of pain in a decrease in the feeling of power. Again, one does *not* react to pain: displeasure is not a "cause" of actions. Pain itself is a reaction, and the reflex is another and *earlier* reaction. The two have distinct origins.

No. 702 *WP* (March-June 1888)

A person does *not* seek pleasure and does *not* avoid displeasure: one will understand what famous prejudice I herewith contradict. Pleasure and displeasure are mere consequences, mere epiphenomena. What each person wants, what every smallest part of a living organism wants, is an increase in power. Both pleasure and displeasure ensue from the striving for this increase; from within that will it seeks resistance, it requires something that opposes. Displeasure, as a hindrance to its will to power, is thus a normal fact, the normal ingredient of every organic event. Human beings do not avoid it; indeed they continuously require it: every victory, every feeling of pleasure, every event presupposes a surmounted resistance.

Let us take the simplest case, that of primitive nourishment: the protoplasm extends its pseudopodia to search for something that resists it—not from hunger but from will to power. Then it attempts to overcome, appropriate, incorporate that entity. What is called "nourishment" is only a resultant phenomenon, a useful application of the original will to become *stronger*.

Thus displeasure so little requires a *reduction in our feeling of power* that in average cases it actually functions as a stimulus to this feeling of power: the hindrance is the *stimulus* of this will to power.

No. 703 *WP* (March-June 1888)

Displeasure has been confused with a specific type of displeasure, with exhaustion; the latter does indeed represent a profound reduction and depression of the will to power, a measurable loss of force. Thus there exist displeasure as a means of stimulating the strengthening of power, and displeasure after a squandering of power: in the first case a stimulus, in the second the result of an excessive stimulation. Inability to resist characterizes the latter type; a challenge to resistance belongs to the former. The only pleasure still felt in a state of exhaustion is falling asleep; the pleasure in the other case is the victory.

A great confusion among psychologists arose in that they did not distinguish these two types of pleasure—that of *falling asleep* and that of *victory*. The exhausted want rest, a chance to stretch their legs, peace, quiet—the happiness of the nihilistic religions and philosophies; the rich and energetic want victory, conquered opponents, an overflowing of the feeling of power over wider domains than before: all healthy functions of the organism have this need, and the whole organism is such a complex of systems struggling for an increase in the feeling of power.

5. *Shock and the Creative Process* (1939)[1]
Walter Benjamin

In seeking a more substantial definition of what appears in Proust's[2] *mémoire de l'intelligence* as a by-product of Bergson's[3] theory, it is well to go back to Freud. In 1921 [sic] Freud published his essay *Beyond the Pleasure Principle*, which presents a correlation between memory (in the sense of the *mémoire involontaire)* and consciousness in the form of a hypothesis. The following remarks based on it are not intended to confirm it; we shall have to content ourselves with investigating the fruitfulness of this hypothesis in situations far removed from those which Freud had in mind when he wrote. Freud's pupils

---

1   From "On Some Motifs in Baudelaire" (1939), *Illuminations*. Trans. Harry Zohn. New York: Shocken, 1955. 160-63.
2   Marcel Proust (1871-1922), French novelist and critic. In his lengthy multi-volume novel, *À la recherche du temps perdu* (1913-27), Proust elaborated the notion of "involuntary memory" in which ordinary experience evokes past recollections without conscious effort.
3   Henri-Louis Bergson (1859-1941), French philosopher. In his writings, Bergson emphasized the notion of free will and the role of intuition in human consciousness.

are more likely to have encountered such situations. Some of Reik's[1] writings on his own theory of memory are in line with Proust's distinction between involuntary and voluntary recollection. "The function of remembrance [*Gedächtnis*]," Reik writes, "is the protection of impressions; memory [*Erinnerung*] aims at their disintegration. Remembrance is essentially conservative, memory is destructive." Freud's fundamental thought, on which these remarks are based, is formulated by the assumption that "consciousness comes into being at the site of a memory trace." (For our purposes, there is no substantial difference between the concepts of *Erinnerung* and *Gedächtnis*, as used in Freud's essay.) Therefore, "it would be the special characteristic of consciousness that, unlike what happens in all other psychical systems, the excitatory process does not leave behind a permanent change in its elements, but expires, as it were, in the phenomenon of becoming conscious." The basic formula of this hypothesis is that "becoming conscious and leaving behind a memory trace are processes incompatible with each other within one and the same system." Rather, memory fragments are "often most powerful and most enduring when the incident which left them behind was one that never entered consciousness." Put in Proustian terms, this means that only what has not been experienced explicitly and consciously, what has not happened to the subject as an experience, can become a component of the *mémoire involontaire*. According to Freud, the attribution of "permanent traces as the basis of memory" to processes of stimulation is reserved for "other systems," which must be thought of as different from consciousness. In Freud's view, consciousness as such receives no memory traces whatever, but has another important function: protection against stimuli. "For a living organism, protection against stimuli is an almost more important function than the reception of stimuli; the protective shield is equipped with its own store of

---

1   Theodor Reik (1888-1969), Viennese lay analyst and early student of Freud. Much of Reik's work examined the role of repressed impulses in everyday behavior including, most notably, those said to be present in the therapist-patient relationship. In 1926 Reik was charged with quackery under an old law prohibiting non-medical treatment of patients. Freud responded in his defense, and the defense of lay analysis, in his "The Question of Lay Analysis" in that same year.

energy and must above all strive to preserve the special forms of conversion of energy operating in it against the effects of the excessive energies at work in the external world, effects which tend toward an equalization of potential and hence toward destruction." The threat from these energies is one of shocks. The more readily consciousness registers these shocks, the less likely are they to have a traumatic effect. Psychoanalytic theory strives to understand the nature of these traumatic shocks "on the basis of their breaking through the protective shield against stimuli." According to this theory, fright has "significance" in the "absence of any preparedness for anxiety."

Freud's investigation was occasioned by a dream characteristic of accident neuroses which reproduce the catastrophe in which the patient was involved. Dreams of this kind, according to Freud, "endeavor to master the stimulus retroactively, by developing the anxiety whose omission was the cause of the traumatic neurosis." Valéry[1] seems to have had something similar in mind. The coincidence is worth noting, for Valéry was among those interested in the special functioning of psychic mechanisms under present-day conditions. (Moreover, Valéry was able to reconcile this interest with his poetic production, which remained exclusively lyric. He thus emerges as the only author who goes back directly to Baudelaire.[2]) "The impressions and sense perceptions of man," Valéry writes, "actually belong in the category of surprises; they are evidence of an insufficiency in man ... [R]ecollection is ... an elemental phenomenon which aims at giving us the time for organizing the reception of stimuli which we initially lacked." The acceptance of shocks is facilitated by training in coping with stimuli, and, if need be, dreams as well as recollection may be enlisted. As a rule, however—so Freud assumes—this training devolves upon the wakeful consciousness, located in a part of the cortex which is "so blown out by the effect of the stimulus" that it offers the most favourable situation for the reception of stimuli. That the shock is thus cushioned, parried by consciousness, would lend the incident that occasions it the character of having been lived in the strict sense. If it were incorporated directly in the

---

1　Paul Valéry (1871-1945), French poet, philosopher, and writer.
2　Charles Pierre Baudelaire (1821-67), controversial French poet, essayist, and critic.

registry of conscious memory, it would sterilize this incident for poetic experience.

The question suggests itself how lyric poetry can have as its basis an experience for which the shock experience has become the norm. One would expect such poetry to have a large measure of consciousness; it would suggest that a plan was at work in its composition. This is indeed true of Baudelaire's poetry; it establishes a connection between him and Poe, among his predecessors, and with Valéry, among his successors. Proust's and Valéry's reflections concerning Baudelaire complement each other providentially. Proust wrote an essay about Baudelaire the significance of which is even exceeded by certain reflections in his novels. In his "Situation de Baudelaire" Valéry supplies the classical introduction to the *Fleurs du mal*. There he says: "The problem for Baudelaire was bound to be this: to become a great poet, yet neither Lamartine nor Hugo nor Musset. I do not claim that this ambition was a conscious one in Baudelaire; but it was bound to be present in him, it was his reason of state." There is something odd about speaking of a reason of state in the case of a poet; there is something remarkable about it: the emancipation from experiences. Baudelaire's poetic output is assigned a mission. He envisioned blank spaces which he filled in with his poems. His work cannot merely be categorized as historical, like anyone else's, but it intended to be so and understood itself as such.

The greater the share of the shock factor in particular impressions, the more constantly consciousness has to be alert as a screen against stimuli; the more efficiently it does so, the less do these impressions enter experience (*Erfahrung*), tending to remain in the sphere of a certain hour in one's life (*Erlebnis*). Perhaps the special achievement of shock defence may be seen in its function of assigning to an incident a precise point in time in consciousness at the cost of the integrity of its contents. This would be a peak achievement of the intellect; it would turn the incident into a moment that has been lived (*Erlebnis*). Without reflection there would be nothing but the sudden start, usually the sensation of fright which, according to Freud, confirms the failure of the shock defence. Baudelaire has portrayed this condition in a harsh image. He speaks of a duel in which the artist, just before being beaten, screams in fright. This duel is the creative process.

6. *Death, Desire, and Freud's Radical Turn* (1954-55)[1]
Jacques Lacan

Where have we got to today? To a theoretical cacophony, to a conspicuous revolution in positions. And why? In the first place, because the metapsychological work of Freud after 1920 has been misread, interpreted in a crazy way by the first and second generations following Freud—those inept people.

Why did Freud think it necessary to introduce these new, so-called structural,[2] metapsychological notions, which we call the ego, the super-ego, and the id? Because, in the experience of the aftermath of his discovery, a turning-point, a real crisis was reached. In short, this new *I*, with whom one was meant to enter into dialogue, after a while refused to answer.

This crisis is clearly expressed in the testimony of historical witnesses of the years between 1910 and 1920. In the course of the first analytical revelation, the subjects recovered more or less miraculously, and this is still apparent when we read Freud's cases with their interpretations which strike lightning and their endless explanations. Well, it is a fact that it worked less and less well, that it ground to a halt in the course of time.

That is what prompted people to think that there is some reality in what I'm saying, that is, in the existence of subjectivity as such, and its modifications in the course of time, in accordance with a specific causality, a specific dialectic, which moves from subjectivity to subjectivity, and which perhaps escapes any kind of individual conditioning. Within the conventional units which we call subjectivities on account of individual particularities, what is happening? What is closing up? What is resisting?

Precisely in 1920, that is just after the change of direction which I have just mentioned—the crisis of analytic technique— Freud thought it necessary to introduce his new metaphysical notions. And if one reads what Freud wrote from 1920 on attentively, you realize that there is a direct link between this crisis in

---

1 From *The Seminar of Jacques Lacan: Book II, The Ego in Freud's Theory and in the Technique of Psychoanalysis, 1954-1955*. Ed. Jacques-Alain Miller. Trans. Sylvana Tomaselli. New York: Cambridge University Press, 1988. 10-12; 36-38; 44-45; 64-65; 75-76; 79-82; 89-90; 232-33; 366.

2 "Topique." Usually referred to as "structural" in English language writings on Freud.

technique which had to be overcome, and the manufacture of these new notions. But for that you must read his writings—to read them in the right order is better still. The fact that *Beyond the Pleasure Principle* was written before *Group Psychology and the Analysis of the Ego*, and before *The Ego and the Id*, should raise questions—no one has ever asked them.

What Freud introduced from 1920 on, are additional notions which were at that time necessary to maintain the principle of the decentring of the subject. But far from being understood as it should have been, there was a general rush, exactly like all the kids getting out of school—*Ah! Our nice little ego is back again! It all makes sense now! We're now back on the well-beaten paths of general psychology.* How could one fail to come back to it with elations when this general psychology is not only stuff from school or a mental commodity, but, what is more, is the psychology of everyman? There was satisfaction in being once again able to believe the ego to be central. And we see its latest manifestations in the amusing lucubrations which come to us at the moment from the other side of the pond.

Mr. Hartmann (1894-1970), psychoanalysis's cherub, announces the great news to us, so that we can sleep soundly—the existence of the *autonomous ego*. This *ego* which, since the beginning of the Freudian discovery, has always been considered as in conflict, which, even when it was located as a function in relation to reality, never ceased to be thought of as something which, like reality, is conquered in a tragedy, is all of a sudden restored to us as a central given. To what inner necessity does the assertion that somewhere there must be an autonomous[1] *ego* answer?

This conviction extends beyond the individual naivity of the subject who believes in himself, who believes that he is himself—a common enough madness, which isn't complete madness, because it belongs to the order of beliefs. Obviously, we are all inclined to believe that we are ourselves. But we aren't so sure of it, take a closer look. In many very specific circumstances we doubt it, without for all that undergoing depersonalisation. It isn't therefore simply to this naive belief that they want us to return. It is properly speaking a sociological phenomenon, which concerns analysis as a technique, or if you prefer, as a ceremony, as a priesthood determined within a certain social context.

---

1 English in the original, and again in what follows.

Why reintroduce the transcendent reality of the autonomous *ego*? Looking at it closely, these autonomous *egos* are more or less equal, according to the individuals. So we are back to an entification according to which not only individuals as such exist, but moreover some exist more than others. That is what contaminates, more or less implicitly, the so-called notions of the strong ego and the weak ego, which are just so many ways of ducking the hard issues raised as much by the understanding of the neuroses as by the handling of the technique.

[17 November 1954, from Lecture 1]

***

I think I can show that in order to gain an idea of the function which Freud designates by the word "ego," as indeed to read the whole of the Freudian metapsychology, it is necessary to use this distinction of planes and relations expressed in the terms, the symbolic, the imaginary and the real.

What's the point? The point is to retain the meaning of a particularly pure symbolic experience, that of analysis. I will give you an example of it, by giving you a foretaste of what I will tell you regarding the ego.

In its most essential aspect, the ego is an imaginary function. This is a discovery yielded by experience, and not a category which I might almost qualify as *a priori*, like that of the symbolic. On account of this point, I would almost say on account of this point alone, we find in human experience a door opened out on to an element of typicality. Of course, to us this element appears on the surface of nature, but in a form which is always misleading. That is what I wanted to insist on when I spoke of the failure of the various philosophies of nature. It is also very misleading with respect to the imaginary function of the ego. But this is a deception to which we are committed up to the hilt. In as much as we are the ego, not only do we experience it, but it is just as much a guide to our experience as the different registers that have been called guides in life, that is, sensations.

The fundamental, central structure of our experience really belongs to the imaginary order. And we can even grasp the extent to which this function is already different in man from what it is in nature as a whole.

We rediscover the imaginary function in nature in a thousand different forms—all the Gestaltist captations linked up to the parade, so essential to sustaining sexual attraction within the species.

Now, in man the function of the ego possesses distinct characteristics. That's the great discovery of analysis—at the level of the generic relation, bound up with the life of the species, man already functions differently. In man, there's already a crack, a profound perturbation of the regulation of life. That's the importance of the notion introduced by Freud of the death instinct. Not that the death instinct is such an enlightening notion in itself. What has to be comprehended is that he was forced to introduce it so as to remind us of a salient fact of his experience, just when it was beginning to get lost.

As I observed a little while ago, when an apperception of the structure is ahead of its time, there is always a moment of weakness when one is inclined to abandon it.

That is what happened in the circle around Freud when the meaning of the discovery of the unconscious was pushed into the background. They reverted to a confused, unitary, naturalistic conception of man, of the ego, and by the same token of the instincts. It was precisely in order to regain the sense of his experience that Freud wrote *Beyond the Pleasure Principle*. I will show you what necessity led him to write those last paragraphs, of whose fate at the hands of the majority of the analytic community you are well aware. It is said that they are incomprehensible. And even when one does show willingness to follow Freud, mouthing *the death instinct*, one doesn't understand it any more than the Dominicans, so prettily riddled by Pascal in *Les Provinciales*, had a clue about sufficient grace. I ask all of you to read this extraordinary text of Freud's, unbelievably ambiguous, almost confused, to read it several times, otherwise you won't understand the literal critique I am going to make of it.

The final paragraphs have quite literally remained a closed book, refusing to speak. As yet they have never been elucidated. They can only be understood if one understands what Freud's experience amounted to. He wanted to save some kind of dualism at all costs, just when this dualism was crumbling in his hands, and when the ego, the libido, etc., all of that was tending to produce a kind of vast whole, returning us to a philosophy of nature.

This dualism is none other than what I am getting at when I emphasize the autonomy of the symbolic. Freud never formulated that. To get you to understand it, a critique and exegesis of his text will be necessary.

[1 December 1954, from Lecture 3]

★★★

That is what happened in analysis the day when realizing that—for a reason which will have to be elucidated in retrospect—the first fruitfulness of the analytic discovery was being exhausted in the practice, people reverted to what is referred to as the analysis of the ego, claiming to find in it the exact inverse of what has to be demonstrated to the subject. Because one has already reached the level of the puzzle, of demonstration. People thought that by analyzing the ego, one would find the reverse-side of whatever it was that had to be made comprehensible. In that way a reduction of the kind I just mentioned was effected—two different images into a single one.

There's no doubt that the real *I* is not the ego. But that isn't enough, for one can always fall into thinking that the ego is only a mistake of the *I*, a partial point of view, the mere becoming aware of which would be sufficient to broaden the perspective, sufficient for the reality which has to be reached in the analytic experience to reveal itself. What's important is the inverse, which must always be borne in mind—the ego isn't the *I*, isn't a mistake, in the sense in which classical doctrine makes of it a partial truth. It is something else—a particular object within the experience of the subject. Literally, the ego is an object—an object which fills a certain function which we here call the imaginary function.

This thesis is absolutely essential to technique. I defy you not to extract this conception from the reading of the post-1920 metapsychological texts. Freud's research on the second topography was undertaken in order to put back in its place an ego which had begun to slide back to its old position. Whereas, through an effort at mental accommodation, one was falling back into the essential element of the classical illusion—I do not say error, it is quite strictly an illusion. Everything Freud wrote aimed at re-establishing the exact perspective of the excentricity of the subject in relation to the ego.

I claim that this is the essential, and that everything must be organized in relation to it.

[8 December 1954, from Lecture 4]

***

Some of you may still have a mnemic trace of what I left you with at the end of our last talk, namely the *Wiederholungszwang*—which we will translate as the *compulsion de répétition* [compulsion to repeat] rather than *automatisme de répétition*. This *Zwang* [compulsion] was singled out by Freud right from the start of his writings, the last to be made public, in the *Project for a Scientific Psychology* to which I frequently allude, an analysis and a critique of which we must undertake here in the weeks to come.

What Freud then defined as the pleasure principle is a principle of constancy. There is another principle, which our theoretician-analysts are as nonplussed by as a fish by a fig, the Nirvana principle. It is remarkable to see how, in the writings of an author like Hartmann, the three terms—principle of constancy, pleasure principle, Nirvana principle—are totally identified, as if Freud has never shifted out of the one mental category with which he sought to put a construction on the facts, and as if it were always the same thing he was talking about. One wonders why all of a sudden he would have called the Nirvana principle the beyond of the pleasure principle.

At the beginning of *Beyond*, Freud gives us a representation of two systems, and shows us that what is pleasure in the one is translated into pain in the other, and conversely. Now, if there were symmetry, reciprocity, a perfect coupling up of the two systems, if the primary and secondary processes were in fact the converse of one another, they would simply become one, and it would be enough to work on one to work on the other at the same time. In working on the ego and resistance, one would by the same token get at the heart of the problem. Freud wrote *Beyond the Pleasure Principle* precisely to explain that the matter can't be left like that.

Indeed, the manifestation of the primary process at the level of the ego, in the form of a symptom, is translated into unpleasure, suffering, and yet, it always returns. This fact alone should give us pause for thought. Why does the repressed system manifest itself with such insistence, as I called it last time? If the nervous system is set to reach a position of equilibrium, why doesn't it attain it? These matters, when put like that, are so obvious.

But that's the point, Freud was a man who, once he had seen something—and he knew how to see, and be the first—would not lose sight of the cutting edge. And that is what makes for the prodigious value of his work. Of course, no sooner had he made a discovery than it would immediately be set upon by the work of gnawing away which always takes place around any kind of speculative novelty, and tends to make everything fit back into the routine. Just look at the first great original notion he contributed at the purely theoretical level, the libido, and the mark, the irreducible character he gives it by saying—*libido is sexual.* These days, in order to make ourselves understood, we would have to say that what Freud put forward is that of the essential motor of human progress, the motor of the pathetic, of the conflictual, of the fruitful, of the creative in human live, is lust. And already, after only ten years, there was Jung ready to explain that the libido is psychic interest. No, libido is sexual libido. When I speak of the libido, I am speaking of the sexual libido.

What everyone acknowledges as the turning-point in the technique of analysis, centring on resistance, was well-founded and proved its fertility, but it lent itself to a theoretical confusion— by working on the ego, it was thought that one was working on one of the two halves of the apparatus. At this point in time, Freud chose to remind us that the unconscious as such cannot be reached and makes itself known in a fashion which is paradoxical, painful, and cannot be reduced to the pleasure principle. He thus brings back into the foreground the essence of his discovery, which one tends to forget.

[...]

Freudian biology has nothing to do with biology. It is a matter of manipulating symbols with the aim of resolving energy questions, as the homeostatic reference indicates, thus enabling us to characterise as such not only the human being, but the functioning of its major apparatuses. Freud's whole discussion revolves around that question, what, in terms of energy, is the psyche? This is where the originality of what in him is called biological thought resides. He wasn't a biologist, any more than any of us are, but throughout his work he placed the accent on the energy function.

If we know how to reveal the meaning of this energy myth, we see the emergence of what was, from the start and without it being understood, implicit in the metaphor of the human body as a machine. Here we see the manifestation of a certain beyond of the inter-human reference, which is in all strictness the symbolic beyond. That is what we are going to study, and surely we will then understand this kind of dawn which the Freudian experience is.

Freud started from a conception of the nervous system according to which it always tends to return to a point of equilibrium. That is what he started with, because it was then a necessity in the mind of any physician of that scientific age concerned with the human body.

Anzieu,[1] look at the *Entwurf,*[2] which is what I am talking about, and give us an account of it. On this foundation, Freud tried to build a theory of the functioning of the nervous system, by showing that the brain operates as a buffer-organ between man and reality, as a homeostat organ. And he then comes up against, he stumbles on, the dream. He realizes that the brain is a dream machine. And it is in the dream machine that he rediscovers what was there all along and which hadn't been noticed, namely, that it is at the most organic and most simple, most immediate and least manageable level, at the most unconscious level, that sense and speech are revealed and blossom forth in their entirety.

Hence the complete revolution in his thinking, and the move to the *Traumdeutung* [*Interpretation of Dreams*]. It is said that he abandons a physiologising perspective for a psychologising perspective. That's not the point. He discovers the operation of the symbol as such, the manifestation of the symbol in the dialectical state, in the semantic state, in its displacements, puns, plays on words, jokes working all on their own in the dream machine. And he has to take a line on this discovery, accept it or ignore

---

1 Didier Anzieu (1923-99), French psychoanalyst. Anzieu worked with Lacan in the early 1950s before breaking off to found (and serve as vice-president for) the French Psychoanalytic Association in 1964.

2 "Draft," by which Lacan presumably means Freud's early and abandoned "Project for a Scientific Psychology" (1895), wherein he tried to bridge psychology and physiology.

it, as all the others had to when they were that close to it. It was such a turning-point that he didn't know anything about what was happening to him. It took him another twenty years of a life which was already quite advanced at the time of this discovery, to be able to look back to his premises and to try to recover what it means in terms of energy. That is what required him to produce the new elaboration of the beyond of the pleasure principle and of the death instinct.

[12 January 1955, from Lecture 6]

★★★

The organism already conceived by Freud as a machine has a tendency to return to its state of equilibrium—this is what the pleasure principle states. Now, at first sight, this restitutive tendency is not clearly distinguishable, in Freud's text, from the repetitive tendency which he isolates, and which constitutes his original contribution. So we ask ourselves the following question—what distinguishes these two tendencies.

In this text, the middle terms are very strange, because they are part of a circular dialectic. Freud is constantly returning to a notion which always seems to elude him. It resists, but he doesn't stop, he tries to maintain the originality of the repetitive tendency at all costs. Without the shadow of a doubt, there was something he lacked, of the order of categories or of images, so as to give us a clear sense of it.

From the beginning of Freud's work to the end, the pleasure principle is explained in the following way—when faced with a stimulus encroaching on the living apparatus, the nervous system is as it were the indispensable delegate of the homeostat, of the indispensable regulator, thanks to which the living being survives, and to which corresponds a tendency to lower the excitation to a minimum. *To a minimum*, what does that mean? There is an ambiguity here, which puts analytic authors under some difficulty. Read them, you'll see them slide down the slope which Freud's way of rendering the question dialectical opens to them.

Freud here offered them the opportunity for yet one more misunderstanding, and in chorus they all succumb to it, in their panic.

The minimum tension can mean one of two things, all biologists will agree, according to whether it is a matter of the minimum given a certain definition of the equilibrium of the system, or the minimum purely and simply, that is to say, with respect to the living being, death.

Indeed one can consider that with death, all tensions are reduced, from the point of view of the living being, to zero. But one can just as well take into consideration the processes of decomposition which follow death. One then ends up defining the aim of the pleasure principle as the concrete dissolution of the corpse. That is something which one cannot but see as excessive.

However, I can cite you several authors for whom reducing the stimuli to the minimum means nothing more or less than the death of the living being. That is to assume that the problem has been resolved, that is to confuse the pleasure principle with what we think Freud designated under the name of the death instinct. I say *what we think*, because, when Freud speaks of the death instinct, he is, thank God, designating something less absurd, less anti-biological, anti-scientific.

There is something which is distinct from the pleasure principle and which tends to reduce all animate things to the inanimate—that is how Freud puts it. What does he mean by this? What obliges him to think that? Not the death of living beings. It's human experience, human interchanges, intersubjectivity. Something of what he observes in man constrains him to step out of the limits of life.

No doubt there is a principle which brings the libido back to death, but it doesn't bring it back any old how. If it brought it back there by the shortest paths, the problem would be resolved. But it brings it back there only along the paths of life, it so happens.

The principle which brings the living being back to death is situated, is marked out behind the necessity it experiences to take the roads of life—and it can only take that way. It cannot find death along any old road.

In other words, the machine looks after itself, maps out a certain curve, a certain persistence. And it is along the very path of this subsistence that something else becomes manifest, sustained by this existence it finds there and which shows it its passage.

There is an essential link which must be made right away—

when you draw a rabbit out of a hat, it's because you put it there in the first place. Physicists have a name for this formulation, they call it the first law of thermodynamics, the law of the conservation of energy—if there's something at the end, just as much had to be there at the beginning.

The second principle—I'll try to give you a striking image of it—stipulates that the manifestation of this energy has undegraded modes and others which aren't. To put it another way, you can't swim against the current. When you do a job, a part of it is expended, as heat for instance—there's a loss. That's called entropy.

There is no mystery to entropy, it's a symbol, a thing you can write on the blackboard, and you'd be very wrong to think it exists. Entropy is a capital E, absolutely indispensable to our thinking. And even if you couldn't care less about this capital E, because a man called Karlus Mayer, a doctor in the navy, founded it, it is the principle, actually, of everything—one cannot avoid taking it into account when one runs a factory, atomic or otherwise, or a country. Karlus Mayer started thinking seriously about it while bleeding his patients—sometimes the paths of thoughts are mysterious, those of the Lord are unfathomable. It is quite striking that having thought this one out, and this is, to be sure, one of thought's great moments, he was extremely enfeebled by it—as if giving birth to capital E might have left its mark on the nervous system.

You'd be wrong to think that, when I take up positions which are commonly thought of as anti-organicist, it is because—as someone I like a lot said one day—the nervous system annoys me. I don't take such sentimental reasons as my guide. I think ordinary organicism is a stupidity, but there is another variety which doesn't in any way neglect material phenomena. Which leads me to tell you—in all honesty, if not in complete truth, for truth would require looking for its traces in experience—that I think that, for an unhappy individual to have been charged by I know not what, *the holy language* as Valéry put it, with the task of bringing capital E to life, doesn't perhaps come about without cost. Karlus Mayer certainly had two parts to his life, the one before and the one after, when nothing else happened—he had said what he had to say.

Well, this entropy, Freud encounters it, and he already does so by the end of the *Wolfman* [case study]. He has a firm sense that it has some kind of relation to his death instinct but without being able, there either, to be quite at ease with it, and throughout this article he pursues his infernal little merry-go-round, like Diogenes[1] seeking a man with his lantern. He was missing something. It would be too easy if I were to tell you—I will tell you—that all you have to do is add a capital *F* or a capital *I* to the capital *E*. That is certainly not it, because it hasn't thereby been entirely elucidated.

Contemporary thought is in the process of trying to get ahold of this down paths which are often ambiguous, even confusional, and you can't be unaware that you are present at its birth. I would go even further—in so far as you are here, following my seminar, you are in the process of see-sawing into this childbirth. You are entering into that dimension in which thought tries to order itself and find its correct symbol, its capital *F* following on from capital *E*. In the present state of things, it's the quantity of information.

Some aren't taken aback by this. Others seem completely baffled.

The great adventure of the research concerning communication began at some distance, at least ostensibly, from our concerns. Rather let's say, for how are we to know where it all began, that one of its significant moments is to be found in the company of telephone engineers.

The Bell Telephone Company needed to economise, that is to say, to pass the greatest possible number of communications down one single wire. In a country as vast as the United States, it is very important to save on a few wires, and to get the inanities which generally travel by this kind of transmission apparatus to pass down the smallest possible number of wires. That is where the quantification of communication started. So a start was made, as you can see, by dealing with something very far removed from what we here call speech. It had nothing to do with knowing whether what people tell each other makes any sense. Besides, what is said on the

---

1   Cynic philosopher Diogenes of Sinope (404-323 BCE). Having considered poverty a great virtue, Diogenes eschewed the social conventions of his day and chose to live in a tub in Athens' marketplace. He was known, among other things, for carrying a lamp in broad daylight which he reportedly said was used in his perpetual search to find "an honest human being."

telephone, you must know from experience, never does. But one communicates, one recognises the modulation of a human voice, and as a result one has that appearance of understanding which comes with the fact that one recognizes words one already knows. It is a matter of knowing what are the most economical conditions which enable one to transmit the words people recognize. No one cares about the meaning. Doesn't this underline rather well the point which I am emphasising, which one always forgets, namely that language, this language which is the instrument of speech, is something material?

[...]

At the point we have reached, I propose, looking ahead, that you conceive of the need for repetition, such as it concretely manifests itself in the subject, in analysis for instance, as the form of behaviour staged in the past and reproduced in the present in a way which doesn't conform much with vital adaptation.

Here we rediscover what I've already pointed out to you, namely that the unconscious is the discourse of the other. This discourse of the other is not the discourse of the abstract other, of the other in the dyad, of my correspondent, nor even of my slave, it is the discourse of the circuit in which I am integrated. I am one of its links. It is the discourse of my father for instance, in so far as my father made mistakes which I am absolutely condemned to reproduce—that's what we call the *super-ego*. I am condemned to reproduce them because I am obliged to pick up again the discourse he bequeathed to me, not simply because I am his son, but because one can't stop the chain of discourse, and it is precisely my duty to transmit it in its aberrant form to someone else. I have to put to someone else the problem of a situation of life or death in which the chances are that it is just as likely that he will falter, in such a way that this discourse produces a small circuit in which an entire family, an entire coterie, an entire camp, an entire nation or half of the world will be caught. The circular form of a speech which is just at the limit between sense and non-sense, which is problematic.

That's what the need for repetition is, as we see it emerge beyond the pleasure principle. It vacillates beyond all the biological mechanisms of equilibration, of harmonisation and of agreement. It is only introduced by the register of language, by the function of the symbol, by the problematic of the question within the human order.

How does Freud project that in the most literal manner on to a level which ostensibly belongs to the order of biology? We will have to come back to that the next few times. Life is only caught up in the symbolic piece-meal, decomposed. The human being himself is in part outside life, he partakes of the death instinct. Only from there can he engage in the register of life.

[19 January 1955, from Lecture 7]

★★★

Oedipus at Colonus,[1] whose being lies entirely within the word [*parole*] proferred by his destiny, makes actual the conjugation of death and life. He lives a life which is dead, which is that death which is precisely there under life. That is also where Freud's lengthy text leads us, where he tells us—*Don't believe that life is an exalting goddess who has arisen to culminate in that most beautiful of forms, that there is the slightest power of achievement and progress in life. Life is a blister, a mould, characterised*—as others besides Freud have written—*by nothing beyond its aptitude for death.*

That is what life is—a detour, a dogged detour, in itself transitory and precarious, and deprived of any significance. Why, in that of its manifestations called man, does something happen, which insists throughout this life, which is called a meaning? We call it *human*, but are we so sure? Is this meaning as human as all that? A meaning is an order, that is to say, a sudden emergence. A meaning is an order which suddenly emerges. A life insists on entering into it, but it expresses something which is perhaps completely beyond this life, since when we get to the root of this life, behind the drama of the passage into existence, we find nothing besides life conjoined to death. That is where the Freudian dialectic leads us.

Up to a certain point, Freudian theory may seem to explain everything, including what's related to death, within the framework of a closed libidinal economy, regulated by the pleasure principle and a return to equilibrium, involving specific relations

---

1 Sophocles (ca. 496-406 BCE), Athenian tragedian, intended this play as the second instalment between *Oedipus the King* and *Antigone*.

between objects. The merging of the libido with activities which on the surface are at odds with it, aggressivity for instance, is put down to imaginary identification. Instead of beating up the other confronting him, the subject identifies himself, and turns against himself this gentle aggressivity, which is thought of as a libidinal object relation, and is founded upon what are called the instincts of the ego, that is to say the need for order and harmony. After all, one must eat—when the pantry is empty, one tucks into one's fellow being [*semblable*]. The libidinal adventure is here objectified in the order of living things, and one assumes that the behaviour of subjects, their inter-aggressivity, is conditioned and capable of explication by a desire which is fundamentally adequate to its object.

The significance of *Beyond the Pleasure Principle* is that that isn't enough. Masochism is not inverted sadism, the phenomenon of aggressivity isn't to be explained simply on the level of imaginary identification. What Freud's primary masochism teaches us is that, when life has been dispossessed of its speech, its final word can only be the final malediction expressed at the end of *Oedipus at Colonus*. Life doesn't want to be healed. The negative therapeutic reaction is fundamental to it. Anyway, what is healing? The realisation of the subject through a speech which comes from elsewhere, traversing it.

This life we're captive of, this essentially alienated life, ex-sisting, this life in the other, is as such joined to death, it always returns to death, and is only drawn into increasingly large and more roundabout circuits by what Freud calls the elements of the external world.

All that life is concerned with is seeking repose as much as possible while awaiting death. That is what devours the time of the suckling baby at the beginning of its existence, with hourly segments which allow him just to take a peep from time to time. You have to try bloody hard to draw him out of this for him to find the rhythm by which we get attuned to the world. If the nameless desire can appear at the level of the desire to sleep, which you mentioned the other day, Valabrega,[1] that's because

---

1 Jean-Paul Valabrega, French psychoanalyst. After the third split of the French psychoanalytic movement in 1969 (fueled in part by criticisms of Lacan's leadership), Valabrega helped to establish the so-called "Fourth group" (or French-Language Psychoanalytic Group).

it is an intermediary state—dozing off is the most natural of all vital states. Life is concerned solely with dying—*To die, to sleep, perchance to dream*, as a certain gentleman put it, just when what was at issue was exactly that—to be or not to be.[1]

[18 May 1955, Lecture 18]

***

Human beings are born with all kinds of extremely heterogeneous dispositions. But whatever the fundamental lot is, the biological lot, what analysis reveals to the subject is its signification. This signification is a function of a certain speech, which is and which isn't the speech of the subject—this speech, he already receives it ready-made, he is its point of passage. I don't know if that is the original master word of the Book of Judgement in the Rabbinical tradition. We aren't searching that far off, we have more limited problems, but ones in which the terms of vocation and of calling have their full value.

If this speech received by the subject didn't exist, this speech which bears on the symbolic level, there would be no conflict with the imaginary, and each of us would purely and simply follow his inclination. Experience shows us that nothing of the sort happens. Freud never renounced an essential dualism as constitutive of the subject. This means nothing other than these intersections. I would like to pursue them.

The ego is inscribed in the imaginary. Everything pertaining to the ego is inscribed in imaginary tensions, like all the other libidinal tensions. Libido and the ego are on the same side. Narcissism is libidinal. The ego isn't a superior power, nor a pure spirit, nor an autonomous agency, nor a conflict-free sphere—as some dare to write—in which we could find some support. What kind of story is this? Do we have to exact from subjects their higher tendencies towards truth? What is this transcendent tendency towards sublimation? Freud repudiates it in the most formal way in *Beyond the Pleasure Principle*. He cannot find the slightest tendency towards progress in any of the concrete and historical manifestations of human functions, and this really has a value for the person who invented our method. All forms of life

---

1 English in the original.

are as surprising, as miraculous, there is no tendency towards superior forms.

This is the point where we open out into the symbolic order, which isn't the libidinal order in which the ego is inscribed, along with all the drives. It tends beyond the pleasure principle, beyond the limits of life, and that is why Freud identifies it with the death instinct. Reread the text, and you'll see whether it seems to you worthy of being endorsed. The symbolic order is rejected by the libidinal order, which includes the whole of the domain of the imaginary, including the structure of the ego. And the death instinct is only the mask of the symbolic order, in so far—this is what Freud writes—as it is dumb, that is to say in so far as it hasn't been realised. As long as the symbolic order hasn't been instituted, by definition, the symbolic order is dumb.

The symbolic order is simultaneously non-being and insisting to be, that is what Freud has in mind when he talks about the death instinct as being what is most fundamental—a symbolic order in travail, in the process of coming, insisting on being realised.

[29 June 1955, from Lecture 24]

7. *On the Development of Mental Functioning* (1958)[1]
Melanie Klein

The paper I present here is a contribution to metapsychology, an attempt to carry further Freud's fundamental theories on this subject in the light of conclusions derived from progress in psychoanalytic practice.

Freud's formulation of mental structure in terms of id, ego and super-ego has become the basis for all psychoanalytic thinking. He made it clear that these parts of the self are not sharply separated from one another and that the id is the foundation of all mental functioning. The ego develops out of the id, but Freud gave no consistent indication at which stage this happens; throughout life the ego reaches deep down into the id and is therefore under the constant influence of unconscious processes.

Moreover, his discovery of the life and death instincts, with their polarity and fusion operating from birth onwards, was a

---

1 "On the Development of Mental Functioning" (1958), *Envy and Gratitude*. London: Delacorte, 1975. 236-46.

tremendous advance in the understanding of the mind. I recognized, in watching the constant struggle in the young infant's mental processes between an irrepressible urge to destroy as well as to save himself, to attack his objects and to preserve them, that primordial forces struggling with each other were at work. This gave me a deeper insight into the vital *clinical* importance of Freud's concept of life and death instincts. When I wrote *The Psycho-Analysis of Children,* I had already come to the conclusion that under the impact of the struggle between the two instincts, one of the ego's main functions—the mastery of anxiety—is brought into operation from the very beginning of life.

Freud assumed that the organism protects itself against the danger arising from the death instinct working within by deflecting it outwards, while that portion of it which cannot be deflected is bound by the libido. He considered in *Beyond the Pleasure Principle* the operation of the life and death instincts as biological processes. But it has not been sufficiently recognized that Freud in some of his writings based his *clinical* considerations on the concept of the two instincts, as for example in "The Economic Problem of Masochism." May I recall the last few sentences of that paper. He said: "Thus moral masochism becomes a classical piece of evidence for the existence of fusion of instinct. Its danger lies in the fact that it originates from the death instinct and corresponds to that part of the instinct which has escaped being turned outwards as an instinct of destruction. But since, on the other hand, it has the value of an erotic component, even the subject of destruction of himself cannot take place without libidinal satisfaction" (Freud, *Standard* 19: 170). In the *New Introductory Lectures,* he put the psychological aspect of his new discovery in even stronger terms. He said: "This hypothesis opens a prospect to us of investigations which may some day be of great importance for the understanding of pathological processes. For fusions may also come apart, and we may expect that functioning will be most gravely affected by defusions of such a kind. But these conceptions are still too new; no one has yet tried to apply them in our work" (22: 105). I would say that in so far as Freud took the fusion and defusion of the two instincts as underlying the *psychological* conflict between aggressive and libidinal impulses, it would be the ego, and not the organism, which deflects the death instinct.

Freud stated that no fear of death exists in the unconscious, but this does not seem compatible with his discovery of the dangers arising from the death instinct working within. As I see it, the primordial anxiety which the ego fights is the threat arising from the death instinct. I pointed out in "The Theory of Anxiety and Guilt" that I do not agree with Freud's view that "the unconscious seems to contain nothing that would lend substance to the concept of the annihilation of life" and that, therefore, "the fear of death should be regarded as analogous to the fear of castration." In "The Early Development of Conscience in the Child," I referred to Freud's theory of the two instincts, according to which at the outset of life the instinct of aggression, or the death instinct, is being opposed and bound by the libido or life instinct—the Eros—and said: "The danger of being destroyed by this instinct of aggression sets up, I think, an excessive tension in the ego, which is felt by it as an anxiety, so that it is faced at the very beginning of its development with the task of mobilizing libido against its death-instinct." I concluded that the danger of being destroyed by the death instinct thus gives rise to primordial anxiety in the ego.[1]

The young infant would be in danger of being flooded by his self-destructive impulses if the mechanism of projection could not operate. It is partly in order to perform this function that the ego is called into action at birth by the life instinct. The primal process of projection is the means of deflecting the death instinct outwards.[2] Projection also imbues the first object with libido. The other primal process is introjection, again largely in the service of the life instinct; it combats the death instinct because it

---

1 Joan Riviere (1952) refers to "Freud's decisive rejection of the possibility of an unconscious fear of death"; she goes on to conclude that "the helplessness and dependence of human children must, in conjunction with their phantasy life, presuppose that the fear of death is even part of their experience" (Riviere). [Klein's footnote]

2 Here I differ from Freud in so far as it seems that Freud understood by deflection only the process whereby the death instinct directed against the self is turned into aggression against the object. In my view, two processes are involved in that particular mechanism of deflection. Part of the death instinct is projected into the object, the object thereby becoming a persecutor; while that part of the death instinct which is retained in the ego causes aggression to be turned against that persecutory object. [Klein's footnote]

leads to the ego taking in something life-giving (first of all food) and thus binding the death instinct working within.

From the beginning of life the two instincts attach themselves to objects, first of all the mother's breast. I believe, therefore, that some light may be thrown on the development of the ego in connection with the functioning of the two instincts by my hypothesis that the introjection of the mother's feeding breast lays the foundation for all internalization processes. According to whether destructive impulses or feelings of love predominate, the breast (for which the bottle can symbolically come to stand) is felt at times to be good, at times to be bad. The libidinal cathexis of the breast, together with gratifying experiences, builds up in the infant's mind the primal good object, the projection on the breast of destructive impulses the primal bad object. Both these aspects are introjected and thus the life and death instincts, which had been projected, again operate within the ego. The need to master persecutory anxiety gives impetus to splitting the breast and mother, externally and internally, into a helpful and loved and, on the other hand, a frightening and hated object. These are the prototypes of all subsequent internalized objects.

The strength of the ego—reflecting the state of fusion between the two instincts—is, I believe, constitutionally determined. If in the fusion the life instinct predominates, which implies an ascendancy of the capacity for love, the ego is relatively strong, and is more able to bear the anxiety arising from the death instinct and to counteract it.

To what extent the strength of the ego can be maintained and increased is in part affected by external factors, in particular the mother's attitude towards the infant. However, even when the life instinct and the capacity for love predominate, destructive impulses are still deflected outwards and contribute to the creation of persecutory and dangerous objects which are reintrojected. Furthermore, the primal processes of introjection and projection lead to constant changes in the ego's relation to its objects, with fluctuations between internal and external, good and bad ones, according to the infant's phantasies and emotions as well as under the impact of his actual experiences. The complexity of these fluctuations engendered by the perpetual activity of the two instincts underlies the development of the ego in its relation to the external world as well as the building up of the internal world.

The internalized good object comes to form the core of the ego around which it expands and develops. For when the ego is supported by the internalized good object, it is more able to master anxiety and preserve life by binding with libido some portions of the death instinct operative within.

However, a part of the ego, as Freud described in the *New Introductory Lectures*, comes to "stand over" against the other part as a result of the ego splitting itself. He made it clear that this split-off part performing many functions is the super-ego. He also stated that the super-ego consists of certain aspects of the introjected parents and is largely unconscious.

With these views I agree. Where I differ is in placing at birth the processes of introjection which are the basis of the super-ego. The super-ego precedes by some months the beginning of the Oedipus complex, a beginning which I date, together with that of the depressive position, in the second quarter of the first year. Thus the early introjection of the good and bad breast is the foundation of the super-ego and influences the development of the Oedipus complex. This conception of super-ego formation is in contrast to Freud's explicit statements that the identifications with the parents are the heir of the Oedipus complex and only succeed if the Oedipus complex is successfully overcome.

In my view, the splitting of the ego, by which the super-ego is formed, comes about as a consequence of conflict in the ego, engendered by the polarity of the two instincts. This conflict is increased by their projection as well as by the resulting introjection of good and bad objects. The ego, supported by the internalized good object and strengthened by the identification with it, projects a portion of the death instinct into that part of itself which it has split off—a part which thus comes to be in opposition to the rest of the ego and forms the basis of the super-ego. Accompanying this deflection of a portion of the death instinct is a deflection of that portion of the life instinct which is fused with it. Along with these deflections, parts of the good and bad objects are split off from the ego into the super-ego. The super-ego thus acquires both protective and threatening qualities. As the process of integration—present from the beginning in both the ego and the super-ego—goes on, the death instinct is bound, up to a point, by the super-ego. In the process of binding, the death instinct influences the aspects of the good objects contained in the super-ego, with the result that the action of the super-ego ranges from restraint of hate and destructive impulses, protection of the good object and self-criticism, to threats, inhibitory complaints and persecution. The super-ego—being bound up with the good object and even striving for its preservation—comes close to the actual good mother who feeds the child and takes care of it, but since the super-ego is also under the influence of the death instinct, it partly becomes the representative of the mother who frustrates the child, and its prohibitions and accusations arouse anxiety. To some extent, when development goes well, the super-ego is largely felt as helpful and does not operate as too harsh a conscience. There is an inherent need in the young child—and, I assume, even in the very young infant—to be protected as well as to be submitted to certain prohibitions, which amounts to a control of destructive impulses. I have suggested in *Envy and Gratitude* that the infantile wish for an ever-present, inexhaustible breast includes the desire that the breast should do away with or control the infant's destructive impulses and in this way protect his good object as well as safeguard him against persecutory anxieties. This function pertains to the super-ego. However, as soon as the infant's destructive impulses and his anxiety are aroused, the super-ego is felt to be strict and overbearing and the ego then, as Freud described it, "has to serve three harsh masters," the id, the super-ego, and external reality.

When at the beginning of the twenties I embarked on the new venture of analysing by play technique children from their third year onwards, one of the unexpected phenomena I came across was a very early and savage super-ego. I also found that young children introject their parents—first of all the mother and her breast—in a phantastic way, and I was led to this conclusion by observing the terrifying character of some of their internalized objects. These extremely dangerous objects give rise, in early infancy, to conflict and anxiety within the ego; but under the stress of acute anxiety they, and other terrifying figures, are split off in a manner different from that by which the super-ego is formed, and are relegated to the deeper layers of the unconscious. The difference in these two ways of splitting—and this may perhaps throw light on the many as yet obscure ways in which splitting processes take place—is that in the splitting-off of frightening figures defusion seems to be in the ascendant; whereas super-ego formation is carried out with a predominance of fusion of the two instincts. Therefore the super-ego is normally established in close relation with the ego and shares different aspects of the same good object. This makes it possible for the ego to integrate and accept the super-ego to a greater or less extent. In contrast, the extremely bad figures are not accepted by the ego in this way and are constantly rejected by it.

However, with young infants, and I assume that this is more strongly the case the younger the infant is, the boundaries between split-off figures and those less frightening and more tolerated by the ego are fluid. Splitting normally succeeds only temporarily or partially. When it fails, the infant's persecutory anxiety is intense, and this is particularly the case in the first stage of development characterized by the paranoid-schizoid position, which I assume to be at its height in the first three or four months of life. In the very young infant's mind the good breast and the bad devouring breast alternate very quickly, possibly are felt to exist simultaneously.

The splitting-off of persecutory figures which go to form part of the unconscious is bound up with splitting off idealized figures as well. Idealized figures are developed to protect the ego against the terrifying ones. In these processes the life instinct appears again and asserts itself. The contrast between persecutory and idealized, between good and bad objects—being an expression of life and death instincts and forming the basis of phantasy life—is to be found in every layer of the self. Among the hated and threatening objects, which the early ego tries to ward off, are also those which are felt to have been injured or killed and which thereby turn into dangerous persecutors. With the strengthening of the ego and its growing capacity for integration and synthesis, the stage of the depressive position is reached. At this stage the injured object is no longer predominantly felt as a persecutor but as a loved object towards whom a feeling of guilt and the urge to make reparation are experienced. This relation to the loved injured object goes to form an important element in the super-ego. According to my hypothesis, the depressive position is at its height towards the middle of the first year. From then onwards, if persecutory anxiety is not excessive and the capacity for love is strong enough, the ego becomes increasingly aware of its psychic reality and more and more feels that it is its own destructive impulses which contribute to the spoiling of its objects. Thus injured objects, which were felt to be bad, improved in the child's mind and approximate more to the real parents; the ego gradually develops its essential function of dealing with the external world.

The success of these fundamental processes and the subsequent integration and strengthening of the ego depend, as far as internal factors are concerned, on the ascendancy of the life instinct in the interaction of the two instincts. But splitting processes continue; throughout the stage of the infantile neurosis (which is the means of expressing as well as working through early psychotic anxieties) the polarity between the life and death instincts makes itself strongly felt in the form of anxieties arising from persecutory objects which the ego attempts to cope with by splitting and later by repression.

With the beginning of the latency period, the organized part of the super-ego, although often very harsh, is much more cut off from its unconscious part. This is the stage in which the child deals with his strict super-ego by projecting it on to his environment—in other words, externalizing it—and trying to come to terms with those in authority. However, although in the older child and in the adult these anxieties are modified, changed in form, warded off by stronger defences, and therefore are also less accessible to analysis than in the young child, when we penetrate to deeper layers of the unconscious, we find that dangerous and persecutory figures still co-exist with idealized ones.

To return to my concept of primal splitting processes, I have recently put forward the hypothesis that it is essential for normal development that a division between the good and bad object, between love and hate, should take place in earliest infancy. When such a division is not too severe, and yet sufficient to differentiate between good and bad, it forms in my view one of the basic elements for stability and mental health. This means that the ego is strong enough not to be overwhelmed by anxiety and that, side by side with splitting, some integration is going on (though in a rudimentary form) which is only possible if in the fusion the life instinct predominates over the death instinct. As a result, integration and synthesis of objects can eventually be better achieved. I assume, however, that even under such favourable conditions, terrifying figures in the deep layers of the unconscious make themselves felt when internal or external pressure is extreme. People who are on the whole stable—and that means that they have firmly established their good object and therefore are closely identified with it—can overcome this intrusion of the deeper unconscious into their ego and regain their stability. In neurotics, and still more in psychotic individuals, the struggle against such dangers threatening from the deep layers of the unconscious is to some extent constant and part of their instability or their illness.

Since clinical developments in recent years have made us more aware of the psycho-pathological processes in schizophrenics, we can see more clearly that in them the super-ego becomes almost indistinguishable from their destructive impulses and internal persecutors. Herbert Rosenfeld,[1] in his paper on the super-ego of the schizophrenic, has described the part which such an overwhelming super-ego plays in schizophrenia. The persecutory anxieties these feelings engender I found also at the root of hypochondria. I think the struggle and its outcome is different in manic depressive illnesses, but must satisfy myself here with these hints.

If, owing to a predominance of destructive impulses which goes with excessive weakness of the ego, the primary splitting processes are too violent, at a later stage integration and synthesis of objects are impeded and the depressive position cannot be worked through sufficiently.

I have emphasized that the dynamics of the mind are the result of the working of the life and death instincts, and that in addition to these forces the unconscious consists of the unconscious ego and soon of the unconscious super-ego. It is part of this concept that I regard the id as identical with the two instincts. Freud has in many places spoken about the id, but there are some inconsistencies in his definitions. In at least one passage, however, he defines the id in terms of instincts only; he says in the *New Introductory Lectures:* "Instinctual cathexes seeking discharge—that, in our view, is all there is in the id. It even seems that the energy of these instinctual impulses is in a state different from that in the other regions of the mind" (22: 74).

My concept of the id, from the time I wrote *The Psycho-Analysis of Children*, has been in accordance with the definition contained in the above quotation; it is true that I have occasionally used the term id more loosely in the sense of representing the death instinct only or the unconscious.

Freud stated that the ego differentiates itself from the id by the repression-resistance barrier. I have found that splitting is one

---

1   Herbert Alexander Rosenfeld (1910-86), German psychoanalyst. Rosenfeld's clinical work on the schizophrenic state of depersonalization led to the first psychoanalytic treatment of psychosis.

of the initial defences and precedes repression, which I assume begins to operate in about the second year. Normally no splitting is absolute, any more than repression is absolute. The conscious and unconscious parts of the ego are therefore not separated by a rigid barrier; as Freud described it, in speaking of the different areas of the mind, they are shaded off into each other.

When, however, there is a very rigid barrier produced by splitting, the implication is that development has not proceeded normally. The conclusion would be that the death instinct is dominant. On the other hand, when the life instinct is in the ascendant, integration and synthesis can successfully progress. The nature of splitting determines the nature of repression. If splitting processes are not excessive, the conscious and unconscious remain permeable to one another. However, whereas splitting performed by an ego which is still largely unorganized cannot adequately lead to modification of anxiety, in the older child and in the adult repression is a much more successful means both of warding off anxieties and modifying them. In repression the more highly organized ego divides itself off against the unconscious thoughts, impulses, and terrifying figures more effectively.

Although my conclusions are based on Freud's discovery of the instincts and their influence on the different parts of the mind, the additions I have suggested in this paper have involved a number of differences, upon which I would now make some concluding remarks.

You may recall that Freud's emphasis on the libido was much greater than that on aggression. Although long before he discovered the life and death instincts he had seen the importance of the destructive component of sexuality in the form of sadism, he did not give sufficient weight to aggression in its impact on emotional life. Perhaps, therefore, he never fully worked out his discovery of the two instincts and seemed reluctant to extend it to the whole of mental functioning. Yet, as I pointed out earlier, he applied this discovery to clinical material to a greater extent than has been realized. If, however, Freud's conception of the two instincts is taken to its ultimate conclusion, the interaction of the life and death instincts will be seen to govern the whole of mental life.

I have already suggested that the formation of the super-ego precedes the Oedipus complex and is initiated by the introjection of the primal object. The super-ego maintains its connection with the other parts of the ego through having internalized different aspects of the same good object, a process of internalization which is also of the greatest importance in the organization of the ego. I attribute to the ego from the beginning of life a need and capacity not only to split but also to integrate itself. Integration, which gradually leads to a climax in the depressive position, depends on the preponderance of the life instinct and implies in some measure the acceptance by the ego of the working of the death instinct. I see the formation of the ego as an entity to be largely determined by the alternation between splitting and repression on the one hand, and integration in relation to objects on the other.

Freud stated that the ego constantly enriches itself from the id. I have said earlier that in my view the ego is called into operation and developed by the life instinct. The way in which this is achieved is through its earliest object relations. The breast, on which the life and death instincts are projected, is the first object which by introjection is internalized. In this way both instincts find an object to which they attach themselves and thereby by projection and reintrojection the ego is enriched as well as strengthened.

The more the ego can integrate its destructive impulses and synthesize the different aspects of its objects, the richer it becomes; for the split-off parts of the self and of impulses which are rejected because they arouse anxiety and give pain also contain valuable aspects of the personality and of the phantasy life which is impoverished by splitting them off. Though the rejected aspects of the self and of internalized objects contribute to instability, they are also at the source of inspiration in artistic productions and in various intellectual activities.

My conception of earliest object relations and super-ego development is in keeping with my hypothesis of the operation of the ego at least from birth onwards, as well as of the all-pervading power of the life and death instincts.

8. *Instinctual Dialectics against Instinctual Dualism* (1959)[1]
Norman O. Brown

If a psychoanalytic theory of the instincts must have the formal characteristics Freud demanded, if it is to trace the conflicts in mental life to basic conflicts in "the demands made upon the

---

1 From *Life Against Death: The Psychoanalytical Meaning of History.* London: Routledge; New York: Vintage, 1959. 79-82.

mind in consequence of its connection with the body," it is difficult to see any way of avoiding Freud's final duality of the life and death instincts. Assuming we have to have a duality, the technical arguments which forced Freud from one duality to another till he reached this final hypothesis are both logically coherent and strongly based on empirical data. Psychoanalysts after Freud, who have not accepted the life-and-death duality, have not been able to produce any alternative. They content themselves with rejecting the death instinct, and thus drift into instinctual monism, as Jung did, or into that general theoretical skepticism or indifference which is so congenial to the practitioner-technician.

The psychoanalytical practitioners have good reason to draw back from Freud's final instinct theory. The theory, as he left it, results in complete therapeutic pessimism, and is therefore worse than useless for therapists. Freud himself was unable to use the death instinct in his own later clinical writings, with one significant exception, namely the essay "Analysis Terminable and Interminable." This essay analyzes the factors preventing complete cure. Freud's therapeutic pessimism is grounded in his hypothesis of the eternal and irreconcilable struggle of life and death in every organism, producing in every human being the "spontaneous tendency to conflict" and manifesting itself in neurotic patients as an unconscious resistance to cure, a kind of "physical entropy" (Freud, *Collected Papers V*: 345, 347).

Quite apart from the specific character of the death instinct—the subject of the next chapter—Freud's system as a whole is given a metaphysical tendency toward pessimism by the formal prerequisite that conflicts in mental life are to be traced to instincts. The aim of the theory of instincts is to build a bridge between mental conflict (neurosis) and human biology, and, at least as Freud handled it, it ends by finding the causes of conflict in the biological domain. But if the causes are biological data, the hope of cure is groundless. It is true that Freud more than once disavows the propriety of giving a biological, as opposed to a psychological, explanation of repression (355). But when, for example in *Civilization and Its Discontents,* he invokes the "primal," "innate" conflict of ambivalence between Eros and Death as the ultimate explanation of the human neurosis, we must assume he means "innate," i.e., biologically given (Freud, *Civilization* 120-21, 136, 144). And the vision of Life and Death in *Beyond the Pleasure Principle* completes the picture by seeing all organic life caught in the conflict of ambivalence.

All organic life is then sick; we humans must abandon hope of cure, but we can take comfort in the conclusion that our sickness is part of some universal sickness in nature. The metaphysical courage, even grandeur, of *Beyond the Pleasure Principle* should not blind us to the fact that it is metaphysics (Freud calls it speculation); it is true religion, in the Spinozistic sense; it is Freud's attempt to see all things in God and *sub specie aeternitatis*. To argue *ad hominem* against a metaphysical system is easy, and psychoanalysis equips us to do so. It is easy to argue that Freud has projected the neurosis of mankind onto the whole organic world, with the effect of exhibiting the inevitability and permanence of the human neurosis. It is easy to argue that this is a rationalization really expressing that unconscious resistance to cure which, according to Freud, makes patients cling tenaciously to illness and suffering and which is a manifestation of the wish to die (Freud, *Introductory* 140-41; *Collected Papers V*: 345). It is less easy to see how the psychoanalytical exploration of the human neurosis leads to any other theoretical conclusion or any other instinctual resolution.

A psychoanalysis which remains psychoanalysis must keep the theory of instincts. In it is contained the commitment to restore to man his animal nature and to eliminate the mystery of the soul. Hence the instincts must be universal biological principles. The question is: What had to happen to an animal in order to make him into a man-animal? And a psychoanalysis which remains psychoanalysis must keep the duality of instincts. The essence of the man-animal is neurosis, and the essence of neurosis is mental conflict. The human neurosis must be traced to an instinctual ambivalence, a conflict between forces inherent in all organic life, unless we are to return to the traditional and stale notion that the psychic conflict in man is due to the ambivalence between his superorganic soul and his animal body.

If, on the other hand, psychoanalysis is to retain hope and keep open the possibility of therapy, it must find a way to avoid Freud's metaphysical vision of all life sick with the struggle between Life and Death. It must hold fast to the vision that man is distinguished from other animals by the privilege of being sick; that there is an essential connection between being sick and being civilized; in other words, that neurosis is the privilege of the uniquely social animal. It must therefore maintain that instinctual ambivalence is a human prerogative.

We need, in fine, a metaphysic which recognizes both the continuity between man and animals and also the discontinuity. We need, instead of an instinctual dualism, an instinctual dialectic. We shall have to say that whatever the basic polarity in human life may be—whether it is the polarity of hunger and love, or love and hate, or life and death—this polarity exists in animals but does not exist in a condition of ambivalence. Man is distinguished from animals by having separated, ultimately into a state of mutual conflict, aspects of life (instincts) which in animals exist in some condition of undifferentiated unity or harmony. Psychoanalysis must find the basis of human neurosis in the animal, and at the same time must recognize that the animal is not neurotic (except when it is brought into contagious contact with man). Since the basis of human neurosis is conflict, the polarities which develop into conflict at the human level must exist, but not as conflict, and therefore somehow undifferentiated, at the animal level.

This dialectical metaphysics is no less metaphysical than the metaphysics of *Beyond the Pleasure Principle*. The difference between the two can be best seen if we relate them to their proper models in pure philosophical speculation. Freud correctly found a model for his own view in the pre-Socratic philosopher Empedocles (490-430 BCE), who found the ultimate principle of the universe to be the eternal conflict between love and strife (348-50). Our speculation has a similar analogy to the philosophy of Empedocles' predecessors—Anaximander (610-546 BCE), who said that the strife of opposites is produced by the separating of opposites out of a primal state of undifferentiated unity, and Heraclitus (535-475 BCE), who asserted the ultimate unity of opposites, including life and death.

The difference between a dualism of the instincts and a dialectical unity of the instincts is small and elusive; but slight shades of difference at this fundamental level can have large consequences. Freud's dualism undermines the distinction between different levels in what is nevertheless the continuous hierarchy of organisms; the shift from the logic of Empedocles to the logic of Anaximander makes it possible to formulate both the continuity and the discontinuity between man and animals. Freud's dualism also leads to suicidal therapeutic pessimism, because it results in representing conflict not as a human aberration but as a universal biological necessity; our modification of Freud's ontology restores the possibility of salvation. It is the distinctive achievement of man to break apart the undifferentiated or dialectical unity of the instincts at the animal level. Man separates the opposites, turns them against each other, and, in Nietzsche's phrase, sets life cutting into life. It is the privilege of man to revolt against nature and make himself sick. But if man has revolted from nature, it is possible for him to return to nature and heal himself. Then man's sickness may be, again in Nietzsche's phrase, a sickness in the sense that pregnancy is a sickness, and it may end in a birth and a rebirth (Nietzsche, *Philosophy* 706, 745). The Freudian dualism prevents us from positing any break with nature, and consequently precludes the notion of a return to nature; and since the failure to posit a break with nature entails the necessity of projecting man's sickness back into nature, a return to nature, even if it were possible, would not be a return to health.

Dialectics rather than dualism is the metaphysic of hope rather than despair. There is no way of eliminating questions of faith from human life as long as human life is subject to general conditions of repression. Or rather—since, as Freud said, faith is a derivative of love—dialectics is the metaphysic of Eros, hoping all things according to St. Paul and seeking reunification according to Freud.

9. *On Death, Time, and Eternity from Hegel to Freud* (1959)[1]
Norman O. Brown

According to Freud, aggressiveness represents a fusion of the life instinct with the death instinct, a fusion which saves the organism from the innate self-destructive tendency of the death instinct by extroverting it, a desire to kill replacing the desire to die (Freud, *Beyond* 73; *Ego* 56-57; *Collected II*: 260). As against Freud, we suggest that this extroversion of the death instinct is the peculiar human solution to a peculiar human problem. It is the flight from death that leaves mankind with the problem of what to do with its own innate biological dying, what to do with its own

---

1   From *Life Against Death: The Psychoanalytical Meaning of History.* London: Routledge; New York: Vintage, 1959. 101-09.

repressed death. Animals let death be a part of life, and use the death instinct to die: man aggressively builds immortal cultures and makes history in order to fight death. Thus Freud's death instinct, if we interpret it dialectically and keep the distinction between men and animals, like the Nirvana-principle and the repetition-compulsion, becomes crucial in the psychology of history, and in fact establishes another crucial link between Freud and the philosopher of history, Hegel (1770-1831).

Existentialist scholarship is discovering a more human Hegel, Hegel the psychologist, Hegel trying to transcend the traditional paranoia of philosophers and find the essence of man not in thinking but in human desires and human suffering. Of Hegel's two systematic attempts to grasp the essence of man, the first identified man with love, and the second identified man with death. Hegel's thought thus passed from Eros to Death, the pair which together form the essence of human nature according to Freud's latest instinct theory. And it was only in his second attempt, through his identification of man with death, that Hegel was able to grasp man as essentially a history-making creature.

At the beginning of his career Hegel shared the sentimental romanticism of the *Sturm und Drang* period, and found the reality of human desire and human action in the microcosm of love. Later, evolving in the same direction as Goethe when he added *Faust* Part II to *Faust* Part I, he found the reality of human action in the macrocosm of human history: man is that unique species of animal which has a history, that is to say, that animal whose essence is not united with his existence as with other animals, but is developed in the dialectic of historical time. In developing his philosophy of man as the animal with a history, Hegel found that his former identification of man with love was inadequate. Love is a little moment in the life of lovers; and love remains an inner subjective experience leaving the macrocosm of history untouched. Human history cannot be grasped as the unfolding of human love.

Hegel was able to develop a philosophy of history only by making a fresh start and identifying man with death. And he develops the paradox that history is what man does with death, along lines almost identical with Freud's. Freud suggests that the aggression in human nature—the drive to master nature as well as the drive to master man—is the result of an extroversion of the death instinct, the desire to die being transformed into the desire to kill, destroy, or dominate. Hegel postulates a transformation of the consciousness of death into a struggle to appropriate the life of another human being at the risk of one's own life: history as class struggle (the dialectic of Master and Slave, in Hegel's terminology) is based on an extroversion of death. And similarly Hegel's other fundamental category of history, human work or labor, is a transformation of the negativity or nothingness of death into the extroverted action of negating or changing nature. More generally, according to Hegel, time is what man makes out of death: the dialectic of history is the dialectic of time, and "time is the negative element in the sensuous world"; time is negativity, and negativity is extroverted death (Kojève 11-34, 364-80, 490-513, 527-73; Marcuse, *Reason* 224, 240; Kroner 153-61).

Freud does not have that concept of historicity which is Hegel's strength: Hegel, although trying to grasp the psychological premises of man's historicity, has only an intuitive psychology. And yet Hegel may help us understand death. Hegel needs reformulation in the light of the psychoanalytical doctrine of repression and the unconscious. It is not the consciousness of death that is transformed into aggression, but the unconscious death instinct; the unconscious death instinct is that negativity or nothingness which is extroverted into the action of negating nature and other men. Freud himself, in his most important addition to the theory of the death instinct after *Beyond the Pleasure Principle*, derived affirmation from Eros and negation from its instinctual opposite (Freud, *Collected Papers V*: 185). On the other hand, Hegel's doctrine of the connection between negation and time is essential if psychoanalysis is to make the breakthrough, which Freud did not make, to a psychoanalytical theory of time.

The relation of the pleasure-principle to the Nirvana-principle suggests that man has a history because the balanced equilibrium between tension and release of tension at the animal level has been disrupted and replaced by a dynamic restless striving. The study of the repetition-compulsion suggests that repression generates historical time by generating an instinct-determined fixation to the repressed past, and thus setting in motion a forward-moving dialectic which is at the same time an effort to recover the past. In that perspective on man's historicity the crucial psychoanalytical concept is fixation to the past. In our new perspective the crucial psychoanalytical concept is the repression of death.

What is the relation between fixation to the past and repression of death? The intermediate term is obvious—the refusal to grow old. At the biological level, organisms live their lives and have no history because living and dying, that is to say growing older, is in them an inseparable unity. With them, in Shakespeare's beautiful phrase, ripeness is all. At the human level, repression produces the unconscious fixation to the infantile past, the instinctual unity of living and dying is disrupted, and both the life instinct and the death instinct are forced into repression. At the biological level, the death instinct, in affirming the road to death, affirms at the same time the road of life: ripeness is all. At the human level, the repressed death instinct cannot affirm life by affirming death; life, being repressed, cannot affirm death and therefore must fly from death; death can only affirm itself (and life) by transforming itself into the force which always denies life, the spirit of Goethe's Mephistopheles.

Then Freud's equivocation with three forms of death—the Nirvana-principle, the repetition-compulsion, and the sado-masochistic complex—turns out to be profoundly suggestive. Man is the animal which has separated into conflicting opposites the biological unity of life and death, and has then subjected the conflicting opposites to repression. The destruction of the biological unity of life and death transforms the Nirvana-principle into the pleasure-principle, transforms the repetition-compulsion into a fixation to the infantile past, and transforms the death instinct into an aggressive principle of negativity. And all three of these specifically human characteristics—the pleasure-principle, the fixation to the past, and the aggressive negativism—are aspects of the characteristically human mode of being, historical time.

The elucidation of Freud's vision of organic life as a dialectical unity of life and death is hampered by the inadequacies in the current philosophy of organism. Psychoanalysis would like to start with a clear idea of the role of death at the organic level. But the great philosopher of organism, Whitehead,[1] has no chapter on death or on the relation between life and death; it seems as if even he bears unconscious witness to the repression of death in the human consciousness. Psychoanalysis therefore cannot proceed without going beyond Whitehead. Not Whitehead but Hegel

---

1 Alfred North Whitehead (1861-1947), English mathematician and philosopher. Whitehead described metaphysical reality in terms of "organic realism"—a form of process philosophy.

puts forward the idea that there is an intrinsic connection between death and that essence of true life, individuality: "The nature of finite things as such is to have the seed of passing away as their essential being: the hour of their birth is the hour of their death" (Hegel 142). The precious ontological uniqueness which the human individual claims is conferred on him not by possession of an immortal soul but by possession of a mortal body. Without death, Hegel argues, individuals are reduced to the status of mere modes in the one infinite and eternal substance of Spinoza (Kojève 517, 549). Whitehead's organisms also, without death, have no individuality: at the simplest organic level, any particular animal or plant has uniqueness and individuality because it lives its own life and no other—that is to say, because it dies.

The intrinsic connection between death and individuality is also suggested by hints contained in Freud's instinct theory. His identification of the life instinct with sexuality identifies it with the force that preserves the immortality of the species. By implication, therefore, it is the death instinct which constitutes the mortal individuality of the particular member of the species. Furthermore, Freud's theorem that Eros or the life instinct, as it operates in the human libido and in the lowest cells, aims to preserve and enrich life by seeking unification implicitly contains the theorem that the aim of the death instinct is separation; and explicitly Freud's theory of anxiety brings birth and death together as separation crises (Freud, *Inhibitions* 91-95). Freud is thus moving toward a structural analysis of organic life as being constituted by a dialectic between unification or interdependence and separation or independence. The principle of unification or interdependence sustains the immortal life of the species and the mortal life of the individual; the principle of separation or independence gives the individual his individuality and ensures his death.

If death gives life individuality and if man is the organism which represses death, then man is the organism which represses his own individuality. Then our proud views of humanity as a species endowed with an individuality denied to lower animals turns out to be wrong. The lilies of the field have it because they take no thought of the morrow, and we do not. Lower organisms live the life proper to their species; their individuality consists in their being concrete embodiments of the essence of their species in a particular life which ends in death.

But if the psychoanalytical doctrine of repression means anything, man never unfolds the mode of being which is proper to his species and given in his body. Repression generates the instinctual compulsion to change the internal nature of man and the external world in which he lives, thus giving man a history and subordinating the life of the individual to the historical quest of the species. History is made not by individuals but by groups; and the cliché-mongers repeat *ad nauseam* that man is by nature a social animal. It is intrinsic to the psychoanalytical point of view to assert the morbidity of human sociability, not just "civilized" as opposed to "primitive" sociability or "class society" as opposed to "primitive communism," but all of human sociability as we have known it. Freud's formulations of the Primal Father and the Primal Horde[1] (in *Group Psychology and the Analysis of the Ego)* may or may not be adequate explanations of the morbidity in group-formation. What is essential is the clinical pronouncement that sociability is a sickness.

The essential point in the Freudian diagnosis of human sociability was seen by Róheim[2]: men huddle into hordes as a substitute for parents, to save themselves from independence, from "being left alone in the dark" (Róheim 77, 79, 98). Society was not constructed, as Aristotle says, for the sake of life and more life, but from defect, from death and the flight from death, from fear of separation and fear of individuality. Thus Freud derives fear of "separation and expulsion from the horde" from castration anxiety, and castration anxiety from the fear of separation from the mother and the fear of death (Freud, *Inhibitions* 93-95, 104-12). Hence there are no social groups without a religion of their own immortality, and history-making is always the quest for group-immortality. Only an unrepressed humanity, strong enough to live-and-die, could let Eros seek union and let death keep separateness.

The unrepressed animal carries no instinctual project to

---

1 Discussion of the "primal horde" and the "primal father" actually begins in Freud's *Totem and Taboo*, although it is picked up again in *Group Psychology*. Freud speculates that civilization owes itself to the rise of guilt and conscience. These characteristics, he claims, are derived historically (phylogenetically) when the primal horde (of sons) banded together and killed their father to gain access to his women. Group psychology is founded, that is, upon an ancient (lost, repressed) murder—the kind of ironical conclusion Freud favored.

2 Géza Róheim (1891-1953), Hungarian lay analyst and anthropologist.

change his own nature; mankind must pass beyond repression if it is to find a life not governed by the unconscious project of finding another kind of life, one not governed by unconscious negativity. After man's unconscious search for his proper mode of being has ended—after history has ended—particular members of the human species can lead a life which, like the lives of lower organisms, individually embodies the nature of the species. But only an individual life in this sense can be satisfactory to the individual who lives it. The attainment of individuality by the human species would therefore mean the return of the restless pleasure-principle to the peace of the Nirvana-principle. The Nirvana-principle regulates an individual life which enjoys full satisfaction and concretely embodies the full essence of the species, and in which life and death are simultaneously affirmed, because life and death together constitute individuality, and ripeness is all. An individual life so regulated is possessed by all organisms below man. Because he too has a body, is an organism, must die, man has also instincts which will not let him rest till he attains individuality.

It is hard, under conditions of general repression, to affirm the death instinct without becoming an enemy of life. For under conditions of general repression the death instinct operates malignantly. In dialectical fusion with the life instinct it is a principle of restless negativity (like Goethe's Mephistopheles); but given the basic unsatisfactoriness of life under conditions of general repression, a defusion into a simple wish to die is always lurking in the background. Thus Schopenhauer seems to affirm death and Nirvana, but because he cannot affirm life, his affirmation of death is spurious. Schopenhauer's hostility to the *principium individuationis*[1] is a hostility to death as well as to life; only he who can affirm birth can affirm death, since birth and death are one. Under conditions of general repression, as long as life is unsatisfactory, death can be affirmed only by those whose life instinct is strong enough to envisage the reconciliation of life and death as a future state of perfection toward which the life instinct strives. Schopenhauer's incapacity to affirm life or death turns on his conviction that "men are so constituted that they could not be happy in whatever kind of world they might be

---

1 Latin phrase meaning "principle of individuation," according to which general or undifferentiated traits are winnowed down to the particular or individual.

placed"; hence all he can say to the dying individual is, "Thou ceasest to be something which thou hadst done better never to become" (Schopenhauer 286, 298, 308).

In contrast with Schopenhauer, Nietzsche, because he envisages the possibility of Superman, can affirm life and therefore death: "What has become perfect, all that is ripe—wants to die." Nietzsche's explanation shows how instinctual repression generates the flight from death, how the flight from death underlies both the religion of immortality and the economic institution of hereditary property: "All that is unripe wants to live. All that suffers wants to live, that it may become ripe and joyous and longing—longing for what is farther, higher, brighter. 'I want heirs'—thus speaks all that suffers; 'I want children, I do not want *myself*'" (in Kaufmann 434). Those prejudiced against Nietzsche might compare his concept of "wanting heirs" to John Maynard Keynes'[1] critique of purposiveness:

> Purposiveness means that we are more concerned with the remote future results of our actions than with their own quality or their immediate effects on our own environment. The "purposive" man is always trying to secure a spurious and delusive immortality for his acts by pushing his interest in them forward into time. He does not love his cat, but his cat's kittens; nor, in truth, the kittens, but only the kittens' kittens, and so on forward forever to the end of cat-dom. For him jam is not jam unless it is a case of jam to-morrow and never jam to-day. Thus by pushing his jam always forward into the future, he strives to secure for his act of boiling it an immortality. (Keynes 370)

In contrast with the neurotic time obsession of repressed humanity, Nietzsche affirms the eternity of repetition: "Joy, however, does not want heirs, or children—joy wants itself, wants eternity, wants recurrence, wants everything eternally the same."

Nietzsche's perfection, which is unrepressed life (joy), wants eternity, but it also wants to die. Eternity is therefore a way of envisaging mankind's liberation from the neurotic obsession with the past and the future; it is a way of living in the present, but also a way of dying. Hence the ultimate defect of all heavens

---

1   John Maynard Keynes (1883-1946), father of modern macroeconomics.

with immortality beyond the grave is that in them there is no death; by this token such visions betray their connection with repression of life. Anxiety about death does not have ontological status, as existentialist theologians claim. It has historical status only, and is relative to the repression of the human body; the horror of death is the horror of dying with what Rilke called unlived lines in our bodies. That perfect, resurrected body which the Christian creed promises would want to die because it was perfect: "All that is perfect wants to die." It takes the greatest strength to accept death, says Hegel (Kojève 546). Following Hegel, the existentialist philosophers have returned to the wisdom of Montaigne, that to learn philosophy is to learn how to die. Lacking Freud's concept of Eros, these philosophers may exhibit the unconscious wish to die, from which even Freud, with his concept of Eros, was not free. Nevertheless, in facing death they are serving the cause of life.

The construction of a human consciousness strong enough to accept death is a task in which philosophy and psychoanalysis can join hands—and also art. It was the poet Rilke who said it was the poet's mission to bind life and death together, and who said, "Whoever rightly understands and celebrates death, at the same time magnifies life" (cf. Rehm 583). But the hard truth which psychoanalysis must insist upon is that the acceptance of death, its reunification in consciousness with life, cannot be accomplished by the discipline of philosophy or the seduction of art, but only by the abolition of repression. Man, who is born of woman and destined to die, is a body, with bodily instincts. Only if Eros—the life instinct—can affirm the life of the body can the death instinct affirm death, and in affirming death magnify life.

If the repression of death and the repression of individuality have this importance in human history, psychoanalysis ought to be able to detect their role in the formation of neurosis in individual lives. Freud, however, perhaps because he lacked the concept of the repression of death, did not make use of his hypothesis of a death instinct (as distinct from an aggressive instinct) in his clinical writings. But if death is the aspect of life which confers on life individuality, independence, and separateness, then *a priori* the repression of death should produce symptoms which exhibit on the one hand a flight from independence and separateness and on the other hand the compulsive return of the repressed instinct. But such an ambivalent attitude toward independence and separateness is at the heart of all neurosis, according to Freud's later clinical writings. The ultimate cause of repression and neurosis is anxiety, and anxiety is "the anxiety of separation from the protecting mother." One of the hallmarks of the neurotic personality is a lifelong fixation to the infantile pattern of dependence on other people.

Although Freud does not make the necessary theoretical links between anxiety and his death instinct, he does say that what the ego fears in anxiety "is in the nature of an overthrow or an extinction" (*Ego* 85). It looks therefore as if the specifically human capacity for anxiety does reflect a revolt against death and individuality, or at least some deep disturbance in the organic unity of life and death. And if there is a connection between the human sense of time and the human use of death, there is also good reason to suspect a connection between time and anxiety. Kierkegaard speaks like a psychoanalyst when he says, "Time does not really exist without unrest; it does not exist for dumb animals who are absolutely without anxiety" (Kierkegaard 253).

10. *Superego and Culture: A Hermeneutic Interpretation* (1965)[1]
Paul Ricoeur

The Death Instinct and the Destructiveness of the Superego

Above we insisted on the excess of meaning that "speculation" gives to the death instinct as compared with the deciphering of that instinct in its representatives, of whatever level or order they may be. We looked upon this discordance as an irreducible given of the theory. We must now try to understand it. Why the absence of symmetry between the hermeneutics of life and the hermeneutics of death? Why does conjecture win out over interpretation when we move from the libido theory, taken at its two earlier stages of elaboration, to the theory of the life and death instincts?

An insistent remark of Freud himself may serve to get us started. On various occasions—already in *Beyond the Pleasure Principle*, but especially in *The Ego and the Id* and *Civilization and*

---

1 From *Freud and Philosophy: An Essay on Interpretation* (1965). Trans. Denis Savage. New Haven: Yale University Press, 1970. 293-309.

Its Discontents—Freud speaks of the death instinct as a "mute" energy, in contradistinction to the "clamour" of life.[1] This disparity between the death instinct and its expressions, between desire and speech—a disparity signified by the epithet "mute"—warns us that the semantics of desire no longer has the same meaning. The desire for death does not speak, as does the desire for life. Death works in silence. Hence the method of deciphering, based on the equivalence of two systems of reference, instincts and meaning, finds itself in difficulty. Yet psychoanalysis has no other recourse than to interpret, that is, to read an interplay of forces in an interplay of symptoms. In his last works, therefore, Freud restricts himself to setting an adventuresome speculation alongside a partial deciphering. Any given representative exhibits only "portions" of the death instinct. But there will be no equivalence between what is deciphered and what has been conjectured.

This point should be kept in mind when one enters into the series of papers that exploited the breakthrough achieved in *Beyond the Pleasure Principle*. One notices a twofold shift of emphasis: first, from the tendency to *repeat* to the tendency to *destroy;* next, from more *biological* to more *cultural* expressions. But this series of manifestations of the death instinct does not exhaust the weight of meaning supplied by speculation; an essential significance may even be lost when this silence is transcribed into clamour. Besides, Freud speaks more readily of the death instincts than of the death instinct (we have ignored this factor in our reconstruction of Freud's speculation), thus reserving the possibility of a great variety of expressions and of a nonexhaustive enumeration of its manifestations.

The first shift of emphasis is already very noticeable in *Beyond the Pleasure Principle*. The death instinct is introduced by the compulsion to repeat; but it is confirmed and verified by aggressiveness, in its two forms of sadism and masochism. These last two examples do not have the same significance: sadism is simply incorporated into the new theory, masochism is reinterpreted in light of the new theory.

The theory of sadism was formulated very early. Ever since the *Three Essays on Sexuality* the term covers three sets of phenomena.

---

1 "The death instincts are by their nature mute ... the clamour of life proceeds for the most part from Eros." (Freud, *Standard* 19: 46). [Ricoeur's note]

First, it designates a more or less perceptible component in any normal and integrated sexuality; second, it designates a perversion, sadism proper,. i.e., a mode of being that has become independent of that sexual component; and last, it also stands for a pregenital organization, the sadistic stage, in which that component plays a dominant role.

The case of masochism is quite different, for up to the present —in the *Three Essays* and in "Instincts and Their Vicissitudes"— masochism was nothing more than sadism "turned round" upon the ego, whereas Freud now regards the forms of masochism as derived phenomena, as a return or regression to a primary masochism. We will soon see the importance this has in the theory of the superego, conscience, and guilt.

All of this is only sketched in a few lines; in 1920, Freud had not yet elaborated the concepts of fusion (*Vermischung*) and defusion (*Entmischung*), by which he will account for the cooperation of the death instinct with sexuality and for its separate functioning.[1] At least these two examples clearly bring out the disparity between the death instinct and its manifestations, where the latter mark the emergence of the instinct at the level of an object-relation. At first view, the case of the death instinct does not seem to differ from that of the life instinct: here too sadism and masochism are able to be interpreted, for they have a particular "aim"—destruction—and definite "objects"—the sexual partner or the ego. But nothing permits one to say that the death instinct is fully manifested in these expressions comparable to the representatives of the life instinct; neither the play of the *fort-da*, nor even the compulsion to repeat can be reduced to destructiveness. Destructiveness is only one of the death instincts.[2]

This double movement—the replacement of the compulsion to repeat by destructiveness, and the switch from a metabiology to a metaculture—will be completed only in *Civilization and Its Discontents*. Sections IV and V of *The Ego and the Id* supply the indispensable transition between the metabiology

---

1 *The Ego and the Id*, Ch. 4, "The Two Classes of Instincts." [Ricoeur's note]

2 "The death instinct would thus seem to express itself—though probably only in part—as an instinct of destruction directed against the external world and other organisms" (41). [Ricoeur's note]

of *Beyond the Pleasure Principle* and the metaculture of *Civilization and Its Discontents*.

The stroke of genius in *The Ego and the Id* was to couple the theory of the three agencies—ego, id, superego—with the dualistic theory of the instincts of *Beyond the Pleasure Principle*. This confrontation makes it possible to pass from mere speculation to actual deciphering. Henceforth, instead of considering the death instincts face to face in a dogmatic mythology, we will approach them in the density of the id, ego, and superego.

Strictly speaking, the dualism of the instincts concerns only the id—it is an internal war of the id.[1] But starting from the instinctual interior, the war spreads out until it finally bursts forth in the higher portions of the psychism, in the "sublime." This process of defusion assures the transition from the biological speculation to the cultural interpretation and enables us to set forth all the representatives of the death instinct, to the point where the death instinct becomes inner punishment.

It is necessary to elaborate the concepts of fusion and defusion; they are, assuredly, economic concepts, as are the concepts of cathexis, regression, and even perversion. To give them an energy basis, Freud adopts a hypothesis not unrelated to Hughlings Jackson's[2] concept of "functional liberation": the defusion of an instinct liberates "a displaceable energy, which, neutral in itself, can be added to a qualitatively differentiated erotic or destructive impulse, and augment its total cathexis" (Freud, *Standard* 19: 44). Have we come back purely and simply to speculation about the quantitative, about free and bound energy? There is no denying the conjectural aspect; Freud himself observes: "In the present discussion, I am only putting forward a hypothesis; I have no proof to offer. It seems a plausible view that this displaceable and neutral energy, which is no doubt active both in the ego and in the id, proceeds from the narcissistic store of libido—that it is desexualized Eros" (44). A sign of this is the looseness or indifference in the "displacements" brought about by the primary process.

---

1   It is in these terms that the *New Introductory Lectures* combine the second topography and the dualistic theory of the instincts. [Ricoeur's note]

2   John Hughlings Jackson (1835-1911), English neurologist. Jackson made numerous contributions toward a scientific understanding of epilepsy and other forms of automatic behavior.

Thus the concepts of fusion and defusion have been constructed in order to state in energy language what happens when an instinct places its energy at the service of forces working in different systems. Consequently they are not based upon anything verifiable at the energy level itself where they are assumed to operate: fusion and defusion are simply the correlates, in energy language, of phenomena discovered by the work of interpretation when it focuses on the area of the instinctual representatives.

To see the sequence of the various representatives of the death instinct, it is necessary to examine them from the bottom up, i.e., to proceed from the more biological to the more cultural.

At the lowest level we meet with the erotogenic form of masochism, pleasure in pain (*Schmerzlust*). It is dealt with very briefly in *The Ego and the Id* and at greater length in "The Economic Problem of Masochism" (19: 159-70). How does it come about that man takes pleasure in pain? It is not enough to say, as in the *Three Essays*, that an excess of pain or unpleasure gives rise to a libidinal sympathetic excitation (*libidinöse Miterregung*) as a concomitant effect (*Nebenwirkung*); granted that this mechanism exists, it provides only a physiological foundation; what is essential takes place elsewhere, on the properly instinctual level. It must be supposed that the destructive instinct is split into two tendencies. One portion, under pressure from the life instinct, which seeks to render it harmless, is diverted outward onto paths of the muscular apparatus; this current of destructiveness places itself in the service of sexuality and constitutes sadism proper. The other portion remains inside the organism and "with the help of the accompanying sexual excitation described above, becomes libidinally bound there"; this constitutes erotogenic masochism, pleasure in pain. Erotogenic masochism is therefore the "residuum," remaining within, of a destructiveness which may be viewed either as primal sadism or as primal masochism. There is clearly much that remains puzzling: we do not know how the "taming" (*Bändigung*) of the death instinct by the libido is effected; we can only assume that the libido is at work not only in sadism, that is, in the portion of the death instinct diverted toward external objects, but in the residuum remaining within, hence in masochism itself, which thus appears as the most primitive "coalescence" (*Legierung*) of love and death. Masochism accompanies the libido through all its developmental phases and derives from them its successive "coatings" (*Umkleidungen*): the fear of being eaten up (oral stage), the wish to be beaten (sadistic-anal stage), castration fantasies (phallic stage), fantasies of being copulated with (genital stage). Thus fusion and defusion pinpoint a difficulty rather than provide the solution to a problem.

In *The Ego and the Id* (Ch. 5), it is basically the theory of the superego that profits from this rereading of the agencies from the viewpoint of death. We recall that for psychoanalysis the superego derives from the father complex and is thus a structure closer to the id than the perceptual ego is. But one trait of the superego remained unexplained: its harshness and cruelty. This strange character rejoins other disconcerting phenomena which at first glance seem unrelated to it, such as the resistance to recovery. When one comes to see that this resistance has a "moral" aspect to it, that it is a form of self-punishment through suffering and that it therefore involves an unconscious sense of guilt finding its satisfaction in the illness, a consistent pattern is revealed which includes such different phenomena as obsessional neurosis and melancholia, the resistance to recovery, and the severity of the normal conscience. Let's not go back over the question of whether it is correct to speak of an "unconscious sense of guilt." What is important is the connection discovered between guilt and death. We touch here upon the most extreme consequence of the relationship between the superego and the id. The instinctual character of the superego implies not only that the superego contains libidinal residues from the Oedipus complex, but that it is charged with destructive rage thanks to the defusion of the death instinct. This goes very far, even to the point of diminishing the importance of instruction or reading, of the "things heard"—in short, of word-presentations—in the development of conscience, to the profit of the great obscure forces rising from below. How is it, Freud asks, that the superego manifests itself essentially as a sense of guilt and develops such extraordinary cruelty toward the ego, to the extent of becoming "as cruel as only the id can be?" (19: 54).[1] The case of melancholia leads us to think that the superego has taken possession of all the available sadism, that the destructive component has entrenched itself in the superego and turned against the ego: "What is now holding sway in the superego is, as it were, a pure culture of the death instinct" (53).

---

1   Freud calls the sense of guilt in certain forms of obsessional neurosis "over-noisy" (überlaut): it is indeed one of the "clamorous voices" of the instinct which itself is "mute." [Ricoeur's note]

In thus emerging at the level of the superego, the death instinct suddenly discloses the dimensions of this pure culture of the death instinct. Caught between a murderous id and a tyrannical and punishing conscience, the ego appears to have no recourse other than self-torment or the torturing of others by diverting its aggressiveness toward them. Hence the paradox: "the more a man checks his aggressiveness towards the exterior the more severe—that is aggressive—he becomes in his ego ideal" (54)—as if aggressiveness either has to be turned outward against others or turned round upon the self. One immediately perceives the religious extension of this ethical cruelty in the projection of a higher being who punishes inexorably.

If we compare the cruelty of the superego with the previous description of "erotogenic masochism," it seems at first glance that any connection with sexuality is lacking; one may assume that there exists a direct link between destructiveness and the superego independently of any erotic factor. In "The Economic Problem of Masochism," Freud attempts to reconstruct the hidden connections between erotism and what he calls "moral masochism"—which, it is true, does not cover the whole domain of the superego.

The unconscious sense of guilt, discovered in the tenacious resistance to recovery and more correctly called the need for punishment (*Strafbedürfnis*), throws light on this hidden link between moral masochism and erotism. The link between the fear of conscience and erotism stems from the deep-seated relationship the superego retains with the id by reason of the libidinal ties with the parental source of prohibition; this is the place to repeat it: the superego is the "representative of the id" (*Vertreter des Es*). This libidinal tie may be drawn out indefinitely, in proportion as the father imago is replaced by increasingly distant and impersonal figures, ending with the dark power of Destiny, which only the fewest of men are able to separate from any parental connection.

But at the same time this comparison affords us the occasion to introduce certain nuances that appear to have been overlooked in *The Ego and the Id*, especially a difference between the superego's sadism and the ego's masochism (i.e., "moral masochism"). What was described in *The Ego and the Id* is the *superego*'s sadism, which is "an unconscious extension of morality" (*eine solche unbewusste Fortsetzung der Moral*). The *ego*'s desire or need for punishment is not exactly the same thing; such a desire is connected with the wish to be beaten by the father, which we have seen to be one of the expressions of "erotogenic masochism." This desire expresses, therefore, a resexualization of morality, in the reverse direction of the normal movement of conscience and morality that arise from the overcoming and hence from the desexualization of the Oedipus complex. With the resexualization of morality the possibility of a monstrous fusion of love and death arises; such a fusion on the "sublime" plane has its counterpart on the "perverse" plane in the phenomena of pleasure in pain.

One can see how dangerous it would be to confuse everything: normal morality, cruelty (the superego's sadism), need for punishment (the ego's masochism). These three tendencies—the cultural suppression of the instincts, the turning back of sadism against the self, and the intensification of the ego's own masochism—do indeed supplement each other and unite to produce the same effects; but, in principle at least, they are distinct tendencies. The sense of guilt results from a combination of these tendencies in various proportions.

If one reexamines the analyses of *The Ego and the Id* in light of the distinctions proposed in "The Economic Problem of Masochism," it must be said that the above description concerns the sadism of the superego rather than the masochism of the ego or "moral masochism." Is this sadism of the superego as clearly opposed to the normal conscience as the masochism characterized above by the resexualization of the Oedipus complex? It is more difficult to decide this. However, it is significant that in Chapter 5 of *The Ego and the Id* Freud limits himself to describing two guilt maladies, obsessional neurosis and melancholia. He shows more interest in their respective differences than in their shared similarity to ordinary morality. In melancholia the superego reveals itself as a pure culture of the death instinct, to the point of suicide. In obsessional neurosis, on the contrary, the ego is protected from self-destruction because of the transformation of its love-objects into objects of hate; the ego struggles against this hate, which is turned outward and which the ego has not adopted, while at the same time the ego undergoes the assaults of the superego which holds the ego responsible; whence the interminable torments of the ego which has to defend itself on two fronts. Are the torments of the obsessed and the melancholic's cultivation of death as clearly opposed to the desexualization of the normal conscience as masochism was? It seems they are not. But the picture is all the more disquieting, for even if the sadism of the superego is independent of any erotic factor, we are presented with a view in which the death instinct is directly included in the sadism of the superego—the result being what might be called a deathly sublimation. Such a view is suggested by the interrelating of defusion, desexualization, and sublimation. Thus the sadism of the superego represents a sublimated form of destructiveness; in proportion as destructiveness becomes desexualized by delusion, it becomes capable of being mobilized to the advantage of the superego; and at this point it becomes a "pure culture of death." The desexualization of sadism is therefore no less dangerous than the resexualization of masochism.[1]

Such is the frightful discovery: the death instinct, too, can be sublimated. To complete this grim picture it might be added that the instinctual basis of this whole process is essentially the fear of castration. In regard to the last text quoted I would like to call notice to a passing remark Freud makes about the relationship between castration and the fear of conscience (a far-reaching remark, if one remembers the role attributed to the dread of castration in "The Dissolution of the Oedipus Complex"). The remark occurs at the end of *The Ego and the Id:* "The superior being, which turned into the ego ideal, once threatened castration, and this dread of castration is probably the nucleus round which the subsequent fear of conscience has gathered; it is this dread that persists as the fear of conscience" (57).

Thus the fear to which we related the genesis of illusions, the properly human fear, the fear of conscience (*Gewissensangst*), remains unintelligible apart from the death instinct.

Culture as Situated Between Eros and Thanatos
We have not yet considered the broadest impact of the new theory of instincts on the interpretation of culture. The destructiveness of the superego is only one of the components of the individual

---

1 "But since the ego's work of sublimation results in a defusion of the instincts and a liberation of the aggressive instincts in the superego, its struggle against the libido exposes it to the danger of maltreatment and death. In the suffering under the attacks of the superego or perhaps even succumbing to them, the ego is meeting with a fate like that of the protista [protozoa] which are destroyed by the products of decomposition that they themselves have created. From the economic point of view the morality that functions in the superego seems to be a similar product of decomposition" (56-57). [Ricoeur's note]

conscience, on the borderline between the normal and the pathological. The death instinct, however, involves a reinterpretation
of culture itself. [...]

Let us consider the new economic interpretation of culture in
Civilization and Its Discontents.

The interpretation is developed in two phases: first, what can
be said without having recourse to the death instinct; second,
what can be said only after its intervention.

Prior to this turning point, which makes the essay terminate
on the tragedy of culture, the essay advances with calculated
ease. The economics of culture is seen to coincide with what
might be called a general "erotics." The aims pursued by the
individual and those which animate culture appear as figures,
sometimes convergent, sometimes divergent, of the same Eros:
"The process of civilization is a modification which the vital
process experiences under the influence of a task that is set it
by Eros and instigated by Ananke—by the exigencies of reality; and ... this task is one of uniting separate individuals into a
community bound together by libidinal ties" (21: 139). Thus the
same "erotism" forms the internal tie of groups and drives the
individual to seek pleasure and flee suffering—the threefold suffering inflicted upon him by the external world, his own body,
and other men. Cultural development, like the growth of the
individual from infancy to adulthood, is the fruit of Eros and
Ananke, of love and work; we must even say, of love more than
of work, for the necessity of uniting in work in order to exploit
nature is but a small thing compared with the libidinal tie which
unites individuals in a single social body. It seems then, that
the same Eros inspires the striving for individual happiness and
wishes to unite men in ever wider groups. But the paradox soon
appears: as the organized struggle against nature, culture gives
man the power that was once conferred on the gods; but this
resemblance to the gods leaves man unsatisfied: civilization and
its discontents ...

Why this dissatisfaction? On the basis of this general "erotics"
alone one can, no doubt, account for certain tensions between
the individual and society, but not for the grave conflict that
makes culture tragic. For example, one can easily explain the
fact that the family bond resists extension to larger groups; to
enter into the wider circle of life necessarily appears to every
young person as a breaking of the earliest and closest ties; it is

also understandable that something in feminine sexuality resists the transfer of libidinal energy from private sex to social aims. One can adduce many other instances of conflict situations and still not encounter any radical contradictions; it is well known that culture imposes sacrifices in enjoyment upon all sexuality: the prohibition of incest, the proscription of childhood sexuality, the arrogant channelling of sexuality into the narrow paths of legitimacy and monogamy, the insistence upon procreation, etc. But, however painful the sacrifices and however complicated the conflicts, they still do not result in a real antagonism. The most that can be said is, first, that the libido resists with all its force of inertia the task culture lays on it to abandon its old positions, and second, that the libidinal ties that constitute society draw their energy from private sexuality, to the extent of endangering the latter with atrophy. But all of this has so little of the tragic about it that we can dream of a sort of armistice or accord between the individual and the social bond.

And so the question arises again: Why does man fail to be happy? Why is man as a cultural being dissatisfied?

The analysis here reaches its turning point. Confronting man is an absurd commandment: to love one's neighbour as oneself; an impossible demand: to love one's enemies; a dangerous order: to turn the other cheek. These precepts squander love, put a premium on being bad, and lead to ruin anyone imprudent enough to obey them. But the truth behind the irrationality of these imperatives is the irrationality of an instinct that lies outside a simple erotics:

> The element of truth behind all this, which people are so ready to disavow, is that men are not gentle creatures who want to be loved, and who at the most can defend themselves if they are attacked; they are, on the contrary, creatures among whose instinctual endowments is to be reckoned a powerful share of aggressiveness. As a result, their neighbor is for them ... someone who tempts them to satisfy their aggressiveness on him, to exploit his capacity for work without compensation, to use him sexually without his consent, to seize his possessions, to humiliate him, to cause him pain, to torture and to kill him. *Homo homini lupus.*[1] (111)

---

1 "Man is a wolf to man," Latin quip attributed to Plautus (ca. 254-184 BCE), Roman playwright.

The instinct that thus disturbs man's relations with man and requires society to rise as the implacable dispenser of justice is, of course, the death instinct, here identified with the primordial hostility of man toward man.

With the death instinct there appears what Freud hencefor-ward calls an "anticultural instinct." From now on social ties cannot be regarded as a mere extension of the individual libido, as in *Group Psychology and the Analysis of the Ego*. They are the expression of the conflict between instincts:

> Man's natural aggressive instinct, the hostility of each against all and of all against each, opposes this program of civilization. This aggressive instinct is the derivative and the main representa-tive of the death instinct which we have found alongside of Eros and which shares world-dominion with it. And now, I think, the meaning of the evolution of civilization is no longer obscure to us. It must present the struggle between Eros and Death, between the instinct of life and the instinct of destruction, as it works itself out in the human species. This struggle is what all life essentially consists of, and the evolution of civilization may therefore be sim-ply described as the struggle for life of the human species. And it is this battle of the giants that our nursemaids try to appease with their lullaby about Heaven. (122)[1]

Thus culture itself has been transported onto the great cosmic stage of life and death! In return, the "mute" instinct speaks in its main derivative and representative. Prior to a theory of culture death is not yet manifested: culture is its sphere of manifestation; that is why a purely biological theory of the death instinct had to remain speculative; it is only in the interpretation of hate and war that speculation about the death instinct becomes a process of deciphering.

There is thus a progressive revelation of the death instinct at three levels, biological, psychological, cultural. Grasped at first in the complexities of Eros, the death instinct remained masked in its sadistic component; sometimes it reinforced object-libido, sometimes it hypercathected narcissistic libido; its antagonism becomes less and less silent as Eros develops,

---

1 *Eiapopeia vom Himmel* is a quotation from Heine's poem *Deutschland*, Caput 1, Strophe 7.

uniting living matter to itself, then the ego to its object, and finally individuals into ever wider groups. At this last level the struggle between Eros and Thanatos becomes declared war; paraphrasing Freud, one might say that war is the clamour of death. The mythical aspect of the speculation is not thereby lessened, however; death now appears not only demonic but demoniacal: Freud now uses the voice of Mephistopheles to speak of death, just as he invoked Plato's *Symposium* to illustrate Eros.

The rebound of the cultural interpretation of the death instinct on the biological speculation has important effects. The final consequence is an interpretation of the sense of guilt quite different from the interpretation in terms of the individual psychology presented in *The Ego and the Id*. Whereas in that essay the sense of guilt leaned toward the pathological, by reason of the resemblance between the cruelty of the superego and the sadistic or masochistic traits of melancholia and obsessional neurosis, Chapters 7 and 8 of *Civilization and Its Discontents* emphasize, to the contrary, the cultural function of the sense of guilt. The sense of guilt is now seen as the instrument which culture uses, no longer against the libido, but against aggressiveness. The switch of fronts is important. Culture now represents the interests of Eros against myself, the center of deathly egoism; and it uses my own self-violence to bring to naught my violence against others.

This new interpretation of guilt entails a complete shift of emphasis. Seen from the point of view of the ego and in the framework of its "dependent relations" (*The Ego and the Id*, Ch. 5), the severity of the superego appeared excessive and dangerous; this remains true and the task of psychoanalysis stays unchanged in this regard: it always consists in attenuating that severity. But seen from the point of view of culture and what might be called the general interests of humanity, that severity is irreplaceable. Thus there is a need to interrelate the two readings of the sense of guilt. Its economics from the point of view of the individual conscience and its economics from the point of view of the task of culture are complementary. So little is the first reading annulled by the second that Freud restates it at the beginning of Chapter 7 of *Civilization and Its Discontents*. According to the second reading, however, the main renunciation culture demands of the individual is the renunciation not of desire as such but of aggressiveness. Consequently, it is no longer sufficient to define the fear of conscience as the tension between the ego and the superego; it must be transported to the larger scene of love and death: "The sense of guilt," we will now say, "is an expression of the conflict due to ambivalence, of the eternal struggle between Eros and the instinct of destruction or death" (132).

The two readings are not merely superimposed, they mesh with one another: the cultural function of guilt necessarily involves the psychological function of the fear of conscience; from the point of view of the psychology of the individual, the sense of guilt—at least in its quasi-pathological form—appears to be merely the effect of an internalized aggressiveness, of a cruelty taken over by the superego and turned back against the ego. But its complete economics is seen only when the need for punishment is placed in a cultural perspective: "Civilization, therefore, obtains mastery over the individual's dangerous desire for aggression by weakening and disarming it and by setting up an agency within him to watch over it, like a garrison in a conquered city" (123-24).

We are thus at the heart of the "malaise" or "discontent" peculiar to the life of culture. The sense of guilt now internalizes the conflict of ambivalence that is rooted in the dualism of the instincts. Hence, in order to decipher the sense of guilt, one must penetrate to this most radical of all conflicts: "It is very conceivable that the sense of guilt produced by civilization is not perceived as such ... and remains to a large extent unconscious, or appears as a sort of *malaise* [*Unbehagen*], a dissatisfaction [*Unzufriedenheit*], for which people seek other motivations" (135-36). The extraordinary complexity of the sense of guilt is due to the fact that the conflict between instincts is expressed by a conflict at the level of the agencies; this is why the reading of *The Ego and the Id* is not abolished but incorporated into the second reading.

The same may be said about the interpretation of the Oedipus complex, on the scale of the individual or the species. The ambivalence peculiar to the oedipal situation—feelings of love and hatred toward the parental figure—is itself a part of the larger ambivalence between the life and death instincts. Taken by themselves, the various genetic considerations, which Freud worked out at different periods and which concern the killing of the primal father and the institution of remorse, remain somewhat problematic, if for no other reason than the contingency introduced into history by the sense of guilt which at the same time presents itself as a "fatal inevitability" (132). The contingent character of this developmental process as reconstructed by the genetic explanation is softened as soon as this explanation is subordinated to the great conflicts that dominate the course of culture; the family, which serves as the cultural framework for the Oedipus episode, is itself simply a figure of the great enterprise of Eros of forming ties and uniting; hence the Oedipus episode is not the only possible path leading to the institution of remorse.

Thus the reinterpretation of the sense of guilt at the end of *Civilization and Its Discontents* is seen to be the climax in the series of figures of the death instinct. By mortifying the individual, culture places death at the service of love and reverses the initial relationship between life and death. We recall the pessimistic formulas of *Beyond the Pleasure Principle:* "The aim of all life is death"; the function of the instincts of self-preservation "is to assure that the organism shall follow its own path to death ... Thus these guardians of life, too, were originally the myrmidons of death." But the same text, having reached this critical point, turns back upon itself: the life instincts struggle against death. And now culture comes upon the scene as the great enterprise of making life prevail against death: its supreme weapon is to employ internalized violence against externalized violence; its supreme ruse is to make death work against death.

That the theory of culture thus finds its completion in the reinterpretation of the sense of guilt is expressly desired by Freud. Apologizing for the troublesome and unexpected detours of the discussion of the sense of guilt, he states: "This may have spoilt the structure of my paper; but it corresponds faithfully to my intention to represent the sense of guilt as the most important problem in the development of civilization and to show that the price we pay for our advance in civilization is a loss of happiness through the heightening of the sense of guilt" (134).

Freud illustrates this ruse on the part of culture by citing in support of his interpretation the famous line of Hamlet's monologue, "Thus conscience does make cowards of us all." But such "cowardice" is also the death of death; it is the work of the spy whom culture, in the service of Eros, has "garrisoned" at the heart of the individual, as in a conquered city; for, in the last analysis, the "discontent of civilization" is "the sense of guilt produced by civilization" (135).

11. *Open Questions: On Negation, Pleasure, Reality* (1965)[1]
Paul Ricoeur

Interrogations

I would like to pay tribute to Freud by gathering together in this chapter some of the questions he opens up for us but does not completely solve. In spite of the trenchant and even intransigent tone of the master who rarely tolerated disagreement or dissent, the final phase of Freud's doctrine terminates on a number of unresolved questions which we will try to assess in a provisional way:

1. Is it certain that we know the death instinct better as it becomes more manifest and is finally revealed at the level of culture as the instinct of destruction? Don't the biological considerations contain a surplusage of speculation not accounted for in cultural deciphering and which presents matter for further thought? Finally, what is negativity in Freud's doctrine?

2. Must we not also doubt our most confident assertions about pleasure? Throughout, we have regarded pleasure as the "watchman over life"; as such, can it express merely the reduction of tensions? If pleasure is connected with life, and not solely with death, must it not be something more than the psychical sign of the reduction of tensions? Indeed, do we ultimately know what pleasure means?

3. Finally, what about the reality principle, which seems indeed to usher in a wisdom beyond illusion and consolation? How does this lucidity, with its attendant pessimistic austerity, ultimately fit in with the love of life which the drama of love and death seems to call for? Does Freudian doctrine finally find a philosophical unity of tone, or does it remain definitively split between the scientism of its initial hypotheses and the *Naturphilosophie* toward which Eros leads it and which, perhaps, had never ceased being the animating force of this tenacious exploration of the universe of desire?

Such is the meaning of the three questions on which, in my opinion, the final reading of Freud terminates: What is the death instinct and how is it connected with *negativity*? What is pleasure and how is it connected with *satisfaction*? What is reality and how is it connected with *necessity*?

---

1   From *Freud and Philosophy: An Essay on Interpretation* (1965). Trans. Denis Savage. New Haven: Yale University Press, 1970. 310-38.

What is Negativity?

The death instinct is a problematic concept in many respects.

First of all there is the problem of the relationship between speculation and interpretation. No reader can be insensible to the uncertain, winding, and even "limping" (18: 64) character of this speculation and its set of heuristic hypotheses. Freud himself admits he does not know to what extent he believes in them (59). At times he talks about an equation with two unknown quantities (57). Again, he says that the supposition of a tendency to restore an earlier state of things, if comparable to a ray of light in the darkness, is nevertheless "a myth rather than a scientific explanation" (57). No treatise of Freud's is so adventurous as *Beyond the Pleasure Principle.* The reason is clear: all *direct* speculation about the instincts, apart from their representatives, is mythical. Thus the third theory of the instincts is more mythical than the earlier ones, for it claims to reach the very substrate of the instincts. The first concept of libido, sharply distinguished from the ego-instincts, was the unifying concept presupposed by the various vicissitudes or destinies of the instincts; the second concept of libido, covering both object-libido and ego-libido, was wider than the first, for it controlled the various distributions of the libidinal cathexes. The speculation on life and death is an attempt to go beneath these two concepts of libido. The network of "analogies, correlations and connections" involved in the hypothesis is far looser than before (60); the speculation is disproportionate to the phenomenon meant to verify it; Freud admits that the hypothesis of the death instinct may have led him to overestimate the significance of the facts concerning the compulsion to repeat (59). We have seen that all the other facts that contribute to this central phenomenon might also be interpreted in another way.

Thus the remainder of our study operated on the plane of analogical interpretation and consisted in a gradual and piece-meal reconquest of what had first been posited on the speculative plane. But we must be aware of the initial excess of speculation over interpretation; from the standpoint of epistemology, this is the most striking feature of the essay. This excess of speculative meaning is essentially due to the fact that the hypotheses at work are directly metabiological in nature: "Biology is truly a land of unlimited possibilities" (60). But the metabiology is itself more mythological than scientific, in spite of the discussions on Weismann and the death of protozoa. The mythical name of Eros is ready proof that we are closer to the poets than to the scientists, closer to the speculative philosophers than to the critical ones. It is no accident that the only philosophical text quoted is taken from the mythical part of Plato's *Symposium* (Aristophanes' discourse about the primeval androgynous men); it is a "poet-philosopher" who teaches that Eros wishes to reunite what a malicious divinity had divided and set asunder. Further, do we not feel that we are listening to one of the pre-Socratics when Eros is called that "which holds all living things together" (50), "the preserver of all things"? (52)

Why did Freud thus venture, hesitancy matching intransigency, into the area of metabiology, speculation, and myth? It is not enough to say that Freud's theorizing was always in excess of interpretation in every field of investigation. What poses a problem is the quasi-mythological nature of this metabiology. Perhaps it must be supposed that Freud was fulfilling one of his earliest wishes—to go from psychology to philosophy—and that in this way he was setting free the romantic demands of his thought which the mechanistic scientism of his first hypotheses had only masked over.

Thus what is most suspect in this essay is also the most revealing: under a scientific surface, or rather under the coating of a scientific mythology, there advises the *Naturphilosophie* which the young Freud admired in Goethe.

But then, must it now be said that the whole libido theory was already under the control of *Naturphilosophie* and that Freud's entire doctrine is a protest on the part of the nature-philosophy against the philosophy of consciousness? The patient *reading* of desire in its symptoms, its fantasies, and in general its signs never equalled the *hypothesis* of the libido, of instincts, of desire. Freud is in line with those thinkers for whom man is desire before being speech; man is speech because the first semantics of desire is distortion and he has never completely overcome this initial distortion. If this is so, then Freud's doctrine would be animated from beginning to end by a conflict between the "mythology of desire" and the "science of the psychical apparatus"—a "science" in which he always, but in vain, tried to contain the "mythology," and which, ever since the "Project," was exceeded by its own contents. This muffled conflict will make its appearance again at the end of this chapter, no longer at the level of the initial hypotheses, but at the level of final wisdom.

But the excess of meaning of the death instinct, taken in its most speculative expressions, as compared with the whole series of its biological, psychical, and cultural expressions, reveals another problematic aspect of this strange concept. Is it certain that all the meaning it carries is fully brought out in the cultural interpretation? The speculation's excess of meaning as compared with the interpretation does not seem to indicate a defect in the theory; on the contrary, it suggests that the death instinct, which is finally regarded as anticultural destructiveness, may conceal another possible meaning, as we will suggest further on in the investigation of "Negation."

If one reads the series of representatives of the death instinct in the reverse order, one is struck by the disparity between three themes: the inertia of life, the compulsion to repeat, and destructiveness. One begins to suspect that the death instinct is a collective term, an incongruous mixture: biological inertia is not pathological obsession, repetition is not destruction. Our suspicion grows stronger when we consider other manifestations of the negative that are irreducible to destructiveness.

Let us return to the intriguing example of the child's *fort-da* play. This game of making the mother symbolically disappear and reappear consists, no doubt, in the repetition of an affective renunciation; but unlike the dreams that occur in traumatic neurosis, the play repetition is not of a forced or obsessive one. To play with absence is already to dominate it and to engage in active behaviour toward the lost object as lost. Hence, as we asked when we presented Freud's analysis of children's play, do we not discover another aspect of the death instinct, a nonpathological aspect, which would consist in one's mastery over the negative, over absence and loss? And is not this negativity implied in every appeal to symbols and to play?

This question ties in with the question we asked earlier concerning Leonardo's creations. With Freud, we said that the lost archaic object has been "denied" and "triumphed over" by the work of art which recreates the object or rather creates it for the first time by offering it to all men as an object of contemplation (11: 117-18). The work of art is also a *fort-da*, a disappearing of the archaic object as fantasy and its reappearing as a cultural object. Thus, does not the death instinct have as its normal, nonpathological expression, the disappearing-reappearing in which the elevation of fantasy to symbol exists?

This interpretation is not without support in Freud. As a final note to the death instinct we have reserved examination of one of the most remarkable of Freud's short essays, entitled "Die Verneinung" (19: 235-39). The word *Verneinung* ordinarily designates the contrary of *Bejahung—affirmation*; thus the title of the paper is correctly translated as "Negation," for the term purely and simply designates the sense of "no" as opposed to "yes." By a series of meanders Freud ends up expressly linking negation, the "no," with the death instinct.

But just what type of negation is this? Very definitely it is not located in the unconscious; the unconscious, let us remember, contains neither negation, nor time, nor the function of reality. Therefore negation belongs to the system *Cs.*, along with temporal organization, control of action, motor inhibition involved in every thought process, and the reality principle itself. Thus we meet with an unexpected result: there exists a negativity that does not belong to the instincts but defines consciousness, conjointly with time, motor control, and the reality principle.

The first manifestation of this negativity of consciousness is seen in the process of becoming aware of what is repressed. As Freud notes in the opening lines of his paper, when a patient accompanies an association of ideas or a dream fragment with a protestation such as "It's *not* my mother," the negation does not actually belong to the association that has just come into consciousness; it is rather a condition on which the repressed idea may make its way into consciousness: "Negation is a way of taking cognizance of what is repressed; indeed it is already a lifting [*Aufhebung*] of the repression, though not, of course, an acceptance [*Annahme*] of what is repressed" (235-36). Freud can even say that "There is no stronger evidence that we have been successful in our effort to uncover the unconscious than when the patient reacts to it with the words 'I didn't think that,' or 'I didn't (ever) think of that'." The "no" is the certificate of origin—the "Made in Germany"—which attests that the thought belongs to the unconscious. "With the help of the symbol of negation [*Verneinungssymbol*], thinking frees itself from the restrictions of repression and enriches itself with material that is indispensable for its proper functioning." Thus "a negative judgment is the intellectual substitute for repression" (236).

The second function of negation has to do with reality-testing. This new function is actually a continuation of the previous one: we know that the conditions of becoming conscious and those of reality-testing are the same, for they are the conditions that govern the differentiation between the internal and the external. The negative judgment "*A* does not possess the attribute *B*" is truly a judgment of real existence only when it goes beyond the viewpoint of the pleasure-ego, for whom to say "yes" means that it wants to introject into itself what is good, i.e., to "devour" it, and to say "no" means that it wants to eject from itself what is bad, i.e., to "spit it out." The judgment of reality is a sign that the "initial pleasure-ego" (*anfängliches Lust-Ich*) has been replaced by the "definitive reality-ego" (*endgültiges Real-Ich*). The question at this point is not whether what has been perceived (*wahrgenommen*) can be taken (*aufgenommen*) into the ego, but whether something that is in the ego as a presentation can be *rediscovered* in reality. Thus is established the differentiation between a presentation, which is only "internal," and the real, which is also "outside." What place does the "no" have in this testing of reality? The function of negation—implicit in every judgment, even positive ones—lies in the interval between "to find" and "to refind" (*wiederfinden*). A presentation is not an immediate presenting of things, but a re-presentation of things that are absent: "A precondition for the setting up of reality-testing is that objects shall have been lost which once brought real satisfaction." It is against this background of absence, of loss, that presentation offers itself to reality-testing: "The first and immediate aim, therefore, of reality-testing is, not to *find* an object in real perception which corresponds to the one presented, but to *refind* such an object, to convince oneself that it is still there" (238).[1] Thus the interval of negation, separating the original presence from the presentation, makes possible the critical testing from which both a *real* world and a *real* ego emerge. If one compares the three analyses—the *fort-da* in *Beyond the Pleasure Principle*, aesthetic creation in the *Leonardo*,[2] and perceptual judgment in "Negation"—the traits of the function of negativity start to become clear. The disappearing-reappearing of play, the deny-

---

1 The same formulation occurs in the *Three Essays*: "The finding of an object is in fact a redefining of it" (7: 222). [Ricoeur's note]
2 "Leonardo da Vinci and a Memory of His Childhood," SE 11, 1910. 57-137.

ing-overcoming of aesthetic creation, and the losing-refinding of perceptual judgment all share a common operation.

What connection does this negativity have with the death instinct? Here is what Freud writes at the end of "Negation":

> The study of judgment affords us, perhaps for the first time, an insight into the origin of an intellectual function from the interplay of the primary instinctual impulses. Judging is a continuation, along lines of expediency [*zweckmässige*], of the original process by which the ego took things into itself or expelled them from itself, according to the pleasure principle. The polarity of judgment appears to correspond to the opposition of the two groups of instincts which we have supposed to exist. Affirmation—as a substitute for uniting—belongs to Eros; negation—the successor to expulsion—belongs to the instinct of destruction. The general wish to negate, the negativism which is displayed by some psychotics, is probably to be regarded as a sign of defusion [*Entmischung*] of instincts that has taken place through a withdrawal of the libidinal components. But the performance of the function of judgment is not made possible until the creation of the symbol of negation has endowed thinking with a first measure of freedom from the consequences of repression and, with it, from the compulsion of the pleasure principle. (238-39)

Freud does not say that negation is another representative of the death instinct; he only says that negation is genetically derived from it by "substitution," as in general the reality principle is substituted for the pleasure principle (or as a character trait, avarice, for example, is substituted for an archaic libidinal constitution, such as anality). We have no right, then, to draw out of this text more than is warranted and to give it a direct Hegelian translation. We may do this on our own, at our own risk, but not as interpreters of Freud. Freud develops an "economics" of negation and not a "dialectic" of truth and certainty, as in the first chapter of *The Phenomenology of Spirit*. Nonetheless, even within these strict limits this short article makes an important contribution: consciousness implies negation—both in the process of "achieving insight" into its own hidden richness and in the "recognition" of what is real.

It is not surprising that negation is derived from the death instinct by way of substitution. On the contrary, what is surprising is that the death instinct is represented by such an important function which has nothing to do with destructiveness, but rather with the symbolization of play, with esthetic creation, and with reality itself. This discovery is enough to throw into flux the whole analysis of the representatives of instincts. The death instinct is not closed in upon destructiveness, which is, we said, its clamour; perhaps it opens out onto other aspects of the "work of the negative," which remain "silent" like itself.

Pleasure and Satisfaction

What has become of the pleasure principle at the end of the essay that claims to go beyond it?

To raise this question is to ask: Exactly what is "beyond the pleasure principle"? But there is no definite answer to this question—a surprising situation, when one thinks of the title of the treatise itself. In point of fact, it turns out that the "beyond" cannot be found. Not only is there no final answer, but along the way we have lost even a provisional answer. This is not the least "problematic" aspect of the essay.

Let us recall the initial question and its provisional answer prior to the introduction of the death instinct.

The question did have a definite meaning, insofar as one admitted the equivalence between the constancy principle and the pleasure principle. This being granted—and Freud will not seriously question it in *Beyond the Pleasure Principle,* but only in "The Economic Problem of Masochism"—to search for something beyond the pleasure principle is to question whether there exist "tendencies more primitive than it and independent of it," that is, tendencies irreducible to the effort of the psychical apparatus to reduce its tensions and keep them at the lowest level (18: 17).

We had found such a tendency, however, even before the introduction of the death instincts. On the one hand, it was manifested by the compulsion to repeat, which operates in spite of the unpleasure which the repetition revives; on the other hand, it was possible to connect it with a task that is prior to the seeking of pleasure, the task of "binding" free energy. Undoubtedly this tendency and this task are not opposed to the pleasure principle; but at least they do not derive from it.

But now the great roles of death and life come upon the scene. Instead of reinforcing the first result, the introduction of the death instinct destroys it. The death instinct turns out to be the most striking illustration of the constancy principle, of which the pleasure principle is always regarded as a mere psychological double. It is impossible not to relate the tendency "to restore an earlier state of things," which defines the death instinct, with the tendency of the psychical apparatus to maintain the quantity of excitation present in it at the lowest possible level or at least to keep it constant. Must one go so far as to say that the principle of constancy and the death instinct coincide? But then the death instinct, introduced precisely in order to account for the instinctual character of the compulsion to repeat, is not beyond the pleasure principle, but is somehow identical with it.

This further step must be taken, I believe, at least so long as one assumes the equivalence of the pleasure principle and the constancy principle. If pleasure expresses a reduction of tension, and if the death instinct marks a return of living matter to the inorganic, it must be said that pleasure and death are both on the same side. More than once Freud touches on this paradox:

> The dominating tendency of mental life, and perhaps of nervous life in general, is the effort to reduce, to keep constant or to remove internal tension due to stimuli (the "Nirvana principle," to borrow a term from Barbara Low)—a tendency which finds expression in the pleasure principle; and our recognition of the fact is one of our strongest reasons for believing in the existence of death instincts. (55-56)

And further on: "The pleasure principle seems actually to serve the death instincts" (63). The same paradox is touched on in *The Ego and the Id*, where the condition that follows complete sexual satisfaction is compared to dying (19: 47).

But then, it will be asked, what is beyond the pleasure principle? All the terms we have thus far opposed to one another have gone over to the same side, the side of death: constancy, the return to an earlier state of things, pleasure ... And if one considers that the task of "binding" free energy is a preparatory act "which introduces and assures the dominance of the pleasure principle" (18: 62), that task is itself in the service of the pleasure principle and consequently of the death instinct. All the differences are annulled in the general tendency toward annulment.

There remains but one possible answer: if the pleasure principle means nothing more than the principle of constancy, must it not be said that only Eros is beyond the pleasure principle? Eros is the great exception to the principle of constancy. I am well aware that Freud writes that all the instincts are conservative (40); but he adds that the life instincts are conservative to a higher degree in that they are peculiarly resistant to external influences, and, in another sense, that they preserve life itself for a comparatively long period. Further, the hypothesis of a "sexuality of cells" allows one to interpret self-preservation and even narcissism as an "erotic" sacrifice of each cell for the good of the whole body, hence as a manifestation of Eros. Finally and above all, if Eros is "the preserver of all things," it is because it "unites all things." But this enterprise runs counter to the death instinct: "Union with the living substance of a different individual increases those tensions, introducing what may be described as fresh 'vital differences' which must then be lived off" (55). Thus we have the sketch of an answer: that which escapes the principle of constancy is Eros itself, the disturber of sleep, the "breaker of the peace." However, doesn't this proposition destroy the hypothesis that lies at the origin of psychoanalysis, namely that the psychical apparatus is regulated quasi-automatically by the principle of constancy?

Actually, the questioning of the initial theory's key concepts extends even further: what becomes most problematic is the meaning of pleasure itself. In *Beyond the Pleasure Principle* Freud does not explicitly question the earliest equivalence of the entire metapsychology, that of the pleasure principle and the constancy principle; but the conclusions he draws from it after the introduction of the death instincts simply make the equivalence untenable. What is on the side of death is the Nirvana principle, the only faithful translation of the constancy principle into human affectivity. But is the pleasure principle completely contained in the Nirvana principle? The supposition that pleasure and love may not be on the same side in the battle of the giants waged by life and death is difficult to maintain to the very end. How could pleasure remain foreign to the creation of tensions, that is to say, to Eros? Is not this creation what is felt even in the discharge of tension? Must we not say, then, with Aristotle, that pleasure completes an activity, a function, an operation, as a supervenient end? But then what becomes suspect is the definition of pleasure in purely quantitative terms as a simple function of the increase or diminution of a quantity described as tension due to stimulus. Freud began to draw this conclusion in 1924, in "The Economic Problem of Masochism": the pleasure principle, he concedes, is not the same thing as the Nirvana principle; it is only the latter that is "entirely in the service of the death instincts" (19: 160). It must be recognized that "in the series of feelings of tension we have a direct sense of the increase and decrease of amounts of stimulus [*Zunahme und Abnahme der Reizgrössen direkt in der Reihe der Spannungsgefühle empfinden*], and it cannot be doubted that there are pleasurable tensions and unpleasurable relaxations of tensions" (160). Pleasure, then, would be linked to a qualitative characteristic of the excitation itself, perhaps to its rhythm, its temporal rise and fall.

However, Freud limits the extent of this concession by tying the pleasure principle back in with the Nirvana principle; the pleasure principle is a modification imposed by the life instinct. In this way the pleasure principle incontestably remains the "watchman" over life. Its role as watchman or guardian expresses its ties with the principle of constancy, but it is the watchman over life and not over death.

Is this not an admission that the great dualism of love and death also cuts across pleasure? And does it not imply that the reason we do not know what is beyond the pleasure principle is that we do not know what pleasure is?

There are numerous reasons in Freud's own writings for having doubts about our knowledge of the nature of pleasure. In the first place it should not be forgotten that the earliest formulation of the pleasure principle is closely connected with a representation of the psychical apparatus which, as we have repeatedly emphasized, is solipsistic in nature. The topographic-economic hypothesis is solipsistic by construction, but this characteristic never attaches to the clinical facts that the hypothesis translates—the relation to the mother's breast, the father, the family constellation, authorities—nor to the analytic experience, dramatized in the transference, in which interpretation takes place. The very notion of impulse or instinct, more basic than all the auxiliary representations of the topography, is distinct from the ordinary notion of instinct inasmuch as an instinct in the Freudian sense involves other persons. Hence, the final meaning of pleasure cannot be the discharge of tensions within an isolated apparatus; such a definition applies only to the solitary pleasure of autoerotic sexuality. Ever since the "Project" Freud used the word "satisfaction" (*Befriedigung*) for that quality of pleasure that requires the help of others.

But then, if we introduce other persons into the circuit of pleasure, other difficulties appear. The structure of *Wunsch* [wish] has taught us that a wish or a desire is not a tension that can be discharged; desire, as Freud himself describes it, reveals a constitution that is insatiable. The Oedipus drama implies that the child desires the unobtainable (to possess his mother, or to have a child by his mother); the "evil infinitude" that dwells in him cuts him off from satisfaction.

Moreover, if man could be satisfied, he would be deprived of something more important than pleasure-symbolization, which is the counterpart of dissatisfaction. Desire, qua insatiable demand, gives rise to speech. The semantics of desire, which we are focusing upon here, is bound up with this postponement of satisfaction, with this endless mediating of pleasure.

Strangely enough, Freud has a more finely developed conception of the evils that are "the burden of existence" than he has of pleasure. While he continues to speak of pleasure as a discharge of tension, he very sharply distinguishes between unpleasure—the simple contrary of pleasure—and numerous forms of suffering: the trilogy of fear, fright, and anxiety; the threefold fear due to dangers from the external world, from instincts, and from conscience. Even the fear of death is differentiated into biological fear and fear of conscience, the latter being related to the threat of castration. Freud also stresses the malaise or discontent (*Unbehagen*) inherent in man's cultural existence; man cannot be satisfied as a member of culture, for he pursues the death of others, and culture turns against him the torments he inflicted on others. There is something contradictory and impossible about the task of culture: to coordinate the ego's egoistic urge, which is biologically turned toward death, and its altruistic urge toward union with others in the community. Ultimately, what makes for endless dissatisfaction is the unresolvable struggle between love and death. Eros wishes union, but must disturb the peace of inertia; the death instinct wishes the return to the inorganic, but must destroy the living organism. This paradox continues on into the higher stages of civilized life: a strange struggle indeed, for civilization kills us in order to make us live, by using, for itself and against us, the sense of guilt, while at the same time we must loosen its embrace in order to live and find enjoyment.

Thus the empire of suffering is more extensive than that of mere unpleasure: it extends to everything that makes up the harshness of life.

What is the meaning, in Freud's works, of this disparity between the diversity of suffering and the monotony of enjoyment? Does Freud stand in need of completion on this point? Must we somehow distinguish as many degrees of satisfaction as there are degrees of suffering? Must we restore the dialectic of pleasure, sketched by Plato in the *Philebus,* or even the dialectic of pleasure and happiness in the manner of Aristotle's *Ethics?* Or does the pessimism of pleasure make us admit that man's capacity for suffering is richer than his power of enjoyment? In the face of manifold suffering, does man's only recourse lie in unvaried enjoyment and in bearing the excess of suffering with resignation? I am inclined to think that the whole of Freud's work tends toward the second hypothesis. This hypothesis brings us back to the reality principle.

What is Reality?
What is, finally, the reality principle? We left the question in suspension at the end of the first chapter, with the hope of discovering a new dimension in the concept of reality that would correspond to the revision of the pleasure principle imposed by the introduction of the death instinct (19: 160).[1]

Let us briefly recapitulate the earlier analysis. We started from an elementary opposition concerning the "functioning of the psychical apparatus." Insofar as the pleasure principle had a simple meaning, the reality principle likewise was without mystery. Freud's direct and indirect interpretations of the reality principle are all extensions of the single line sketched by the 1911 article, "The Two Principles of Mental Functioning"—the

---

1 "In this way we obtain a small but interesting set of connections. The *Nirvana* principle expresses the trend of the death instinct; the *pleasure* principle represents the demands of the libido; and the modification of the latter principle, the *reality* principle, represents the influence of the external world" (19: 160). [Ricoeur's note]

line of the useful; whereas the pleasure principle is biologically dangerous, the useful represents the organism's true and proper interests. All the various levels of meaning of the reality principle that we went on to consider lie within the limits of this notion of utility. Thus, reality is first of all the opposite of fantasy—it is facts, such as the normal man sees them; it is the opposite of dreams, of hallucination. In a more specifically analytical sense, the reality principle indicates adaptation to time and the demands of life in society; thus reality becomes the correlate of consciousness, and then of the ego. Whereas the unconscious—the id—is ignorant of time and contradiction and obeys only the pleasure principle, consciousness—the ego—has a temporal organization and takes account of what is possible and reasonable.

As may be seen, nothing in this analysis bears a tragic accent; nothing foreshadows the world view dominated by the struggle between Eros and death.

Now, what happens to this simple opposition between desire and reality when it is shifted to the area of the new theory of instincts? This question arises because the first term of the pair, pleasure, vacillates in its most basic meaning, and also because reality contains death. However, the death that reality holds in reserve is no longer the death instinct, but my own death, death as destiny; this is what gives reality its inexorable and tragic sense; because of death-destiny reality is called necessity and bears the tragic name Ananke. Let us ask ourselves, then, to what extent the oldest theme of Freudianism—that of the double functioning of the psychical apparatus—was raised to the level of the great dramaturgy of Freud's later writings.

The fact is that Freud's later philosophy did not truly transform, but rather reinforced and hardened the early characteristics of the reality principle. It is only within very narrow and very strict limits that one may say that the "romantic" theme of Eros transformed the reality principle. But this discrepancy between the relative mythicizing of Eros and the cold consideration of reality deserves attention and reflection: this fine discordance reveals perhaps the essence of the philosophical tone of Freudianism.

While emphasizing the dualism of Eros and death, Freud also emphasized the struggle against illusion, the last entrenchment of the pleasure principle; he thus reinforced what might be called his "scientific conception of the world," the motto of which could be, "beyond illusion and consolation."

The last chapters of *The Future of an Illusion* are very significant in this respect. Religion, Freud states, has no future; it has
exhausted its resources of constraint and consolation. Thus
the reality principle, in which *Totem and Taboo* had already
recognized a stage of human history parallel to a stage of the
libido, becomes the principle that presides over the postreli-
gious age of culture. In this age to come, the scientific spirit
will replace religious motivation and moral prohibitions will
be motivated by social interests alone. Coming back to his earlier views about the excessive demands of the superego, Freud
suggests that, along with their sanctity, commandments will
lose their rigidity and intolerance as well; instead of dreaming
of their abolition, it is possible that man will work toward their
improvement, finding them in the end reasonable and perhaps
even friendly.

All this might make one think of the rationalistic and optimistic prophecies of the last century. But Freud himself objects that
prohibitions have never been founded on reason but on powerful
emotional forces, such as remorse for the primal killing; besides,
was it not Freud who revealed the power of the destructive forces
working against the ethical, and even worse, within the ethical?
Freud is mindful of all this and will express it even more forcefully
a few years later in *Civilization and Its Discontents.* His timid hope
is pinned to a single point: if religion is the universal neurosis of
mankind, it is partly responsible for the intellectual retardation
of mankind; it is as much the expression of the powerful forces
that arise from below as it is their educator. The possibility of a
nonreligious mankind is supported and measured by the parallelism between the growth of mankind and the growth of the
individual: "But surely infantilism is destined to be surmounted.
Men cannot remain children forever; they must in the end go out
into 'hostile life.' We may call this *'education to reality.'* Need I
confess to you that the sole purpose of my book is to point out the
necessity for this forward step?" (21: 49). Such is the restrained
but hazardous optimism underlying this prophecy of the positive age. Addressing himself to a hypothetical opponent [in *The
Future of an Illusion*] who suggests that religion be retained as a
pragmatic illusion, Freud in his reply ventures to give the name
of a god—the god Logos—to the central idea of his sober prophecy; but I think this must be looked upon merely as a bit of irony
inserted in an *ad hominem* argument:

The voice of the intellect is a soft one, but it does not rest till it has gained a hearing. Finally after a countless succession of rebuffs, it succeeds.... Our god, Λόγος [Logos], will fulfill whichever of these wishes nature outside us allows, but he will do it very gradually, only in the unforeseeable future, and for a new generation of men. He promises no compensation for us, who suffer grievously from life.... Our god Λόγος is perhaps not a very almighty one, and he may only be able to fulfill a small part of what his predecessors have promised. If we have to acknowledge this we shall accept it with resignation. (53-54)

This kinship between Logos and Ananke—the twin gods of the Dutch writer Multatuli—excludes all lyricism about the totality. Moreover, a proud closing protestation is meant to set the tone for the whole book: "No, our science is no illusion. But an illusion it would be to suppose that what science cannot give us we can get elsewhere" (56).

This text leaves no doubt; reality has the same meaning at the end of Freud's life as it had at the beginning: reality is the world shorn of God. Its final meaning does not contradict but rather extends the concept of utility, long since opposed to the fictions created by desire. This coherence between the final and the initial meanings is borne out by the plea for this world, on which Freud ends one of the last chapters of *The Future of an Illusion*. Borrowing a couplet from Heine, Freud states: "Then, with one of our fellow-unbelievers (*Unglaubensgenossen*), they will be able to say without regret:

Den Himmel überlassen wir
Den Engeln und den Spatzen" (50).[1]

The notion of reality that results from this critique of religion is the least romantic of ideas and seems to have no connection with the term Eros. Even the word Ananke—as set within this context—seems to designate the visage of reality after reality has been stripped of any analogy with the father figure. If religious illusion stems from the father complex, the "dissolution" of the

---

1 Strachey translates Heine's verse (*Deutschland* [Caput 1]) thus: "We leave Heaven to the angels and the sparrows."

Oedipus complex is attained only with the notion of an order of things stripped of any paternal coefficient, an order that is anonymous and impersonal. Ananke is therefore the symbol of disillusion. This was the sense in which I believe the term made its first appearance in the *Leonardo* (11:125), even before *Totem and Taboo*. Ananke is the name of nameless reality, for those who have "renounced their father." It is also chance, the absence of relationship between the laws of nature and our desires or illusions.

Is this Freud's final statement on the matter? The very expression "resignation" or "submission" to Ananke points to a total wisdom that is more than the mere reality principle, psychologically considered as the perceptual testing of reality. Is it not the case that it is only when reality is accepted with resignation that it becomes Ananke?

Ananke, it seems to me, is a symbol of a world view, and not merely the symbol of a principle of mental functioning; in it is summed up a wisdom that dares to face the harshness of life. Such wisdom is an art of "bearing the burden of existence," according to Schiller's remark cited in *Beyond the Pleasure Principle*.

One can thus find in Freud the sketch of a Spinozistic meaning of reality, a meaning that is connected, as in the great philosopher, with an ascesis of desire restricted to the body's perspective and with an ascesis of the imaginative knowledge arising from that perspective; is not necessity the second kind of knowledge, knowledge according to reason? And if there is in Freud—we shall go on to discuss this point—the first step of a reconciliation in the form of resignation, is this not an echo of the third kind of knowledge? This sketch, it is true, is so little developed philosophically, that one might just as well speak of a love of fate in a Nietzschean sense. The touchstone of the reality principle, thus interpreted philosophically, would be the victory of the love of the whole over my narcissism, over my fear of dying, over the resurgence in me of childhood consolations.

Let us essay this "second wave," as Plato would have said, taking as our clue the gap the previous analysis kept widening—in spite of the continuity of meaning—between mere perceptual reality-testing and resignation to the inexorable order of nature. Without forcing the texts, I wish simply to gather together certain remarks, certain signs and tentative indications, that broaden this respect for nature in such a way that the reality principle is brought in harmony with the themes of Eros and death.

Perhaps the most direct approach to the theme of resignation is through the question of death, or rather of dying. Resignation is basically a working upon desire that incorporates into desire the necessity of dying. Reality, insofar as it portends my death, is going to enter into desire itself.

In 1899 Freud recalled the phrase of Shakespeare: "Thou owest Nature a death" (Freud, *Origins* 276).[1] He alludes to it again at the beginning of the second essay of "Thoughts for the Times on War and Death," written shortly after the outbreak of World War I (Freud, *Standard* 14: 275-300).

The natural tendency of desire, he explains, is to put death to one side, to exclude it from the purview of life; desire has the conviction of its own immortality. Such an attitude is an aspect of the absence of contradiction in the unconscious. And so we disguise death in innumerable ways, reducing it from a necessity to a chance event. But in return, "life is impoverished, it loses in interest, when the highest stake in the game of living, life itself, may not be risked" (290). Thus paralyzed, when we exclude death from life, we no longer understand the proud motto of the Hanseatic League: *Navigare necesse est, vivere non necesse* ("It is necessary to sail the seas, it is not necessary to live"). We content ourselves with dying fictionally with our heroes of literature and the theatre, while preserving our lives intact.

When Freud wrote these lines he had in mind the lie war deals to this conventional treatment of death; and he dared to write: "Life has, indeed, become interesting again; it has recovered its full content" (291). Of course, Freud knew how odious a remark from the home front, from a noncombatant, could be. What mattered to him was the attainment—through the cruelty of the remark—of truthfulness. When death is acknowledged as the termination of life, finite life recovers its significance.

But the recognition of death is obscured by the fear of death no less than by the disbelief on the part of our unconscious concerning our own death; the fear of death has a different source: it is a by-product of the sense of guilt (297). At the end of *The Ego and the Id*, Freud will state even more firmly: "I believe that

---

1   The actual line in Shakespeare runs: "Thou owest God a death" (*Henry IV*, V. i.126).

the fear of death is something that occurs between the ego and the superego.... These considerations make it possible to regard the fear of death, like the fear of conscience, as a development [*Verarbeitung*] of the fear of castration" (19: 58). The fear of death is therefore no less an obstacle than the invulnerability of the unconscious which proclaims, "Nothing can happen to *me*." If it be added, finally, that we quite readily put to death enemies and strangers, it appears that the number of inauthentic attitudes in the face of death is considerable; the immorality of the id, the fear of death stemming from guilt, the urge to kill—these are so many screens between the destined meaning of death and ourselves. One thus sees that the acceptance of death is a task: *Si vis vitam, para mortem.* If you want to endure life, be prepared for death (14: 300).

But then, just what is resignation?

The integration of death into life is symbolically proposed to us by "The Theme of the Three Caskets" (12: 291-300), that admirable short essay Ernest Jones[1] was so fond of. The third casket, neither of gold nor silver but of lead, contains the portrait of the bride; the suitor who chooses it will also have the beautiful girl as his wife. But if the caskets are women, according to a well-known dream symbol, cannot this comic theme be related to the tragic theme of old King Lear who, to his own ruin, does not choose the third daughter, Cordelia, who was the only one that really loved him? A survey of folklore and literature discloses a series of "the choice of the third woman": the Aphrodite of the Judgment of Paris, Cinderella, the Psyche of Apuleius ... But who is the third woman? The fairest one, of course, but also the one who "loves and is silent." Now, in dreams, dumbness is a common symbol of death. Hence, are not the three sisters the Moerae, the Fates, the third of whom is called Atropos, the inexorable? If the comparison is correct, "the third woman" signifies that man realizes the full seriousness of the laws of nature only when he has to submit to them by accepting his own death.

It will be objected, however, that no one chooses death, nor did Paris choose death, but the most beautiful of women!

---

1 Ernest Jones (1879-1958), the first English-speaking psychoanalyst. Jones presided over both the British Psycho-Analytical Society and the International Psychoanalytic Association and wrote the "official" biography of Freud in the 1950s.

Substitution, replies Freud: our wishes substitute for death its contrary, beauty, perhaps in accordance with the confusion of contraries in the unconscious; but above all in accordance with the primeval identity of life and death preserved in the myth of the Great Goddess. But if the most beautiful woman is the substitute for death, what does it mean to choose death? Again a substitution, under the dominance of desire: instead of accepting the worst, we substitute the choice of the best. Freud's answer merits quotation:

> Here again there has been a wishful reversal. Choice stands in the place of necessity, of destiny. In this way man overcomes death, which he has recognized intellectually. No greater triumph of wish-fulfillment is conceivable. A choice is made where in reality there is obedience to a compulsion; and what is chosen is not a figure of terror, but the fairest and most desirable of women. (12: 299)

If, then, Shakespeare achieves a profound effect upon us in *King Lear*, it is because he has known how to revert to the primeval myth: if one does not choose the fairest woman, one is necessarily driven to the third, to unhappiness and death. But that is not all: the relation between death and women is still not clear; once again it is Shakespeare who discloses it: Lear is both the lover and the dying man: Lear is doomed to death, yet he insists on being told how much he is loved. What is, then, the relation between death and woman? The third woman, we said, is death; but if the third woman is death, one must also say, conversely, that death is the third woman, the third form or figure of woman: after the mother, after the beloved mate chosen on the pattern of the mother, finally "the Mother Earth who receives him once more" (301).

Does this mean that man can "choose death and make friends with the necessity of dying" (301) only through regression to the mother figure? Or is it to be understood that the woman figure must become the figure of death for man, so as to cease being fantasy and regression? Freud's final words do not provide a clear answer: "But it is in vain that an old man yearns for the love of a woman as he had it first from his mother: the third of the Fates alone, the silent Goddess of Death, will take him into her arms" (301).

Of course, one might add, along the lines of *The Future of an Illusion,* that the true acceptance of death is distinct from a regressive return in fantasy to the mother's breast only if that acceptance has stood the test of a scientific view of the world. I think this is Freud's actual thought. Even in a Freudian perspective, however, the answer does not completely exhaust the problem; resignation to the ineluctable is not reducible to a mere knowledge of necessity, i.e., to a purely intellectual extension of what we called perceptual reality-testing; resignation is an affective task, a work of correction applied to the very core of the libido, to the heart of narcissism. Consequently, the scientific world view must be incorporated into a history of desire.

The appeal to the poets, to Shakespeare in *King Lear,* invites us to try another path equally familiar to Freud, the path of art. We did not [earlier in *Freud and Philosophy*] exhaust the resources of Freud's esthetics when we treated the work of art from the standpoint of artistic creation. Because of its analogical character, the investigation of aesthetic phenomena remained cautious and fragmentary: the work of art entered the field of psychoanalysis as the analogue of dreams and the neuroses. Nevertheless we did gain two insights into the specificity of works of art: by means of the forepleasure (or pleasure bonus) that the artist's technique offers us, profound sources of tension are liberated; on the other hand, through symbolism, the fantasies of the abolished past are recreated in the light of day.

If we now take up these fragmentary insights from the point of view of the task of culture defined above—to diminish instinctual charges, to reconcile the individual with the ineluctable, to compensate for irreparable losses through substitute satisfactions—it is reasonable to ask whether art, now considered from the standpoint of the user or viewer, does not derive its meaning from its intermediate position between illusion represented by religion and reality represented by science. Might it not be that the task of reconciliation and compensation, withdrawn from religion, devolves upon this intermediate function? Is not art an aspect of the education to reality spoken of in the 1911 article, "The Two Principles of Mental Functioning"?

To understand the esthetic function in Freud one would have to locate the exact place of the *seduction* or *charm* of the work of art on the path leading from the pleasure principle to the reality principle. It is certain that Freud's severity toward religion is equaled only by his sympathy for the arts. Illusion is the way of regression, the "return of the repressed." Art, on the contrary, is the nonobsessional, non-neurotic form of substitute satisfaction; the "charm" of esthetic creations does not stem from the memory of parricide. We recall our earlier analysis of forepleasure or the incentive bonus: the artist's technique creates a formal or esthetic pleasure which brings about a general lowering of the thresholds of inhibition and thereby enables us to enjoy our fantasies without shame. No fictive restoration of the father enters in here to make us regress toward the submissive state of childhood. Instead, we play with the resistances and impulses and in this way achieve a general relaxation of our conflicts. Freud comes very close here to the cathartic tradition of Plato and Aristotle.

What is the relation, then, between esthetic seduction and the reality principle? Freud explicitly treats this point in the 1911 article. In Paragraph 6 he says that art brings about a reconciliation between the two principles in a peculiar way: the artist, like the neurotic, is a man who turns away from reality because he cannot come to terms with the renunciation of instinctual satisfaction that reality demands, and who transposes his erotic and ambitious desires to the plane of fantasy and play (12: 24). By means of his special gifts, however, he finds a way back to reality from this world of fantasy: he creates a new reality, the work of art, in which he himself becomes the hero, the king, the creator he desired to be, without having to follow the roundabout path of making real alterations in the external world. In this new reality other men feel at home because they "feel the same dissatisfaction as he does with the renunciation demanded by reality, and because that satisfaction, which results from the replacement of the pleasure principle by the reality principle, is itself part of reality."

As may be seen, if art initiates the reconciliation between the pleasure and the reality principles, it does so mainly on the basis of the pleasure principle. In spite of his great sympathy for the arts, Freud has none for what might be described as an esthetic world view. Just as he distinguishes esthetic seduction from religious illusion, so too he lets it be understood that the esthetic—or, to be more exact, the esthetic world view—goes only halfway toward the awesome education to necessity required by the harshness of life and the knowledge of death, an education impeded by our incorrigible narcissism and by our thirst for childhood consolation.

I will give only one or two indications of this. In his interpretation of humor, at the end of his book *Jokes and the Unconscious*, Freud seemed to make much of the ability to create pleasure as a substitute for the release of painful affects. The humor that smiles through tears, and even the dreadful gallows humor (according to which the rogue, who was being led out to execution on a Monday, says: "Well, this week's beginning nicely") seemed to have some credit in his eyes. Interpreted economically, the pleasure of humor arises from an economy in the expenditure of painful feelings. Yet, a brief remark in the 1905 text sets us on guard:

> We can only say that if someone succeeds, for instance, in disregarding a painful affect by reflecting on the greatness of the interests of the world as compared with his own smallness, we do not regard this as an achievement of humour but of philosophical thought, and if we put ourselves into this train of thought, we obtain no yield of pleasure. (8: 233)

In 1927, Freud wrote a separate short paper entitled "Humour," which is much more severe, and in which he extends humor to all the sentiments of the sublime. Humor elevates us above misfortune only by saving our narcissism from disaster:

> The grandeur in it clearly lies in the triumph of narcissism, the victorious assertion of the ego's invulnerability. The ego refuses to be distressed by the provocations of reality, to let itself be compelled to suffer. It insists that it cannot be affected by the traumas of the external world; it shows, in fact, that such traumas are no more than occasions for it to gain pleasure.... Humour is not resigned; it is rebellious. It signifies not only the triumph of the ego but also of the pleasure principle, which is able here to assert itself against the unkindness of the real circumstances. (21: 161-66)

And where does humor get this power of withdrawal and rebellion? From the superego, which condescends to allow the ego a small yield of pleasure. Freud concludes: "In bringing about the humorous attitude, the superego is actually repudiating reality and serving an illusion.... And finally, if the superego tries, by means of humor, to console the ego and protect it from suffering, this does not contradict its origin in the parental agency."

I am well aware that one cannot judge the whole of art and all of the arts by such a narrow feeling as humor. Still, we had found that humor seems to be a point where the pleasure of esthetic seduction borders on philosophical resignation. It is precisely at this point that Freud opposes a strong negation, as if he said to us: The acceptance of life and death? Yes, but not so cheaply! Everything in Freud implies that true resignation to necessity, active and personal resignation, is the great work of life and that such a work is not of an esthetic nature.

But if art cannot take the place of wisdom, it does lead to it in its own way. The symbolic resignation of conflicts through art, the transfer of desires and hatreds to the plane of play, day-dreams, and poetry, borders on resignation; prior to wisdom, while waiting for wisdom, the symbolic mode proper to the work of art enables us to endure the harshness of life, and, suspended between illusion and reality, helps us to love fate.

Let us make a final effort to reach the undiscoverable point in Freud's work where his early and unchanged view concerning the reality principle would be rejoined by his later views concerning the struggle between Eros and Death. Must we leave these two lines of thought unconnected—the one which I will call the path of disillusion, the other that of the love of life? Is it possible that the acceptance of reality has nothing to do with "the battle of the giants"? If the meaning of culture is a struggle of the human species for existence, if love is to be the stronger of the two, what is the meaning of the acceptance of death in relation to the enterprise of Eros? Does not the acceptance of death have to overcome a final counterfeit which would be precisely the death instinct, the wish to die, *against which* Eros is aimed?

I see nothing explicit along these lines in Freud's writings except for some early allusions in the *Leonardo* and a few remarks in *The Ego and the Id* and *Civilization and Its Discontents*. Leonardo's conversion of libido into intellectual curiosity, into the scientific investigation of the external world, teaches us that the force of reflection must express the power of loving, for otherwise it will kill the libido and itself fall into decline; Leonardo himself neither lived nor created according to the standard of the hymn he addresses to "the sublime law of nature (*O mirabile necessità*)" (11: 75). Whereas Faust transformed intellectual curiosity back into an enjoyment of life, Leonardo devoted himself to investigation rather than to loving; and Freud observes: "Leonardo's development approaches Spinoza's mode of thinking" (75)—which would imply that Freud was not satisfied with Spinoza's intellectual love. He continues:

> Lost in admiration and filled with true humility, he all too easily forgets that he himself is a part of those active forces and that in accordance with the scale of his personal strength the way is open for him to try and alter a small portion of the destined course of the world—a world in which the small is still no less wonderful and significant than the great. (76)

Does this mean that the knowledge of necessity, separated from Eros, is also lost in an impasse? Is the sublimation of the libido into the instinct for research, as in the case of Leonardo, already in betrayal of Eros? Which is the true twin of Ananke—is it Logos, as described at the end of *The Future of an Illusion*, or Eros, as implied in the *Leonardo*? Should we not once again pay heed to the old androgynous myths, evoked in the *Leonardo* (93-98), which signify the primal creative force of nature? Do they not say the same thing as the myth of the *Symposium*, cited at length in *Beyond the Pleasure Principle*, the myth of the primeval confusion of the sexes? In short, does not Eros strive to convert the reality principle also, just as it transformed the pleasure principle? Let us listen once more to the *Leonardo*:

> We all still show too little respect for Nature which (in the obscure words of Leonardo which recall Hamlet's lines) "is full of countless causes that never enter experience." (*La natura è piena d'infinite ragioni che non furono mai in isperienza.*) Every one of us human beings corresponds to one of the countless experiments in which these *ragioni* of nature force their way into experience. (137)

This was the final statement of the *Leonardo*.

If these lines have a meaning, do they not say that what is greater than the reality principle, understood as the scientific view of the world, is the respect for nature and for the "countless causes" that "force their way into experience"? But nothing indicates that Freud finally harmonized the theme of the reality principle with the theme of Eros—the first being an essentially critical theme directed against archaic objects and illusions, the second an essentially lyrical theme of the love of life and thus a theme directed against the death instinct. In Freudianism there is undoubtedly no "beyond the reality principle," as there is a "beyond the pleasure principle"; but there is a concurrence of scientism and romanticism. Freud's philosophical temperament consists perhaps in this delicate equilibrium—or subtle conflict?—between lucidity free of illusion and the love of life. It is perhaps in the resignation to death that this equilibrium finds its most fragile expression; but here death figures twice and with different meanings: lucidity without illusion invites me to accept my death, that is to say, to regard it as one of the necessities of blind nature; but Eros, which wishes to unite all things, calls upon me to struggle against the human instinct of aggression and self-destruction, hence never to love death, but to love life, in spite of my death. It would seem that Freud never unified his early world view, expressed from the beginning in the alternation of the pleasure principle and the reality principle, with the new world view, expressed by the struggle of Eros and Thanatos. That is why he is neither Spinoza nor Nietzsche.

Let us give Freud the last word—which is also his concluding remark in *Civilization and Its Discontents*: "And now it is to be expected that the other of the two 'Heavenly Powers,' eternal Eros, will make an effort to assert himself in the struggle with his equally immortal adversary" (21: 145).[1]

12. *Sadism, Masochism, and the Death Instinct* (1967)[2]
Gilles Deleuze

Of all the writings of Freud, the masterpiece which we know as *Beyond the Pleasure Principle* is perhaps the one where he engaged most directly—and how penetratingly—in specifically philosophical reflection. Philosophical reflection should be understood as "transcendental," that is to say concerned with a particular kind of investigation of the question of principles. It soon becomes

---

1 In 1931, when the menace of Hitler was beginning to be apparent, Freud added a final sentence terminating the work in the second edition: "But who can foresee with what success and with what result?" (Freud, *Standard* 21: 145) [Ricoeur's note]
2 From *Masochism* (1967). New York: Zone, 1991. 111-21.

apparent that in *Beyond the Pleasure Principle*, Freud is not really preoccupied with the exceptions to that principle; they are not what he means by the "beyond" of the title. All the apparent exceptions which he considers, such as the unpleasure and the circuitousness which the reality principle imposes on us, the conflicts which cause what is pleasurable to one part of us to be felt as unpleasure by another, the games by means of which we try to reproduce and to master unpleasant experiences, or even those functional disturbances or transference phenomena from which we learn that wholly and unequivocally unpleasurable events are nevertheless reproduced with obstinate regularity—all these are treated by Freud as merely apparent exceptions which could still be reconciled with the pleasure principle. In other words there are no exceptions to the principle—though there would indeed seem to be some rather strange complications in the workings of pleasure. This is precisely where the problem arises, for though nothing contradicts the pleasure principle and everything can always be reconciled with it, it is far from obvious that it can account for all the various elements and processes which go to make its application so complicated. Everything might well be governed by the pleasure principle without therefore being finally dependent on it, and since the demands of the reality principle are no more adequate to account for the complications involved, these being more often the products of fantasy, we must conclude that the pleasure principle, though it may rule over all, does not have the final or highest authority over all. There are no exceptions to the principle but there is a residue that is irreducible to it; nothing contradicts the principle, but there remains something which falls outside it and is not homogeneous with it—something, in short, *beyond....*

At this point we need to resort to philosophical reflection. What we call a principle or law is, in the first place, that which governs a particular field; it is in this sense that we speak of an empirical principle or a law. Thus we say that the pleasure principle governs life universally and without exception. But there is another and quite distinct question, namely in virtue of what is a field governed by a principle; there must be a principle of another kind, a second-order principle, which accounts for the necessary compliance of the field with the empirical principle. It is this second-order principle that we call transcendental. Pleasure is a principle insofar as it governs our psychic life. But we must still ask what is the highest authority which subjects our psychic life to the dominance of this principle. Already Hume[1] had remarked that though psychic life clearly exhibits and distinguishes between pleasures and pains, we could never, no matter how exhaustively we examined our ideas of pain and pleasure, derive from them a *principle* in accordance with which we seek pleasure and avoid pain. We find Freud saying much the same: we continually encounter pleasures and pains in psychic life, but they are found scattered here and there in a free state, "unbound." That the pleasure principle should nevertheless be so organized that we systematically seek pleasure and avoid pain makes it imperative that we should look for a higher type of explanation. For there is in short *something* that the pleasure principle cannot account for and that necessarily falls outside it, namely its own particular status, the fact that it has dominance over the whole of psychic life. In virtue of what higher connection—what "binding" power—is pleasure a principle, with the dominance that it has? Freud's problem, we may say, is the very opposite of what it is often supposed to be, for he is concerned not with the exceptions to the principle but with its *foundation*. His problem is a transcendental one: the discovery of a transcendental principle—a problem, as Freud puts it, for "speculation."

Freud's answer is that the binding of excitation alone makes it "resolvable" into pleasure, that is to say makes its discharge possible. Without the process of binding, discharges and pleasures would still no doubt occur but only in a scattered, haphazard manner, with no systematic value. It is the binding process which makes pleasure as the principle of mental life possible. Eros thus emerges as the foundation of the pleasure-principle behind the twin aspects of the binding process—the energetic which binds excitation, and the biological which binds the cells (the first being perhaps dependent on, or at least helped by specially favourable conditions obtaining in the second). The "binding" action of Eros, which is constitutive of the pleasure principle may, and indeed must, be characterized as "repetition"—repetition in

---

1   David Hume (1711-76), Scottish empiricist philosopher. The second book of Hume's *Treatise of Human Nature* (1739), "Of the Passions," is sometimes regarded as a work of protopsychology insofar as it attempts to trace the effects of the passions on human thought and behavior.

respect of excitation, and repetition of the *moment* of life, and the necessary union—necessary indeed even in the case of unicellular organisms.

It is in the nature of a transcendental inquiry that we cannot break it off when we please. No sooner have we reached the condition or ground of our principle than we are hurled headlong beyond to the absolutely unconditioned, the "ground-less" from which the ground itself emerged. Musil (1880-1942) wrote: "What fearful power, what awesome divinity is repetition! It is the pull of the void that drags us deeper and deeper down like the ever-widening gullet of a whirlpool.... For we knew it well all along: it was none other than the deep and sinful fall into a world where repetition drags one down lower and lower at each step...."[1] We remarked earlier that repetition characterized the binding process inasmuch as it is repetition of the very moment of excitation, the moment of the emergence of life; repetition is what holds together the instant; it constitutes *simultaneity*. But inseparable from this form of the repetition we must conceive of another which in its turn repeats *what was before the instant* —before excitation disturbed the indifference of the inexcitable and life stirred the inanimate from its sleep. How indeed could excitation be bound and thereby discharged except by this double action of repetition, which on the one hand binds the excitation and on the other tends to eliminate it? Beyond Eros we encounter Thanatos; beyond the ground, the abyss of the groundless; beyond the repetition that links, the repetition that erases and destroys. It is hardly surprising that Freud's writings should be so complex; sometimes he suggests that repetition is one and the same agency, acting now demonically, now beneficently, in Thanatos and in Eros; elsewhere he contradicts this by insisting on the strictest qualitative difference between Eros and Thanatos, the difference being that between union, the construction of ever larger units, and destruction; elsewhere again he tones down the strictly dualistic hypothesis by suggesting that what probably underlies the qualitative difference is a difference in rhythm and amplitude, a difference on a time-scale—according as repetition is repetition *at* the origination of life, or before. It

---

1   Musil, *The Man without Qualities*. [Deleuze's note] This passage does not seem to be included in the English translation of this work.

should be understood that repetition as conceived by Freud's genius is in and of itself a synthesis of time—a "transcendental" synthesis. It is at once repetition of *before, during* and *after,* that is to say it is a constitution in time of the past, the present and even the future. From a transcendental viewpoint, past, present and future are constituted in time *simultaneously,* even though, from the natural standpoint, there is between them a qualitative difference, the past following upon the present and the present upon the future. Hence the threefold determination which we brought out in Freud's treatment: a monism, a qualitative dualism and a difference in rhythm. If it is possible to add the future (i.e., *after*) to the other two dimensions of repetition (i.e., *before* and *during*), it is because these two correlative structures cannot constitute the synthesis of time without immediately opening up to and making for the possibility of a future in time. To repetition that binds—constituting the present—and repetition that erases—constituting the past—we must add a third, that saves or fails to save, depending on the modes of combination of the other two. (Hence the decisive role of transference as a progressive repetition which liberates and saves—or fails.)

We saw that repetition came before the pleasure principle as the unconditioned condition of the principle. If we now return to experience, we find that the order is reversed, and repetition subordinated to the principle; it is now at the service of the pleasure, since we tend to repeat what has been found to be pleasurable, or is anticipated to be. Our transcendental inquiry showed that while Eros is what makes possible the establishment of the empirical pleasure principle, it is always necessarily and inseparably linked with Thanatos. Neither Eros nor Thanatos can be given in experience; all that is given are combinations of both—the role of Eros being to bind the energy of Thanatos and to subject these combinations to the pleasure principle in the id. This is why Eros, although it is no more given in experience than Thanatos, at least makes its presence felt; it is an active force. Whereas Thanatos, the ground-less, supported and brought to the surface by Eros, remains essentially silent and all the more terrible. Thanatos *is*; it is an absolute. And yet the "no" does not exist in the unconscious because destruction is always presented as the other side of a construction, as an instinctual drive which is necessarily combined with Eros.

What then is the meaning of *defusion* of the instincts? We may put it differently and ask what becomes of the combination of the instincts when we no longer consider the id but the ego, the superego and their complementarity. Freud showed how the formation of the narcissistic ego and of the superego both implied a "desexualization." A certain quantity of libido (Eros-energy) is neutralized, and becomes undifferentiated and freely mobile. The desexualization process would seem to be profoundly different in each case: in the first it is the equivalent of a process of *idealization,* which can perhaps constitute the power of the imagination in the ego; in the second it is the equivalent of *identification,* which would constitute the power of thought in the superego. Desexualization has two possible effects on the workings of the pleasure principle: either it introduces functional disturbances which affect the application of the principle, or else it promotes a sublimation of the instincts whereby pleasure is transcended in favour of gratifications of a different kind. In any case it would be a mistake to view defusion in terms of invalidation of the pleasure principle, as though the combinations that are subject to it were destroyed in favour of the emergence of Eros and Thanatos in their pure form. Defusion, with respect to the ego and the superego, simply means the formation of this freely mobile energy within the various combinations. The pleasure principle in itself is not in the least invalidated, however serious the disturbances which may affect the function responsible for its application. (Thus Freud could still maintain his wish-fulfillment theory of the dream, even in those cases of traumatic neurosis where the dream function is most seriously perturbed.) Nor is the pleasure principle overturned by the renunciations which reality imposes upon it, or by the spiritual extensions brought about by sublimation. We may never encounter Thanatos; its voice is never heard; for life is lived through and through under the sway of the empirical pleasure principle and the combinations that are subject to it—though the formulae governing the combinations may vary considerably.

Is there no other solution besides the functional disturbance of neurosis and the spiritual outlet of sublimation? Could there not be a third alternative which would be related not to the functional interdependence of the ego and the superego, but to the structural split between them? And is not this the very alternative indicated by Freud under the name of perversion? It is remarkable that the process of *desexualization* is even more pronounced than in neurosis and sublimation; it operates with extraordinary coldness; but it is accompanied by a *resexualization* which does not in any way cancel out the desexualization, since it operates in a new dimension which is equally remote from functional disturbances and from sublimations: it is as if the desexualized element were resexualized but nevertheless retained, in a different form, the original desexualization; the desexualized has become in itself the object of sexualization. This explains why coldness is the essential feature of the structure of perversion; it is present both in the apathy of the sadist, where it figures as theory, and in the ideal of the masochist, where it figures as fantasy. The deeper the coldness of the desexualization, the more powerful and extensive the process of perverse resexualization; hence we cannot define perversion in terms of a mere failure of integration. Sade[1] tried to demonstrate that no passion, whether it be political ambition, avariciousness, etc., is free from "lust"—not that lust is their mainspring but rather that it arises at their culmination, when it becomes the agent of their instantaneous resexualization. (Juliette, when she discoursed on how to maximize the power of sadistic projection, began by giving the following advice: "For a whole fortnight abstain from all lustful behaviour; distract and entertain yourselves with other things....") Although the coldness of the masochist is totally different from the sadist's, the desexualization process in masochism is equally the precondition of instantaneous resexualization, as a result of which all the passions of man, whether they concern property, money, the State, etc., are transformed and put at the service of masochism. The crucial point is that resexualization takes place instantaneously, in a sort of leap. Here again, the pleasure principle is not overthrown, but retains its full empirical dominance. The sadist derives pleasure from other people's pain, and the masochist from suffering pain himself as a necessary precondition of pleasure. Nietzsche stated the essentially religious problem of the meaning of pain and gave it the only fitting answer: if pain

---

1   Marquis de Sade (1740-1814), French nobleman and writer, renowned for his scandalous libertine lifestyle and equally controversial erotic writings. The term "sadism"—as the derivation of pleasure from the pain of others—is coined from his name.

and suffering have any meaning, it must be that they are enjoyable to someone. From this viewpoint there are only three possibilities: the first, which is the "normal" one, is of a moral and sublime character; it states that pain is pleasing to the gods who contemplate and watch over man; the other two are perverse and state that pain is enjoyable either to the one who inflicts it or to the one who suffers it. It should be clear that the normal answer is the most fantastic, the most psychotic of the three. So far as the structure of perversion is concerned, given that the pleasure principle must retain its dominance here as elsewhere, we must ask what has happened to the combinations which are normally subject to the principle. What is the significance of the resexualization, the *leap*? Earlier we became aware of the particular role played by the function of *reiteration* in masochism no less than in sadism: it takes the form of quantitative accumulation and precipitation in sadism and qualitative suspense and "freezing" in masochism. In this respect the manifest content of the perversion is liable to obscure the deeper issues, for the apparent link of sadism with pain and the apparent link of masochism with pain are in fact subordinate to the function of reiteration. Evil as defined by Sade is indistinguishable from the perpetual movement of raging molecules; the crimes imagined by Clairwil[1] are so intended as to ensure perpetual repercussions and liberate repetition from all constraints.

Again, in Saint-Fond's system, the value of punishment lies solely in its capacity for infinite reproduction through the agency of destructive molecules. In another context we noted that masochistic pain depends entirely on the phenomenon of waiting and on the functions of repetition and reiteration which characterize waiting. This is the essential point: *pain only acquires significance in relation to the forms of repetition which condition its use.* This is pointed out by Klossowski [1905-2001], when he writes with reference to the monotony of Sade: "The carnal act can only constitute a transgression if it is experienced as a spiritual event; but in order to apprehend its object it is necessary to circumscribe and reproduce that event in a reiterated description

---

1 Clairwil and Saint-Fond are debauched characters in Sade's novel *Histoire de Juliette ou les Prospérités du vice*, published anonymously in 1797-1801. Sade was arrested and, without trial, jailed for the remaining thirteen years of his life.

of the carnal act. This reiterated description not only accounts for the transgression but it is in itself a transgression of language by language." Or again when he emphasizes the role of repetition, in relation this time to masochism and the frozen scenes of masochism: "Life reiterating itself in order to recover itself in its fall, as if holding its breath in an instantaneous apprehension of its origin" (Klossowski *Funeste* 127; *Révolution* 17).

Such a conclusion would nevertheless seem to be disappointing, insofar as it suggests that repetition can be reduced to a pleasurable experience. There is a profound mystery in the *bis repetita*.[1] Beneath the sound and fury of sadism and masochism the terrible force of repetition is at work. What is altered here is the normal function of repetition in its relation to the pleasure principle: instead of repetition being experienced as a form of behaviour related to a pleasure already obtained or anticipated, instead of repetition being governed by the idea of experiencing or reexperiencing pleasure, repetition runs wild and becomes independent of all previous pleasure. It has itself become an idea or ideal. Pleasure is now a form of behaviour related to repetition, accompanying and following repetition, which has itself become an awesome, independent force. Pleasure and repetition have thus exchanged roles, as a consequence of the instantaneous leap, that is to say the twofold process of desexualization and resexualization. In between the two processes the Death Instinct seems about to speak, but because of the nature of the leap, which is instantaneous, it is always the pleasure principle that prevails. There is a kind of mysticism in perversion: the greater the renunciation, the greater and the more secure the gains; we might compare it to a "black" theology where pleasure ceases to motivate the will and is abjured, disavowed, "renounced," the better to be recovered as a reward or consequence, and as a law. The formula of perverse mysticism is coldness and comfort (the coldness of desexualization, on the one hand, and the comfort of resexualization, on the other, the latter being clearly illustrated by Sade's characters). As for the anchoring of sadism and masochism in pain, this cannot really be understood so long as it is considered in iso-

---

1 "Bis repetita placent" is Latin, meaning "Things twice repeated are pleasing."

lation: pain in this case has no sexual significance at all; on the contrary it represents a desexualization which makes repetition autonomous and gives it instantaneous sway over the pleasures of resexualization. Eros is desexualized and humiliated for the sake of a resexualized Thanatos. In sadism and masochism there is no mysterious link between pain and pleasure; the mystery lies in the desexualization process which consolidates repetition at the opposite pole to pleasure, and in the subsequent resexualization which makes the pleasure of repetition seemingly proceed from pain. In sadism no less than in masochism, there is no direct relation to pain: pain should be regarded as an *effect* only.

13. *Freud's Mystic Writing Pad* (1967)[1]
Jacques Derrida

All that Freud had thought about the unity of life and death [...] should have led him to ask other questions here. And to ask them explicitly. Freud does not explicitly examine the status of the "materialized" supplement which is necessary to the alleged spontaneity of memory, even if that spontaneity were differentiated in itself, thwarted by a censorship or repression which, moreover, could not act on a perfectly spontaneous memory. Far from the machine being a pure absence of spontaneity, its *resemblance* to the psychical apparatus, its existence and its necessity bear witness to the finitude of the mnemic spontaneity which is thus supplemented. The machine—and, consequently, representation—is death and finitude *within* the psyche. Nor does Freud examine the possibility of this machine, which, in the world, has at least begun to *resemble* memory, and increasingly resembles it more closely. Its resemblance to memory is closer than that of the innocent Mystic Pad: the latter is no doubt infinitely more complex than slate or paper, less archaic than a palimpsest; but, compared to other machines for storing archives, it is a child's toy. This resemblance—i.e., necessarily a certain Being-in-the-world of the psyche—did not happen to memory from without, any more than death surprises life. It founds

---

1 From *Writing and Difference* (1967). Trans. Alan Bass. Chicago: University of Chicago Press, 1978. 227-29.

memory. Metaphor—in this case the analogy between two apparatuses and the possibility of this representational relation—raises a question which, despite his premises, and for reasons which are no doubt essential, Freud failed to make explicit, at the very moment when he had brought this question to the threshold of being thematic and urgent. Metaphor as a rhetorical or didactic device is possible here only through the solid metaphor, the "unnatural," historical production of a *supplementary* machine, *added to* the psychical organization in order to supplement its finitude. The very idea of finitude is derived from the movement of this supplementarity. The historico-technical production of this metaphor which survives individual (that is, generic) psychical organization, is of an entirely different order than the production of an intrapsychical metaphor, assuming that the latter exists (to speak about it is not enough for that), and whatever bond the two metaphors may maintain between themselves. Here the question of *technology* (a new name must perhaps be found in order to remove it from its traditional problematic) may not be derived from an assumed opposition between the psychical and the nonpsychical, life and death. Writing, here, is *techne*—as the relation between life and death, between present and representation, between the two apparatuses. It opens up the question of technics: of the apparatus in general and of the analogy between the psychical apparatus and the nonpsychical apparatus. In this sense writing is the stage of history and the play of the world. It cannot be exhausted by psychology alone. That which, in Freud's discourse, opens itself to the theme of writing results in psychoanalysis being not simply psychology—nor simply psychoanalysis.

Thus are perhaps augured, in the Freudian breakthrough, a beyond and a beneath of the closure we might term "Platonic." In that moment of world history "subsumed" by the name of Freud, by means of an unbelievable mythology (be it neurological or metapsychological: for we never dreamed of taking it seriously, outside of the question which disorganizes and disturbs its literalness, the metapsychological fable, which marks perhaps only a minimal advance beyond the neurological tales of the *Project*), a relationship to itself of the historico-transcendental stage of writing was spoken without being said, thought without being thought: was written and simultaneously erased, metaphorized; designating itself while indicating intrawordly relations, it *was represented*.

This may perhaps be recognized (*as an example and let this be understood prudently*) insofar as Freud too, with admirable scope and continuity, *performed for us the scene of writing*. But we must think of this scene in other terms than those of individual or collective psychology, or even of anthropology. It must be thought in the horizon of the scene/stage of the world, as the history of that scene/stage. Freud's language is *caught up* in it.

Thus Freud performs for us the scene of writing. Like all those who write. And like all who know how to write, he let the scene duplicate, repeat, and betray itself within the scene. It is Freud then whom we will allow to say what scene he has played for us. And from him that we shall borrow the hidden epigraph which has silently governed our reading.

In following the advance of the metaphors of path, trace, breach, of the march treading down a track which was opened by effraction through neurone, light or wax, wood or resin, in order violently to inscribe itself in nature, matter, or matrix; and in following the untiring reference to a dry stylus and a writing without ink; and in following the inexhaustible inventiveness and dreamlike renewal of mechanical models—the metonymy perpetually at work on the same metaphor, obstinately substituting trace for trace and machine for machine—we have been wondering just what Freud was doing.

And we have been thinking of those texts where, better than anywhere else, he tells us *worin die Bahnung sonst besteht*. In what pathbreaking consists.

Of the *Traumdeutung* ["Interpretation of Dreams"]: "It is highly probable that all complicated machinery and apparatuses occurring in dreams stand for the genitals (and as a rule male ones), in describing which dream-symbolism is as indefatigable as the joke-work *(Witzarbeit)*" (Freud, *Standard* 5: 356).

Then, of *Inhibitions, Symptoms, and Anxiety*: "As soon as writing, which entails making a liquid flow out of a tube onto a piece of white paper, assumes the significance of copulation, or as soon as walking becomes a symbolic substitute for treading upon the body of mother earth, both writing and walking are stopped because they represent the performance of a forbidden sexual act" (20: 90).

14. *"A Decisive Correction": Non-Repressive Progress and Freud's Instinct Theory* (1970)[1]
Herbert Marcuse

To summarize: progress itself, according to its explicit concept, is laden with disturbing activity, transcendence for its own sake, unhappiness, and negativity. It becomes an unavoidable question whether the negativity inherent in the principle of progress is perhaps the motive force of progress, the force that makes it possible. Or, to formulate it in another way that establishes the link to Freud: Is progress necessarily based on unhappiness and must it necessarily remain connected to unhappiness and the lack of gratification? John Stuart Mill (1806-73) once said: "Nothing is more certain than that all improvement in human affairs is without exception the work of discontented characters." If this is true, then inversely it can also be said—and this would be in the strictest sense the other face of this idea of progress—that contentment, gratification, and peace may afford happiness, but in a definite sense they are unsuited for progress; that war in the sense of the struggle for existence is the father of all progressive inventions, which then incidentally and often at a late date contribute to the improvement and gratification of human needs, and that both lack of fulfillment and suffering have been the permanent impulse to all of the previous work of civilization.

Here we come to the center of the problem as posed by Freud. According to him, happiness is as little a product of civilization as is freedom. Happiness and freedom are incompatible with civilization. The evolution of civilization is based on the suppression, limitation, and repression of sensual, instinctual wishes and is unthinkable without a repressive modification of the instincts. This follows from what according to Freud is a very clear and unchangeable principle, namely that the human organism is originally ruled by the "pleasure principle" and wants nothing but to avoid pain and obtain pleasure, and that civilization cannot afford this principle. Because men are too weak and the human environment too poor and cruel, the denial and suppression of instincts became from the beginning fundamental conditions of all the unpleasurable work, the denials

---

1 From *Five Lectures* (1970). Trans. Jeremy J. Shapiro and Shierry M. Weber. Beacon Press: Boston, 1970. 32-43.

and renunciations that, as repressively transformed instinctual energy, make the progress of civilization at all possible. The pleasure principle must be replaced by the "reality principle" if human society is to progress from the animal to the human level. I have formulated this so emphatically only to counteract once more, in passing, the widespread misunderstanding that Freud is in any sense an irrationalist. There is perhaps no more rationalistic thinker of the past decades than Freud, whose entire endeavor is aimed at showing that the irrational forces that still operate in men must be subjected to reason if human conditions are to improve in any way, and whose statement, "Where id was, ego shall develop" is perhaps the most rational formulation I can imagine finding in psychology (see Freud *Standard* 22).

Why does civilization require that the reality principle overcome the pleasure principle? What actually is the reality principle as the principle of progress? According to Freud's later instinct theory, which will be the basis of my argument here, the organism with its two basic instincts, Eros and the death instinct, cannot be socialized as long as these instincts remain uncontrolled. As such they are unsuited for the construction of a human society in which a relatively secure satisfaction of needs is to be possible. Eros, when uncontrolled, strives for nothing further than obtaining more intensive and perpetual pleasure, and the death instinct, if uncontrolled, is simple regression to the state that preceded birth and therefore tends toward the annihilation of all life. Thus, for culture and civilization to emerge, the pleasure principle has to be replaced by another principle, one which makes society possible and sustains it: the reality principle. This is, according to Freud, nothing other than the principle of productive renunciation developed as the system of all of the modifications, denials, diversions, and sublimations of instinct that society must impose on individuals in order to transform them from bearers of the pleasure principle into socially utilizable instruments of labor. In this sense the reality principle is identical with the principle of progress, because it is through the repressive reality principle that instinctual energy first becomes released for unpleasurable labor, for labor that has learned to renounce, to deny instinctual wishes and that can become and remain socially productive only in this way.

What is the psychic result of the rule of the reality principle? The repressive transformation of *Eros*, which begins with the incest taboo, leads, even in early childhood, to fundamentally overcoming the Oedipus complex and therewith to the internalization of the father's domination. At this time the decisive modification of Eros under the reality principle occurs: its transformation into sexuality. Eros is originally more than sexuality in the sense that it is not a partial instinct but rather a force that governs the entire organism and that only later is put into the service of reproduction and localized as sexuality. This decisive modification of Eros means a desexualization of the organism, and only this change can make the organism as bearer of the pleasure principle into an organism that is a possible instrument of labor. The body becomes free for the expenditure of energy that otherwise would only have been erotic energy. It becomes, so to speak, free of the integral Eros that originally governed it and thereby free for unpleasurable labor as the content of life. To the extent that individuals themselves are affected by it, the repressive transformation of the fundamental psychic structure is the individual psychological basis of the work of civilization and of progress in culture. Its result is not only the conversion of the organism into an instrument of unpleasurable labor but also and above all the devaluation of happiness and pleasure as ends in themselves, the subordination of happiness and gratification to social productivity without which there is no progress in civilization. With this devaluation of happiness and instinctual gratification and their subordination to socially tolerable satisfaction, however, occurs the transformation and progression from the human animal to the human being, the progression from the necessity of mere instinctual gratification, which is not really enjoyment, to the reflective behavior and *mediated* enjoyment characteristic of and particular to man.

What is the result of the repressive modification of the death instinct? Here, too, the first step is the incest taboo. The final deprival of the mother enforced by the father signifies the permanent mastery of the death instinct, the Nirvana principle, and its subordination to the life instincts. For the incestuous desire for the mother also contains the ultimate goal of the death instinct, regression to the painless, need-less, and in this sense pleasurable state before birth, which becomes instinctually more desirable the more unpleasurable and painful the experience of life itself becomes. The remaining energy of the death instinct is then made socially useful in two ways. As socially useful destructive energy it is directed outwards, that is, the goal of the death instinct is no longer the annihilation of one's own life through regression, but of other life: the annihilation of nature in the form of the domination of nature and the annihilation of socially sanctioned enemies inside and outside the nation. But almost more important than this external licensing of the death instinct is an internal one. It consists in the utilization of destructive energy as social morality, as conscience, which is localized in the superego and carries out the demands and claims of the reality principle against the ego. The result of the social transformation of the death instinct is thus destruction. In the forms of useful aggression and the domination of nature destruction is one of the main sources of work in civilization. As moral aggression, unified in conscience as the claims of morality against the id, it is an equally indispensable factor of civilization.

It is crucial that through the repressive modification of instincts, and through it alone, progress in civilization becomes not only possible but also automatic. Once the former has been successfully achieved, the latter is reproduced by the instinctually modified individuals themselves. But just as progress becomes automatic through the repressive modification of instincts, so it cancels itself and negates itself. For it prohibits the enjoyment of its own fruits and in turn, precisely through this prohibition, it augments productivity and thus promotes progress. More precisely, this peculiar and antagonistic dynamic of progress comes into being as follows. Progress is only possible through the transformation of instinctual energy into the socially useful energy of labor, that is, progress is only possible as sublimation. Sublimation, however, is only possible as expanded sublimation. For, once it is in effect, it is subject to its own dynamic, which extends the sphere and intensity of sublimation. Under the reality principle the libido diverted from originally pleasurable but socially useless or even harmful instinctual goals becomes social productivity. As such it improves the material and intellectual means for the gratification of human needs. But at the same time it denies men the full enjoyment of these goods because it is *repressive* instinctual energy and has already so preformed men that they do not know how to value life except in accordance with the hierarchy of values that rejects enjoyment, peace, and gratification as goals or subordinates them to productivity. With the growth of the quantum of energy stored up through renunciation comes a growth of productivity that does not lead to individual gratification. The individual denies himself the enjoyment of productivity and thereby provides the resources for new productivity, propelling the process to an ever higher level both of production and of the renunciation of what is produced. This psychic structure reflects the specific organization of progress in advanced industrial society. We can speak here of a *vicious circle of progress*. The rising productivity of social labor remains linked to rising repression, which itself in turn contributes to raising productivity. Or, put another way, progress must continually negate itself in order to remain progress. Inclination must continually be sacrificed to reason, happiness to transcendental freedom, in order that through the promise of happiness men can be maintained in alienated labor, remain productive, keep themselves from the full enjoyment of their productivity, and thereby perpetuate productivity itself.

The self-renunciation in the principle of progress is not, I grant, formulated by Freud in this manner. But I am convinced that it is grounded in Freudian theory and appears perhaps most strikingly in the dialectic of patriarchal authority as explained by Freud. This process is of decisive import for the concept of progress. Freud's hypothesis about the origins of human history, regardless of its possible empirical content, compresses the *dialectic of domination*, its origins, transformation, and development in the progress of civilization into a unique image. Its main features are known. Human history begins with a primal horde in which the strongest, the primal father, rose to autocracy and stabilized his domination by monopolizing woman, the mother of mothers, for himself and excluding all other members of the horde from their enjoyment. And that means that neither nature nor poverty nor weakness compels the first suppression of instincts, which is the most important one for the evolution of culture, but rather the despotism of domination: the fact that a despot unequally distributes and exploits poverty, scarcity, and weakness, that he reserves enjoyment for himself and imposes labor on the other members of the horde. This first, still prehistoric step in instinctual repression compels the second: the rebellion of the sons against the father's despotism. According to Freud's hypothesis the father is killed by the sons and devoured in a communal funeral feast. The first attempt to liberate the instincts and to generalize instinctual gratification, to eliminate the despotic, hierarchical, and privileged distribution of happiness and labor, is liberation from domination.

It ends, according to Freud, when the rebellious sons or brothers see, or think they see, that they cannot do without domination and that the father was not really dispensable, no matter how despotically he ruled. The father is now voluntarily reestablished by the sons and, as it were, generalized—as morality. That is, the brothers freely impose upon themselves the same instinctual renunciations and denials that the father had previously imposed upon them. Culture and civilization begin with this internalization of paternal domination, which is the origin of morality and conscience. The human-animalistic primal horde has become the first and the most primitive human society. The repression of instincts becomes the voluntary achievement of individuals and is internalized. At the same time patriarchal domination is established as the many fathers who—each for himself—carry over the morality of patriarchal domination and therefore instinctual repression to their own clans or groups, where they are implanted in the young generation.

This dynamic of domination, which begins with the institution of despotism, leads to revolution and ends after the first attempt at liberation with the reestablishment of the father in internalized and generalized form, i.e., rational form, repeats itself, according to Freud, during the entire history of culture and civilization, although in diluted form. It does so as the rebellion of all sons against all fathers in puberty, as the disavowal of this rebellion after overcoming puberty, and finally as the integration of the sons into the social framework in voluntary subjection to socially required instinctual renunciation, whereby the sons themselves become fathers. This psychological repetition of the dynamic of domination in civilization finds its world-historical expression in the ever recurring dynamic of revolutions in the past. These revolutions manifest an almost schematic development. Insurrection succeeds and certain forces attempt to drive the revolution to its extreme point, from which the transition to new, not only quantitatively but qualitatively different conditions could perhaps proceed. At this point the revolution is usually vanquished and domination is internalized, reestablished, and continued at a higher level. If Freud's hypothesis is really legitimate, then we can raise the question whether alongside the socio-historical Thermidor that can be demonstrated in all past revolutions there is not also a *psychic* Thermidor. Are revolutions perhaps not only vanquished, reversed, and unmade from outside, is there perhaps in individuals themselves already a dynamic at work that *internally* negates possible liberation and gratification and that supports external forces of denial?

If the repression of instincts, even according to the Freudian hypothesis, is not only a natural necessity, if it has its roots at least just as much and perhaps primarily in the interest of domination and the maintenance of despotic authority, if the repressive reality principle is not only a result of historical reason without which no progress would have been possible, but above and beyond this the result of a particular historical form of domination; then we must in fact undertake a decisive correction of Freudian theory. For if the repressive modification of the instincts, which has until now constituted the main psychological content of the concept of progress, is neither naturally necessary nor historically immutable, then it has its quite definite limit. This becomes apparent after instinctual repression and progress have fulfilled their historical function and mastered the condition of human impotence and the scarcity of goods, and when a free society for all has become a real possibility. The repressive reality principle becomes superfluous in the same measure that civilization approaches a level at which the elimination of a mode of life that previously necessitated instinctual repression has become a realizable historical possibility. The achievements of repressive progress herald the abolition of the repressive principle of progress itself. It becomes possible to envisage a state in which there is no productivity resulting from and conditioning renunciation and no alienated labor: a state in which the growing mechanization of labor enables an ever larger part of the instinctual energy that had to be withdrawn for alienated labor to return to its original form, in other words, to be changed back into energy of the life instinct. It would no longer be the case that time spent in alienated labor occupied the major portion of life and the free time left to the individual for the gratification of his own needs was a mere remainder. Instead, alienated labor time would not only be reduced to a minimum but would disappear and life would consist of free time.

Crucial here is the comprehension that such a development is not equivalent to an extension and increase of present conditions and relations. Instead a *qualitatively different reality principle* would replace the repressive one, transmuting the entire human-psychic as well as socio-historical structure. What really happens when this state, today still repudiated as utopia, becomes continually more real? What happens when more or less total automation determines the organization of society and reaches into all areas of life? In depicting the consequences I keep to the fundamental Freudian concepts. The first consequence would be that the force of the instinctual energy released by mechanized labor would no longer have to be expended on unpleasurable activity and could be changed back into erotic energy. A reactivation would be possible of all those erotic forces and modes of behavior that were blocked off and desexualized under the repressive reality principle. I should like to emphasize sharply, because the greatest misunderstanding is possible on this point, that sublimation would not cease but instead, as erotic energy, would surge up in new forces of cultural creation. The result would not be pansexualism; which rather belongs to the image of repressive society (for pansexualism is conceivable only as an explosion of repressive instinctual energy, not as the fulfillment of non-repressive instinctual energy). To the extent that erotic energy were really freed, it would cease to be mere sexuality and would become a force that determined the organism in all its modes of behavior, dimensions, and goals. In other words the organism would be able to admit what it could not admit under the repressive reality principle. Striving for gratification in a happy world would be the principle according to which human existence would develop.

The order of values of a non-repressive principle of progress can be determined on almost all levels in opposition to that of its repressive counterpart. Men's basic experience would be no longer that of life as a struggle for existence but rather that of the enjoyment of life. Alienated labour would be transformed into the free play of human faculties and forces. In consequence all contentless transcendence would come to a close, and freedom would no longer be an eternally failing project. Productivity would define itself in relation to receptivity, existence would be experienced not as continually expanding and unfulfilled becoming but as existence or being with what is and can be. Time would not seem linear, as a perpetual line or rising curve, but cyclical, as the return contained in Nietzsche's idea of the "perpetuity of pleasure."

You can see that the non-repressive principle of progress along with its own order of values is in a fundamental sense conservative. And none other than Freud himself stressed that in their innermost nature the instincts are conservative. What they really want is not unending and eternally unsatisfying change, not striving for what is endlessly higher and unattained, but rather a balance, a stabilization and reproduction of conditions within which all needs can be gratified and new wants only appear if their pleasurable gratification is also possible. If, however, this striving for gratification according to the conservative nature of the instincts can fulfill itself in actual existence under a non-repressive principle of progress, then one of the main objections against its possibility becomes invalid, namely the assertion that, once a pacified state were attained, men would no longer have any motivation to work and would degenerate to the dull, static enjoyment of whatever they could have without work. The exact opposite seems to be the case. Incentives to work are no longer necessary. For if work itself becomes the free play of human abilities, then no suffering is needed to compel men to work. Of themselves, and only because it fulfills their own needs, they will work at shaping a better world in which existence fulfills itself.

The hypothesis of a civilization governed by a non-repressive principle of progress, in which work becomes play, has been suggested, interestingly enough, by just those thinkers in the tradition of Western thought who can in no other respect be considered as representatives and propagandists of sensuality, pansexualism, or the inadmissible liberation of radical tendencies. I shall mention only two examples.

In his letters *On the Aesthetic Education of Man* Schiller[1] developed the idea outlined here in Freudian terms of an aesthetic, sensuous civilization in which reason and sensuality are reconciled. The crucial thought is that of the transformation of labor into the free play of human faculties as the authentic goal of existence, the only mode of existence worthy of man. Schiller emphasizes that this idea can only be realized at a level of civilization on which the highest development of intellectual and mental capacities goes hand in hand with the presence of the material means and goods for the gratification of human needs.

Another thinker, who can be suspected even less than can Schiller of being the spokesman of pansexualism or the unjustified liberation of instincts and who is perhaps one of the —at least traditionally—most repressive thinkers, namely Plato, has expressed this idea in its perhaps most radical form: and in

---

1 Johann Christoph Friedrich von Schiller (1759-1805), German poet, playwright, and philosopher. Together with Goethe, Schiller founded the famed Weimar Theater.

the book that of all his books is by far the most repressive, in which the idea of a totalitarian state is presented in unequalled detail. Precisely in this context he said the following (the discussion is about the determination of what existence is actually the most worthy of man, and the Athenian speaks):

> Why, I mean we should keep our seriousness for serious things, and not waste it on trifles, and that, while God is the real goal of all beneficent serious endeavour, man, as we said before, has been constructed as a toy for God, and this is, in fact, the finest thing about him. All of us, then, men and women alike, must fall in with our role and spend life in making our *play* as perfect as possible—to the complete inversion of current theory.... It is the current fancy that our serious work should be done for the sake of our play; thus it is held that war is serious work which ought to be well discharged for the sake of peace. But the truth is that in war we do not find, and we never shall find, either any real play or any real education worth the name, and *these* are the things I count supremely serious for such creatures as ourselves. Hence it is peace in which each of us should spend most of his life and spend it best. What, then, is our right course? We should pass our lives in the playing of games—*certain* games, that is, sacrifice, song, and dance—with the result of ability to gain heaven's grace, and to repel and vanquish an enemy when we have to fight him.... (Plato, *Laws* 1375)

The interlocutor has exactly the same reaction that we have. For he says, "... You have but a poor estimate of our race." The Athenian answers, "Do not be amazed by that, Megillus. Bear with me. I had God before my mind's eye, and felt myself to be what I just said." You see that Plato is being perhaps more serious than ever, when at this point, in a consciously provocative formulation, he celebrates and defines work as play and play as the main content of life, as the mode of existence most worthy of man.

In conclusion I should like to defend myself against the reproach that I hope you have long been addressing to me, that we live in a reality that has nothing to do with the happiness presented here but is rather in all its aspects its exact opposite and promises to remain so, and that in this condition it is unjustified and irresponsible to portray a utopia in which it is asserted that modern industrial society could soon reach a state in which the principle of repression that has previously directed its development will prove itself obsolete. Certainly the contrast of this utopia with reality can scarcely be imagined as greater than it now is. But perhaps the very extent of this gap is a sign of its limit. The less renunciation and denial are biologically and socially necessary, the more must men be made the instruments of repressive policies that restrain them from realizing the social potentialities they would otherwise think of by themselves. It may be less irresponsible today to depict a utopia that has a real basis than to defame as utopia conditions and potentials that have long become realizable possibilities.

15. *Economic Paradox of the Death Drive* (1970)[1]
Jean Laplanche

Beyond the Pleasure Principle, which in 1920, one year after "A Child Is Being Beaten," introduces the death drive, remains the most fascinating and baffling text of the entire Freudian *corpus*. Never has Freud shown himself to be as profoundly *free* and as audacious as in that vast metapsychological, metaphysical, and metabiological fresco. Terms which are entirely new appear: Eros, the death drive, the repetition compulsion. Old and apparently forgotten ideas, in particular those of the *Project for a Scientific Psychology*, are taken up again and renewed. More than ever, the problem of Freud's "biologism" exercises, in this text, a global pressure: what is the function of recourse to the life sciences, manifest at times as unrestrained speculation, at others, as a series of references to precise experimentation? A dialectical move "beyond" *Beyond the Pleasure Principle*, if it is to be convincing, will be possible only after the meaning of that biologism has been elucidated.

★★★

Profoundly baffling, Freud's discourse is only sporadically and superficially subordinated to logical imperatives: it constitutes a mode of thought that is free (in the sense of free associations), is undertaken "in order to see," and implies a series of "about-faces," acts of virtual repentance, and denials. *That* (equally attractive) counterpart of the freedom of Freud's style of inquiry may well disappoint the

---

1 From *Life and Death in Psychoanalysis* (1970). Trans. Jeffrey Mehlman. Baltimore: Johns Hopkins, 1976. 106; 107; 110-11; 122-24.

reader who fails to identify with that style: the holes in the reasoning constitute so many traps; the sliding of concepts results in blurring terminological points of reference; the most far-reaching discussions are suddenly resolved in the most arbitrary manner. If one resists the inherent movement of the text, one may derive the impression that every question in it is poorly posed and in need of reformulation.

Seductive and traumatic as it was, the forced introduction of the death drive could only provoke on the part of Freud's heirs every conceivable variety of defence: a deliberate refusal on the part of some; a purely scholastic acceptance of the notion and of the dualism: Eros-Thanatos on the part of others; a qualified acceptance, cutting the notion off from its philosophical basis, by an author like Melanie Klein;[1] and, most frequently of all, a passing allusion to or a total forgetting of the notion.

★★★

A hypothesis emerges that calls everything into question. A hypothesis? It is presented without restraint, with arguments of every kind, frequently borrowed from fields outside of psychoanalytic practice, calling to the rescue biology, philosophy, and mythology. The argument progresses through a series of interruptions, obstinately following the details of a scientific debate only in order to abandon it abruptly, like an unlucky gambler who suddenly kicks over the table. We are thinking here of the extremely long and highly documented discussion of the problem of the immortality of the living cell in the light of experiments on protista, in which abruptly, when the reader has an impression that an examination of the various theses would end up refuting the existence of an *internal* tendency towards death, Freud breaks off his argument with an *ad hoc* invocation of the metaphysics of entities:

It becomes a matter of complete indifference to us whether natural death can be shown to occur in protozoa or not.... The drive forces which seek to conduct life into death may also be operating in protozoa from the first, and yet their effects

---

1 Psychoanalyst Melanie Klein (1882-1960), one of the founders of object relations theory although deeply committed to the death drive theory. Klein is perhaps best known for using traditional psychoanalytic methods with young children. See Appendix B7, 175.

may be so completely concealed by their life-preserving forces that it may be very hard to find any direct evidence of their presence.... But even if protista turned out to be immortal in Weismann's sense, his assertion that death is a late acquisition would apply only to its *manifest* phenomena and would not make impossible the assumption of processes *tending* towards it. (Freud, *Standard* 18: 48)[1]

This hypothesis is presented under the cover of an extremely "liberal" argument: the universal right to pursue a train of thought as far as one wants, the sovereign freedom to philosophize and to dream.

Soon, however, the *Zwang* [compulsion] appears; the metaphysical reverie becomes dogma, as much for Freud as in relation to his disciples: "To begin with it was only tentatively that I put forward the views I have developed here, but in the course of time they have gained such a hold upon me that I can no longer think in any other way" (21: 119).

A second and opposite index of the same *Zwang*: this veritable dogma, which seems ineluctable at the level of the systematicity of Freud's thought, has only a relatively slight repercussion on the totality of his work as soon as that work moves closer to clinical practice: the new "dualism" is poorly integrated into the theory of conflict, in which the old oppositions of drives subsist, while the death drive is invoked as a last recourse and generally remains in the background: "Theoretical speculation [as opposed to 'empirical analysis'] leads to the suspicion that there are two fundamental drives which lie concealed behind the manifest ego-drives and object-drives" (20: 265).

---

1   The discussion of biological experiments on the survival of unicellular organisms in a suitably nourishing milieu resulted in the conclusion that the organisms would perish only if the milieu was not periodically purged of the toxins produced by the cellular metabolism. Freud sees this as proof that "an infusorian ... if it is left to itself, dies a natural death owing to its incomplete voidance of the products of its own metabolism" (Freud, *Standard* 48). Thus the cell dies for "internal reasons provided that we leave it in the midst of its wastes—that is, provided that we enlarge the organism so that it includes its surroundings. In this kind of argument we recognize the metaphorical pendant of the internalization—in trauma—of the "irreconcilable" drive and of the element of strife that it conveys. [Laplanche's note]

The pleasure principle, radicalized as the Nirvana principle, was discovered and is valid only at the level of ideational representatives, and cannot be merged haphazardly—lest the most utter confusion ensue for psychoanalysis—with apparently similar principles observed within the "vital order."

And yet it is indeed with principles from the vital order that Freud, from the very beginning, would establish a kind of continuity. It is to them that, in *Beyond the Pleasure Principle,* he attributes, as a tendency towards death, a repetition compulsion whose major piece of supporting evidence is, however, the psychoanalytic phenomenon par excellence: transference. We are thus posing the most difficult question when we inquire as to the internal exigency that leads Freud to carry back to the biological level two theses that can be justified only in relation to the discovery of psychoanalysis.

To be sure, the necessity of *affirming the primal or originary,* both in the form of the "individual myth"[1] and in historical or prehistorical myth, may be identified as one of the fundamental, founding orientations of Freud's thought. And asserting the biological myth of the emergence of a living form from a chaos of energy is indeed tantamount to projecting into the same dimension, beyond our grasp, the individual event effecting the coagulation—within what we can imagine only with difficulty under the rubric of the primary process—of the first nucleus of an ego.

And yet if we consider that this carrying back of the present into the past, of ontogeny into phylogeny, is also, in the case at hand, a carrying back of death into life, we are hard put to avoid a more specific interpretation of that movement towards the originary. It is as though there were in Freud the more or less obscure perception of a necessity to refute every vitalistic interpretation, to shatter life in its very foundations, with its consistency, its adaptation, and, in a word, its instinctuality—concerning which we have noted how problematical it is in the case of humans. And in order to do so, to carry death back (and such, of course, is the paradox) to the very level of biology, as an *instinct.* It is not without good reason that the

---

1 See Lacan, "Le Mythe individual du nérvosé ou poésie vérité dans la nérvosa" (Lecture at the Collège Philosophique). In a similar way, Freud had already spoken of the neurotic's "family romance." (*Standard* 9: 235-41).

commentators have on more than one occasion noted that at the level of Freud's last "dualism," it is perhaps no longer drives in the "Freudian" sense of the term that are in question, but instincts, in a kind of hyperbolical transcendence of the banal meaning assumed by that term within the life sciences. In order better to understand how this compulsion to demolish life comes to the surface precisely in the year 1919, with the ascendancy of the death drive, several additional considerations concerning the evolution and structure of Freud's theory would be indispensable.

In 1914, "Narcissism: An Introduction" appeared; in 1923, *The Ego and the Id.* This is the period in which, with the development of the theory of the ego and of its narcissistic libidinal cathexis, "life" imposes itself as more pressing and encroaching. The ego now seems to pride itself on all the powers and delegations it has accumulated: the delegations of self-preservation, but also those of sexuality, even including love and object-choice, which are always marked, as we observed, by the stigma of narcissism. Concomitantly, we now observe the emergence of Eros, the divine force that we were not able to examine at any length, but only to emphasize how it differs from sexuality, the first discovery of psychoanalysis. Eros is what seeks to maintain, preserve, and even augment the cohesion and the synthetic tendency of living beings and of psychical life. Whereas, ever since the beginnings of psychoanalysis, sexuality was in its essence hostile to binding—a principle of "un-binding" or unfettering (*Entbindung*) which could be bound only through the intervention of the ego—what appears with Eros is the *bound and binding form* of sexuality, brought to light by the discovery of narcissism. It is that form of sexuality, cathecting its object, attached to a form, which henceforth will sustain the ego and life itself, as well as any specific form of sublimation.

In the face of this triumph of the vital and the homeostatic, it remained for Freud, in keeping with the structural necessity of his discovery, to reaffirm, not only within psychoanalysis, but even within biology (by means of a categorical disregard for epistemological distinctions), a kind of antilife as sexuality, frenetic enjoyment [*jouissance*], the negative, the repetition compulsion. Strategically, the carrying back of the principles of psychoanalysis into the vital order is tantamount to a counterattack, a means of wreaking havoc in the very bases from which one risked being invaded. A subjective strategy? A strategy of the thing itself if it is indeed true that this carrying back into life of an intensely human war was already at the origin of the generalized subversion introduced by sexuality.

The energy of the sexual drive, as is known, was called "libido." Born of a formalistic concern for symmetry, the term "destrudo," once proposed to designate the energy of the death drive, did not survive a single day. For the death drive does not possess its own energy. Its energy is libido. Or, better put, the death drive is the very soul, the constitutive principle, of libidinal circulation.

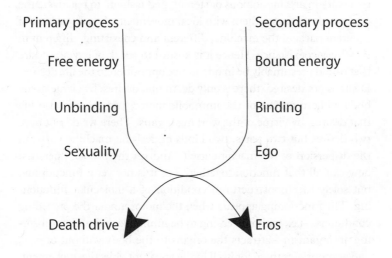

Primary process   Secondary process

Free energy   Bound energy

Unbinding   Binding

Sexuality   Ego

Death drive   Eros

The genealogy of the final instinctual dualism? If we place face to face the terms constituting the constant pairs of opposites in Freud's thought, that genealogy takes the form of a strange chiasmus whose riddle we, as Freud's successors, are beginning to decipher.

16. *First Positive Task of Schizoanalysis* (1972)[1]
Gilles Deleuze and Félix Guattari

The body without organs is the model of death. As the authors of horror stories have understood so well, it is not death that serves

---

1 From *Anti-Oedipus: Capitalism and Schizophrenia* (1972). Trans. Robert Hurley, Mark Seem, and Helen R. Lane. Minneapolis: University of Minnesota Press, 1983. 329-37.

as the model for catatonia, it is catatonic schizophrenia that gives its model to death. Zero intensity. The death model appears when the body without organs repels the organs and lays them aside: no mouth, no tongue, no teeth—to the point of self-mutilation, to the point of suicide. Yet there is no real opposition between the body without organs and the organs as partial objects; the only real opposition is to the molar organism that is their common enemy. In the desiring-machine, one sees the same catatonic inspired by the immobile motor that forces him to put aside his organs, to immobilize them, to silence them, but also, impelled by the working parts that work in an autonomous or stereotyped fashion, to reactivate the organs, to reanimate them with local movements. It is a question of different parts of the machine, different and coexisting, different in their very coexistence. Hence it is absurd to speak of a death desire that would presumably be in qualitative opposition to the life desires. Death is not desired, there is only death that desires, by virtue of the body without organs or the immobile motor, and there is also life that desires, by virtue of the working organs. There we do not have two desires but two parts, two kinds of desiring-machine parts, in the dispersion of the machine itself. And yet the problem persists: how can all that function together? For it is not yet a functioning, but solely the (nonstructural) condition of a molecular functioning. The functioning appears when the motor, under the preceding conditions—i.e., without ceasing to be immobile and without forming an organism—attracts the organs to the body without organs, and appropriates them for itself in the apparent objective movement. Repulsion is the condition of the machine's functioning, but attraction is the functioning itself. That functioning depends on repulsion is clear to us, inasmuch as it all works only by breaking down. One is then able to say what this running or this functioning consists of: in the cycle of the desiring-machine it is a matter of constantly translating, constantly converting the death model into something else altogether, which is the experience of death. Converting the death that rises from within (in the body without organs) into death that comes from without (on the body without organs).

But it seems that things are becoming very obscure, for what is this distinction between the experience of death and the model of death? Here again, is it a death desire? A being-for-death? Or rather an investment of death, even if speculative? None of the above. The experience of death is the most common of occurrences in the unconscious, precisely because it occurs in life and for life, in every passage or becoming, in every intensity as passage or becoming. It is in the very nature of every intensity to invest within itself the zero intensity starting from which it is produced, in one moment, as that which grows or diminishes according to an infinity of degrees (as Klossowski noted, "an afflux is necessary merely to signify the absence of intensity"). We have attempted to show in this respect how the relations of attraction and repulsion produced such states, sensations, and emotions, which imply a new energetic conversion and form the third kind of synthesis, the synthesis of conjunction. One might say that the unconscious as a real subject has scattered an apparent residual and nomadic subject around the entire compass of its cycle, a subject that passes by way of all the becomings corresponding to the included disjunctions: the last part of the desiring-machine, the adjacent part. These intense becomings and feelings, these intensive emotions, feed deliriums and hallucinations. But in themselves, these intensive emotions are closest to the matter whose zero degree they invest in itself. They control the unconscious experience of death, insofar as death is what is felt in every feeling, *what never ceases and never finishes happening in every becoming*—in the becoming-another-sex, the becoming-god, the becoming-a-race, etc., forming zones of intensity on the body without organs. Every intensity controls within its own life the experience of death, and envelops it. And it is doubtless the case that every intensity is extinguished at the end, that every becoming itself becomes a becoming-death! Death, then, does actually happen. Maurice Blanchot[1] distinguishes this twofold nature clearly, these two irreducible aspects of death; the one, according to which the apparent subject never ceases to live and travel as a *One*—"*one* never stops and never has done with dying"; and the other, according to which this same subject, fixed as *I*, actually dies—which to say it finally ceases to die since it ends up dying, in the reality of a last instant that fixes it in this way as an *I*, all the while undoing the intensity, carrying it back to the zero that envelops it (Blanchot 104, 106).

---

1   Maurice Blanchot (1920-2003), novelist, literary critic, and philosopher, perhaps best known for interrogating the barriers between literature and philosophy. Blanchot was indebted to the ethical philosophy of his friend Emmanuel Levinas (1906-1995), and in the 1960s became a major influence for post-structuralists.

From one aspect to the other, there is not at all a personal deepening, but something quite different: there is a return from the experience of death to the model of death, in the cycle of the desiring-machines. The cycle is closed. For a new departure, since this *I* is another? The experience of death must have given us exactly enough broadened experience, in order to live and know that the desiring-machines do not die. And that the subject as an adjacent part is always a "one" who conducts the experience, not an *I* who receives the model. For the model itself is not the *I* either, but the body without organs. And *I* does not rejoin the model without the model starting out again in the direction of another experience. Always going from the model to the experience, and starting out again, returning from the model to the experience, is what *schizo-phrenizing death* amounts to, the exercise of the desiring-machines (which is their very secret, well understood by the terrifying authors). The machines tell us this, and make us live it, feel it, deeper than delirium and further than hallucination: yes, the return to repulsion will condition other attractions, other functionings, the setting in motion of other working parts on the body without organs, the putting to work of other adjacent parts on the periphery that have as much a right to say *One* as we ourselves do. "Let him die in his leaping through unheard-of and unnamable things: other horrible workers will come; they will begin on the horizons where the other collapsed!" (Rimbaud). The Eternal Return as experience, and as the deterritorialized circuit of all the cycles of desire.

How odd the psychoanalytic venture is. Psychoanalysis ought to be a song of life, or else be worth nothing at all. It ought, *practically*, to teach us to sing life. And see how the most defeated, sad song of death emanates from it: *eiapopeia* [lullaby]. From the start, and because of his stubborn dualism of the drives, Freud never stopped trying to limit the discovery of a subjective or vital essence of desire as libido. But when the dualism passed into a death instinct against Eros, this was no longer a simple limitation, it was a liquidation of the libido. Reich[1] did not go wrong

---

1 Wilhelm Reich (1897-1957), Austrian-American psychiatrist and psychoanalyst. Close to the inner circle of Freudians in the 1920s, Reich was one of the first to put Freud and Marxism together. Freud rejected this idea and by the early 1930s their relationship soured. Reich left for America in 1939 where his militant politics and work on "character analysis" gave way to increasingly eccentric work on orgone energy and therapy, UFOs, and cloud-busting.

here, and was perhaps the only one to maintain that the product of analysis should be a free and joyous person, a carrier of the life flows, capable of carrying them all the way into the desert and decoding them—even if this idea necessarily took on the appearance of a crazy idea, given what had become of analysis. He demonstrated that Freud, no less than Jung and Adler, had repudiated the sexual position: the fixing of the death instinct in fact deprives sexuality of its generative role on at least one essential point, which is the genesis of anxiety, since this genesis becomes the autonomous cause of sexual repression instead of its result; it follows that sexuality as desire no longer animates a social critique of civilization, but that civilization on the contrary finds itself sanctified as the sole agency capable of opposing the death desire. And how does it do this? By in principle turning death against death, by making this turned-back death (*la mort retournée*) into a force of desire, by putting it in the service of a pseudo life through an entire culture of guilt feeling.

There is no need to tell all over how psychoanalysis culminates in a theory of culture that takes up again the age-old task of the ascetic ideal, Nirvana, the cultural extract, judging life, belittling life, measuring life against death, and only retaining from life what the death of death wants very much to leave us with—a sublime resignation. As Reich says, when psychoanalysis began to speak of Eros, the whole world breathed a sigh of relief: one knew what this meant, and that everything was going to unfold within a mortified life, since Thanatos was now the partner of Eros, for worse but also *for better*.[1] Psychoanalysis becomes the training ground of a new kind of priest, the director of bad conscience: bad conscience has made us sick, but that is what will cure us! Freud did not hide what was really at issue with the introduction of the death instinct: it is not a question of any fact whatever, but merely of a principle, a question of principle. The death instinct is pure silence, pure transcendence, not givable and

---

1 Reich, *The Function of the Orgasm*. A correct interpretation—marked throughout by idealism—of Freud's theory of culture and its catastrophic evolution concerning guilt feeling, can be found in Paul Ricoeur: on death and "the death of death," see *De l'interprétation* (Paris: Editions du Seuil) pp. 299-303. [Deleuze and Guattari's note; see Appendix B10 and B11.]

not given in experience. This very point is remarkable: it is because death, according to Freud, has neither a model nor an experience, that he makes of it a transcendent principle (Freud, *Inhibitions*). So that the psychoanalysts who refused the death instinct did so for the same reasons as those who accepted it: some said that there was no death instinct *since* there was no model or experience in the unconscious; others, that there was a death instinct precisely *because* there was no model or experience. We say, to the contrary, that there is no death instinct because there is both the model and the experience of death in the unconscious. Death then is a part of the desiring-machine, a part that must itself be judged, evaluated in the functioning of the machine and the system of its energetic conversions, and not as an abstract principle.

If Freud needs death as a principle, this is by virtue of the requirements of the dualism that maintains a qualitative opposition between the drives (you will not escape the conflict): once the dualism of the sexual drives and the ego drives has only a topological scope, the qualitative or dynamic dualism passes between Eros and Thanatos. But the same enterprise is continued and reinforced—eliminating the machinic element of desire, the desiring-machines. It is a matter of eliminating the libido, insofar as it implies the possibility of energetic conversions in the machine (Libido-Numen-Voluptas). It is a matter of imposing the idea of an energetic duality rendering the machinic transformations impossible, with everything obliged to pass by way of an indifferent neutral energy, that energy emanating from Oedipus and capable of being added to either of the two irreducible forms—neutralizing, mortifying life.[1] The purpose of the topological and dynamic dualities is to thrust aside the point of view of *functional multiplicity* that alone is economic (Szondi situates the problem clearly: why two kinds of drives qualified as molar, functioning mysteriously,

---

1   On the impossibility of immediate qualitative conversions, and the necessity for going by way of neutral energy, see Sigmund Freud, *The Ego and the Id*. This impossibility, this necessity is no longer understandable, it seems to us, if one agrees with Jean Laplanche that "the death drive has no energy of its own" (*Vie et mort en psychanalyse* [Paris: Flammarion, 1970], 211). Therefore the death drive could not enter into a veritable dualism, or would have to be confused with the neutral energy itself, which Freud denies. [Deleuze and Guattari's note]

which is to say oedipally, rather than *n* genes of drives—eight molecular genes, for example—functioning machinically?).

If one looks in this direction for the ultimate reason why Freud erects a transcendent death instinct as a principle, the reason will be found in Freud's practice itself. For if the principle has nothing to do with the facts, it has a lot to do with the psychoanalyst's conception of psychoanalytic practice, a conception the psychoanalyst wishes to impose. Freud made the most profound discovery of the abstract subjective essence of desire—Libido. But since he realienated this essence, reinvesting it in a subjective system of representation of the ego, and since he recoded this essence on the residual territoriality of Oedipus and under the despotic signifier of castration, he could no longer conceive the essence of life except in a form turned back against itself, in the form of death itself. And this neutralization, this turning against life, is also the last way in which a depressive and exhausted libido can go on surviving, and dream that it is surviving: "The ascetic ideal is an artifice for the *preservation* of life ... even when he *wounds* himself, this master of destruction, of self-destructing— the very wound itself compels him *to live* ..." (Nietzsche, *Genealogy* 13). It is Oedipus, the marshy earth, that gives off a powerful odor of decay and death; and it is castration, the pious ascetic wound, the signifier, that makes of this death a conservatory for the Oedipal life. Desire is in itself not a desire to love, but a force to love, a virtue that gives and produces, that engineers. (For how could what is in life still desire life? Who would want to call that a desire?) But desire must turn back against itself in the name of a horrible Ananke, the Ananke of the weak and the depressed, the contagious neurotic Ananke; desire must produce its shadow or its monkey, and find a strange artificial force for vegetating in the void, at the heart of its own lack. For better days to come? It must—but who talks in this way? What abjectness—become a desire to be loved, and worse, a sniveling desire to have been loved, a desire that is reborn of its own frustration: no, daddy-mommy didn't love me enough. Sick desire stretches out on the couch, an artificial swamp, a little earth, a little mother. "Look at you, stumbling and staggering with no use in your legs.... And it's nothing but your wanting to be loved which does it. A maudlin crying to be loved, which makes your knees go all ricky" (Lawrence 101). Just as there are two stomachs for the ruminant, there must also exist two abortions, two castrations for sick desire: once in the family, in the familial scene, with the knitting mother; another time in an aseticized clinic, in the psychoanalytic scene, with specialist artists who know how to handle the death instinct and "bring off" castration, "bring off" frustration.

Is this really the right way to bring on better days? And aren't all the destructions deformed by schizoanalysis worth more than this psychoanalytic conservatory, aren't they more a part of an affirmative task? "Lie down, then, on the soft couch which the analyst provides and try to think up something different ... if you realize that he is not a god but a human being like yourself, with worries, defects, ambitions, frailties, that he is not the repository of an all-encompassing wisdom [= code] but a wanderer, along the [deterritorialized] path, perhaps you will cease pouring it out like a sewer, however melodious it may sound to your ears, and rise up on your own two legs and sing with your own God-given voice [Numen]. To confess, to whine, to complain, to commiserate, always demands a toll. To sing it doesn't cost you a penny. Not only does it cost nothing—you actually enrich others (instead of infecting them).... The phantasmal world is the world which has not been fully conquered over. It is the world of the past, never of the future. To move forward clinging to the past is like dragging a ball and chain.... We are all guilty of crime, the great crime of not living life to the full" (Miller 429-30). You weren't born Oedipus, you caused it to grow in yourself; and you aim to get out of it through fantasy, through castration, but this in turn you have caused to grow in Oedipus—namely, in yourself: the horrible circle. Shit on your whole mortifying, imaginary, and symbolic theater. What does schizoanalysis ask? Nothing more than a bit of a *relation to the outside*, a little real reality. And we claim the right to a radical laxity, a radical incompetence—the right to enter the analyst's office and say it smells bad there. It reeks of the great death and the little ego.

Freud himself indeed spoke of the link between his "discovery" of the death instinct and World War I, which remains the model of capitalist war. More generally, the death instinct celebrates the wedding of psychoanalysis and capitalism; their engagement had been full of hesitation. What we have tried to show apropos of capitalism is how it inherited much from a transcendent death-carrying agency, the despotic signifier, but also how it brought about this agency's effusion in the full immanence of its own system: the full body, having become that of capital-money, suppresses the distinction between production and antiproduction; everywhere it mixes antiproduction with the productive forces in the immanent reproduction of its own always widened limits (the axiomatic). The death enterprise is one of the principal and specific forms of the absorption of surplus value in capitalism. It is this itinerary that psychoanalysis rediscovers and retraces with the death instinct: the death instinct is now only pure silence in its transcendent distinction from life, but it effuses all the more, throughout all the immanent combinations it forms with this same life. Absorbed, diffuse, immanent death is the condition formed by the signifier in capitalism, the empty locus that is everywhere displaced in order to block the schizophrenic escapes and place restraints on the flights.

The only modern myth is the myth of zombies—mortified schizos, good for work, brought back to reason. In this sense the primitive and the barbarian, with their ways of coding death, are children in comparison to modern man and his axiomatic (so many unemployed are needed, so many deaths, the Algerian War doesn't kill more people than weekend automobile accidents, planned death in Bengal, etc.). Modern man "raves to a far greater extent. His delirium is a switchboard with thirteen telephones. He gives his orders to the world. He doesn't care for the ladies. He is brave, too. He is decorated like crazy. In man's game of chance the death instinct, the silent instinct is decidedly well placed, perhaps next to egoism. It takes the place of zero in roulette. The house always wins. So too does death. The law of large numbers works for death" (Céline 171). It is now or never that we must take up a problem we had left hanging. Once it is said that capitalism works on the basis of decoded flows as such, how is it that it is infinitely further removed from desiring-production than were the primitive or even the barbarian systems, which nonetheless code and over-code the flows? Once it is said that desiring-production is itself a decoded and deterritorialized production, how do we explain that capitalism, with its axiomatic, its statistics, performs an infinitely vaster repression of this production than do the preceding regimes, which nonetheless did not lack the necessary repressive means? We have seen that the molar statistical aggregates of social production were in a variable relationship of affinity with the molecular formations of desiring-production. What must be explained is that the capitalist aggregate is the least affinal, at the very moment it decodes and deterritorializes with all its might.

The answer is the death instinct, if we call instinct in general the conditions of life that are historically and socially determined by the relations of production and antiproduction in a system. We know that molar social production and molecular desiring-production must be evaluated both from the viewpoint of their identity in nature and from the viewpoint of their difference in régime. But it could be that these two aspects, nature and régime, are in a sense potential and are actualized, only in inverse proportion. Which means that where the régimes are the closest, the identity in nature is on the contrary at its minimum; and where the identity in nature appears to be at its maximum, the régimes differ to the highest degree. If we examine the primitive or the barbarian constellations, we see that the subjective essence of desire as production is referred to large objectities, to the territorial or the despotic body, which act as natural or divine preconditions that thus ensure the coding or the overcoding of the flows of desire by introducing them into systems of representation that are themselves objective. Hence it can be said that the identity in nature between the two productions is completely hidden there: as much by the difference between the objective socius and the subjective full body of desiring-production, as by the difference between the qualified codes and overcodings of social production and the chains of decoding or of deterritorialization belonging to desiring-production, and by the entire repressive apparatus represented in the savage prohibitions, the barbarian law, and the rights of antiproduction. And yet the difference in régime, far from being accentuated and deepened, is on the contrary reduced to a minimum, because desiring-production as an absolute limit remains an exterior limit, or else stays unoccupied as an internalized and displaced limit, with the result that the machines of desire operate on this side of their limit within the framework of the socius and its codes. That is why the primitive codes and even the despotic overcodings testify to a polyvocity that functionally draws them nearer to a chain of decoding of desire: the parts of the desiring-machine function in the very workings of the social machine; the flows of desire enter and exit through the codes that continue, however, to inform the model and experience of death that are elaborated in the unity of the sociodesiring-apparatus. And it is even less a question of the death instinct to the extent that the model and the experience are better coded in a circuit that never stops grafting the desiring-machines onto the social machine and implanting the social machine in the desiring-machines. Death comes all the more from without as it is coded from within. This is especially true of the system of cruelty, where death is inscribed in the primitive mechanism of surplus value as well as in the movement of the finite blocks of debt. But even in the system of despotic terror, where debt becomes infinite and where death experiences an elevation that tends to make of it a *latent* instinct, there nonetheless subsists a model in the over-coding law, and an experience for the overcoded subjects, at the same time as antiproduction remains separate as the share owing to the overlord.

17. *A Humanist Response to the Death Instinct Theory* (1973)[1]
Erich Fromm

In the previous pages [of *The Anatomy of Human Destructiveness*] I have pointed to the immanent contradictions into which Freud was forced when he changed from the libido theory to the Eros-death-instinct theory. There is another conflict of a different kind in the latter theory which must attract our attention: the conflict between Freud the theoretician and Freud the human-ist. The theoretician arrives at the conclusion that man has only the alternative between destroying himself (slowly, by illness) or destroying others; or—putting it in other words—between causing suffering either to himself or to others. The humanist rebels against the idea of this tragic alternative that would make war a rational solution of this aspect of human existence.

Not that Freud was averse to tragic alternatives. On the contrary, in his earlier theory he had constructed such a tragic alternative: repression of instinctual demands (especially pre-genital ones) was supposed to be the basis of the development of civilization; the repressed instinctual drive was "sublimated" into valuable cultural channels, but still at the expense of full human happiness. On the other hand, repression led not only to increasing civilization, but also to the development of neurosis among the many in whom the repressive process did not work

---

1 From *The Anatomy of Human Destructiveness* (1973). New York: Holt, Reinhart and Winston, 1973. 463-69; 471.

successfully. Lack of civilization combined with full happiness, or civilization combined with neurosis (and even general diminished happiness) seemed to be the alternative.[1]

The contradiction between the death instinct and Eros confronts man with a real and truly tragic alternative. A real alternative because he can decide to attack and wage war, to be aggressive, and to express his hostility because he prefers to do this rather than to be sick. That this alternative is a tragic one hardly needs to be proven, at least not as far as Freud or any other humanist is concerned.

Freud makes no attempt to befog the issue by blurring the sharpness of the conflict. As quoted earlier, in the *New Introductory Lectures* he wrote:

> And now we are struck by the significance of the possibility that the aggressiveness may not be able to find satisfaction in the external world because it comes up against real obstacles. If this happens, it will perhaps retreat and increase the amount of self-destructiveness holding sway in the interior. We shall hear how this is in fact what occurs and how important a process this is. (Freud, *Standard* 22: 105)

In *An Outline of Psychoanalysis* he wrote: "Holding back aggressiveness is in general unhealthy and leads to illness" (23: 150). After having thus drawn the lines sharply, how does Freud respond to the impulse not to leave human affairs in such a hope-

---

1   Cf., for instance, *Civilized Sexual Morality and Modern Nervous Illness* where Freud wrote: "We may justly hold our civilization responsible for the threat of neurasthenia" (179–204). Herbert Marcuse makes the point that Freud said that full happiness requires the full expression of all sexual instincts (which in Freud's sense would mean particularly the pregenital components) (Marcuse 1955). Regardless of whether Freud is right in this opinion, Marcuse overlooks the fact that Freud's main point was that of the tragic alternatives. Hence, it is not at all a Freudian view that the goal should be the unlimited expression of all components of the sexual instinct. On the contrary, Freud— being on the side of civilization against barbarism—prefers repression to its opposite. Besides, Freud always spoke of the repressive influence of *civilization* on the instincts, and the idea that this happens only in capitalism and need not happen in socialism is completely contrary to his thinking. Marcuse's ideas on this subject suffer from insufficient knowledge of the details of Freud's theory. [Fromm's note]

less view, and to avoid siding with those who recommend war as the best medicine for the human race?

Indeed, Freud made several theoretical attempts to find a way out of the dilemma between the theoretician and the humanist. One attempt lies in the idea that the destructive instinct can be transformed into conscience. In *Civilization and Its Discontents* Freud asks: "What happens to him [the aggressor] to render his desire for aggression innocuous?" Freud answers thus:

> Something very remarkable, which we should never have guessed and which is nevertheless quite obvious. His aggressiveness is introjected, internalized; it is in point of fact, sent back to where it came from—that is, it is directed towards his own ego. There it is taken over by a portion of the ego which sets itself over against the rest of the ego as super-ego, and which now, in the form of "conscience," is ready to put into action against the ego the same harsh aggressiveness that the ego would have liked to satisfy upon other, extraneous individuals. The tension between the harsh super-ego and the ego that is subjected to it, is called by us the sense of guilt; it expresses itself as a need for punishment. Civilization, therefore, obtains mastery over the individual's dangerous desire for aggression by weakening and disarming it and by setting up an agency within him to watch over it, like a garrison in a conquered city. (*Standard* 21: 123-24)[1]

The transformation of destructiveness into a self-punishing conscience does not seem to be as much of an advantage as Freud implies. According to his theory conscience would have to be as cruel as the death instinct, since it is charged with its energies, and no reason is given why, under the rule of this cruel "garrison" the death instinct should be "weakened" and "disarmed." It would rather seem that the following analogy would express the real consequences of Freud's thought more logically: a city that has been ruled by a cruel enemy defeats him with the help of a dictator who then sets up a system that is just as cruel as that of the defeated enemy; and thus, what is gained?

---

1   Freud's concept of conscience as essentially punishing is surely a very narrow one, in the tradition of certain religious ideas; it is that of an "authoritarian," not a "humanistic" conscience. Cf. E. Fromm (1947). [Fromm's note]

However, this theory of the strict conscience as a manifestation of the death instinct is not the only attempt Freud makes to mitigate his concept of a tragic alternative. Another less tragic explanation is expressed in the following: "The instinct of destruction, moderated and tamed, and, as it were, inhibited in its aim, must, when it is directed towards objects, provide the ego with the satisfaction of its vital needs and with control over nature" (*Standard* 21). This seems to be a good example of "sublimation"[1]; the aim of the instinct is not weakened, but it is directed toward other socially valuable aims, in this case the "domination over nature."

This sounds, indeed, like a perfect solution. Man is freed from the tragic choice between destroying either others or himself, because the energy of the destructive instinct is used for the control over nature. But, we must ask, can this really be so? Can it be true that destructiveness becomes transformed into constructiveness? What can "control over nature" mean? Taming and breeding animals, gathering and cultivating plants, weaving cloth, building huts, manufacturing pottery, and many more activities including the construction of machines, railroads, airplanes, skyscrapers. All these are acts of constructing, building, unifying, synthesizing, and, indeed, if one wanted to attribute them to one of the two basic instincts, they might be considered as being motivated by Eros rather than by the death instinct. With the possible exception of killing animals for their consumption and killing men in war, both of which could be considered as rooted in destructiveness, control and mastery over nature is not destructive but constructive.

Freud makes one other attempt to soften the harshness of his alternative in his answer to Albert Einstein's letter on the topic

---

1 Freud did not use the term "sublimation" in connection with the death instinct, but it seems to me that the concept with which the following paragraph deals is the same as that which Freud calls sublimation in relation to the libido. The concept of "sublimation" is questionable even when Freud applied it to sexual, and especially to pregenital instincts. In terms of the older theory, the example was popular that a surgeon uses the sublimated energy of his sadism. But is this really true? After all, the surgeon does not only cut: he also mends, and it is more likely that the best surgeons are not motivated by sublimated sadism, but by many other factors, such as having manual dexterity, the wish to heal through immediate action, the capacity for making quick decisions, etc. [Fromm's note]

Why War? Not even on this occasion, when confronted with the question of the psychological causes of war by one of the greatest scientists and humanists of the century, did Freud try to hide or mitigate the harshness of his previous alternatives. With the fullest clarity he wrote:

> As a result of a little speculation, we have come to suppose that this instinct is at work in every living creature and is striving to bring it to ruin and to reduce life to its original condition of inanimate matter. Thus it quite seriously deserves to be called a death instinct, while the erotic instincts represent the effort to live. The death instinct turns into the destructive instinct when, with the help of special organs, it is directed outwards, on to objects. The organism preserves its own life, so to say, by destroying an extraneous one. Some portion of the death instinct, however, remains operative *within* the organism, and we have sought to trace quite a number of normal and pathological phenomena to this internalization of the destructive instinct. We have even been guilty of the heresy of attributing the origin of conscience to this diversion inwards of aggressiveness. You will notice that it is by no means a trivial matter if this process is carried too far: it is positively unhealthy. On the other hand if these forces are turned to destruction in the external world, the organism will be relieved and the effect must be beneficial. *This would serve as a biological justification for all the ugly and dangerous impulses against which we are struggling. It must be admitted that they stand nearer to Nature than does our resistance to them for which an explanation also needs to be found.* (22: 211, italics added)

After having made this very clear and uncompromising statement summing up his previously expressed views about the death instinct, and after having stated that he could hardly believe the stories about those happy regions where there are races "who know neither coercion nor aggression," Freud tried toward the end of the letter to arrive at a less pessimistic solution than the beginning seemed to foreshadow. His hope is founded on several possibilities: "If willingness to engage in war," he wrote, "is an effect of the destructive instinct, the most obvious plan will be to bring Eros, its antagonist, into play against it. Anything that encourages the growth of emotional ties between men must operate against war" (212).

It is remarkable and moving how Freud the humanist and, as he calls himself, "pacifist," tries here almost frantically to evade the logical consequences of his own premises. If the death instinct is as powerful and fundamental as Freud claims throughout, how can it be considerably reduced by bringing Eros into play, considering that they are both contained in every cell and that they constitute an irreducible quality of living matter?

Freud's second argument in favour of peace is even more fundamental. At the end of his letter to Einstein he writes:

> Now war is in the crassest opposition to the psychical attitude imposed on us by the process of civilization, and for that reason we are bound to rebel against it; we simply cannot any longer put up with it. This is not merely an intellectual and emotional repudiation; we pacifists have a *constitutional* intolerance of war, an idiosyncrasy magnified, as it were to the highest degree. It seems indeed, as though the lowering of aesthetic standards in war plays a scarcely smaller part in our rebellion than do its cruelties. And how long shall we have to wait before the rest of mankind become pacifists too? There is no telling. (215)

And at the end of this letter Freud touches upon a thought found occasionally in his work, that of *the process of civilization as a factor leading to a lasting, as it were, a "constitutional," "organic" repression of instincts.*

Freud had already expressed this view much earlier, in the *Three Essays,* when he spoke of the sharp conflict between instinct and civilization: "One gets an impression from civilized children that the construction of these dams is a product of education, and no doubt, education has much to do with it. But in reality *this development is organically determined* and fixed by heredity, and it can occasionally occur without any help at all from education" (7: 177-78, italics added).

In *Civilization and Its Discontents* Freud continued this line of thinking by speaking of an "organic repression," for instance in the case of the taboo related to menstruation or anal erotism, thus paving the way to civilization. We find, even as early as 1897, Freud expressed himself in a letter to Fliess (14 November 1897; Letter 75) that "something organic played a part in repression" (S. Freud, 1897).

The various statements quoted here show that Freud's reliance on a "constitutional" intolerance to war was not only an attempt to transcend the tragic perspective of his death instinct concept produced *ad hoc*, as it were, by his discussion with Einstein, but was in accord with a line of thinking that, although never dominant, had been in the background of his thoughts since 1897.

If Freud's assumptions were right, that civilization produces "constitutional" and hereditary repressions, that is, that in the process of civilization certain instinctual needs are in fact weakened, then indeed he would have found a way out of the dilemma. Then civilized man would not be prompted by certain instinctual demands contrary to civilization to the same degree as primitive man. The impulse to destroy would not have the same intensity and power in civilized man that it would have in primitive man. This line of thinking would also lead to the speculation that certain inhibitions against killing might have been built up during the process of civilization and become hereditarily fixed. However, even if one could discover such hereditary factors in general, it would be exceedingly difficult to assume their existence in the case of the death instinct.

According to Freud's concept the death instinct is a tendency inherent in all living substance; it seems to be a theoretically difficult proposition to assume that this fundamental biological force could be weakened in the course of civilization. With the same logic one could assume that Eros could be constitutionally weakened and such assumptions would lead to the more general assumption that the very nature of living substance could be altered by the process of civilization, by means of an "organic" repression.[1]

However this may be, today it would seem to be one of the most important subjects for research to try to establish the facts with regard to this point. Is there sufficient evidence to show that there has been a constitutional, organic repression of certain instinctual demands in the course of civilization? Is this repression one that is different from repression in Freud's usual sense, inasmuch as it weakens the instinctual demand, rather than removing it from consciousness or diverting it to other aims? And more specifically, in the course of history have man's destructive impulses become weaker, or

---

1 What speaks most against Freud's assumption was that pre-historic man was not more but less aggressive than civilized man. [Fromm's note]

have inhibitory impulses developed that are now hereditarily fixed? To answer this question would require extended studies, especially in anthropology, sociopsychology, and genetics.

Looking back at the various attempts Freud made to mitigate the sharpness of his fundamental alternative—destruction of others or of oneself—one can only admire his persistence in trying to find a way out of the dilemma and, at the same time, his honesty in having refrained from believing that he had found a satisfactory solution. Thus, in the *Outline* he no longer makes reference to the factors limiting the power of destructiveness (except the role of the superego) and concludes this topic by saying: "This is one of the dangers to health by which human beings are faced on their path to cultural development. Holding back aggressiveness is in general unhealthy and leads to illness (to mortification)" (23: 150).[1]

★★★

Where are we left after this analysis of Freud's theory of the death instinct? Is it essentially different from the construct of a "destructive instinct," that many psychoanalysts make, or from Freud's earlier construct, that of the libido? We have in the course of this discussion pointed out subtle changes and contradictions in Freud's development of the theory of aggression. We have seen, in the answer to Einstein, that Freud for a moment indulged in speculations that tended to make his position less harsh and less apt to be used as a justification of war. But when we look over Freud's theoretical edifice once more, it becomes clear that in spite of all this, the basic character of the death instinct follows the logic of the hydraulic model that Freud had originally applied to the sexual instinct. A striving for death is constantly generated in all living substance, leaving only one alternative: either to do the silent work of man's destruction from within, or to turn toward the outside as "destructiveness" and to save man from self-destruction by the destruction of others. As Freud put

---

1 I want to point out once more the change in Freud's view concerning the relationship between instinct and civilization. In terms of the libido theory, civilization results in the repression of *sexual* strivings and may cause *neurosis*. In the new theory, civilization leads to the holding back of *aggressiveness* and results in *physical illness*. [Fromm's note]

it: "Holding back aggressiveness is in general unhealthy and leads to illness (to mortification)" (23: 150).

Summing up this examination of Freud's theory of life and death instinct, it is hard to avoid the conclusion that Freud, since 1920, got entangled in two basically different concepts and in two distinct approaches to the problem of human motivation. The first, the conflict between self-preservation and sexuality, was the traditional concept, reason versus passion, duty versus natural inclination, or hunger versus love, as the driving forces in man. The later theory, based on the conflict between the inclination to live and the one to die, between integration and disintegration, between love and hate, was entirely different. While one may say that it was based on the popular concept of love and hate as the two forces driving man, it was in fact more profound and original; it followed the Platonic tradition of Eros and considered love as the energy that binds all living substance together and is the guarantor of life. More specifically even, it seems to follow Empedocles' idea that the world of living creatures can exist only as long as the struggle between the contrary forces of Strife and Aphrodite, or love, the power of attraction and repulsion are active together.[1]

18. *Scientific Discourse in the Light of Metapsychological Speculation* (1974)[2]
Rodolphe Gasché

The witch metapsychology! Without metapsychological speculation and theorizing—I had almost said "phantasying"—we shall not get another step forward.
        Freud, "Analysis Terminable and Interminable"

Let us define a little more closely this extraordinary discourse called speculation.

---

1 The similarities between Empedocles' and Freud's concepts are perhaps not as real as they appear at first glance. For Empedocles, Love is attraction between dissimilars; Strife is attraction of like to like. A serious comparison requires the examination of Empedocles' whole system. (Cf. W.K.C. Guthrie, 1965.) [Fromm's note]

2 From "The Witch Metapsychology" (1974). *Returns of the "French Freud": Freud, Lacan and Beyond*. Trans. Julian Patrick. Ed. Todd Dufresne. New York: Routledge, 1997. 183-85; 187-88; 193-97; 200-01; 202-05.

In *Beyond,* evoking the obscurity that perpetually cloaks the nature of the instincts, Freud goes so far as to valorize even the merest of incidental ideas [*Einfall*]: "In the obscurity that reigns at present in the theory of the instincts, it would be unwise to reject any idea that promises to throw any light on it" (Freud, *Standard* 18: 53).

The explanatory value derives its emphasis not only from the sudden occurrence of such an idea, through the unexpected light that it promises, but also from the fact that the sudden indication is, as the German term *Einfall* suggests, a happening, an interpolation, an irruption or breach in the discourse in question. The power of such an incidental idea results moreover from that which comes from a *somewhere or other* [See Freud Standard 14: 117], but this time from a place that, insofar as it is a presupposition, is already inscribed in the beyond of the dichotomy: leading sciences versus metatheoretical or philosophical speculation.

The existing obscurity of the theory of the instincts remains opaque despite the introduction of the opposition between life instincts and death instincts. For, having already displaced the earlier opposition between the ego-instincts and the sexual instincts, this later opposition ends up, nevertheless, by making the life instincts prevail, by all its explanation via the biological sciences, and by the attempt to found the opposition on biology. However, what Freud was looking for was a way to reconstitute the original opposition he had left behind, that he had dropped in the hope of finding another that would be sharper, more radical, and more decisive. That the incidental idea, the isolated, exemplary idea has to do with an example, and that the example is that of another opposition—the ambivalence between hate and love affecting object relations[1]—is not arbitrary. In fact, it leads on to primary sadism, to the force of destruction and aggression that facilitates the relation to an object, in whose wake what will come to slip through after the fact will be only affection towards the object. The same example will later lead to the supposition

---

1   The opposition between hate and love, the incidental idea, comes already from a beyond of what one might properly call philosophy. It descends from mythic, pre-Socratic philosophemes, more precisely from the philosophy of Empedocles. In this respect, we refer to the text of Sarah Kofman, "Freud and Empodocles." [Gasché's note]

of a primary masochism. This example, which gives prominence to an unheard of force of destruction, is an example undiscoverable within the register of the biological sciences. It belongs to another order, to the order of an interpolation and, beyond that, is recognizable only as an incidental idea.

The *Voraussetzung* [presupposition] of which the example is but an index, and which from now on is going to regulate the movements of the text of *Beyond*, is a presupposition of metapsychological discourse (of which this one here will be the representation), a presupposition which structures it from an earlier time to the time proper of its discursive elaboration, from a time neither logical nor spatio-temporal in the sense in which this presupposition would have already obviously existed in another discourse. Or again, the presupposition in question that structures the metapsychological quest is a before that is constituted only in the elaboration of the metapsychological and speculative "science," for which it provides a place, a time, and a "logic."

It is mainly because of the ineffectiveness of the established sciences, of the vague notions of common sense, of the impossibility of starting only from the material of observation, that Freud will give a different status to metapsychological speculation. But we must also be aware that the necessity of speculation is based on the object itself of psychoanalysis, which is certainly not an object in the traditional sense, not allowing itself to be clearly objectified, but occurring rather, in the psychoanalytical situation for example, as a lacuna, omission, or fault within the discourse: this "object" is the unconscious. If the unconscious is one of those presuppositions of analytical and metapsychological discourse, then evidently it is a question of an earlier state of which no scientific discourse had given an explicit sign until now, these discourses always obeying the rules and dominant logic of consciousness. Thus all the deductions that one can make from these discourses remain necessarily inadequate: as a consequence, they will have only a provisional status, even though we have already suspected that the fact that they must be replaced cannot be reduced only to their unsuitability, but that it is dictated by the very nature of the object of metapsychological discourse.

Chapter Four of *Beyond* begins in this way:

What follows is speculation, often far-fetched speculation [*oft weitausholende Spekulation*], which the reader will consider or dismiss according to his individual predilection. It is further an attempt to follow out an idea consistently, out of curiosity to see where it will lead.

Psychoanalytic speculation takes as its point of departure the impression, derived from examining unconscious processes, that consciousness may be, not the most universal attribute of mental processes, but only a particular function of them. (18: 24)

Freud's liberalism here should not mislead us. It has everything to do with the nature, let us say the expressed form, of speculation. As it is a question of bringing the death instinct to the fore (which we know never shows itself in a pure state, its appearance remaining always doubtful), the tolerance invoked by Freud concerns exclusively its representations, and not the "source" from which these developments draw their vigor.

In the passage cited, Freud mentions curiosity, *Neugier*, the ardent desire for the new, the unappeasable desire that incites him to follow an idea to the end, to its extreme consequences. Curiosity, in effect, has been one of the most conspicuous ideological motifs of the birth of science. It should be noticed, though, that this motif cannot account for the arguments elaborated in *Beyond*. When he has concluded the debate over the death instinct, Freud writes this:

It may be asked whether and how far I am myself convinced of the truth of the hypotheses that have been set out in these pages. My answer would be that I am not convinced myself and that I do not seek to persuade other people to believe in them. Or, more precisely, that I do not know how far I believe in them. There is no reason, as it seems to me, why the emotional factor of conviction should enter into this question at all. It is surely possible to throw oneself into a line of thought and to follow it wherever it leads out of simple scientific curiosity, or, if the reader prefers, as an *advocatus diaboli*, who is not on that account himself sold to the devil. (59)

Freud adds that scientific curiosity excludes all sentiment, even all belief. Now, if curiosity were purely scientific, it would have to be crowned with a pleasure bonus and would not be without affect as a consequence. In "Formulations on the Two Principles of Mental Functioning," Freud notes that science is the first to get the better of the pleasure principle but remarks immediately that it yields an intellectual pleasure and the promise of a practical gain in addition (12: 222). If, therefore, in *Beyond*, curiosity has nothing to do with affect, we must conclude that it is not scientific curiosity merely, and that the lack of sentiment results from the fact that an affect of a different nature is at stake. Hence curiosity would be following another motif. It would perhaps be a demoniacal motif (remember that Freud several times designated the compulsion to repeat with this word), of which the devil's advocate would be the representative, in the figure of a witch not entirely abandoned to the devil, since science always gets itself involved throughout this project. The witch metapsychology, emphasized in the epigraph, is thus revealed as the hybrid product of a scientificity denuded of affect and without advantage: a scientificity that this time would have radically overcome the pleasure principle, and a demoniacal curiosity prompted also by a beyond of the pleasure principle stronger than the pleasure imputed to properly scientific discourse.

Metapsychological discourse is directed at the silent, subterranean work of the death instinct: hence, the pleasure linked to metapsychological speculation will also be unobtrusive, the imperceptible work of the death instinct manifesting itself only in its repetition through isolated examples and never in a pure state. Freud's pleasure, quite as much as the status of metapsychological discourse, is affected by the exemplary and the temporary, remaining essentially incommunicable and having to forego any hope of persuasion at the level of examples, which can always turn out to be motivated by the pleasure principle and the life instinct. And assuming the role of devil's advocate, to be summoned to defend a thing unworthy of being defended by proposing objections to and disputing the unreserved acceptance of the pleasure principle in psychoanalysis (this is how the text of *Beyond* begins)—is this not to expose himself to incredulity and incomprehension, thus furthering, more or less without knowing it, as a thing unquestionable, the very universality the devil's advocate wanted to challenge?

The text of *Beyond* is the scene of this (dialectical?) conflict between the witch and the man of science, taking shape in the figure of the devil's advocate. This struggle would perhaps be dialectical to the extent that the man of science would seem always to win. Now, the text is also a struggle of the two instincts that he dramatizes: the death instinct and the life instinct. Since the latter is the only one to show itself to the senses, since it seems to take charge of the pleasure principle, since it assumes the function of countering any possible agreement on the evidence of a contrary tendency that might weaken the apparent primacy of this principle, the silent work of the death instinct has perhaps appealed to the dialectic in question from the outset.

***

Freud's speculative, metapsychological discourse is, as a consequence, subdued to the very structure of its "object": the unconscious, the repetition compulsion, the (death) instinct. It shows its discontinuous nature in leaps and jumps, in bounds and rebounds, in detours and returns of all sorts, the purpose being to subvert the different forms that the *Darstellung* [presentation/representation] of these "objects" takes. The movements in question shape the text, without, for all that, being set out in a network of definitions. This operation becomes inevitable from the moment at which one decides not to stop the regressive movement to which the death instinct, with its endless reiteration, attests. Therefore, the death instinct cannot be a scientific object to the same degree as the life instinct (as long, to be sure, as this latter is not yet weakened by the death instinct). The non-objectivizable nature of this nonobject, fleeing, in the name of its regressive movement, without ceasing, without any possible place to stop, the dead products of its *Darstellung*, remaining like the traces of its impossible representation,[1] displays itself only in the interval of different repetitions. It is not only all certainty that thus collapses in this circumstance; the degree itself, or margin, of uncertainty remains impossible to determine.

Freud's breaking off at the end of his argument, before he proposes his critical remarks, is not a final result [*Endergebnis*] in the strict sense. The breaking off, and even its result, can only be provisional, for the process of combination, of repeated grafts, is not limited theoretically by an agency internal to the repetition.

---

1 Not only these varied and successive representations, but also the ceaseless repetition of one of these particular and concrete representations. [Gasché's note]

A result so much less definitive that the successive movement of combination provokes a growth, a fatal augmentation of uncertainty. Irrevocable, ineluctable uncertainty, to which has just been added as a supplement complete doubt in knowing whether one has guessed correctly or shamefully lost one's way, a doubt so powerful that it even abrogates all the rights of intuition: "One may have made a lucky hit or one may have gone shamefully astray [*in die Irre gegangen sein*]" (18: 59).

The breaking off, the interruption of the exposition concerning repetition and the life and death instincts, "mimics" a final result, which is nothing, however, but a figure articulating a non-object. The pretense of making critical observations bathes this apparent result in a critical light after the fact, in the light of theory. The breaking off constitutes a well drawn figure, resembling an experience, on which the light of critique can halt in its turn. Precisely because of the uncertainty, of the fugitive and fictive character of the result, this breaking off does not equally leave the light of theory intact. Freud writes:

> Since we have such good grounds for being distrustful, our attitude towards the results of our own deliberations [*eigenen Denkbemühung*] cannot well be other than one of cool benevolence [*ein kühles Wohlwollen*]. (59)

And again: "I hasten to add, however, that self-criticism such as this is far from binding one to any specific tolerance towards dissentient opinions" (59).

The critical remarks function to cut short any divergent opinion that might come from elsewhere. It appears, then, that the critical supplement, which seemed to be concerned with the final result, stigmatizing the undeniable uncertainty, is in fact a criticism addressed to the theoretical function itself. The critical supplement makes noticeable the undoubtedly provisional character of the final result, necessarily provisional, but not invalidating in any way the "logic," doubtful in itself, from which the result comes. Each representation of the death instinct, of the repetition compulsion, is in effect problematic; each *Endresultat* of their representation constitutes only a mixture motivated by the two originary instincts. The movement of these two articulated instincts, invalidating any stopping at a definitive result, is in effect the most powerful demonstration of the beyond—of the beyond of the pleasure principle, of the laws that regulate scientific discourse.

★★★

[P]hilosophy, for Freud, despite its incapacity to pronounce on the question of the phenomena indicated, becomes a part of the non-space from which ideas indispensable to metapsychological speculation are drawn. The reduction of philosophy to a domain of reference, to a reservoir of metaphors, to a region divided up by the fact that Freud refuses to rely on a well established philosophical system, both weakens and provokes the priority and originality recommended by philosophy. *Nor will philosophy escape the destiny inflicted on the sciences of being made use of and used up in the web of metapsychological discourse.*

On the first pages of *Beyond*, Freud writes that in his psychoanalytic work he is aiming neither at priority nor originality. This implies that even metapsychological speculation—to the extent that it shuffles the materials of observation unceasingly, where it is always ready to substitute new ideas for its ideas—has nothing definitive about it, in the sense of an original response to the desire for subjective comprehension of the significance of the phenomena analyzed. At a pinch, its originality could only be that of an original borrowing, inasmuch as it might adhere to a particular philosophical system, to a philosophy that would think the origin in a manner both fresh and original. Never paying attention, however, to such a significance, metapsychological speculation gives up altogether a final response to major questions. The borrowings and their successive multiplications endlessly displace any possible stopping at a specific significance. Mixed with large questions about the origin of life and death, metapsychological discourse, as an exhaustive description (through its topographical, dynamic, and economic viewpoints), cannot claim priority and originality, because it is going to have to give an account of the origin of originality and priority, an origin, however, whose mode will no longer be that of a definitive pronouncement.

Why then would Freud appear grateful to a philosophical system that would bring him an answer as to the significance of the sensations of pleasure and unpleasure? Would it not be because he could then have a response for his own use that, by its necessarily subjective and imaginary nature, could be submitted to metapsychological treatment?

Nietzsche, whose decisive importance for Freud is well known, appears in the text of *Beyond* without, however, being named, on the occasion of a reference to "the eternal return of the same" (22). On this subject, it is astonishing that the recourse to "lofty thought" comes in a context in which Freud is talking about utterly banal phenomena of repetition. In effect, it is a question of a series of examples of people continually deceived by repeated, fateful setbacks, examples belonging to the experience of daily life. If the Nietzschean thought of the eternal return arises precisely on this occasion, a mere banal reflection on unsurprising facts, then we must believe that for Freud the idea of "the eternal return of the same" has an explanatory value of the same order as what it is clarifying here: it is not more surprising than the facts to which it refers and which it does nothing but duplicate. Compared to the repetition compulsion and to what is reiterated in regressive repetition—death—the thought of the eternal return, a thought so close to Freud that it can seem to be Freud's, is nevertheless nothing but a deceptive figure. A philosopheme such as Nietzsche's in no way overtakes the belief in fate in the Freudian design, which common sense calls on in similar cases. In the argument of *Beyond*, the lofty thought of Nietzsche becomes only a sort of coin in exchange, a mere coin among others. Now if, despite everything, all interchange between Nietzschean philosophy and the speculation of Freud remains undeniable, it is not to be found at the level of declaration and of citation, but in a movement common to the two texts, *Beyond* and of *Zarathustra*, namely, in the fundamental impossibility of saying in a clear and distinct manner, of summarizing in *one* figure, the thought of return.[1]

What about Schopenhauer? After the reply, addressed to Weismann, that the forces of the death instinct are already right at work in the life of protozoa, after having reprivileged the dualistic conception of the two sorts of original instincts, Freud writes this:

---

1 In this regard, one should read Bernard Pautrat's "Nietzsche Medused." [Gasché's note]

    We skip over the references to Kant in the text of *Beyond*, which would require a more extended treatment than we can produce here.

There is something else, at any rate, that we cannot remain blind to. We have unwittingly steered our course into the harbour of Schopenhauer's philosophy. For him death is the 'true result and to that extent the purpose of life,' while the sexual instinct is the embodiment of the will to live. (49-50)

The passage cited is preceded by the refutation of Weismann's thesis concerning the immortality of the protozoa. Biology has demonstrated its incapacity to reject the supposition of a death instinct intrinsic to living matter from the moment of its origin. This powerlessness then becomes for Freud the negative condition for starting the speculation rolling again. For, notwithstanding the facts that he (along with other researchers) opposes to Weismann's theses, the facts themselves could not be relevant. Their irrelevance emerges with evidence of an opposition that Freud constructs on this occasion, between manifest signs of death [*manifeste Aeusserung des Todes*] and internal, latent processes pressing towards death. The first, the manifest signs, are acquired late, while the latter are earlier, innate to living matter. The distinction in question is not based on the facts that Freud has used to refute the thesis of immortality: it is only the negative character of certain facts that has made it conceivable.

Freud revalorizes after the fact the distinction between soma and germ-plasm. Here he emphasizes the striking likeness [*auffällige Aehnlichkeit*] to his distinction between the life and death instincts. But in fact, if there is an analogy, is it not exclusively in the idea of a dualism in general, to which the two sets of oppositions would only be bearing witness? One would be thus led to affirm that anything dualistic could do the job. Therefore, the taking up again of the Weismannian dualism is not a return to this author's mode of enunciation, a mode that Freud has not ceased refuting throughout the preceding. On the contrary, this reprise splits Weismann's dualism. That is to say that, rejected initially for its lack of a clear contrast, the Weismannian dualism is undermined by a dualism more radical still, which not only splits the opposed terms with more vigour, but which, with the opposition between the manifest exteriorization and latent impulsion of the death instinct, dualizes the very terms of the originating opposition:

We may pause for a moment over this pre-eminently dualistic view of instinctual life. According to E. Hering's theory, two kinds of processes are constantly at work in living substance, operating in contrary directions, one constructive or assimilatory and the other destructive or dissimilatory. May we venture to recognize in these two directions taken by the vital processes the activity of our two instinctual impulses, the life instincts and the death instincts? (49)

A proper name, that of Weismann, is replaced by another, the name of Hering. Is there development, or simple analogical substitution? Or do these two conceptions, those of Hering and those of Weismann, function in the text to exclude one another, the one representing principally the constructive and progressive tendency (the thesis of the immortality of the germ-plasm), the other going rather in a direction already opposed? A displacement of the limited dualistic conception of Weismann towards a balanced dualism, giving equal importance to assimilatory and to dissimilatory tendencies, has certainly taken place. The response to the question of a possible identification of these two tendencies with the Freudian dualism remains again in suspense, however, for as elegant as Hering's dualism may be, it has not yet been shaped by the distinction between manifest sign and imperceptible impulsion of death.

If assimilation means rendering similar, and if dissimilation (in German, *Dissimilation*) implies differentiation, difference, and if this last marks a movement of deanalogization, then the so-called striking analogy between the Freudian conception of the nature of the instincts and the dualism of Weismann or of Hering ought necessarily to be dissimilated. This will take place surreptitiously. Being the characteristic, in the sense attached here to this term, of a textual practice that, by the play of substituting analogies, provokes their subversion from another register—that of a radicalized and generalized dualism—the dissimilation in question happens noiselessly. This practice—interior to language, to its structure—that pulls to pieces the dualisms of the two authors named, so that they appear like belated manifestations of the undermining impulse in the substitutive structure of language, is the erosion of analogism, insofar as it would be the mimesis of an earlier plenitude. *Dissimilation is, at the level of the text, the silent and imperceptible work of the death instinct.*

The work of death happens in silence. In order to fill this gap, to say it in the very impossibility of saying it—for it invalidates every expression, linguistic or other, every possible signification—all analogies are good so long as they are ceaselessly replaced, unceasingly dissimilated. By this bias alone—and let us not forget that the term, dissimilation, is only a figure, no less an analogy—the metapsychological text, whose discourse has to do with the repetition of death, "manifests" this death and its silence in submitting itself from the outset to the "laws" that govern the instincts.

On the other hand, what do they do, the philosophers and certain psychoanalysts as well? They invent new distinctions and metaphors for their own pleasure, busying themselves [*wirtschaften*] in manipulating them "and juggled with them like the ancient Greek natural philosophers with their four elements" (51). With psychoanalysis, they have in common the profusion of distinctions, the production of substitutes, in order to saturate a domain where one marks time in complete obscurity. But the philosophers try to fill in the hole, to cover it over, to muffle the silence in the jumble of productive significations. They make use of the substitutive nature of language as it suits them and unknown to themselves are subjected to its ascendency and its dissimilating structure. By the denial or repression of this undermining activity, they are subject to the lure of signification. On the other hand, metapsychological speculation produces an effusion of substitutes, but doesn't retain them long enough to establish significations. Through its elaboration of a radical dualism, and its always already undermining of the set of oppositions produced by the philosophers, it gets at the veiled nudity of the instinctual structure of language. It does not reach it through the enunciation of this dualism, but insofar as it repeats, through its consuming and dissimilating of the analogies it finds ready made or which it invents in its turn, the instinctual structure of language. In this repetition, by this return to the fatal anteriority of signification, metapsychological discourse prepares for its own exhaustion. Thus it does not represent, it does not signify this approximative activity the philosophers busy themselves with; it demonstrates the work of the instinct in the putting to death of signification and of representation.[1]

---

1 For a more exhaustive analysis of the destabilization of signification and of representation, one reads the decisive texts of Jacques
   Derrida, "Freud and the Scene of Writing" and Jean-Michel Rey
   (1974), especially the chapter, "De la dénégation." [Gasché's note]

In return for which, metapsychology can go to the point of accommodating itself, without the sin of arbitrariness, to the very material of familiar beliefs. From this point of view, it can equally do without any philosophical reflection of its own: it finds it always already elaborated somewhere, even though it is powerless, as are other discourses, to respond to the large questions. It finds it ready for the work of misappropriation.

After the developments that we have put forward, the name of Schopenhauer arises. Just like the others, his proper name is only a piece of money to spend. It is worth our while, nonetheless, to stop a moment at this name, so that we may analyze the stunning metaphorics that emerges with him, and finally, because we find ourselves at a decisive turning point in the text that announces itself as follows: "Let us make a bold attempt at another step forward" (50).

After the elegant dualisms of Weismann and Hering have been advanced, the Schopenhauerian dualism turns up: one dualism more, but a dualism where the accents have perhaps been displaced. If the dualism of Weismann was limited because he privileged the life instinct, and if that of Hering balanced the two terms of the opposition, Schopenhauer's dualism lends itself to reinforcing the primacy of the death instinct. With him, this appears to be the "true result" of life. The conception in question seems to have something in common with that of Freud insofar as it would perhaps already obey the distinction made between manifest death and its latent work. It is to the will to live (in the sexual instinct) that the act of incarnation [*Verkörperung*], and therefore, of manifestation, is imputed. It is the will to live that again puts flesh on death, which is then able to take on the apparition of a manifest sign. Death, on the other hand, is defined by Schopenhauer as result and telos. The "true result" would then manifest death as a last compromise of death with life, as an incarnation that signifies again the primacy of the force of life. The purpose [*Zweck*], on the other hand, the telos, would be understood as the silent work of the death instinct, playing around with its incarnation in the manifest sign under the apparent primacy of the life instinct. All that remains clearly undecidable, if one keeps strictly to the text of Freud alone.

But what matters is that Schopenhauer's philosophy represents a harbor for Freud where his speculations can end up [*einlaufen*]. As if Freud, wandering on the seas, lost amid the uncertainties of speculation, has been conducted without perceiving it to a secure place, that of a particular philosophy. Towards a port, notwithstanding the diverse wanderings, whose bay would have always already embraced him. Towards a harbour that understood his speculations even before their beginning and which marks them with originality after the fact. Does the wandering that led him as unexpectedly [*unversehens*] to the harbour of Schopenhauer's philosophy, to the conception of a philosophical dualism (that by its ambiguity, however, remains very close to Hering's), does it guarantee indemnity, does it assure the safe and sound passage of the traveller? In this way, Freud would not be susceptible to any reproach, all that he had advanced up to that point being already canonized. No recourse properly speaking to philosophy therefore, but an unwished for result, unknown to Freud and, consequently, all the more reassuring! Always already supported by philosophy, the arbitrary and fantastical speculations of metapsychology would see themselves justified after the fact. The harbour of Schopenhauer's philosophy seems then to promise nothing less than an intact disembarking on well established ground.

Now, Freud will immediately propose an audacious step forward, one step more and leading further [*weiter*]. Would this be a step onto the continent of the terra firma of Schopenhauerian philosophy, or would it be rather a question of a step leading beyond the dichotomy: wandering on a sea, wandering that leads the traveller always without his knowledge to the shore of terra firma and the assurance of stepping on this earth? Namely, beyond the dichotomy of an opposition whose terms are equivalent, imbricating itself in a well balanced interdependence?

The one step beyond, following the entry [*einlaufen*] into port, could be of such a sort that this engagement would only be provisional [*vorläufig*]. The ambiguity of Freud with regard to Schopenhauer shows well that he is going to take a supplementary step in and outside this philosophy, thus leaving the promised terra firma. In effect, the step sketched in the rest of *Beyond* is a step that, after developing unprecedented speculations concerning the transposition of narcissism to cellular life, ends up after some detours in another harbour, already less reassuring—namely the myth of Aristophanes in the *Symposium*. Thus, Schopenhauer will only have been a springboard on which one never again falls back once the leap has been taken. But this springboard will have been useful for, and will have been inscribed in, the wasting and consuming movement of speculation.

***

In the light of speculation, the special place of the sexual instincts collapses, as well as the theoretical discourse that has granted them this status. If theoretical discourse is founded on an intellectual predisposition [*Streben*]—which obliges us to notice that *streben* signifies also "to buttress," "to prop up," a movement by which theoretical and scientific discourse substantiates, supports the sexual instincts as if it sought to preserve, to re-establish the earliest propping [*Anlehnung*] of the sexual instincts on the ego instincts, to avoid the dissolution, the uncoupling of the two sorts of instincts and the forced entry of the sexual as phantasm, extending beyond the purely reproductive function of sexuality— in that case, it must be considered one of the substitutes for repression of the instincts, of their regressive aspect.

It is uniquely in the strange light of speculation and of its presuppositions, a light which focuses on the algebraic sign x that the instincts represent, that their "real" nature can appear.

Bathed in this unusual light, the life instincts cease to play the role of peace breaker [*Störenfried*] that they represent as much in psychic life as in the theoretical discourse charged with giving an account of them:

> Another striking fact is that the life instincts have so much more contact with our internal perception—emerging as breakers of the peace and constantly producing tensions whose release is felt as pleasure—while the death instincts seem to do their work unobtrusively. (63)

The strange light of the hypothesis makes a *tabula rasa* of what absorbs the theoretical, of what troubles its reasoning [*empfindliche Störung unseres Gedankenganges*], of the pleasure that science experiences again in its work, in order to displace it at once beyond the pleasure principle. What lies beyond the philosophic and the metatheoretical speculative is the myth, which thus responds to the desire for a certain silence of scientific discourse, fulfilling in its work the loss of profit and the victory over the pleasure principle. Therefore, the myth will be this disquieting light that for a moment will throw light on obscure origins. The myth will have the power to pierce the darkness because it is spoken: words of *Aristophanes* who brought a light regarding origins while distinguishing himself by his prophetic force; words, therefore, that will definitely re-establish the silence by making the repetition of the death instinct be repeated. In other terms, the myth repeated by Freud, and which he draws from an earlier scene than scientific discourse strictly speaking, a fantastic and phantasmatic myth representing a primitive scene—the separation of a unity that afterwards tends to reconstitute itself—(is) the repetition in a figure which, as an image, illuminates and makes visible that aspect of the origin that cannot be spoken of except in figures or in scenes. As a consequence, the mythic light reestablishes the obscurity, its word reinstates the initial silence, having suspended it and displaced it for an instant only. In the slender break that separates the two obscurities, the initial obscurity and the obscurity after the illumination, the presuppositional, parenthetical hypothesis looms up, like a flash [*Lichtstrahl*] that repeats death in its obliteration. By the division that is reiterated and that reiterates obscurities, the phantasmatic hypothesis becomes the lot of scientific discourse and exploits the repetition compulsion as the repetition of the death of this discourse. The way scientific discourse finds of dying in its own way [*der eigene Todesweg*] is its reinscription within the order of the phantasmatic, within the regime of a certain mythic quality, which is not the myth of the philosophy or of the science which would have preceded them as their disfiguration.

★★★

Let us try to make operative—now that the mechanism is in place—a series of signifiers that continuously mark the text of *Beyond*: the provisional, the vacillating, the patient.

Before committing himself to a discussion of the possibly progressive character of certain instincts (other than the conservative instincts), Freud writes:

> [F]or the moment it is tempting to pursue to its logical conclusion the hypothesis that all instincts tend toward the restoration of an earlier state of things. The outcome may give an impression of mysticism of or sham profundity; but we can

feel quite innocent of having had any such purpose in view. We seek only for the sober results of research or of reflection based on it; and we have no wish to find in those results any quality other than certainty. (37)

A note at the bottom of the page warns the reader that eventually such an extreme way of conceiving the conservative character of the instincts will be toned down. Nevertheless, nothing of the sort happens, and, on the contrary, this aspect will become more insistent when the subject is the repetitive nature of the sexual instincts. For Freud, speculation and its development are in the service of a larger certainty. The correction that is later brought to speculation suggests that here it is a question only of heuristic theses that will require verification and limitation by the material of observation. On the contrary, the extreme theses will not be falsified, nor toned down, nor limited in the text of *Beyond*, but will be extended more widely. Therefore, the promised recasting of the thesis by means of the material of observation doesn't come about, for the thesis is so extreme that it renews itself at each confrontation with new material of observation.

If, therefore, there is a place to speak of certainty, it is here that we should pin it down. The requirement of a wider certainty must be understood as the power to repeat the same thesis. A thesis like this can only belong to the order of speculation. In its successive realizations, each one more radical than the last, it in no way abandons its "profound," even its slightly mystical, aspect.

From the beginning, therefore, there is a kind of seduction, a temptation to trap oneself [*verlocken*] into following the paths of wandering deliberately. These ways, and the results to which they lead, are evidence of a certainty—of a certainty that is nevertheless the product of the uncontrollable reappearance of these results after each new confrontation with the facts. This certainty, moreover, in itself uncertain, is a "provisional certainty" [*vorläufig*]. The reason for it being so must be imputed to the fact that absolutely nothing is known of what the speculation is supposed to be giving an account. It is the big X, the original chiasmus, the bar that crosses out all knowledge about the nature of the instincts, about the nature of excitatory phenomena in the elements of psychic systems, the shortcoming of a well defined, clear and distinguishable object, that makes all speculation, however certain it may be, remain nonetheless indefinitely provisional and indeterminate:

> The indefiniteness of all our discussions on what we describe as metapsychology is of course due to the fact that we know nothing of the nature of the excitatory process that takes place in the elements of psychic systems, and that we do not feel justified in framing any hypothesis on the subject. We are consequently operating all the time with a large unknown factor [in Richter: "a large X"], which we are obliged to carry over into every new formula. (30-31)

Therefore, there is no object that might serve to validate speculative considerations once and for all. The emptiness of the knowledge they are concerned with will repeat itself ceaselessly in each new construction—reason enough why speculations are based only on their substitutive, progressively radical movements—incorporating and manipulating all the available material in its regressive movement. It is only by locating and repeating their movements in different facts that the speculations are assured of a certain certainty. It is also provisional, however, for sidestepping the big X is also their product. Because one must serve as a substitute for the other, metapsychological speculations work to break the object down. They are caught between two provisional arrangements: one that aims at and anticipates a presence—the impossible chance arrival of the object X—and another that runs [*läuft*] before [*vor*] even the possibility of representation. This last provisionality is bound by its very nature, because it belongs to the primary process, to all that has been said concerning the character of the instincts. This implies a repetitive character, one that tends to re-establish a prior state, to return to what takes place before the process, before the *Vorgang*.

What leads metapsychological speculations, originating in profound prejudices, to be engulfed immediately in an earlier time, only to set out again by representing themselves in figures and new constructions, is the fact of their not being bound, of their looking for an immediate satisfaction, obeying the economy of the primary process. It is what gives them their floating character. The wandering, floating aspect, the fact of not being bound, no longer shares the fragile relation of metatheoretical speculation to scientific empiricism. Strictly speaking, it is beyond that dichotomy and all that it implies. For metapsychological speculations do not float above established empirical facts; rather, they propel and set the facts going by a process of brewing them together, using them up, consuming them as representations of the big X, perpetually different and deferred. They consume them as they are themselves engulfed.

Speaking then at the beginning of *Beyond,* of the most obscure region of psychic life, Freud remarks that the vaguest and most indeterminate suppositions [*Annahmen*] are best suited to prepare an approach to this fleeting domain:

> This is the most obscure [the meaning of the feelings of pleasure and unpleasure—R.G.] and inaccessible region of the mind, and, since we cannot avoid contact with it, the least rigid hypothesis, it seems to me, will be the best [*so wird die lockerste Annahme, so meine ich, die beste sein*]. (7)

The most vague and indeterminate supposition defers certainty; it belongs to the order of speculation. It will not bring a definitive solution to the great questions. It is nothing but the always provisional substitute for such a response, a substitute that is therefore indefinitely replaceable. Scientific progress, then, is nothing other than this infinite movement of substitutions of always provisional responses. Patience, then, is indispensable, a patience that will have no limit. Let us read, at the end of *Beyond:*

> We must be patient and await fresh methods and occasions of research. We must be ready, too, to abandon a path that we have followed for a time, if it seems to be leading to no good end. Only believers, who demand that science shall be a substitute for the catechism they have given up, will blame an investigator for developing or even transforming his views. (64)

What is not bound as supposition, what has no basis in any belief, what witnesses solely to profound prejudices in the resolution of the great problems is what lends itself very particularly, however paradoxical this may appear, to substitution and expenditure.

The remark about the necessity for vague suppositions is followed by the development of the first speculative thesis, namely the pleasure principle:

We have decided [*entschlossen*] to relate pleasure and unpleasure to the quantity of excitation that is present in the mind but is not in any way "bound"; and to relate them in such a manner that unpleasure corresponds to an *increase* in the quantity of excitation and pleasure to a *diminution*. (7-8)

If "decided" [*entschlossen*] is the contrary of *verschlossen*, of "reserved," of "restrained," then the decision in question obeys the acceptance of a floating supposition in theoretical discourse, similar in this way to the apparatus not being able to avoid the irruption of a quantity of unbound energy that requires to be discharged in order to be able to return after to a state of instinctual silence. Now, the instincts only keep silent for a little while before appearing again with renewed vigour. Patience is indispensable as well with regard to their definitive reduction in the silence of death. What is instinctively seductive [*verlocken*] about getting oneself trapped into adopting, into introducing vague [*locker*] suppositions into discourse, is the pleasure in what is vague, in digression, in wandering. Wandering, being always in a position to dispense with the accepted suppositions, is quite obviously governed by the pleasure principle; but it is a pleasure without profit. It is born of the tension that defers its immediate abolition, following in that fashion the proper manner for theoretical discourse to be engulfed by its own death, to waste away in non-significance.

The detours that lead theoretical discourse to its death are the paths of wandering, of the infinitely provisional. It can only attain this death by limping. The text of *Beyond* breaks off by being conciliatory over the slowness of scientific progress, which is that of a course full of obstacles, towards [*vorlaufen*] a "knowledge" of death in the phantasmatic framework, and towards the abolition of theoretical discourse in the mythic silence. Attesting to this silence are the *Vorlieben*, the prejudices that already shape the text of *Beyond* in silence, and which reduce it, which try to reduce it to silence in a certain writing and a certain speech, which is only its effect. Consolation comes, incidentally, from a writer:

What we cannot reach flying, we must reach limping.
The Book tells us it is no sin to limp.

19. *The Metaphor of the Death Drive and Its Counter-Finality* (1976)[1]

Jean Baudrillard

With Freud we pass from philosophical death and the drama of consciousness to death as a pulsional process inscribed in the unconscious order; from a metaphysics of anguish to a metaphysics of the pulsion. It's just as if death, *liberated from the subject*, at last gained its status as an *objective* finality: the pulsional energy of death or the principle of psychical functioning.

Death, by becoming a pulsion, does not cease to be a finality (it is even the only end from this standpoint: the proposition of the death drive signifies an extraordinary simplification of finalities, since even Eros is subordinate to it), but this finality sinks, and is inscribed in the unconscious. Now this sinking of death into the unconscious coincides with the sinking of the dominant system: death becomes simultaneously a "principle of psychical functioning" and the "reality principle" of our social formations, through the immense repressive mobilisation of labour and production. In other words, with the death drive, Freud installs the process of *repetition* at the core of objective determinations, at the very moment when the general system of production passes into pure and simple *reproduction*. This coincidence is extraordinary, since we are much more interested in a *genealogy* of the concept of the death drive than in its metaphysical status. Is the death drive an anthropological "discovery" which supplants all the others (and which can from now on provide a universal explanatory principle: we can imagine political economy entirely governed and engendered by the death drive), or is it *produced* at a given moment in relation to a particular configuration of the system? In this case, its radical nature is simply the radical nature of the system itself, and the concept merely sanctions a culture of death by giving it the label of a trans-historical pulsion. This operation is characteristic of all idealist thought, but we refuse to admit this with Freud. With Freud (as with Marx), Western reason will stop rationalising and idealising its own principles, it will even stop idealising reality through its critical effect of "objectivity."

---

1   From *Symbolic Exchange and Death* (1976). Trans. Iain Hamilton Grant. London: Sage, 1993. 148-54.

Ultimately, reality will designate unsurpassable pulsional or economic structures: thus the death drive as the *eternal* process of desire. But how is it that this proposition is itself not a matter of a secondary elaboration?

It is true that, at first, the death drive breaks with Western thought. From Christianity to Marxism and existentialism: either death is openly denied and sublimated, or it is dialecticised. In Marxist theory and practice, death is already conquered in the being of the class, or it is integrated as historical negativity. In more general terms, the whole Western practice of the domination of nature and the sublimation of aggression in production and accumulation is characterised as constitutive Eros: Eros makes use of sublimated aggression for its own ends and, in the movement of becoming (this applies just as much to political economy), death is distilled as negativity into homeopathic doses. Not even the modern philosophies of "being-towards-death" reverse this tendency: here death serves as a tragic haunting of the subject, sealing its absurd liberty.

In Freud it is quite another matter. A dialectic with the death drive is no longer possible; there is no longer any sublimation, even if it is tragic. For the first time, death appeared as an indestructible *principle*, in opposition to Eros. The subject, class and history are irrelevant in this regard: the irreducible duality of the two pulsions, Eros and Thanatos, reawakens the ancient Manichean version of the world, the endless antagonism of the twin principles of good and evil. This very powerful vision comes from the ancient cults where the basic intuition of a specificity of evil and death was still strong. This was unbearable to the Church, who will take centuries to exterminate it and impose the pre-eminent principle of the Good (God), reducing evil and death to a negative principle, dialectically subordinate to the other (the Devil). But there is always the nightmare of Lucifer's autonomy, the Archangel of Evil (in all their forms, as popular heresies and superstitions that always have a tendency to take the existence of a principle of evil literally and hence to form cults around it, even including black magic and Jansenist theory, not to mention the Cathars), which will haunt the Church day and night. It opposes the dialectic as an institutional theory and as a deterrent to a radical, dualistic and Manichean concept of death. History will bring victory to the Church and the dialectic (including the "materialist" dialectic). In this sense, Freud breaks quite profoundly with Christian and Western metaphysics.

The duality of the life and death instincts corresponds more precisely to Freud's position in *Beyond the Pleasure Principle*. In *Civilisation and Its Discontents,* the duality completes itself in a cycle dominated solely by the death drive. Eros is nothing but an immense detour taken by culture towards death, which subordinates everything to its own ends. But this last version does not, however, revert to an inverted dialectic between the two terms of the duality, since dialectics can only be the constructive becoming of Eros, whose goal is "to establish ever larger unities and to bind and regulate energies." Two principal characteristics oppose the death drive to this:

1. It dissolves assemblages, unbinds energy and undoes Eros's organic discourse by returning things to an inorganic, *ungebunden*, state, in a certain sense, to utopia as opposed to the articulate and constructive topics of Eros. Entropy of death, negentropy of Eros.

2. This power of disintegration, disarticulation and *defection* implies a radical counter-finality in the form of an involution towards the prior, inorganic state. The compulsion to repeat (*Wiederholungszwang*), or the "tendency to reproduce and revive even those past events that involve no satisfaction whatsoever," is primarily, for every living being, the tendency to reproduce the non-event of a prior inorganic state of things, that is to say, death. It is thus always as a repetitive cycle that death comes to dismantle the constructive, linear or dialectical finalities of Eros. The viscosity of the death drive and the elasticity of the inorganic is everywhere victorious in its resistance to the structuration of life.

In the proposed death drive therefore, whether in its duel form or in the incessant and destructive counter-finality of repetition, there is something irreducible to all the intellectual apparatuses of Western thought. Freud's thought acts fundamentally as the death drive in the Western theoretical universe. But then, of course, it is absurd to give it the constructive status of "truth": the "reality" of the death instinct is indefensible; to remain faithful to the intuition of the death drive, it must remain a deconstructive hypothesis, that is, it must be adopted solely within the limits of the deconstruction that it carries out on all prior thought. As a concept, however, it too must be immediately deconstructed. We cannot think (other than as the ultimate subterfuge of reason) that the principle of deconstruction is all that escapes it.

The death drive must be defended against every attempt to redialecticise it into a new constructive edifice. Marcuse is a good example of this. Concerning repression through death, he writes: "Theology and philosophy today compete with each other in celebrating death as an existential category. Perverting[!] a biological fact into an ontological essence, they bestow transcendental blessing on the guilt of mankind which they help to perpetuate" (Marcuse, *Eros* 188). Thus it is for "surplus-repression." As for fundamental repression:

> The brute fact of death denies once and for all the reality of a non-repressive existence. For death is the final negativity of time, but 'joy wants eternity'.... Time has no power over the Id, the original domain of the pleasure principle. But the Ego, through which alone pleasure becomes real, is in its entirety subject to time. The mere anticipation of the inevitable end, present in every instant, introduces a repressive element into all libidinal relations. (185)

We will overlook the "brute fact of death": it is never a brute fact, only a social relation is repressive. What is most curious is the way in which death's primal repression exchanges signs with the "liberation" of Eros:

> The death instinct operates under the Nirvana principle: it tends towards... a state without want. This trend of this instinct implies that its *destructive* manifestations would be minimised as it approached such a state. If the instinct's basic objective is not the termination of life but of pain—the absence of tension—then paradoxically, in terms of the instinct, the conflict between life and death is the more reduced, the closer life approximates the state of gratification.... Eros, freed from surplus-repression, would be strengthened, and the strengthened Eros would, as it were, absorb the objective of the death instinct. *The instinctual value of death would have changed.* (187, emphasis added)

Thus we will be able to change the instinct and triumph over the brute fact, in accordance with good old idealist philosophy of freedom and necessity:

Death can become a token of freedom. The necessity of death does not refute the possibility of final liberation. Like the other necessities, it can be made rational—painless. (188)

The Marcusean dialectic therefore implies the total restoration of the death drive (in *Eros and Civilisation*, however, this passage is immediately followed by the "Critique of Neo-Freudian Revisionism"!), thus limiting the resistances this concept provokes in pious souls. Here again, it is not too much for dialectics—the "liberation" of Eros in this instance; in others the "liberation" of the forces of production—to bring about the end of death.

The death drive is irritating, because it does not allow of any dialectical recovery. This is where its radicalism lies. But the panic it provokes does not confer the status of truth on it: we must wonder if, in the final instance, it is not itself a rationalisation of death.

This is first of all the conviction that we hear in Freud (elsewhere he will talk of a speculative hypothesis):

> The dominating tendency of mental life ... is the effort to reduce, to keep constant or to remove internal tension due to stimuli (the 'Nirvana principle', to borrow a term from Barbara Low) ... [which] is one of our strongest reasons for believing in the existence of death instincts. (Freud, *Standard* 18: 55-56)

Why, then, all Freud's efforts to ground the death instinct in biological rationality (Weismann's analysis, etc.)? This positivist effort is generally deplored, a little like Engels'[1] attempt to dialecticise Nature that we agree to ignore out of affection for him. However:

> If we are to take it as a truth that knows no exception that everything living dies for *internal* reasons—becomes inorganic once again—then we shall be compelled to say that *'the aim of all life is death'* and, looking backwards, that *'inanimate things existed before living ones'*.... Thus these guardians of life [instincts], too, were originally the myrmidons of death. (38)

---

1 Friedrich Engels (1820-95) German political theorist and co-author, with Marx, of *The Communist Manifesto* (1848).

It is difficult to rid the death drive of positivism here in order to turn it into a "speculative hypothesis" or "purely and simply a principle of psychical functioning" (Pontalis). Moreover, at this level there is no longer any real pulsional duality: death alone is finality. But it is this finality that in turn poses a crucial problem, since it inscribes death as anterior, as psychical and organic destiny, almost like programming or genetic code, in short, as a *positivity* that, unless we believe in the scientific reality of this pulsion, we can only take it as a myth. We can only set Freud against what he himself says:

> The theory of the drives is so to say our mythology. Drives are mythical entities, magnificent in their indefiniteness. (22: 95)

If the death drive is a myth, then this is how we will interpret it. We will interpret the death drive, and the concept of the unconscious itself, as myths, and no longer take account of their effects or their efforts at "truth." A myth *recounts* something: not so much in the content as in the form of its discourse. Let's make a bet that, under the metaphoric species of sexuality and death, psychoanalysis tells us something concerning the fundamental organisation of our culture, that when the myth is no longer told, when it establishes its fables as axioms, it loses the "magnificent indefiniteness" that Freud spoke of. "The concept is only the residue of a metaphor," as Nietzsche said. Let's bet then on the *metaphor* of the unconscious, on the *metaphor* of the death drive.

Eros in the service of death, all cultural sublimation as a long detour to death, the death drive nourishing repressive violence and presiding over culture like a ferocious super-ego, the forces of life inscribed in the compulsion to repeat; all this is true, but true of *our* culture. Death undertakes to abolish death and, for this very purpose, erects death above death and is haunted by it as its own end. The term "pulsion" or "drive" is stated metaphorically, designating the contemporary phase of the political economic system (does it then remain political economy?) where the law of value, in its most terroristic structural form, reaches completion in the pure and simple compulsive reproduction of the code, where the law of value appears to be a finality as irreversible as a pulsion, so that it takes on the figure of a destiny for our culture. Stage of the immanent repetition of one and the same law, insisting on its own end, caught, totally invested by death as objective finality, and total subversion by the death drive as a deconstructive process—the metaphor of the death drive says all of this simultaneously, for the death drive is at the same time the system and the system's *double,* its doubling into a radical counter-finality (see the Double, and its "worrying strangeness," *das Unheimliche* [the Uncanny]).

This is what the myth recounts. But let's see what happens when it sets itself up as the objective discourse of the "pulsion." With the term "pulsion," which has both a biological and a psychical definition, psychoanalysis settles down into categories that come straight from the imaginary of a certain Western reason: far from radically contradicting this latter, it must then interpret itself as a moment of Western thought. As for the biological, it is clear that scientific rationality produces the distinction of the living and the non-living on which biology is based. Science, producing itself as a code, on the one hand literally produces the dead, the non-living, as a conceptual object, and, on the other, produces the separation of the dead as an axiom from which science can be legitimated. The only good (scientific) object, just like the only good Indian, is a dead one. Now it is this inorganic state to which the death drive is oriented, to the non-living status that only comes about through the arbitrary decrees of science and, when all's said and done, through its own phantasm of repression and death. Ultimately, being nothing but the cyclical repetition of the nonliving, the death drive contributes to biology's arbitrariness, doubling it through a psychoanalytic route. But not every culture produces a separate concept of the non-living; only our culture produces it, under the sign of biology. Thus, suspending the discrimination would be enough to invalidate the concept of the death drive, which is ultimately only a theoretical agreement between the living and the dead, with the sole result that science loses its footing amongst all the attempts at articulation. The nonliving is always permanently sweeping science along into the axiomatics of a system of death.

The problem is the same as regards the psychical, putting the whole of psychoanalysis into question. We must ask ourselves when and why our system began to produce the "psychical." The psychical has only recently become autonomous, doubling biology's autonomy at a higher level. This time the line passes between the organic, the somatic and "something else." There is nothing psychical save on the basis of this distinction. Hence the ensuing insoluble difficulty of linking the two parts together again; the precise result of this is the concept of the pulsion, which is intended to form a bridge between the two, but which merely contributes to the arbitrariness of each. Here the meta-psychology of the pulsion reverts to mind-body metaphysics, rewriting it at a more advanced stage.

The separated order of the psychical results from our precipitate desire, in our (conscious or unconscious) "heart of hearts," for everything that the system prohibits from collective and symbolic exchange: it is an order of the repressed. It is hardly astonishing that this order is governed by the death drive, since it is nothing but the precipitate individual of an order of death. Psychoanalysis, like every other discipline, theorises the death drive as such within its own order, and so merely sanctions this mortal discrimination.

Conscious, unconscious, super-ego, guilt, repression, primary and secondary processes, phantasm, neurosis and psychosis: yes, all this works very well *if we consent to* the circumscription of the psychical as such, which circumscription produces our system (not just any system) as the immediate and fundamental form of intelligibility, that is to say, as *code.* The omnipotence of the code is precisely the inscription of separate spheres, which then justifies a specialised investigation and a sovereign science; but it is undoubtedly the psychical that has the best future. All the savage, errant, transversal and symbolic processes will be inscribed and domesticated within it, *in the name of the unconscious itself,* which, like an unexpected joke, is generally considered today as the leitmotiv of radical "liberation"! Death itself will be domesticated under the sign of the death drive!

In fact the death drive must be interpreted against Freud and psychoanalysis if we wish to retain its radicality. The death drive must be understood as acting against the scientific positivity of the psychoanalytic apparatus as developed by Freud. The death drive is not just the limit of psychoanalysis's formulations nor its most radical conclusion, it is its reversal, and those who have rejected the concept of the death drive have, in a certain sense, a more accurate view than those who take it, as even Freud himself did, in their psychoanalytic stride without, perhaps, understanding what he had said. The death drive effectively goes far beyond all previous points of view and renders all previous apparatuses, whether economic, energetic, topological or even the psychical apparatus itself, useless. All the more reason, of course, for the pulsional logic it draws on, inherited from the scientific mythology of the nineteenth century. Perhaps Lacan guessed this when he spoke of the "irony" of the concept of the death drive, of the unheard of and insoluble paradox that it poses. Historically, psychoanalysis has taken the view that this is its strangest offspring, but death does not allow itself to be caught in the mirror of psychoanalysis. It acts as a total, radical, functional principle, and has no need of the mirror, repression, nor even a libidinal economy. It merely meanders through successive topologies and energetic calculi, ultimately forming the economics of the unconscious itself, denouncing all that *as well* as Eros's positive machinery, as the positive interpreting machine that it disrupts and dismantles like any other. A principle of counter-finality, a radical speculative hypothesis, meta-economic, metapsychical, meta-energetic, metapsychoanalytic, the death (drive) is beyond the unconscious: it must be wrested from psychoanalysis and turned against it.

20. *The Work of Death* (1976)[1]
J.-B. Pontalis

Whatever the personal motives (mournings) or collective motives (the hecatomb of the Great War, which had not yet been given a number, and which made a corpse of Reason) which may have pushed Freud to propose a principle going beyond the coupling pleasure principle/reality principle without any decisive clinical proof, it is clear that these pages (I have in mind the essay written in 1920), so close in their movement, not in their style, to associative discourse, are sustained throughout by a *demand* for thought, analogous to a desire that irrepressibly seeks out the path of truth: "It's as though I'm obliged to believe it."

This path was not followed by disciples of the time, or else it was diverted in another direction, in my opinion, by those who, like Melanie Klein, seemed to be profoundly committed to it while focussing the death instinct on the object (external or internal), thus reducing it to a force aiming at *destroying* this object.

---

1 From "On Death Work" (1976 [1977])." *Frontiers in Psychoanalysis: Between the Dream and Psychic Pain.*" Trans. Catherine Cullen and Philip Cullen. London: Hogarth Press, 1981. 190-91.

Everything about this notion is disturbing: its speculative air (which Freud admitted), the coupling of the terms instinct and death in just one word *Todestrieb*. Instinct was until then associated with self-preservation, with life, above all with sexuality, but it was now associated with death—death, traditionally associated with the cessation of life and attributed to the expected but *denied* intervention of an outside agent. But what is concerned here? The desire for death, or the death of desire? And how can one tolerate the assertion, itself repetitive, that "every being dies necessarily from internal causes?" (Was this an oblique message to psychoanalysis, that entity conceived, made and maintained alive by Freud, an admission of his disillusionment as to the creative abilities of its members, the presentiment that the death instinct would turn against the psychoanalytical edifice, against its Eros?)

The term "instinct" is also awkward here. Where is one to find the source, the object and the aim of the death instinct? Which are its delegates? Which representations and which affects?

There lies the error made as much by those who refute the death instinct as by those upholding it on the grounds of a *destrudo*, as opposed to a *libido*: they act as though it were a question of a particular form of instinct, and they then seek to establish what *represents* it:

—Is it aggressive and destructive behaviour (which Freud could bear out), above all self-destructive, or is it a state of apathy?

—Is it unrestrained violence or the temptation of nirvana (each generation finding or rediscovering its own)?

—Is it an overabundance, an excess of excitation inducing a devastating acting out, or a scarcity of excitation inducing the feeling of non-existence, a void of thoughts and of affects?

—Is it for Narcissus, a fascinated self-sufficiency or an omnipotent and raging hold over the object?

—Is it zero or infinity?

So many possible apprehendable *figures*, but ones which threaten to make us lose what is essential in Freud's intuition: the death instinct asserts itself in a radical *unbinding process*, a process of *enclosure* that has no aim but its own accomplishment and whose repetitive nature is the sign of its instinctivity. This is a process that no longer has anything to do with conscious death anxiety but which *mimics death* in the being's very nucleus, and this led Freud to assign it to the cell, the nucleus of the living being. Then the psyche is no longer a substitutive representative of the body. It *is* body. The unconscious can no longer be deciphered through its *formations*, in a mobile and articulable logic of "signifiers," it is realized and immobilized in the logic of the psychical body. This process of functioning has a secondary effect on reality, provoking splittings in the object, in the ego, in every individual or group agency which claims to achieve an ever increasingly embracing unity.

No psychopathological structure is exempted from this unbinding and unchaining force operating at the heart of a more and more limited closed system through a set of increasingly elementary oppositions, like an organism traversed by energies. All one can say is that the frequency of these states or the limits of the analysable has made analysts more receptive to its modes of operation and to its effects. But it is found in the most certain, the most straightforward neurotic organizations, for example, in obsessional neurosis, where mental activity is literally fenced in. Freud had more than a vague feeling about this; one has but to refer to his "Analysis Terminable and Interminable," particularly to what is said about the "alterations of the ego" compared to "anachronistic institutions."

Every psychoanalyst talks about death insinuated into life. And if the psychoanalyst's work has as its goal a psychical space that is not just a surface, but one that has some consistency, some flesh to it, some body, and that acquires some freedom of movement and flexibility, then this implies that he cannot evade the antagonistic work of death, he must go out to meet it.

21. *Freud, Aristophanes, and the Phantastic Hypothesis* (1979)[1]
Samuel Weber

Replacing the "phantastic hypothesis" by a theory placed in the mouth of a fictional character by "the poet-philosopher," Freud seeks to surmount the fiction and to restore the truth behind it: an original unity, "living substance," is split apart at the moment of its birth; repetition thus appears, once again, as the restoration of a previous unity, as a "reunification."

---

1 From *The Legend of Freud* (1979). Minneapolis: University of Minnesota Press, 1982. 149-63.

If this interpretation seeks to authorize itself by appealing to the authority of the author, the "poet-philosopher," this gesture both repeats and initiates what it seeks to confirm: repetition as a movement of the same, originating and seeking to return to a founding identity.

The text, as the expression of the "poet-philosopher" repeats what the latter intended to say: namely, that all repetition repeats an original identity, that it seeks to restore: the lovers, their original unity; life, its original death; the text, the original intention of its author. Freud's interpretation thus presupposes the authority of an original identity, the Author, and more precisely, an authorial consciousness and intention as the ground and guarantee of the meaning it attributes to the text. The essence of that meaning, and perhaps of meaning as such, is to portray repetition as a movement of sameness, deriving from an original identity.

But in thus interpreting the story of Aristophanes as a repetition of the same, Freud, curiously enough, alters that story. We need only reread the opening lines of the *Symposium* to discover that the question of who said what is just what sets the scene of the text, and sets it up so as to exclude the possibility of its ever being authoritatively resolved. This is why all the speeches of the *Symposium* are reported in a blend of direct and indirect discourse, something that Plato, the poet-philosopher, will specifically condemn in the *Republic*.[1]

The *Symposium,* of course, is generally considered to be an *early* text of the poet-philosopher. But just how early is precisely the question. For the text begins with Apollodorus telling Glaucon that just two days earlier he recounted the very same story Glaucon asks him to tell. The story concerns a dinner given by Agathon, which Glaucon assumes to have taken place in the recent past, with Apollodorus an invited guest. The latter, however, is quite amused at the assumptions of his interlocutor, whom he astonishes by informing that he was not present at the gathering and could not have been, since the banquet took place

---

1 Cf. Plato's *Republic*; see *Republic* III, 392-97b, where the distinction is made between *diagetic* and *mimetic* discourses, and the latter excluded from the Republic because in it the poet "delivers a speech as though he were someone else" (393c) and thus, through mimesis, refuses to assume responsibility for his words. Overt narration is thus acceptable, whereas mimetic attribution of discourse to another must be condemned. [Weber's note].

many years ago, "when we were still children" (Plato, *Republic* 173a). Apollodorus, it turns out, does know the story, but only through others, above all, through a certain Aristodemos, who, it appears, really did attend the dinner. "But even Aristodemos did not remember any more everything that was said," Apollodorus adds, "nor do I recall everything that he said to me" (178a).

This, then, is the starting-point, the point of departure for the speech that will constitute the major portion of the *Symposium*, and nothing is therefore less certain than what Freud so readily takes for granted: who precisely said what. For everything that is recounted is a repetition of a repetition, Apollodorus recounting the words of Aristodemos. And what really was said may never be certain, for it all took place "long ago, when we were still children."

The *Symposium*, then, begins with a series of repetitions, and it is difficult to know where, if anywhere, they stop. Freud, by contrast, is looking for something quite different: an authoritative account *of* repetition, not one that merely repeats what others (may) have said. He therefore needs authors and authorities and invokes as one such, "Prof. Heinrich Gomperz of Vienna,"[1] to establish the authenticity of the myth. The Professor is cited in order to situate the myth of the *Symposium* as the development of an earlier one, found in the *Upanishads*, which tells of the "emergence of the world from the Atman" (the Self or the Ego), as Freud recounts in a long footnote.

It is as though Freud, backed by the scientific authority of Prof. Gomperz, once again seeks to retrace a repetition (the myth of the *Symposium*) back to its source and origin (the *Upanishads*), to establish it as a repetition of the same. And yet, right from the start, something very curious happens: Freud invokes the authority of the specialist, Prof. Gomperz, to whom he attributes "the following suggestions concerning the derivation (Herkunft) of the Platonic myth"; but when he then proceeds to those "suggestions" ("I would like to call attention to the fact that"), he renders them "only in part in his (Prof. Gomperz's) words." It thus becomes virtually impossible to discern with certainty just who, in this long footnote, is saying what; that is, where the discourse of Professor Gomperz stops and where that of Professor

---

1 Heinrich Gomperz (1873-1942), professor of Greek philosophy at University of Vienna and patient of Freud.

Freud begins—or vice versa. In itself, of course, this would be a trivial matter, but where questions of authority and authenticity are at stake, it becomes an important, if undecidable, question. For the entire footnote serves primarily to line up authoritative support for Freud's interpretation of the "Platonic" myth by demonstrating the latter to be merely a repetition of another, an earlier story, whose meaning is clear, once and for all. It is to this end that Freud invokes Professor Gomperz, however vague that invocation turns out to be:

> I have to thank Professor Heinrich Gomperz, of Vienna, for the following discussion of the origin of the Platonic myth, which I give partly in his own words. It is to be remarked that what is essentially the same theory is already to be found in the Upanishads. For we find the following passage in the *Brihadâranyaka-upanishad,* 1, 4, 3, where the origin of the world from the Atman (the Self or Ego) is described: "But he (the Atman, the Self or the Ego) felt no joy [*hatte auch keine Freude*]; therefore [*darum*] a man has no joy when he is alone. Thereupon [*Da*] he desired a second. You see, he was as large as a woman and a man intertwined. This his Self he sunders in two parts; out of this [*Daraus*] husband and wife emerged. Therefore [*Darum*], measured against the Self this body is as it were a half, thus explained Yagnâvalkya. Therefore [*Darum*] this empty space here is filled by woman." (*Standard* 18: 52)

No doubt that Freud here recognizes the possibility of escaping from the joyless solitude of the Fort! Da!, and, with the authority of Prof. Gomperz, of transforming it into a "There-fore" (darum), a logically compelling way of departing from the "there" (daraus). No doubt that this version of the myth provides Freud with a mirror-image of the fulfillment he desires: a self or ego alone is no more cause for rejoicing than is a death drive all by itself. For there to be joy, Freude, there must be a second, a double, a pair of opposites, joined together, to be sure, in holy matrimony. The other must be different, and yet dominated by the law of the same—that is the condition that Freud's speculation desires to fulfill.

But if the story he thus retells, partially in the words of another, authorizes such a desire, it also repeats the very problem that Freud has been seeking to avoid: for this narcissistic account of the creation of difference from identity cannot account for the creation—i.e., separation—itself. Except, that is, by pointing to the lack of Freude that renders that separation necessary, but not necessarily intelligible. The gap, in short, between a "therefore" and a "thereupon," a darum and a da, remains to be bridged. And yet, without this bridge, the fortress of the Fort! Da! has not really been breached.

This is why Freud may find comfort in discovering an earlier origin of the myth he seeks to found, but also why he cannot dispense with its "Platonic" repetition. For although the story that furnishes him with the hypothesis he desires is spoken by Aristophanes, Freud persists in treating the latter as a mere spokesman for the "poet-philosopher," for whom, as is well known, the comic dramatist had little sympathy. Yet this attribution—of Aristophanes' discourse to Plato—is only one of a number of alterations that Freud's reading of the *Symposium* imposes upon its "original" text. Let us, therefore, reread the latter as literally as possible, without prejudging the question of who, in the final analysis, im letzten Grunde, is really speaking, or who has the *last word*. Let us, in short, allow Aristophanes, at least for the moment, speak for himself. He begins his story thus: "Our body, you see, was at first not formed as it is now; it was utterly different." Wilamowitz, whose translation Freud cites, renders the Greek "physis" not, as is often the case, by "nature" but, more concretely, by "body." The story shows that the choice was a good one. For, in contrast to the alleged source in the Upanishad, Aristophanes' story concerns not abstract or incorporeal beings, a "self" or an "ego," but *bodies*. His story of love begins with the body. Not with the body as we know it today, to be sure, but with one that was "utterly different." Once upon a time (*pálai*). Einmal....

And yet, when those bodies begin to be described, we discover that they were not quite so different after all. What was different was a certain duplication: a double-male, double-female, and that third kind, combining half of each, and which survives only as a name, androgyne. Everything was doubled in these beings, with one notable exception: the head. They kept their heads, as it were, single. Once upon a time, long ago.

In the context of Freud's speculations, one might be tempted to see in this initial state not merely duplication, doubling, but also: repetition. Repetition of the same, at the very beginning. But instead of jumping to conclusions, let us listen to Aristophanes, and to what he has to say at the end of his tale. The moral of the story, as Aristophanes describes it, seems to be not so very different from the interpretation of Freud:

> The cause of all this is that our original nature was thus, and we were whole, and this very yearning and striving for wholeness is what we call love. And before this, as I have said, we were one, but now, because of injustice, we have been taken apart by the God and dispersed like the Arcadians before the Spartans. (Plato, *Symposium* 192-193a)

Like Freud, and most other commentators of this text,[1] Aristophanes seems to state unequivocally that human beings were originally whole and one, and that only as a result of "injustice" were they condemned, punished and estranged from their original unity; that Eros entails the striving to return to this lost unity, to restore that original wholeness. This, at least, is what Aristophanes seems to want to say. Indeed, he seems to leave little room for doubt,

> that our race would be blessed if we could succeed in love, and everyone was able to win his particular beloved, in order thus to return to our original nature. If this would be best, under the prevailing conditions the best will be what comes closest to that ideal, and that is to find the beloved who most conforms to our wishes. And therefore if we wish to celebrate in song the God to whom we owe this, we must indeed sing the praises of Eros, who nowadays shows us so much good in leading us to those for whom we bear affinities, but who also gives us hope that in the future, if only we prove our respect for the Gods, our original nature will be healed and restored, and we will be made happy and blessed. (193c-d)

Who would wish to spoil such a Happy Ending, or want to say anything different? This, at least, seems to be the effect intended by Aristophanes, for immediately after proclaiming this to be the moral of his story, he turns to the previous speaker, Eryximachos, the physician, with a remark that casts a somewhat different light

---

1   See, however, the discussion of the *Symposium* in Stanley Rosen's *Plato's Dialogues*. [Weber's note]

on that moral:

> This, oh Eryximachos, he said, is my discourse on Eros, one
> that is quite different from yours. As I asked you before, please
> don't make fun of it. (193d)

In view of this plea to be taken seriously, Aristophanes' commentary on his tale now appears as something of a *captatio
benevolentiae*.[1] And, as readers of the *Symposium* already know,
his fears are not unfounded. Nor is he himself innocent in
the affair. For earlier in the evening, as it had come time for
him to speak, Aristophanes suddenly seemed taken by a fit of
hiccoughs which caused him to change places in the order of
speakers with Eryximachos, who also gave him the professional
advice of sneezing and holding his breath in order to get over the
attack. That such remedies were not without their effect can be
surmised from the fact that Aristophanes is able to reply to the
physician immediately after the latter has concluded his speech.
But Aristophanes' response to the well-meaning inquiry of the
doctor as to the state of his hiccoughs, can only be considered an
impertinent provocation:

> Of course it stopped, but not before it was treated with sneez-
> ing; and this, he added, makes me wonder why it is that the
> harmony of the body [one of the basic positions outlined by
> Eryximachos in the speech he has just delivered] should desire
> the kind of noise and tickling involved in sneezing; for as soon
> as I began to sneeze, it stopped straightaway. (189a)

Having presumably sneezed and snorted throughout much of the
good doctor's discourse, Aristophanes now has the effrontery to
cite his own cure as evidence against Eryximachos's panegyrics
to love as the harmony of the body. Small wonder, then, that
Aristophanes concludes his own speech with an eye cast anx-
iously in the direction of the physician. For the latter has already
given him fair warning:

> My good Aristophanes, take care! You mock me, as you are

---

1 To "catch benevolence," a rhetorical and legal term for attempting
   to win influence or persuade others of your case.

about to speak, and compel me therefore to become the judge of your discourse and to make sure that you too do not say anything laughable [*geloion*], whereas otherwise you could have spoken in peace. (189a-b)

If the scene of the *Symposium* is from the very beginning agonistic, with the different speakers vying with one another in their praises of Eros, the interchange of Aristophanes and Eryximachos introduces an unmistakable tone of aggressiveness. Henceforth, the speeches will not merely be in competition with one another, and therefore directed at addressees who are also judges: they will also engage the prestige and standing of those who deliver them. Which is why Aristophanes' reply to the physician's warning, while ironically half-hearted, touches the core of the problem:

Thereupon Aristophanes laughingly [*gelásanta*] replied: Well said, Eryximachos, and as far as I am concerned, let what I have said be unsaid. So don't lie in wait for me, since in any case I shall be concerned, not that what I intend to say will turn out to be laughable [*geloia*], for that would be all to the good and in accordance with my muse, but rather ridiculous [*katagélasta*]. (189b)

But if Aristophanes seeks to unsay what he has said, he knows, no less than Freud, that such an attempt at "undoing" must always leave traces. And if he thus chooses the physician, Eryximachos, to be his privileged addressee and judge, is this not his attempt to displace the verdict, upon which his joke, like all jokes, depend, from that other listener, who, for the moment at least, remains silent, awaiting his turn. For if Aristophanes insults and provokes Eryximachos, the author of the *Clouds* knows full well that his most redoubtable antagonist lies elsewhere. Eryximachos, however, speaks also for the silent Socrates when he reminds the satirist that, notwithstanding his efforts to unsay what he has said, he can expect to be held responsible for his words:

Now that you have done, Eryximachos replied, do you think you can get away as easily as that, Aristophanes? Take care, rather, to speak as one who will have to answer for what he says. (189b-c)

It is not simply fortuitous if it is a physician, Eryximachos, who is first charged with calling the mocking Aristophanes to order. From Plato to the present, the doctor has stood as one of the chief guardians of order in the *physis,* and hence as a model for order in the *polis* as well. It was Eryximachos who first launched the idea of replacing the usual after-dinner entertainment, music, with serious discourse:

> Now that it has been decided ... that each shall drink only as much as he likes ... I would like to propose that we ask the lady flutist who has just entered to leave and either play for herself or, if she prefer, for the women inside, and that this evening we entertain ourselves with speeches. (176e)

The lady flutist having thus been excluded, the men, left to themselves, begin to speak seriously their *logoi* about Love. It is only consistent, then, that it is Eryximachos who has the task of calling Aristophanes to order in the name of seriousness and of reponsibility. And it is no less consistent that Aristophanes should therefore conclude his speech with a moral designed to disarm the suspicions he himself has provoked.

But what, then, of that speech itself? Aristophanes, it will be recalled, concludes by stressing that it has been very different from that of Eryximachos; he introduces it, however, in precisely the same way:

> To be sure, Aristophanes said, I intend to speak very differently from the way both you and Pausanias have spoken. For it seems to me that so far people have not at all perceived the true force of Eros. Had they done so, they would have certainly built him the most marvellous temples and altars and made the greatest sacrifices in his honor. (189c)

If Aristophanes declares that he intends to speak in a very different manner from that of his predecessors, it is because he is convinced that there has been a problem of perception: the true power of Eros has not yet been properly recognized and therefore remains to be revealed. The discourse of Aristophanes, then, will be different in not taking Eros for granted, for self-evident, but rather as the object of a certain blindness, a kind of malady that he sets about to remedy. Aristophanes, therefore, repeats the gesture of the physician but at the same [time] extends it to cover the operation in which he and the other speakers are engaged. For one can only seriously sing the praises of Eros if one knows what one is talking about. And this, Aristophanes insists, is precisely the problem. His discourse will thus be both revelatory, and pedagogic:

> I will therefore try to explain his power as well, and you can then be teachers of the others. (189d)

This pedagogic intention, therefore, to reveal the true nature and power of Eros, to remove, that is, a certain blindness, may be what explains the vivid quality of Aristophanes' description of those ancient beings, whom he asserts, were so utterly different *(all'alloia)* from those we see today. And yet as we have already remarked, the difference to which Aristophanes refers is rather one of quantity than of quality: a difference, one might say, in economy. For if we look closely at Aristophanes' description of those double-beings, we discover them to have been very similar: to us, to themselves and to their parents:

> Because the male was originally an offspring of the sun, and the female a child of the earth, while that participating in both was sired by the moon, which itself participates in both sexes. And they were round and went round, thus resembling their parents. (190b)

The world of the double-beings was one of resemblances, family and otherwise; and like their parents, they moved in circles, "making cartwheels," as children do "even today." If we compare Aristophanes' double-being with the Atman of the Upanishad, we can see that the solitude of the latter would seem out of place in the world of the former: never being alone, they would never need to create others. And if there is a beginning, it is already doubled, duplicated, full of repetition and of resemblance, circular: for "they were round and they went round"—while keeping their heads, that single, "common head shared by the opposing faces."

They kept their heads—or did they?

Freud's version of the story grows strangely vague at this point: that is, at precisely the point where the actual story, the dramatic conflict as it were, sets in: "Thereupon Zeus was moved ..." The German is even more suggestive: "*Da* liess sich Zeus bewegen...." But where, *da?* If Freud is notably imprecise, Aristophanes is less so. What he has to say shows that Zeus had good reason to be moved. For the double-beings had begun to grow tired of the same, of turning around in circles, and had cast their eyes upward instead:

> Now their force and strength were enormous, and their thoughts no less so, and what Homer tells of Ephialtes and Otos applies to them as well, for they wanted to invade the heavens and attack the gods. (190b)

Freud's "thereupon," that indeterminate but indicative "da," spatial and temporal at once, covers a desire that is distant and yet familiar: the striving to transgress the boundaries separating gods from men, rulers from ruled, the other from the same. And although Freud in his account omits the deliberations that lead Zeus to "be moved," Aristophanes does not:

> For it was not expedient to kill them [the double-beings], and, as in the case of the Titans, exterminate the entire race, since that would have also meant the loss of all the tributes and sacrifices men give to the gods: but they could not simply be permitted to continue their blasphemous doings either. (190c)

The deliberations of Zeus indicate what Freud is at pains to ignore: that the law presiding over the *Fort(ress)-Da!* is none other than that of the *oikos:* the economy of appropriation and assimilation that characterizes the organization of the ego; in short, the economy of narcissism. In that distant place, utterly different from all that is familiar, we therefore encounter something all too familiar: the narcissistic effort to keep the other in its (proper) place, to subordinate alterity to an economy of the same. In the case, however, of an other that is all the more difficult to control because it is already a mirror-image of the same, radical measures are called for. The other must be altered, in accordance with the laws of narcissistic economics, and this is precisely what Zeus proposes:

I think, then, that I have found a means that will allow humans to survive and still compel them to cease their excesses for lack of strength. For now, he said, I shall cut each of them into two halves, which will make them weaker and also more useful to us, since there will be more of them, and they will walk upright on two legs. Should I observe, however, that they continue their blasphemous doings and refuse to keep still, he said, I shall cut them apart once again, and then they can hop around on one leg, like tops. (190c)

Zeus' strategy is doubtless decisive: by dividing the doubles he ups the ante while lowering the risk, and the move can be repeated. It is also fully in accord with the economic law that calls for a lowering in (unbound) energy and an increase in binding. If the energy of the doubles is dangerously unbound, bounding back and forth, as it were, through a mirroring in which the same becomes other and the other, the same, what Zeus suggests is to create a different kind of image; the image of difference "itself." Zeus therefore proposes, but it is Apollo—god of the sun, father of the male—who disposes; for after Zeus has made the first incision,

he ordered Apollo to turn the face and the half-neck around towards the cut, so that man, confronted with his cleavage, would become more moral, and the rest he ordered Apollo to heal. (190e)

"In the final analysis [*im letzten Grunde*], it must have been the history of our earth and its relation to the sun that has left us its mark ..." Aristophanes, here, tells us just that story of the mark, left by wounds not of the spirit, but of the body; and these wounds, as both Freud and Aristophanes well knew, do not heal without leaving scars. Or "blisters," as with the scorched crust-scab?—of the Blaschen. Or finally, without marking the place in which all these strands come together to form a single, inextricable knot.

[Apollo] therefore turned the face around, pulled the skin from all sides up over what today we call the belly, and just as when one pulls together the strings of a purse, he drew the ends together and tied them up in the middle of the belly in what today we call the navel. The resulting wrinkles he smoothed out for the most part, and moulded the chest with the aid of a tool like that used by shoemakers to smoothe out creases in the leather, except for a few wrinkles that he left around the belly and navel to serve as a reminder of the ancient accident. (190e-191a)

The navel is left wrinkled, knotted, interrupting the smooth surface of the body, which, as Freud knew, serves the ego as its model.[1] The closure of the body, paradigm of the ego's organization, is both accomplished and interrupted by Apollo, the "sun," the intervention of an exteriority, and serves as reminder "of the ancient accident." No matter how economical the ego may be, its "purse" can never be hermetically sealed, for just in the place where everything comes together, we find the scar and stigma of an ancient wound, an ancient striving. And it is precisely this striving that emerges from the operation of Zeus and Apollo:

> Once the figure had thus been cut in two, each part yearned for its other half, and so they came together, held each other in their arms and pressed together, intertwined. (191a)

This marks the spot where Freud *seems* to have found what he was looking for: the derivation of life as a process of repetition from the tendency to restore a previous unity. It is here, then, that he believes that he has found Eros. But in Aristophanes' story, Eros is not yet mentioned, and with good reason. For the striving that Freud takes to be Eros is, in the version of the comic-dramatist, nothing other than Thanatos, in the purest and most irresistible of forms. The sundered bodies, he relates,

> intertwined, and out of the desire to grow together they died from hunger and other neglect, for they would not do anything apart. If, now, the one half was dead and the other remained, the survivor sought out another and embraced it ... and thus they perished. (191b)

Had Aristophanes' tale ended here, as Freud's version does, there would have never been Eros at all, but only death. The story would have merely repeated, or rather anticipated, the Freudian

---

1 "The Ego ... may thus be regarded as a mental projection of the surface of the body" (Freud, *Standard* 19: 26). [Weber's note]

black hole, fortress of the impervious *da!* and, in the end, nothing would have been left, not even death itself. But Aristophanes continues his story, just as Freud must continue his search. And it is just possible that it is precisely this continuation that provides what Freud so deeply desires. For Aristophanes tells of a second, repeated intervention, designed to save the moribund bodies from themselves, from their deadly desire to be reunified and whole—to be, in short, a self:

> Thereupon Zeus took pity and placed another means at their disposal, by shifting their private parts to the front, instead of on the side where they were before, since previously they had reproduced not in one another but in the earth, like crickets. Now, however, he shifted them to the front and thus allowed them to reproduce in one another. (191b-c)

This second intervention does not merely repeat the first; it adds a new direction: instead of dividing, cutting, and separating, it shifts, dislocates, and rearranges the reproductive organs, bringing repetition, as it were, to the fore. It is only with this dislocation, with the advent of a certain Entstellung, that the fort(ress) da! is finally and irrevocably breached. And only here, in the story of Aristophanes, is Eros finally named:

> Ever since this distant time, therefore, love is inborn in man, attempts to make one of two and to heal human nature. (191c-d)

Therefore, henceforth, the da! is fort!: not simply as a unity that has been lost, or a wholeness that has been separated from itself, but as an Entstellung that reinscribes the stories of loss and of separation in another text, one in which displacement becomes the "origin" of eros. For it is only when the organs have been displaced that they become capable of generating eros, and not merely thanatos; only then do they become *erogenous:*

> Each of us is therefore a fragment of a man [*anthropou sýmbolon*], since we are cut like flatfish, and have become two from one. Therefore everyone is always seeking his other part. (191d)

For Aristophanes, it would seem, this erogenous, symbolic striving can never be separated from the narcissistic desire to become one; for him, the Symbolic therefore is indissociable from narcissism, from a certain mirror-image of the other. And yet, his story also marks indelibly the site, and the sight, of that image as the *navel*, reminder of the ancient accident or incident by which the sun left its imprint for us to decipher.

But what of that cipher left in just the place where we straddle, or fall for, the unknown? What of the "capital X" in which so much energy is bound up, the variable that both permits the "equations" of metapsychology and also casts them in doubt?

In short, can we be sure, as Freud seems to be (but only by not reading the story he recites), that we know just where the story stops, or where it is going? Where the myth ends, and where theory begins? The lovers, at any rate, are least able to say what it is they really desire:

> When, then, one meets its true, proper half, be he a pediast or anyone else, the two are overcome by amorous union and love and do not wish to part for even the shortest time; and those who spend their entire lives together would not even be able to say what they want from one another. For this can hardly be the community of amorous delight ... but rather it is clear that the soul of each desires something else, which however it cannot explicitly utter but only hint at. (192b-c)

The lovers cannot explicitly utter what it is that they desire from each other, because what they desire is so utterly different that it can only be uttered by someone else. This, at least, would seem to be the reason why, at the very end of his tale, Aristophanes recounts the intervention of yet another figure—or is it rather a *hypothesis,* a supposition that suddenly makes its appearance here, to guide the story toward its happy end?

> And if, while they lay together, Hephaistos was to step before them, tools in hand, and was to ask them: What is it then really, people, that you want from each other? And if they then had no answer, and he asked further: Is what you desire something like this, that you may be together as much as possible, and never part, either day or night? For if this is your desire, then I will melt and weld you so that you are one instead of two, and may live together as one, and so that when you have

died, even in the underworld you will be dead not as two but as one. (192d-e)

Hephaistos, the god of binding and unbinding,[1] often pictured with his tools slung over his shoulder like a capital X, appears here on the scene to assure the binding that the lovers, it would seem, so desire, and also to guarantee the moral of the story, that both Aristophanes, and Freud, cannot do without. But if Hephaistos thus ties up the loose ends of the story into a seemingly neat knot, the lovers, it should be observed, remain silent. And since they cannot say what it is that they want, Hephaistos must do it for them. For he does not merely pose his question, he *imposes* the response, putting his answer into the mouths of the lovers just as Plato, according to Freud at least, put his story into the mouth of Aristophanes. Is this, then, the mouth that gives us the *true* sense of the story?

Hearing this, we know for certain, not even one (of the lovers) would refuse or indicate that he wanted something different, but rather each would be sure to have heard just what he had wanted to hear, what he had always yearned for, that is, by being close to, and melting into the beloved, to make two into one. (192e)

Does Aristophanes speak for Plato here, for himself, or for Hephaistos, who speaks for, and in the name of, the lovers? Will we ever know for certain? "Each would be sure to have heard just what he had wanted to hear, what he had always yearned for." This, Aristophanes concludes, "we know for certain." But does that not mean that all we know for certain is what we desire to hear?

The lovers, in any case, remain silent. They must be spoken *for;* but their silence speaks *to* us, through the voice of a narrator, about whose status we grow increasingly uncertain:

It must therefore be feared that if we do not behave properly towards the gods, that we will once again be rendered asunder, and have to go about like the figures carved out of tombstones, which are divided at the nose, and that we will then become just like split dice, each of which possesses its other half. (193e)

1   See Marie Delcourt, *Hephaistos, ou la légende du magicien.* Paris, 1957. [Weber's note]

The fate of the lovers, Aristophanes makes clear here, at the end, is ours as well: the mark they leave us, imprint of the sun and its relation to the earth, of a violent intervention of powerful forces, is a signal that suspends us somewhere between symbols and "split dice," in the silence of a figure engraved on a tombstone. The danger with which the signal confronts us is that, like Nietzsche's "female," we shall be neither deep, nor even flat, but rather twisted, distorted, entstellt. And that we shall move about like Hephaistos himself, who, it should be recalled, is the only Greek god known to limp.

And perhaps it is this, more than anything else, that binds the Greek god of binding and unbinding, bearer of the great X, to Freud, who concludes his speculative way *Beyond the Pleasure Principle* with the following remark:

> This is tied up with countless other questions which are impossible to answer now. We must be patient and await further means and occasions for research. Also ready to forsake a way that we have followed for a while if it seems to be leading to no good end.... Moreover, for the slow advances of our scientific knowledge we may take comfort in the words of a poet:
>
>> "What we cannot reach flying, we must reach limping.
>> Scripture tells us it is no sin to limp." (Freud, *Standard* 18:64 [translation modified])

Again, it is the words of a poet (Rückert), philosophizing, that provides Freud with comfort. Or is it really a poet that Freud cites, here at the end of his speculative way? For, many years before, he had cited the same poet, and the same passage, but at a time when he was less concerned with death and with repetition than with the machine he was in the process of constructing, a machine that seemed almost ready to "fly" by itself. This machine, or more properly, this automat (Hephaistos, we recall, is said to have been the founder of automats) was none other than Freud's first attempt to elaborate a psychological system. As the "Project" drew ever nearer to completion, Freud wrote of his feelings in a letter to his friend, Fliess:

> Now listen to this. One strenuous night last week, when I was in the stage of painful discomfort in which my brain works best, the

barriers suddenly lifted, the veils dropped, and it was possible to see from the details of neurosis all the way to the very conditioning of consciousness. Everything fell into place, the cogs meshed, one had the impression that the thing was now really a machine which in a moment would begin to go by itself. The three systems of neurones, the "free" and "bound" state of quantity, the primary and secondary processes, the main and compromise tendencies of the nervous system, the two biological rules of attention and of defence, the indications of quality, reality and thought, the state of the psycho-sexual group, the sexual condition of repression, finally the conditions of consciousness as a perceptual function—that all fit together and still does. I can, of course, hardly contain myself for delight. *(Origins,* 129)

Freud, who can hardly contain himself, nevertheless wishes he had waited before sending his friend and first reader an early draft of his "machine," one that was still incomplete:

Had I only waited a fortnight with the communication to you, everything would have turned out so much clearer. But it was only in attempting to communicate it to you that the thing became clear to me in the first place. So it could not have been otherwise. Now I shall hardly find the time to give you a proper account. If only I had forty-eight hours to talk with you about this and nothing else [*und nichts anderes*], the thing could probably be finished up. But that is impossible. "What we cannot reach flying ..." (*Ibid.*)

In the absence of the cherished friend, "first reader" and "representative of the others," Freud turned to the poet for comfort. And if the latter, repeating Scripture—*Die Schrift*—could tell him that it is not a sin to limp, Freud was far from limping in 1895. Rather, he was flying high: "Other neurotic confirmations deluge me. The thing is really true and genuine" (*Ibid.*). In 1920, however, in the absence of the Friend, Freud still sought solace from the poets, and confirmation from the neurotics. And in the "transference" of the latter—precisely, that is, in their refusal to confirm—Freud seemed to distinguish the true and genuine machine behind it all: the driving force of the repetition-compulsion, working automatically, flying, as it were, in the face of the pleasure principle. If the psychoanalytical machine might falter as therapy, it would fly as theory, as speculation, if need be. But the latter, like the automat, still needed a start from somewhere else—a start, which would also be a finish—and so Freud found himself on the way to an utterly different place, where he thought he discerned the authoritative voice of the poet-philosopher.

But if the figure he found there was indeed a "poet," it was no philosopher but rather their antagonist, a man of the theater, a storyteller with a sense for the absurd. And the legend he told only repeated what Freud himself had thought and written elsewhere, long ago; repeated, that is, but also and inevitably transformed.

22. *"A Kind of Discourse on Method": Freud's Performative Writing* (1980)[1]
Jacques Derrida

Thus, *Beyond the Pleasure Principle.* Which I open to the first page, without any other precaution, as naively as possible. Without having it, I am giving myself the right to jump over all the methodological or juridical protocols which, with all the legitimacy in the world, could slow me down to the point of paralysis here. So be it.

Nevertheless, the first page of the first chapter already contains: 1. a certain reminder: of the present state and acquisitions of analytic theory. Psychoanalytic theory exists. The performance of the first words implies this fact in any event: "In the theory of psychoanalysis we have no hesitation in assuming ..." Etc. One is not obliged to believe that it exists, one does not have to consider it valid, yet one must nevertheless rest assured—as is implied by the reception of this *speech act*—that Freud means to say that it exists, and that things are happening in it. His statement is not *stricto sensu* a performative, he is allegedly declaring and attesting. But he is attesting to an act whose producing agent and first subject the speaker knows himself to be, wishes himself to be, or alleges himself to be. Which he will have been; and those whom he has associated, or who have associated themselves with the movement of this production have all accepted, in principle and consciously, the contract which institutes him as producer.

---

1 From *The Post Card* (1980). Trans. Alan Bass. Chicago: University of Chicago Press, 1987. 273-74; 283-85; 298-304; 320-21; 322-23; 344-45; 358-59; 369-75; 377; 383-84; 385; 391; 405-06; 408.

Whence the singularity of this performance. When Freud advances a statement implying that psychoanalytic theory exists, he in no way is in the situation of a theoretician in the field of another science, nor is he any more in the position of an epistemologist or of a historian of the sciences. He is attesting to an act whose contract implies that the act come back [*revienne*] to him, and that he answer for it. In a certain way he seems to have contracted only with himself. *He would have written himself.* To himself, as if someone were sending himself a message informing himself by certified letter, on an official document, of the attested existence of a theoretical history to which he himself—such is the content of the message—gave the send-off [*coup d' envoi*].

2. the taking of a position as concerns philosophy. This is also the taking of a non-position, the placarded neutrality of a declaration of indifference which, if not indifferent in itself, must take its determination from elsewhere. In any event, Freud insists: the question of knowing whether the establishment of the pleasure principle is or is not close to a given philosophical system is "of no concern."

3. a concept of reflection which, under the heading "speculative," henceforth derives neither from metaphysical philosophy, nor from experimental science, even if linked to psychoanalytic experience as such.

★★★

In sum, Freud could have stopped there (and in a certain way he does, I think that everything is played out in these first pages, in other words that everything will only repeat his arrest, his *pas de marche,* but it is repetition, precisely, that is in question here): the speculative possibility of the totally-other (*than* the pleasure principle) is in advance inscribed within it, in the letter of engagement that it believes it sends to itself circularly, specularly, inscribed as that which is not inscribed within it, the opener of a scription of the other that *overlaps* [*à même*] the principle. The very surface of the "overlap" no longer belongs to itself, is no longer what it is as such. Writing affects the very surface of its support. And this nonbelonging unleashes speculation.

You must already find that I myself am corrupting the "properly Freudian" usage of "speculation," of the notion or the concept, and of the word. Where Freud seems to make of it a mode of research, a theoretical attitude, I am also considering it as the object of his discourse. I am acting *as if* Freud were not only pre-paring himself to speak *speculatively* of this or that (for example of a beyond of the pleasure principle), but were already speaking *of* speculation. As if he did not content himself to move *within speculation,* but insisted upon treating of it also, on the bias. And it is the bias of this procedure which interests me. I am acting as if the very thing he appears to analyze, for example the relation between the two principles, were already an element of specula-tive structure in general: simultaneously in the senses of specular reflection (the pleasure principle can recognize itself, or no longer at all recognize itself, in the reality principle); of the production of surplus value, of calculations and bets on the Exchange, that is, the emission of more or less fictive shares; and finally in the sense of that which overflows the (given) presence of the present, the given of the gift. I am doing all this, and I am alleging that this must be done in order to gain access to that which is played out here beyond the "given," to that which is rejected, withheld, taken back, beyond the principle of what Freud presently *says,* if such a thing were possible, *about speculation.* In what he writes something must derive from the speculation of which he speaks. But I will not content myself with this corruption by reapplication. I am alleging that speculation is not only a mode of research named by Freud, not only the oblique object of his discourse, but also the opera-tion of his writing, the scene (of that) which he makes by writing what he writes here, that which makes him do it, and that which he makes to do, that which makes him write and that which he makes—or lets—write. To make to do, to make write, to let do, or to let write: the syntax of these operations is not given.

No *Weg* [path] without *Umweg* [detour]: the detour does not overtake the road, but constitutes it, breaks open the path. Freud here does not seem to interrogate the graphics of this *différant*[1]

---

1 Derrida's neologism, *différance,* is derived from *différant,* present participle of *différer*—which means both "to differ" and "to defer." With this term Derrida is gesturing toward the "undecidable" space between binaries; the space of a "detour" that in Freud, Derrida claims, constitutes path-breaking (i.e., proto-deconstructive) thought. Freud thus goes "beyond" conceptual, logical pathways. Like similar concept-busting terms throughout Derrida's oeuvre, différance exposes the unstructured ground out of which concepts (and thus metaphysics) are constructed. Hence the philosophical, rather than merely literary, significance of his work of "de-construction."

detour *for itself*. But can it be interrogated for *itself*? Itself, it is not. Nevertheless it can eventually account for the interminable detour of this text (is it itself here?), and for its speculative athesis.

Pure pleasure and pure reality are ideal limits, which is as much as to say fictions. The one is as destructive and mortal as the other. Between the two the *différant* detour therefore forms the very actuality of the process, of the "psychic" process as a "living" process. Such an "actuality," then, is never present or given. It "is" that which in the gift is never presently giving or given. There is (*es gibt*)—it gives, *différance*. Therefore one cannot even speak of effective actuality, of *Wirklichkeit*, if at least, and in the extent to which, it is coordinated with the value of presence. The detour thereby "would be" the common, which is as much as to say the *différant*, root of the two principles, the root uprooted from itself, necessarily impure, and structurally given over to compromise, to the speculative transaction. The three terms—two principles plus or minus *différance*—are but one, the same divided, since the second (reality) principle and *difference* are only the "effects" of the modifiable pleasure principle.

But from whichever *end* one takes this structure with one-two-three terms, it is death. *At the end,* and this death is not opposable, does not differ, in the sense of opposition, from the two principles and their *différance*. It is inscribed, although non-inscribable, in the process of this structure—which we will call later stricture. If death is not opposable it is, already, *life death*.

This Freud does not say, does not say it presently, here, nor even elsewhere in this form. It gives (itself to be) thought without ever being given or thought. Neither here nor elsewhere. But the "hypothesis" with which I read this text and several others would go in the direction of disengaging that which is engaged here between the first principle and that which appears as *its other*, to wit, the reality principle as *its* other, the death drive as its *other*: a structure of alteration without opposition. That which seems, then, to make the belonging—a belonging without interiority—of death to pleasure more continuous, more immanent, and more natural too, also makes it more scandalous as concerns a dialectics or a logic of opposition, of position, or of thesis. There is no thesis of this *différance*. The thesis would be the death sentence (*arrêt de mort*) of *différance*. The syntax of this *arrêt de mort,* which arrests death in two *différant* senses (a sentence which condemns to death and an interruption suspending death), will be in question elsewhere.[1]

My "hypothesis," and you can see in what sense I will use this word henceforth, is that the speculative structure has its place and its necessity in this graphics.

★★★

Let us begin then with the "normal" and the "original": the child, the child in the typical and normal activity usually attributed to him, play. Apparently this is an activity entirely subject to the PP—and it will be shown that indeed it is, and entirely under the surveillance of a PP which (who) nevertheless permits it(him)self to be worked upon in silence by its (his) other—and as unaffected as possible by the second principle, the PR.

And then the argument of the spool. I am saying argument, the legendary argument, because I do not yet know what name to give it. It is neither a narrative, nor a story, nor a myth, nor a fiction. Nor is it the system of a theoretical demonstration. It is fragmentary, without conclusion, selective in that it gives something to be read, more an argument in the sense of a schema made of dotted lines, with ellipses everywhere.

And then what is given to be read here, this legend, is already too legendary, overburdened, obliterated. To give it a title is already to accredit the deposit or the consignment, that is, the investiture. As for the immense literature whose investment this legendary argument has attracted to itself, I would like to attempt a partial and naive reading, as naive and spontaneous as possible. As if I were interesting myself for the first time in the first time of the thing.

Initially, I remark this: this is the first time in this book that we have an apparently autobiographical, that is domestic, piece. The appearance is veiled, of course, but all the more significant. Of the experience Freud says he has been the witness. The

---

1 *Arrêt de mort* means "death sentence" but can also be translated as "arrest of death." Derrida is referring to Blanchot's *Arrêt de mort,* and to his analysis of it in "Living On—Borderlines," translated by James Hulbert in *Deconstruction and Criticism* (New York: Seabury Press, 1979). [Translator's note]

motivated witness. It took place in his family, but he says nothing about this. Moreover we know this just as we know that the motivated witness was none other than the child's grandfather. "... I lived under the same roof as the child and his parents for some weeks ..." (Freud, *Standard* 18: 14). Even if an experiment[1] could ever be limited to observation, the conditions as they are defined were not those of an observation. The speculator was not in a situation to observe. This can be concluded in advance from what he himself says in order to accredit the seriousness of his discourse. The protocols of experimentation, including sufficient observation ("It was more than a mere fleeting observation, for I lived under the same roof as the child and his parents for some weeks ..."), guarantee the observation only by making of the observer a participant. But what was his part? Can he determine it himself? The question of objectivity has not the slightest pertinence here—nor does any epistemological question in canonic form—for the primary and sole reason that the experiment and its account will pretend to nothing less than a genealogy of objectivity in general. How, then, can they be subject to the authority of the tribunal whose institution they repeat? But inversely, by what right is a tribunal forbidden to judge the conditions of its establishment? and, what is more, forbidden to judge the account, by a motivated witness, a participant, of the so-called establishment? Especially if the involved witness gives all the signs of a very singular concern: for example, that of producing the institutions of his desire, of grafting his own genealogy onto it, of making the tribunal and the juridical tradition his inheritance, his delegation as a "movement," his legacy, his *own*.[2] I will indeed refrain from insisting on the syntax of his *own*. Both so that you will not get lost right away, and because I suspect that he *himself* has a hard time recognizing *himself* among his own. Which would not be unrelated to the origin of objectivity. Or at least of this experiment, and the singular account we are given of it.

What is given is first filtered, selected, actively delimited. This discrimination is in *part* declared at the border. The speculator

---

1 Experiment in French is *expérience*, and has the cognate double meaning. [Translator's note]
2 "His own" here are *les siens*, which has the sense of one's closest relations. This is the syntax that is referred to in the next sentence. [Translator's note]

who does not yet say that he has truly begun to speculate (this will be on the fourth day, for there are seven chapters in this strangely composed book: we will come back to this), acknowledges this discrimination. He has not sought "to include the whole field covered by these phenomena." He has only retained the characteristics pertinent to the economic point of view. Economic: this might already be translated, if one plays a bit (play is not yet forbidden in this phase of the origin of everything, of the present, the object, language, work, seriousness, etc.), but not gratuitously, as point of view of the *oikos*,[1] law of the *oikos*, of the proper as the domestico-familial and even, by the same token, as we will verify, as the domestico-funerary. The grandfather speculator does not yet say that he has begun to speculate in broad daylight (the daylight will be for the fourth day, and yet), he will never say that he is the grandfather, but he knows that this is an open secret, *le secret de Polichinelle*. Secret for no one. The grandfather speculator justifies the accounts he is giving, and the discrimination he operates in them, in broad daylight. The justification is precisely the economic point of view. Which until now has been neglected by the "different theories of children's play," and which also constitutes the privileged point of view for *Beyond* ..., for what he who here holds or renders the accounts is doing, to wit, writing. "These theories attempt to discover the motives which lead children to play, but they fail to bring into the foreground the *economic* motive, the consideration of the yield of pleasure (*Lustgewinn*) involved. Without wishing to include the whole field covered by these phenomena, I have been able, through a chance opportunity which presented itself, to throw some light upon the first game invented by himself (*das erste selbstgeschaffene Spiel*) that was played by a little boy of one and a half. It was more than a mere fleeting observation, for I lived under the same roof as the child and his parents for some weeks, and it was some time before I discovered the meaning of the puzzling activity which he constantly repeated" (14, trans. sl. modified).

He has profited from an opportunity, a chance, he says. About the possibility of this chance he says nothing. From the immense discourse which might inundate us here, but which is held back, let us retain only this: the opportune chance has as its propitious

---

1   Household or family.

terrain neither the family (the narrow family, the small family in its nucleus of two generations: Freud would not have invoked the opportune chance if he had observed one of his nearest, son, daughter, wife, brother or sister, mother or father), nor the non-family (several weeks under the same roof is a familial experience). The field of the experiment is therefore of the type: family vacationcy.[1]

A supplement of generation always finds here reason to employ or deploy its desire.

From the first paragraph of the account on, a single trait to characterize the object of the observation, the action of the game: repetition, repeated repetition (*andauernd wiederholte Tun*). That is all. The other characteristic ("puzzling," *rätselhafte*) describes nothing, is void, but with a vacancy that calls out, and calls for, like every enigma, a narrative. It envelopes the narrative with its vacancy.

It will be said: yes, there is another descriptive trait in this first paragraph. The game, of which the repetition of repetition consists, is a *selbstgeschaffene* game, that the child has produced or permitted to be produced by itself, spontaneously, and it is the first of this type. But none of all this (spontaneity, autoproduction, the originality of the first time) contributes any descriptive content that does not amount to the self-engendering of the repetition of itself. Hetero-tautology (definition of the Hegelian speculative) of repeated repetition, of self-repetition. In its pure form, this is what play will consist of.

It gives time. There is time.

The grandfather (who is more or less clandestinely the) speculator (although not yet) repeats the repetition of repetition. A repetition between pleasure and unpleasure, of a pleasure and an unpleasure whose (agreeable/disagreeable) content, however, is not added to repetition. It is not an additive but an internal determination, the object of an analytic predication. It is the possibility of this analytic predication which slowly will develop the hypothesis of a "drive" more original than the PP and independent

---

1   *Vacance* in French is both vacation and a state of vacancy. Derrida is punning on the fact that Freud observed Ernst while on vacation with a grandson who is also somewhat outside the family, in that he has a different last name. And of course vacation is the time when the family is *away* (fort). [Translator's note]

of it (him). The PP will be overflowed, and is so in advance, by the speculation in which it (he) engages, and by its (his) own (intestine, proper, domestic, familial, sepulchral) repetition.

Now—fold back (reapply) what the grandfather, who still is hiding from himself that he is the grandfather, says here without hiding it from himself, reapply what he has said, by repeating it, about the repetition of the grandson, the eldest of his grandsons, Ernst. We will come back to this in detail. Fold back what he says his grandson is doing, with all the seriousness appropriate to an eldest grandson called Ernst (*the importance of being earnest*),[1] but not Ernst Freud, because the "movement" of this genealogy passes through the daughter, the daughter wife who perpetuates the race only by risking the name, (I leave it to you to follow this factor[2] up to and including all of those women about whom it is difficult to know whether they have maintained the movement without the name or lost the movement in order to maintain, in that they have maintained, the name; I leave it to you to follow this up, suggesting only that you not forget, in the question of the analytic "movement" as the genealogy of the son-in-law, Judaic law), fold back, then, what he says his grandson is doing seriously on what he himself is doing by saying this, by writing *Beyond* ..., by playing so seriously (by speculating) at writing *Beyond*.... For the speculative heterotautology of the thing is that the beyond is *lodged* (more or less comfortably for this *vacance*) in the repetition of the repetition of the PP.

Fold back: *he* (the grandson *of* his grandfather, the grandfather *of* his grandson) compulsively repeats repetition without it ever advancing anywhere, not one step. He repeats an operation which consists in distancing, in pretending (*for a time*, for time: thereby writing and doing something that is not being talked about, and which must give good returns) to distance pleasure, the object or principle of pleasure, the object and/or the PP, here represented by the spool which is supposed to represent the mother (and/or, as we will see, supposed to represent the father, in the place of the son-in-law, the father as son-in-law, the other family name), in order to bring it (him) back indefatigably. It (he) pretends to distance the PP in order to bring it (him) back

---

1 In English in the original. [Translator's note]
2 Factor is *facteur*, which is also the mailman, as in *le facteur de la vérité*. [Translator's note]

ceaselessly, in order to observe that itself it (himself he) brings itself (himself) back (for it (he) has in it(him)self the principal force of its (his) own economic return, to the house, his home, near it(him)self despite all the difference), and then to conclude: it (he) is still there, I am always there. *Da.* The PP maintains all its (his) authority, it (he) has never absented it(him)self.

One can see that the description to follow of the *fort/da* (on the side of the grandson of the house) and the description of the speculative game, so painstaking and so repetitive also, of the grandfather writing *Beyond* ... overlap down to their details. They are applied to the same thing. I have just said: one can see that they overlap. Rigorously speaking, it is not an overlapping that is in question, nor a parallelism, nor an analogy, nor a coincidence. The necessity that binds the two descriptions is of another kind: we would have difficulty naming it; but of course this is the principal stake for me in the selective and motivated reading that I am repeating here. Who causes (himself) to come back [*revenir*], who makes who come back [*revenir*] according to this double *fort/da* which conjugates into the same genealogical (and conjugal) writing the narrated *and* the narrating of this narrative (the game of the "serious" grandson with the spool and the serious speculation of the grandfather with the PP)?

This simple question in suspense permits us to foresee: the description of Ernst's serious game, of the eldest grandson of the grandfather of psychoanalysis, *can no longer be read solely* as a theoretical argument, as a strictly theoretical speculation that tends to *conclude* with the repetition compulsion *or* the death drive *or* simply with the internal limit of the PP (for you know that Freud, no matter what has been said in order vehemently to affirm or contest it, *never concludes on this point*), but can also be read, according to the supplementary necessity of a *parergon*,[1] as an autobiography of Freud. Not simply an autobiography confiding his life to his own more or less testamentary writing, but a more or less living description of his own writing, of his way of writing what he writes, most notably *Beyond* ... In question is not

---

1 Derrida in *The Truth in Painting* (1987) encounters this word in Kant's three critiques. It signifies for Derrida that which is outside a work and yet is essential to it, like an artist's signature or the frame of a painting. The metaphysics-busting word functions in Derrida's work like *différance* (see p. 333, note 1).

only a folding back or a tautological reversal, as if the grandson, by offering him a mirror of his writing, were in advance dictating to him what (and where) he had to set down on paper; as if Freud were writing what his descendence prescribed that he write, in sum holding the first pen, the one that always passes from one hand to another; as if Freud were making a return to Freud through the connivance of a grandson who dictates from his spool and regularly brings it back, with all the seriousness of a grandson certain of a privileged contract with the grandfather. It is not only a question of this tautological mirror. The autobiography *of the writing* posits and deposits simultaneously, in the same movement, the psychoanalytic movement. It performs, and bets on that which gave its occasional chance. Which amounts [*revenant*] to saying in sum, (but who is speaking here?), I bet that this double *fort/da* cooperates, that this cooperation cooperates with initiating the psychoanalytic cause, with setting in motion the psychoanalytic "movement," even being it, even *being* it, in its being *itself*, in other words, in the singular structure of its tradition, I will say in the proper name of this "science," this "movement," this "theoretical practice" which maintains a relation to its history like none other. A relation to the history of its writing and the writing of its history also. If, in the unheard-of event of this cooperation, the unanalyzed remainder of an unconscious remains, if this remainder works, and from its alterity constructs the autobiography of this testamentary writing, then I wager that it will be transmitted blindly by the entire movement of the return to Freud.

★★★

The serious play of the *fort/da* couples absence and presence in the *re-* of returning [*revenir*]. It overlaps them, it institutes repetition as their relation, relating them the one and the other, the one to the other, the one over or under the other. Thereby it plays with itself *usefully*, as if with its own object. Thus is confirmed the abyssal "overlapping" that I proposed above: of the object or the content of *Beyond* ..., of what Freud is supposedly writing, describing, analyzing, questioning, treating, etc., and, on the other hand, the system of his writing gestures, the scene of writing that he is playing or that plays itself. With him, without him, by him, or all at once. This is the same "complete game" of the *fort/da*. Freud does with (without) the object of his text exactly what Ernst does with (without) his spool. And if the game is called complete on one side and the other, we have to envisage an eminently symbolic completion which itself would be formed by these two completions, and which therefore would be incomplete in each of its pieces, and consequently would be completely incomplete when the two incompletions, related and joined the one to the other, start to multiply themselves, supplementing each other without completing each other. Let us admit that Freud is writing. He writes that he is writing, he describes what he is describing, but this is also what he is doing, he does what he is describing, to wit, what Ernst is doing: *fort/da* with his spool [*bobine*]. And each time that one says *to do,* one must specify: *to allow* to do (*lassen*). Freud does not do *fort/da,* indefatigably, with the object that the PP is. He does it with himself, he recalls himself. Following a detour of the *télé*,[1] this time an entire network. Just as Ernst, in recalling the object (mother, thing, whatever) to himself, immediately comes *himself* to recall *himself* in an immediately supplementary operation, so the speculating grandfather, in describing or recalling this or that, recalls *himself.* And thereby makes what is called his text, enters into a contract with himself in order to hold onto all the *strings/sons* [*fils*] of the descendance. No less than of the ascendance. An *incontestable* ascendance. The incontestable is also that which needs no witness. And which, nevertheless, cannot not be granted its rights: no counter-testimony appears to have any weight before this teleological auto-institution. The net [*filet*] is in place, and one pulls on a string [*fil*] only by getting one's hand, foot, or the rest, caught. It is a lasso or a lace.[2] Freud has not positioned it. Let us say that he has known how to get caught in it. But nothing has been said yet, nothing is known about this knowledge, for he

---

1 *Télé* is the French equivalent of the American expression TV—the English "telly" is almost perfect here—as well as the prefix to "tele-communication," communication at a distance, from the Greek *tele* (distant, *loin, fort*). "Network" at the end of this sentence translates chaîne, which has the sense of chain and network, as in a television or radio station, one of the télé's byways or detours. [Translator's note]
2 Concerning the double stricture of the *lace* in relation to the *fort:da,* I must refer to *Glas* (Paris: Galilee, 1974) and to "Restitutions—de la vérité en pointure" in *La vérité en peinture* (Paris: Flammarion, 1978). [Derrida's note]

himself has been caught in advance by the catching. He could not have or foresee this knowledge entirely, such was the condition for the overlapping.

Initially this is imprinted in an absolutely formal and general way. In a kind of *a priori*. The scene of the *fort/da*, whatever its exemplary content, is always in the process of describing in advance, as a deferred overlapping, the scene of its own description. The writing of a *fort/da* is always a *fort/da*, and the PP and *its* death drive are to be sought in the exhausting of this abyss.

★★★

The speculator himself recalls himself. He describes what he is doing. Without doing so *explicitly*, of course, and everything I am describing here can do without a thoroughly auto-analytic calculation, whence the interest and necessity of the thing. It speculates without the calculation itself analyzing itself, and from one generation to another.

He recalls *himself*. Who and what? Who? himself, of course. But we cannot know if this "himself" can say "myself"; and, even if it did say "myself," which me then would come to speak. The *fort/da* already would suffice to deprive us of any certainty on this subject. This is why, if a recourse, and a massive recourse, to the autobiographical is necessary here, the recourse must be of a new kind. This text is autobiographical, but in a completely different way than has been believed up to now. First of all, the autobiographical does not overlap the auto-analytical without limit. Next, it demands a reconsideration of the entire *topos* of the *autos*. Finally, far from entrusting us to our familiar knowledge of what autobiography means, it institutes, with its own strange contract, a new theoretical and practical charter for any possible autobiography.

Beyond ..., therefore, is not an *example* of what is allegedly already known under the name of autobiography. It writes autobiography, and one cannot conclude from the fact that in it an "author" recounts a bit of his life that the document is without value as truth, science, or philosophy. A "domain" is opened in which the inscription, as it is said, of a subject in his text, (so many notions to be reelaborated), is also the condition for the pertinence and performance of a text, of what the text "is worth" beyond what is called an empirical subjectivity, supposing that such a thing exists as soon as it speaks, writes, and substitutes one object for another, substitutes and adds itself as an object to another, in a word, as soon as it *supplements*. The notion of truth is quite incapable of accounting for this performance.

Autobiography, then, is not a previously opened space within which the speculating grandfather tells a story, a given story about what has happened to him in his life. What he recounts is autobiography. The *fort/da* in question here, as a particular story, is an autobiography which instructs: every autobiography is the departure/return of a *fort/da,* for example this one. Which one? The *fort/da* of Ernst? Of his mother conjoined with his grandfather in the reading of his own *fort/da?* Of *her* father, in other words of *his* grandfather? Of the great speculator? Of the father of psychoanalysis? Of the author of *Beyond* ...? But what access is there to the latter without a spectral analysis of all the others?

Elliptically, lacking more time, I will say that the graphics, the autobiographics of *Beyond* ..., of the word *beyond* (*jenseits* in general, the step beyond in general), imprints a prescription upon the *fort/da,* that of the overlapping by means of which proximity distances itself in *abyme* (*Ent-fernung*). The death drive is *there*, in the PP, which is a question of a *fort/da.*

***

A short paragraph opens chapter IV. It pronounces the new beginning, the step further, the beginning of the passage beyond, the passage finally freed. But it announces the step beyond as that which follows, gives it to follow, making it follow, forwarding it, but not yet effectively taking it: "What now follows is speculation, *Was nun folgt ist Spekulation* ..."

What follows now is Speculation. In a word. This is why the French translation says "pure speculation" ("*Ce qui suit doit être considéré comme de la pure speculation*"). Speculation pure and simple. And Freud adds, after the comma, "often far-fetched speculation (*oft weitausholende Spekulation*), which the reader will consider or dismiss according to his individual predilection" (24).

In other words: the "author" already is no longer there, no longer responsible. He has absented himself in advance, leaving the document in your hands. At least this is what he states. He does not seek to convince you of a truth. He does not seek to detract anything from the power, the proprietary investments, that is, the associations and projections of anyone. Association is free, which holds also for the contract between the writing and the reading of this text, along with the exchanges, engagements, and gifts, along with everything whose performance is attempted. At least this is what he says. The speculative discourse would have the value of what is performed in analysis, or in the field called "literary": you make of it what you like or what you can, it no longer concerns me, it has no law, especially scientific law. It concerns you. But the "it no longer concerns me," "it concerns you," more than ever compels you to the thing. Heteronymy is almost naked in the dissymmetry of the "it concerns." Given over to yourself, you are more than ever bound to the cause, autonomy is the autonomy of a "movement" prescribed by the thing which concerns you, concerns only you. You can no longer get rid of the uncontestable inheritance. The last free will in person (the signer of the will) no longer has anything to do with it or with anyone. You carry his name.

In a procession. On your shoulders, until the end of time you will formulate the theory carrying his name.

★★★

What has been translated as the "authenticity" of *Dasein* "resolutely" assuming its Being-for-death in the original (non-"vulgar") temporality of its "care," was also a certain quality of the relation to the proper: *Eigentlichkeit* [authenticity] assumed. Beyond the metaphysical categories of the subject, of consciousness, of the person, beyond the metapsychological categories which would be, to corrupt slightly the joke in *The Psychopathology of Everyday Life*, but the conversions of metaphysics, this movement of propriation would come back [*reviendrait*] to the Da of *Sein* and the Da of *Dasein*.[1] And the existential analytic of *Da-sein* is inseparable from an analysis of distancing and proximity which would not be so foreign to the analysis of the *fort:da*, at least such as we are

---

1   "Dasein," or "being," refers to Martin Heidegger's early existential work. Presumably, Derrida is also playing with the "da" (there) of Freud's "fort/da" (a child's game of there/gone he describes in *BPP*), and the "sein" of Heidegger's discussion of authentic existence, being.

reading it here. And that we can also follow on the track [*à la trace*], up to the relation to one's own death as a condition of authenticity (*Eigentlichkeit*). When Freud speaks of *Todestrieb*, *Todesziel*, *Umwege zum Tode*, and even of an "*eigenen Todesweg des Organismus*," he is indeed pronouncing the law of life-death as the law of the proper. Life *and* death are opposed only in order to serve it. Beyond all oppositions, without any possible identification or synthesis, it is indeed a question of an *economy* of death, of a law of the proper (*oikos*, *oikonomia*) which governs the detour and indefatigably seeks the proper event, its own, proper propriation (*Ereignis*) rather than life *and* death, life *or* death. The prolongation or abbreviation of the detour would be in the service of this properly economic or ecological law of oneself as proper, of the auto-mobile auto-affection of the *fort/da*. Does not everything that Freud ventures on the subject of time in these environs have to be related to the auto-affective structure of time (that which there gives itself to receive is no present-being) such as it is described in Husserl's *Lectures on Internal Time Consciousness* or Heidegger's *Kantbuch*?

***

It is exactly *there* (where? *there*), in the paralysis of this further step that always has to be taken away, it is there (but why there? why not one more or one less step? Where, there? *there*, answers life-death), when Freud's step cannot go on having to walk further for nothing, it is exactly there, by virtue of an apparently external constraint (fatigue? lack of time? rules of composition for the last or next to last chapter, etc.?), that Freud calls upon a "myth": Aristophanes' discourse in the *Symposium*. One no longer dares say anything about it. After the story of the spool, this place is the one most well trodden in the psychoanalytic literature, and how could the grass grow again in such a spot? Therefore, I will say almost nothing about this too familiar story. It is true that whatever becomes *too* familiar can always be suspected of jealously keeping a secret, of standing guard over the unexpected. This could have been the case, already, of the so familiar and so familial story of the *fort/da* and of the grandson's spool. It has in common with the recourse to the myth from the *Symposium* of also being a "story." Which is the more mythic of the two, and of a "fantastic kind" (*phantastischer Art*), as Freud says only about the second? Each time, there is the moment of the interruption of a certain type of questioning in order to recount a narrative. Pause: I am going to tell you a story. In both cases, the content of the story, narrative, or citation of the narrative, comes to us *filtered:* the most active selection is marked by ellipses in great number, and the most efficacious lacunae are not punctuated by the author. In different narrative modes, certainly, which themselves deserve a minute analysis, a tissue of lacunae tends to compose another fable. In both cases, the narrative is concerned with the theme of repetition, of relation, of the narrative as a return to a previous state. This is too evident for the *fort/da* of the spool. Here, the only characteristic that Freud says he is retaining from the *Symposium,* the only one that corresponds to the "condition whose fulfillment we desire," is the characteristic which makes the drive derive from the need to restore "an earlier state of things" (57). *Fort:da.* Rest assured, I am not going to hunt too far and too long for the analogy between the two fabulous narratives. I will not look for the androgyne in the triangle of the first scene, nor for the couple which desperately seeks to reconstitute itself. Nevertheless, these two "narrative" moments must be brought together: if they are the most famous and fabulous moments of the book, it is not only because they seem to interrupt a scientific or speculative discourse, thereby making us dream. It is also because they reveal and reconstitute the narrative necessity, or rather the structure as "narrative" at the limit of which, and with which, "speculation" constantly has to deal throughout the "book." The *fort:da* is a narrative. This is a reminder which can only be recalled, fabulously, from before memory, just as the entire book is concerned with what comes back from further away than the simple origin.

The origin is a speculation.

Whence the "myth" and the *hypothesis.* If there is no thesis in this book, it is because its proper object cannot be the object of any thesis. It will have been noticed that the concept of *hypothesis* is the most general "methodological" category of the book: all the "methodical" procedures amount to [*reviennent à*] hypotheses. And when science leaves us in the dark, providing us, for example as concerns the origin of sexuality, "not so much as a ray of a hypothesis" (*nicht der Lichtstrahl einer Hypothese*), it is again to a "hypothesis," of another order certainly, that we must recur. Aristophanes' myth is presented as a *"Hypothese"* of a "fantastic" kind. It is fantastic only in an accessory way, Freud wants to emphasize, because it seriously meets the required condition: to make the drive derive from a need to restore a previous state. In effect, this is the only service that Freud at first seems to expect from this hypothesis. In any event, this is what he begins by saying: "In quite a different region, it is true, we do meet with such a hypothesis; but it is of so fantastic a kind—a myth rather than a scientific explanation—that I should not venture to produce it here, were it not that it fulfills precisely the one condition whose fulfillment we desire. For it traces the origins of a drive to *a need to restore an earlier state of things*" (57). But already in the next paragraph, a secondary profit seems to be expected from Aristophanes. Is it secondary? Is it otherwise? In question is "the most important of [the drive's] variations in relation to its object." This myth's "theory"—and Freud indeed says "theory"—the theory which Plato "lets Aristophanes develop" [mod.] "deals not only with the *origin* of the sexual drive but also with the most important of its variations in relation to its object" (*seiner wichtigsten Variation in Bezug auf das Objekt*). Is this another goal of the same demonstration? an accessory or a principal goal? or a supplementary one, and in what sense then? And if they were the same? If there were no origin of the sexual drive except in this variation, in the variability which conditions it, in other words in the play of vicariance and of the supplement?

Rushing to extract a fragment of it, to retain only its *discursive* content—a "hypothesis," a "theory," a "myth," all three at once, for such are his own words in the lines preceding the citations—completely preoccupied by the consideration of this fragment, which moreover he has punctured with ellipses after lifting it out of the body of the text, Freud seems barely attentive to what the *Symposium* puts onstage or hides from view in its theater. He is interested in this theater as barely as possible. Here, I am not only speaking of what by convenience might be called the literary or fictional "form" of this theater, the form of this narrative of narratives, interlacing *diagesis* with *mimesis*, and also inscribing the one in the other, thus calling for the greatest possible circumspection in listening to the invisible quotation marks. I am also speaking of the "content" of this theater, of the stories told by the narrators or speakers, stories in which other stories are told. I am speaking of the "stories," the "affairs" between the characters of the *Symposium*, of what is placed on stage within it or is hidden from sight. Now, this is not without relation to the *origin-of-the-sexual-drive*, that is to the *variation-of-the-trait-in-relation-to-the-object*. This variation is not only the theme of the symposium, as is also the birth of Eros, it is also its performance, its condition, its milieu.

Now, in the time of this performance, Aristophanes' discourse represents only one episode. Freud is barely interested in this fact, and he retains only those shards of a fragment of this episode which appear to him pertinent to his own hypothesis, to what he *says* he means. Once again, he sets himself to relating a piece of a piece of a narrative related in the *Symposium*. This is a habitual operation. Who does not do so? And the question is not one of approving or disapproving in the name of the law. Of what law? Beyond any criteria of legitimation, we can nevertheless attempt to understand what is going on in a putting into perspective, in a reading, a writing, in citations, liftings, omissions, suspensions, etc. To do this, one must set oneself to it, in the same perspective, but one must also make the relation to the object vary. Without these two conditions, the very identity of the perspective could not appear as such. As concerns Freud and Plato, the *Symposium* and *Beyond* ..., the variety of possible perspectives is inexhaustibly rich. Obeying a law of selective economy (the limits of what I can say here, in this context whose givens are too complex for me even to attempt to reassemble them) as much as the rightful pleasure that I can give myself tonight, I will limit myself to the following traits.

First, if Aristophanes' discourse represents only a limited episode, notably as concerns what is to occur afterward, it is to limit it even more to reduce it to ten lines; but what to say then about the gesture which consists in taking no account of the person who holds the floor, of the person whom Plato "lets develop" the "theory"? No allusion to Aristophanes, save [*fors*] his name. No allusion to Socrates, who is not even named. Now, Aristophanes is not just anyone. Not just anyone for Socrates. Or for Plato. He is the other. In *The Clouds* he had violently attacked Socrates. In the *Apology*, Plato accuses him of the worst: of having been the first accuser of Socrates, or even his betrayer. He would have lent his hand to the murder, or even the suicide. And Plato, in accusing Aristophanes, defends Socrates, is behind him. Or in *front* of him, showing him with his finger as a lawyer presents the defendant: here is the innocent man, the martyr, admire him, be pardoned by him, *he* is judging you. But what is he doing by "letting" Aristophanes "develop" what Freud calls the "theory"? Alcibiades too will be behind Socrates. Further on in the *Symposium* his praise of Socrates will be a response to the calumnies of *The Clouds*, etc.

For the moment, let us be content with the following indices. In order to suggest that an immense reconstitution around these lacunae certainly would be necessary, but above all, primarily, in order to become attentive to the abyssal structure of the lacunary phenomenon. The corpus from within which Freud operates his fragmentary and lacunary liftings will never have been a complete body whose integral reconstitution would be promised to us. Narratives of mimetico-diagetic narratives, opened by a "mimed" demand for "diagesis" ("it is from you that I expect this narrative ..."), for diageses which relate "*logoi*" ("... *alla diegesai tines esan oi logoi* ..."), but *logoi* which are also performing gestures; these tales begin by stating their lacunae, if not by taking an exact account of them, since this is impossible. One cannot remember everything. Even before relating the first discourse on love, Phaedrus', the lacunae are pointed out, as well as the lapses of memory, but one insists: the essential has been maintained. Of course, and Freud too will maintain the "essential." Of what was said by each Aristodemus did not remember everything (*oute panu o Aristodemos ememneto*). And I, Apollodorus, I did not remember everything that Aristodemus had said to me (*out au ego a ekeinos elege panta, a de malista*), but the most important things—who could doubt it?—and so on, up to Freud and beyond, right here. Each one makes himself into the *facteur,* the postman, of a narrative that he transmits by maintaining what is "essential" in it: underlined, cut out, translated, commented, edited, taught, reset in a chosen perspective. And occasionally, within the narrative, lacunae are again pointed out, which makes a piece of supplementary history. And this supplement can embed itself in *abyme* within another lacuna that is bigger or smaller. Bigger or smaller because here we are within a logic that makes possible the inscription of the bigger in the smaller, which confuses the order of all limits, and forbids the *arrangement of bodies.*

Which is indeed what is going on here—the bodies are not very well arranged—and if Aristophanes' discourse is cut out of the great lacunary body of the *Symposium*, it happens that it comes as a response, in the *mise en scène*, to a demand concerning the lacuna, precisely, and the ellipsis of memory: if I have omitted or elided something, let it be your job, Aristophanes, to supplement it and to fill in the lacuna (Plato, *Symposium* 188e). And what is Aristophanes going to recount, in order to supplement the lacuna? A story of a lacuna and of supplementation at the origin of love, of sexual difference, and of variation in relation to the object. Etc.

Thus, Freud omits the scene of the text, including the placing in *abyme* of the memories of lacunae. In this great omission, he forgets Socrates. He leaves Plato alone with Aristophanes, he leaves it to Plato to leave it to Aristophanes to develop the theory. Why? The most banal answer certainly is not incorrect. For his purpose this little extract sufficed, and let us not make mountains of molehills. Nothing else has happened. This is true. But why did nothing else happen? Why has the relation to the object not been different? Why has it not varied? What has immobilized it?

To omit Socrates when one writes, is not to omit just anything or anyone, especially when one is writing about Plato. Especially when one is writing about a dialogue of Plato's in which Socrates, a Socrates and the Socrates, is not a simple supernumerary. This omission is not a murder, of course, let us not overdramatize. It erases a singular character written or described by Plato as a character in the *Symposium*, but also as the one who will have caused or let the *Symposium* be written without writing himself, an infinitely complex scene of the signature in which the inscription arrives only to erase itself, engraves itself in depth in proportion to its erasure. Plato remains *behind* Socrates' signature, but what is this position? What does "behind" mean in this case? What does it sign, and what does it signify?

If Freud in his turn erases Socrates, which only accentuates his profile in what remains here of a *Symposium*, is this in order to pay homage to Plato for an acknowledgment of debt? Is it in order to praise an inheritance, a genealogy, a descendance? Is it in order to trace a tradition back to Plato, and to constitute himself as its heir? Is it in order to attribute to Plato the merit of an inauguration, or even a paternity? No, on the contrary. It is in order to take the origin away from Plato, and to make him, already, an heir. Not of Socrates, who is too close and too proper to him. But of someone much further away. It would be to exaggerate—a bit—to read this passage as a destitution of Plato. It would be to exaggerate, a bit, to say that Freud is vehemently determined to secondarize, to minimize, to devalue, but in the end he does insist a great deal on the fact that Plato has invented nothing, that his lack of originality is indeed the sign of the truth of what he says, that he had to inherit an entire tradition, etc. This is the object of a note which is not only the longest in the book, but also much longer than the passage it annotates. It begins curiously with the acknowledgment of a debt: not a debt to Plato, but to the person who helped Freud to think that he owed nothing to Plato, and that Plato himself was indebted to the Hindu tradition: "I have to thank Professor Heinrich Gomperz, of Vienna, for the following discussion on the origin (*Herkunft*) of the Platonic myth ..." (Freud, *Standard* 18: 58). The note then follows, more than twice as long as the citation from the *Symposium*. It gives the impression that Freud, in effect, is more worried about "the origin of the Platonic myth" (*Herkunft des platonischen Mythus*), than about the Platonic myth of "the origin of the sexual drive" (*Herkunft des Geschlechtstriebes*). Freud compulsively seeks, q.e.d., to displace the object and to restore an "earlier state." Which is rather laborious, we are rather uneasy about this, please rest assured that we are giving you Gomperz's own words, a tug on your sleeve: I would like to draw your attention to the fact that essentially, *wesentlich*, this same theory is already to be found in the Upanishads, etc., and that "in contradiction to the prevailing opinion" I will not purely and simply deny the possibility of Plato's "dependence" (or subjection, *Abhängigkeit*), even indirectly, upon Indian thought. The word "*Abhängigkeit*" comes back further on, in the middle of confused concessions: Plato would not have appropriated (*sich nicht zu eigen gemacht*) this story through some "oriental tradition" if he had not been in a situation to be illuminated by its tenor of truth. Etc. One's eyes widen.[1]

***

---

1   This is doubtless not the only place in which I must have intersected, I am pleased to say, with several of Samuel Weber's analyses in a very recent book, analyses certainly both different and much richer than the ones I was attempting here. On all these questions it seems to me that *The Freud Legend* (Minneapolis: University of Minnesota Press, [1979] 1982) will become uncircumventable. [Derrida's note; see Appendix B21]

What does a scene of writing like this one consist of? What is its structure, and the condition for it as an event? Where, how, when, to what, and to whom does it happen?

By all rights these questions have precedence over any possible debate on the subject of the alleged theses of this book, the theses too precipitously perceived in it, as I am attempting to demonstrate. Prior questions which, to my knowledge, have never been asked. They have never even bothered all those, especially within the analytic movement, who since 1920 have entered into a battle with (very) well-drawn lines around these "theses."

There are those who have taken them "seriously," and have constructed an entire discourse about the seriousness of *Beyond* ... In this respect, the most interesting and spectacular case, I believe, is that of Lacan.

Others, more light- or heavy-handedly, as you will, have shrugged their shoulders and politely looked away from this attack of mysticism, speculative deviation, mythological dreaming: the master has played, he was not serious, etc.

But no one on either side has examined the testamentary singularity of this scene of writing. For itself, and for its consequences for the psychoanalytic context in general. At the most, some have contented themselves with remarking on the mythological or literary *ornaments* with which Freud's thetic prose is supposed *surrounded*.

This is why we must insist upon the textual (autobiographical, heterobiographical, thanatographical, all of this in the same framework) procedure, *dé-marche,* and particularly upon this kind of postscript to the next to last chapter.

★★★

The word transference reminds one of the unity of its metaphoric network, which is precisely metaphor and transference (*Übertragung*), a network of correspondences, connections, switch points, traffic, and a semantic, postal, railway sorting without which no transferential destination would be possible, in the strictly technical sense that Freud's psychoanalysis has sought to assign to this word (see the end of chapter III).

The corresponding "concept" remains no less enigmatic, and when Freud or others attempt to define the "strict" sense of the word, they call upon an entire stock of metaphors and of metaphors of metaphors. This is not fortuitous. All these metaphors regroup themselves around the notions of repetition, of analogy, of correspondence in view of a destination, of relay, of reedition or corrected and revised edition, transcription, translation from an "original." The passage between transference (in every sense) and speculation that we are situating here perhaps becomes more salient. Speculative transference orients, *destines*, calculates the most original and most passive "first step" on the very threshold of perception. And this perception, the desire for it or its concept, belongs to the destiny of this calculation. As does every discourse on this subject. This one, of course, Freud's, of which he speaks also. Freud designates the "predilections" which orient speculative transference, shows their necessity and their effects only by speaking of himself, in the self-critical movement which at no moment alleges that it escapes from the fatalities that it defines. Once the term and the oppositional limit are erased, and replaced by an entirely other structure, the suspensive procedure [*démarche*] appears interminable. The interminable is not accidental, does not come, as if from the outside, to mark incompletion and infirmity. Speculative repetition and transference start the march.

Thus, one is less surprised to see that Freud does not expect from scientific progress a finally proper language, purified of every metaphor, and finally *surpassing* its *trans*ference: even if one could replace the terms of psychology with those of physiology or chemistry, one would dispose only of more "familiar" and "simpler" significations, but not of appropriated significations. The language of physiology or of chemistry is also a "*Bildersprache*." Therefore, progress can be made only within metaphoric transference. *To borrow* is the law. Within every language, since a figure is always a borrowed language, but also from one discursive domain to another, or from one science to another. Without borrowing, nothing begins, there is no proper fund/foundation [*fonds*]. Everything begins with the transference of funds, and *there is interest in borrowing*, this is even its initial interest. To borrow yields, *brings back*, produces surplus value, is the prime mover of every investment. Thereby, one begins by speculating, by betting on a value to be produced as if from nothing. And all these "metaphors" confirm, as metaphors, the necessity of what they state.

★★★

These are the last words of the chapter. To every chagrined, anxious or pressing objection, to every attempt at scientistic or philosophizing intimidation, this is how I hear Freud's answer resonate, at my own risk and peril, and I translate it: "go look for yourself, as for me I like it, the beyond of the PP is my rightful pleasure. The hypothesis of the death drive: for myself I like it, and above all it interests me, I find, and thus I take my interest there." Here is the original text that I have just translated, and that I translate now in another way. If one has confidence in certain norms, one will doubtless find it more faithful. "If so, it may be asked why I have embarked upon efforts such as those consigned to this chapter, and why they are delivered for publication. Well—I cannot deny that some of the analogies, correlations and connections which it contains *seemed* to *me* to deserve consideration" (18: 60; mod.). My emphasis: *mir* der Beachtung würdig *erschienen sind*. Period, the end. This is the final point, the last words of the chapter.

★★★

When Freud says "we find ourselves before an unresolved problem ...," the state he is then describing must correspond to what he says in the same book about the resolution of a problem or of a difficulty or of a tension in general. In any event, this state must be put to the test of such a correspondence and such a responsibility. But is the question of such a correspondence or such a responsibility solvable? What happens when acts or performances (discourse or writing, analysis or description, etc.) are part of the objects they designate? When they can be given as examples of precisely that of which they speak or write? Certainly, one does not gain an auto-reflective transparency, on the contrary. A reckoning is no longer possible, nor is an account, and the borders of the set are then neither closed nor open. Their trait is divided, and the interlacings can no longer be undone.[1] Perhaps this where the ultimate resistance to the solution is found, and to make it appear more clearly, or rather to infer it more accurately, for it never appears, one must place in relation the procedure

---

1 Other essays analyze this figure under the heading of "double chiasmatic invagination of the borders." [See Derrida *Law*.] [Derrida's note]

of *Beyond* ... and the structure of its objects, the irresolution of its problems (in its procedure) and what the book says about the solution of problems in general (in its objects). Its procedure [*démarche*] is one of its objects, whence its pace (*allure*), and this is why it does not advance [*aller*] very well, or work [*marcher*] by itself. One of its objects among others, but also the object for which there are other objects with which to effect *trans-* and to speculate. This object among others is not just any object. Thus it limps and is hard to close.

***

This seminar will have played the *fort/da* of Nietzsche.

Which is rhythm.

Pleasure is a kind of rhythm, says a fragment from 1884.

Is what we have retained from *Beyond* ... anything other than a rhythm, the rhythm of a step which always *comes back* [*revient*], which again has just left? Which has always just left again? And if there is a theme, in the interpretation of this piece, a theme rather than a thesis, it is perhaps *rythmos,* and the rhythm of the theme no less than the theme of a rhythm.

Fort:da. The most normal step has to bear disequilibrium, within itself, in order to carry itself forward, in order to have itself followed by another one, the same again, that is a step, and so that the other comes back, amounts to [*revienne*] the same, but as other. Before all else limping has to be the very rhythm of the march, *unterwegs.* Before any accidental aggravation which could come to make limping itself falter. This is rhythm.

If speculation necessarily remains unresolved because it plays on two boards, band contra band, losing by winning and winning by losing, how can one be surprised that it advances painfully [*que ça marche mal*]? But it has to advance painfully in order to advance; if it has to, if it has to advance, it must advance hesitatingly. It limps well, no?

The allusion to limping, on the last line of the book, has an oblique, lateral, winking *relation* to Freud's very procedure [*démarche*]. It designates first, obviously, a law of scientific *progress*; to this extent it belongs to a kind of discourse on *method.* But it is also to be read in relation to the procedure [*démarche*] of Freud's *fort:da.* I would even say that it is also the relation of it, the contracted narrative. And the translation. The citation of the poet remarks everything in a scene of writing without border, without theoretical suture, disjointed according to the aspect and pace [*allure*] of a prosthetic graft.

It is suddenly immobilized over limping, at the moment of stepping across the last line of the text. But wait, it was going to start up again, it had left in order to start up one more time. He was going to begin again. On the last page, just before the great speculator decides, will we ever know why, "enough," he had almost proposed another step forward, which would have been, we cannot doubt, once again, a step forward for nothing, only rhythm.

★★★

Can one think pleasure?

One can think about it. Thus it cannot be a question of asking oneself, properly, what it is. It is that which asks itself.

One can still compare, translate, transfer, traffic, sort [*trier*]. *Fort:da* of Nietzsche according to the rhythm. He compares pleasure, he says that it compares *itself* to a "kind of rhythm" in the series of lesser pains, and always according to differences of degree, "more or less." He says "perhaps," and does so in a context in which his rhetoric purposely appears more disconcerting than ever; he says perhaps, and he says it in parentheses "(One might perhaps characterize pleasure in general as a rhythm of small painful excitations.)" Elsewhere he speaks of pleasure, of a "kind of pleasure" and in certain "cases," on the condition of a "certain rhythmic series of small painful excitations." We are henceforth in a logic of difference—which can be radical alterity—and no longer in a logic of opposition or contradiction: "Pain is something other than pleasure, I mean that it is *not* the opposite of pleasure."

Other aphoristic lines appear to essentialize the beyond of the pleasure principle: pain is due to the very essence of existence, the will to suffer would inhabit life fundamentally, constituting the very aspiration of the will to power, the *differential* necessity which does not go without resistance. If one follows this series of statements, the beyond of the pleasure principle would be the affirmation of life rather than the aspiration to return to the inorganic. But, as we have verified, this latter motif is far from being absent in Nietzsche's texts. Therefore it is necessary (q.e.d.) to take into account precisely, within reading itself, both serial *différance* and rhythm. For other lines also come to deride all those, men and women, who are worried by the question of knowing what *carries the day* in the end, and what *commands* in this world, of pleasure or of pain. Such a question is to be abandoned: to philosophical dilettantism, to women, he says, and once again, why not, to the poets, to certain poets (he specifies).

23. *The Pleasures of Repetition: A Phenomenological Perspective* (1987)[1]
Judith Butler

Although one might discount Freud's postulation of the death instinct from the outset, maintaining that it is a purely speculative notion that cannot be justified, it seems wiser to concede Freud the speculative license he claims and to question instead whether this principle and instinct does the explanatory work that he claims it does. The challenge to that explanatory power that I wish to pursue here is embodied in those experiences that are both pleasurable *and* repetition-compulsive. If Freud is right, then repetition compulsion is not motivated by pleasure, but by the Thanatic wish for a complete regression to a time before life. But what do we make of *the pleasures of repetition* themselves, the compulsive and defeated pleasures that not only accompany various forms of neurosis, but nourish and sustain them as well? In *Beyond the Pleasure Principle*, Freud searches for a manifestation of the death instinct that will support his point, and the example he lights upon is sadism. By claiming that sadism is not motivated by pleasure, Freud is forced to revise the theory articulated in *Three Essays on the Theory of Sexuality* and "Instincts and Their Vicissitudes," that sadism is a strategy of self-preservation and not, as he comes to claim, a strategy of self-annihilation. Although this article will consider some of the key shifts within his theory that culminate in this view of sadism as emblematic of the death instinct, it will in no way represent a comprehensive summary of Freud's various insights into the psychosexual meaning of

---

1   From "The Pleasure of Repetition" (1987), *Pleasure Beyond the Pleasure Principle*. Ed. Robert A. Glick and Stanley Bone. New Haven: Yale University Press, 1990. 260-61; 267-70; 271-73; 274-75.

sadism. Instead, we will consider the ways in which sadism as pleasurable repetition might well disprove the very construct of the death instinct that Freud assumes it will confirm. I will suggest how the phenomenon of compulsively repetitive pleasures confounds and challenges some of the speculative notions that lead Freud's theory astray, and I will sketch an alternative point of departure based on phenomenological grounds. The invocation of phenomenology is not intended to displace the psychoanalytic framework—indeed, points of comparison between the doctrine of intentionality and the psychoanalytic school of object relations will be explored—but to ground psychoanalytic insights in experience rather than in wholly speculative constructs. Indeed, the phenomenological approach offered here is one which in fact characterizes much of Freud's own analytic work to understand those peculiarly (self-)destructive postures of pleasure as the dramatized fantasies of traversing time in order to repeat and repair a history that one wishes never was.

★★★

As an explanatory principle, the notion of an instinctual drive toward death is no doubt comprehensive. But the problem of establishing the ontological validity of such a construct is notoriously difficult. Freud knows his inquiry to be speculative, and he knows as well that the usefulness of his theoretical constructs consists in their capacity to illuminate those aspects of repetition compulsion that have previously remained opaque. Indeed, he suggests at the end of his inquiry that his theory of instincts belongs to "the figurative language peculiar to psychology" (Freud, *Beyond2* 83). The question, however, is whether the intellectual breadth afforded by this avowedly speculative construct diminishes the analytic practicability of his theory. In developing this instinctual theory of sadism, Freud moves away from a position which took the desire for mastery and reparation as the key to understanding the origins and strategies of sexual sadism. That the sadist now manifests the generalized urge of the organism to return to its original stasis leaves the interpretation of the sadist at a generalized level.

But consider the possibility that Freud's reversal of his own position might well require a further reversal, in order that its analytic usefulness be restored. We might go along with Freud and argue that the sadist first seeks his or her own death, albeit unconsciously; that this aim conflicts with the sexual instinct, which seeks cathexis and hence life-affirming connections; and that the resolution of this conflict is achieved through the subordination of the sexual strategy to the overall plan of restoring the stasis characteristic of the organism prior to its individuation. As such, the sexual dimension of sadism would always be considered a mere channel or vehicle for the death instinct, its instrument and cover, as it were. In Freud's own words, this death instinct, first "forced" out of the ego, "has pointed the way for the libidinal components of the sexual instinct, and ... these follow after it to the object" (74). This tagging along of sexuality suggests its inadvertent and unnecessary function in the strategy of sadism and suggests as well that both the sexual and the sadistic dimensions might be understood as organized and regulated by the death instinct.

This explanation has impressive existential dimensions, and one might also account for a variety of religious experiences on the basis of this universally human urge to restore the organism to its original state. But though we have explained the phenomenon of sadism through recourse to a universal principle, it seems that we have lost the capacity to explain it on the level of the individual. Indeed, what framework is left to us to explain the specificity of sadistic strategies in the biographical context of the individual? Inasmuch as human beings are sadists, are they sadists for the same reasons? It appears that Freud's move to a universal grounding of sadism deprives his theory of the capacity to discern the particular forms of sadism, their origins, and the specific content of their aims. Is it purely tangential that sadism takes a sexual form, or is the relation between pleasure and pain more closely interrelated than Freud at this point in his theory seems ready to acknowledge?

As was suggested above, we might well reverse Freud's ever-reversible theory yet another time and ask: What conditions within the biographical experience of the individual occasion both the desire to die and the externalization of this desire in the form of sadism? Clearly, I have already reinterpreted Freud's vocabulary, renouncing the naturalistic lexicon of instinct for the more phenomenologically familiar notion of desire. But this reworking of Freud's vocabulary is crucial, if we are to retain the experiential insights he offers and yet to escape the unfortunate implications of his speculative naturalism. We might well concur with Freud that there is a significant connection between a desire for death and the sadistic effort to master or injure another human being, but we might remain skeptical with regard to the ontological primacy attributed to the death instincts and the subsidiary, even inadvertent, role assigned to the sexual instincts. In his earlier theory, he suggested that sadism is the effort to master the love-object that has resisted and escaped the strategy of appropriation and incorporation. Indeed, if I cannot make the object into a part of me, then I will subdue it through force or coercion, and thereby I will make it into an instrument of my will. Sadism would then appear as the failure of incorporation, the effort to maintain the Other as an extension of my will, a refusal to grant the Other its Otherness. Moreover, in both the earlier theory and in *Beyond the Pleasure Principle*, Freud maintains that sadism is structured by repetition, that sadistic acts are efforts to recover a time past in order to gain satisfaction for a wish previously unsatisfied. Here Freud suggests the crucial link between sadism and *reparation* that is lost from the theory developed in 1920, unless of course we understand life itself as a damage for which one seeks reparation.

According to the theory of primary narcissism, all externality provokes a hostile reaction on the part of the established ego, and Freud said as much in 1914. But what of the peculiar history of hostilities that comes to structure the sadistic aims of an individual's sexual desire? How does hostility become incorporated into desire, if it was not always there, and does a schematic rendering of the universal basis of hostility do enough to explain the particular forms of sadism that appear in human sexual behaviour?

As a repetitive pleasure, sadism is both cathexis and regression at once; it is a binding activity that regularly unbinds itself, a connection that reasserts distance, a sexual act that seeks to repudiate sexuality. The paradoxical character of sadism reveals the conflict that it expresses, but there is no good reason to assume that this conflict rests in instinctual life per se. The negation of pleasure at the heart of sadism may not readily be equated with the desire to die; what is intended is primarily the death of pleasure in the midst of pleasure. We may subsequently interpret this effort to negate pleasure as an effort to negate life and this attempt to negate life as a regressive effort to recover a time before the anxieties and hostilities associated with pleasure, sexuality, and loving emerge. But the latter two conclusions in no way follow necessarily from the phenomenological description of the paradoxes of sadism. We can further conclude that the effort to subdue or even injure the body of the Other in and through sexual acts is an externalized relation of the ego to itself, that the body which is being subdued and repudiated is only *secondarily* the body of the Other, but it is primarily the body of the sadist himself. But here again, to argue on behalf of the primary reflexivity of the sadistic relation in no way compels an acceptance of any postulation regarding the instinctual basis of sadism.

Toward a Phenomenological Interpretation of Repetitive Pleasures

Freud's route for providing a universal basis for sadism is through the theory of instincts, a theory he knows to be speculative, but one that he considers to be part of the necessarily "figurative language of psychology." Although Freud occasionally wrote that he hoped to ground that theory of instinct in a neurophysiological framework, he also appeared to be prepared to settle for a certain necessary ambiguity in the language that describes psychic and affective life. Rather than enter into the debate over whether Freud intended psychoanalytic theory to be a science and, if so, in what its scientific character consists, I would like to suggest an alternative point of departure for understanding the particular phenomenon under investigation here: the pleasures of repetition. In claiming that this alternative point of departure is phenomenological, I mean simply that it takes its bearings within experience and that it subscribes to a view of psychic life as *intentional*. Although the term "intentional" is often equated with the mental disposition of having a clear and conscious intention to do *x* or *y*, its usage within phenomenology is significantly different. As Edmund Husserl[1] has argued, the intentional character of consciousness is its *relatedness* to the world in which it is found and which offers up the various objects of its experience. In Husserl's words, "consciousness is always consciousness of," meaning that consciousness is never wholly self-referential, that it can only take itself as its object once that "self" is projected or determined in a countervailing world. With the presumption

---

1 Edmund Husserl (1895-1938), German mathematician and philosopher. Founder of "phenomenology," which sides with human experience against positivism.

of *intentionality*, philosophical and psychological theories can no longer claim that our various ways of being conscious or aware of the world are merely mental representations that have no bearing or relation to an objective field. Our conscious thoughts and various modalities of awareness are related to an exterior field, whether it is existent or not. This relationship is characteristic of human existence. Indeed, it constitutes the primary structure of human experience and consequently all interpretations of psychological life must in some way presuppose this relationship.

The phenomenological doctrine of intentionality is comparable to that tenet of object relations theory which assumes that concrete relationships, whether in memory or fantasy, provide the point of departure for psychological interpretation. According to Jean-Paul Sartre,[1] within a phenomenological framework it is no longer possible to describe a human being as solely concerned with himself or herself. Even the most reclusive or monastic of human beings maintains a relation to the world, even if in the mode of denial. The refusal to be in the world is but one way of maintaining a relation to that world, as the "negation" of others is still a vital and significant way of being related to them. This effort to deny connection emerges within Sartre's analysis as a connection that is specified as denial. According to Sartre's psychological extension of phenomenological philosophy, human beings are inevitably and, indeed, unbearably *in the world*. Whether in a posture of rejection, hatred, or indeed, sadism, the individual endeavors to break the intentional bond with the world that constitutes the ineradicable structure of his or her experience. Turning against intentionality itself, the individual attempts to deny its own connectedness but necessarily fails. Not unlike Freud's view of Eros, the doctrine of intentionality assumes a primary and difficult connectedness with the external objects of the world. Indeed, if sadism is, as Freud argues, a turning of Eros against itself, the phenomenological explanation is not far afield: sadism would be the effort to break a connection which, in effect, can

---

1 Jean-Paul Sartre (1905-80), French existentialist philosopher. For Sartre, the intentional nature of consciousness necessarily and continuously directs the human subject outward and beyond itself; all consciousness is consciousness of some*thing*. This fundamental principle renders absurd the notion of an "unconscious."

never be broken precisely because connection is, as intentional, constitutive of human experiences itself [...]

★★★

[...] [P]leasure is not a substance or state that has any meaning outside of the context in which it is related to an object. Indeed, the physiological or somatic preconditions of pleasure are not identifiable with pleasure itself, for pleasure denotes an experience, and hence, an intentional relation. The consequence of this view is that we cannot meaningfully speak of pleasure as a principle or instinct that maintains ontological integrity before experience itself; the attribution of pleasure to a pre-experiential set of processes is an inappropriate transposition of a term applicable only to lived and knowable experience to the physiological conditions of that experience. Although Sartre's argument relies unfortunately on a refutation of the unconscious, his theory makes some more general points about the applicability of terms such as "pleasure," "desire," and "emotion" that do not require us to corroborate his misunderstanding of unconscious processes. At its best, his theory offers an insight which object relations theory specifies and demonstrates in terms of early childhood: that the structure, aim, and strategies of pleasure are developed in relation to the earliest objects of love. The consequence of this claim is that pleasure is only and always understandable in relation to an object, that it is referential and intentional in its ontology, that it is neither instinct nor state but a relation to an object repeated and elaborated over time.

Because intentionality, according to Husserl, is a polyvalent structure, the intentional structure of pleasure may well have a variety of objects. The problem of compulsively repeated pleasures that Freud describes in *Beyond the Pleasure Principle* might be described, then, as maintaining at least a twofold intentional object: the uncathected object of love and temporality itself. For the individual who suffers this repeated and frustrated effect of pleasure, it is not only the object of the past that cannot be recovered, nor the relation that cannot be restored or reconstructed, but it is time itself that resists the human will and proves itself unyielding. Between pleasure and satisfaction, a prohibition or negation of pleasure is enacted which necessitates the endless repetition and proliferation of thwarted pleasures. The repetition is a vain effort to stay, or indeed, to reverse time; such repetition reveals a rancor against the present which feeds upon itself.

Resisting the present is, from a phenomenological point of view, a useless effort to exercise control over the structure of temporality as necessarily expressed in time past, time present, and time future. The effort to stop or break this temporal continuity is, in effect, the self-defeating strategy of the individual. To be an individual is to be *in time*: to be subject to the exigencies of time; to refuse the temporal continuity of experience is to refuse the very structure of the self.

From the viewpoint of phenomenology, then, pleasure is polyvalent in its intentional structure; it relates not only to an object—present, past, or both—but to temporality and to the world as such. These last two objects of pleasure constitute the existential dimension of the intentionality of pleasure. The Sartrian question—what kind of relation to the world is expressed in this posture of self-defeat?—suggests that the selfsame agency that pursues pleasure also interrupts and rejects that pleasure and that this fundamental ambivalence is an intentional relation rather than a phenomenal expression of a wholly instinctual source. Again, to claim that this ambivalence emerges from a relationship is not to offer a causal account of the origins of pleasures and their repetitive character. Indeed, such a claim merely designates the operative intentional relationship as an ambivalent one and poses the question of what sort of necessarily failed effort to eradicate the ineradicable structure of intentionality is here under way. The primacy of intentionality suggests that connectedness is insuperable and that the effort to deny connection is always and only a manner of being engaged in the world in the mode of denial. Clearly, the phenomenological conclusion to the problem of repetitive pleasures is to assert as primary what Freud would have called Eros, the intimate involvement with exteriority which, despite its best efforts, the human subject cannot overcome within the confines of lived experience.

From the terms of Sartre's phenomenology, then, the pleasures of compulsive repetition constitute a crisis of intentionality but not its refutation. Only through the contention that a nonintentional break with exteriority is possible does the problem of rival drives or instincts become possible. In other words, only if we fail to understand disconnection as a mode of connection does the question of opposing human drives or tendencies become possible. With intentionality as the theoretical point of departure, however, we can understand the negation of pleasure and connection as its own kind of connection and, in psychoanalytic terms, its own peculiar kind of pleasure.

★★★

Just as Freud maintained that sadism maintains hostility toward external objects per se, Sartre would argue that sadism exemplifies an unresolved quarrel with exteriority, and hence, with the intentional structure of pleasure itself.

In reversing his earlier position, which argued that masochism was but the internalization of a primarily sadistic relation, Freud opened the way for a consideration of sadism as an externalized relation to oneself. Here it is clear that for Sartre, sadism signifies a rebellion against intentionality that can never wholly succeed (even in the desire to obliterate the object, it is still the object whose obliteration is sought). Freud's theory in *Beyond the Pleasure Principle* does not entail a controversial rehabilitation of primary masochism as a way of explaining the reflexive relations, those which the ego maintains toward itself, characteristic of sadistic acts. In postulating the death instinct as the primary basis of sadism, Freud suggests that sadism is inadvertently sexual only in its expression and that this destructive urge is conditioned by the innate physiological constitution of human beings. By relinquishing the postulation of an instinct as the origin of sadism, we free the analysis to consider whether sadism, although grounded in a posture of self-hatred, might be further explained as an internalized relation, the repetition of an originally external abuse as a self-inflicted injury, that is, the internalization of abuse as self-punishment. Moreover, by disputing the dualistic account of sexual instincts and death instincts, we allow for the possibility that pleasure is not arbitrarily associated with sadism, neither tagging along behind it as a separate instinctual force nor serving as a mere channel for the expression of a death instinct. On the contrary, the unhappy repetitions of sadistic acts bear out a useless desire to repeat and repair a history of dissatisfaction. The effort to comprehend this pleasure that goes nowhere, that repeats itself endlessly as the infinite stutter of desire, requires a turn: not to instinct but to the particular history of injury which, internalized then externalized, becomes the focus of a sexual battle.

24. *"The Possibility of Happiness": Absolute Narcissism and the Problem of Sociality* (2000)[1]
Todd Dufresne

> Such a limitation of narcissism can, according to our theoreti-
> cal views, only be produced by one factor, a libidinal tie with
> other people. Love for oneself knows only one barrier—love
> for others, love for objects.
>
> Sigmund Freud, *Group Psychology and the Analysis of the Ego*
> (*Standard* 18: 102)

It is well known that Freud, in the misnamed "cultural" or
"sociological" works that follow *Beyond the Pleasure Principle*,
was obsessed with the perverted and perverting, socialized and
socializing Others, and with their collective psychology. This
is no accident, since for Freud the social is always a function
of the individual; it is only amid the group that pleasure in death
becomes for the "individual" such a pain in the ass—that is, where
everything natural or biological is turned on its head. Death is
the essence of an authentic individuality that is denied under
the compulsion or threat of a society that demands for every
subject a group identity—to wit, a life. Only thereafter is the
primacy of the inner world redirected or projected outward
onto the screen of the external world; a stage upon which the
essential war of self against self has raged since the beginning
of time. Time, indeed, is the measure of this trauma called
life, and Freud went out of his way to destroy its history and
obliterate its baneful influence upon the mass individual. To
this apocryphal end he erected a theory of the free, ahistorical,
lifeless "subject," a subject that precedes time and subjectivity,
a subject, silent as mum, that is already an inanimate object,
"dead."

Given the extreme aims of this metapsychological fantasy, it
cannot be surprising that Freud at times expressed deep pessimism about therapeutic interventions of any kind. For if death
is conceived as the ultimate relief from the unhappy tensions of
life, then any therapy less than euthanasia is bound to be at best

---

1 From *Tales From the Freudian Crypt: The Death Drive in Text and
   Context*, foreword M. Borch-Jacobsen, Stanford: Stanford University
   Press, 2000. 158-64.

partially effective and, thus, interminable. The best of all possible therapies is always the one that does the least to interfere with, or the most to promote, the patient's bid to re-member or re-cognize the ultimate basis of existence: silence, nonreciprocity, inanimacy, mother earth. Hence the theatrical death that characterizes the analytic encounter, where the analyst (as Lacan understood best), like the death drive, always does his best work in silence. A theatrical taste of the real thing, analytic therapy thus treads upon the existential ground that metapsychology, as suggested, can quite simply do without.

Freud's growing pessimism about psychoanalysis and society—and in the end, frankly, there is no difference between these two—is reflected in his own critical appraisal of *Civilization and Its Discontents* during a gathering of colleagues on March 20, 1930. These remarks, attributed to Freud by the analyst Richard Sterba (1898-1989), are significant. Freud begins his self-critique by complaining that he did not deal substantially enough in this work with the subject of guilt (in Sterba *Reminiscences*: 113). Freud's second criticism is indirectly connected to this concern, but is altogether more serious and more extreme:

> None of you has noted one omission in the work, and this is a gigantic disgrace. I myself only noticed it after the book was already printed. My omission is excusable, but not yours. I had good reason to forget something that I know very distinctly. If I had not forgotten it, but had written it down, it would have been unbearable. Thus, it was an opportunistic tendency that expressed itself through this forgetting. The forgotten piece belongs to the possibilities of happiness; in fact, this is the most important possibility because it is the only one that is psychologically unassailable. Thus, the book does not mention the only condition for happiness that is really sufficient. (114)

At this point Freud, with a flair for the dramatic, recites an ode from Horace in Latin, "Si fractus inlabatur [sic] orbis / impavidum ferient ruinae" (Horace *Odes* 3.3.7-8), which he apparently translates for his colleagues along the lines of: "If the firmament [i.e., the sky] should break to pieces over him / the fragments will bury a fearless man." He continues: "This possibility of happiness is so very sad. It is the person who relies completely upon himself. A caricature of this type is Falstaff. We can tolerate him as a caricature, but otherwise he is unbearable. This is the absolute narcissist. My omission was a real defect in the presentation" (in *Reminiscences*: 114).

This is a remarkable and telling criticism of Freud's part, first of all, because the limits of psychoanalysis and sociality in general are exposed by the "sad" fiction of the "absolute narcissist." And what is absolute narcissism? According to Freud in "An Outline of Psycho-analysis," when the "whole available quota of libido is stored up" we have a state of "absolute, primary *narcissism*. It lasts till the ego begins to cathect the ideas of objects with libido, to transform narcissistic libido into object-libido" (Freud *Standard* 23: 150; his emphasis). The situation is nicely summarized by [Sandor] Ferenczi, who writes: "We are able to love (recognize) objects only by a sacrifice of our narcissism, which is after all but a fresh illustration of the well-known psychoanalytical fact that all object-love takes place at the expense of narcissism" (Ferenczi *Problem*: 377).

Not incidentally, it was the problem of narcissism that complicated Freud's early dualism in the first place and that encouraged him to postulate the more distinct dualism of the life and death drives. But by the time Freud wrote his metapsychology papers he was obviously intrigued with the problem of a *primary* or *fundamental* narcissism, a new and abstract foundation that, as suggested, raised considerably the stakes of his speculative ambitions. In the popular *Introductory Lectures on Psycho-Analysis* that immediately follow his meta-psychological papers of 1915, Freud declares that self-love "cannot be an exceptional or trivial event. On the contrary it is probable that this narcissism is the universal and original state of things, from which object-love is only later developed, without the narcissism necessarily disappearing on that account" (*Standard* 16: 416; see also 13: 89). Or as Freud puts it in "Instincts and Their Vicissitudes": "Hate, as a relation to objects, is older than love. It derives from the narcissistic ego's primordial repudiation of the external world with its outpouring of stimuli" (14: 139). Basically Freud contends that narcissism is a form of psychosis that is antisocial and, like death, "beyond" the interventions of any Other—including the psychoanalyst. It therefore follows that *absolute* narcissism is the only possibility for a type of happiness in civilization that "is psychologically unassailable." Why? Again, because absolute narcissism is quite literally beyond society, love, and the pleasure principle: untouchable, unapproachable, even unimaginable. Freud adopts similar language in *Totem and Taboo*—where he speaks of love, and self-love in particular, as "psychologically so remarkable" and "the normal prototype of the psychoses" (13: 89)—and again in his essay "On Narcissism," where he discusses the enviable narcissism of the child: "an unassailable libidinal position which we ourselves have since abandoned" (14: 89).

Yet the "so very sad" ideal of an original and absolute narcissism is, as Freud admits, a "caricature." More exactly put, it is a parody of an ideal, if not a reduction ad absurdum of a wild train of thought. All fantasy aside, Freud is careful to admit that no social being could be an absolute narcissist and, in any case, no one could bear his presence if he arrived on the scene at this late date. For if it is already difficult to tolerate the narcissistic infant, it would be all the more "unbearable" to tolerate the similarly asocial adult. His character would be "in the profoundest sense hostile to civilization" (23: 185), essentially "unready" for and "insusceptible" to culture (see 201). Nonetheless, Freud maintains a very special role for the absolute narcissist in a place, time, or theory of splendid isolation set far apart from the energetic mass of Others, the maddening horde, society. It is no doubt for this very reason that he chastises himself and his followers especially for "forgetting" this well-established piece of the metapsychological puzzle. I am of course thinking of the primal father first introduced in *Totem and Taboo* as the original condition of guilt and, thus, of civilization. But I am also thinking of his return nine years later, *after* the publication of *BPP*, in a chapter from *Group Psychology* called "The Group and the Primal Horde." The father, Freud tells us in this later work, was "free," that is, "he loved no one but himself" (18: 123).

He, at the very beginning of the history of mankind, was the "superman" whom Nietzsche only expected from the future. Even to-day the members of a group stand in need of the illusion that they are equally and justly loved by their leader; *but the leader himself need love no one else, he may be of a masterful nature, absolutely narcissistic, self-confident and independent.* We know that love puts a check upon narcissism, and it would be possible to show how, operating this way, it became a factor of civilization. (123-24; my emphasis)

Since things are not spelled out in *Civilization and Its Discontents*, about which Freud modestly claims to have "discovered afresh the most banal truths" (Freud and Andreas-Salomé 1966: 181), it may be helpful to put this entire paradox of *Kultur* (society or civilization) another way. According to Freud, the absolute narcissist is the sole condition of the possibility of happiness in civilization and yet his is an untenable and impossible condition. For just as the father's death at the hands of his parricidal sons brings about, retrospectively, guilt and renunciation and, thus, repressive civilization, it simultaneously brings about the death of true happiness: absolute narcissism. Or, more precisely, his death brings about homosexual group love as a "check on narcissism," an expression of guilt that plagues the sons and becomes "a factor of civilization"—and, thus, an enemy of the most pure or absolute expression of happiness: death. In any case, Freud insists that the father's narcissism lingers in society as a latent principle of destruction among the unhappy band of brothers. "Some portion of self-destructiveness remains within," as Freud put it in 1938, "till at last it succeeds in killing the individual" (23: 150).

At the risk of being pedantic, I should emphasize that everything metapsychological boils down to the difference between the dead but authentic individual and the alive but inauthentic group. In point of fact, the drives of death and life are basically derives of radical individualism and mass individualism (i.e., group identity), the second derivative upon and contaminated by the first. Against our traditionally inverted perspective, "freedom" in this view is always a freedom *from* a group identity based on life, love, libido, sexuality, and Eros: biologically speaking, that is, the mass individual is driven away from sociality and toward the freedom of true individuality qua death. Such freedom is reflected in the simple facts of sleep, parapraxis, and similar features of ego functioning that are the meat and potatoes of analytic interpretation. Psychic determinism in this view is nothing but the inevitable and finally total failure of the individual to maintain an illusory identity with the group. The psychopathology of everyday life is thus found in the many cracks along the seams of group relations; or, if you prefer, it is destruction that wins the day, every day, because death, not love, conquers all.

It is certainly true that Freud, in the very first paragraph of *Group Psychology*, admits that "only rarely and under exceptional conditions is individual psychology in a position to disregard the relations of this individual to others" (18: 68). Yet as rare and exceptional as this condition may be, it becomes for Freud nothing less than the rule—the so very sad ideal—by which he measures all social relations in his *Massenpsychologie*. Freud matter-of-factly rejects the possibility of a "*social* instinct," by which he means the popular "herd instinct" as developed by the English surgeon Wilfred Trotter, and directs his attention, as usual, "towards two other possibilities: that the social instinct may not be a primitive one and insusceptible of dissection, and that it may be possible to discover the beginnings of its development in a narrower circle, such as that of the family" (70). As Freud suggests, this "narrower circle" coincides with the "narrow dimension of this little book" on group psychology, by which he means the truth of individual psychology understood via the privileged tools of psychoanalysis.

As complicated a picture as this is, it requires one final clarification. If life is but a "detour" on the path leading toward death, and if it is a path determined on some level by one's own choice, as Freud argues in *BPP* (see 18: 38-39), then the act of parricide which is supposed to form the back-bone of society is obviously an illusion. Indeed, it is the greatest illusion of all: namely, the illusion that the environment (in this case a murderous one) really matters, first, for the group (or horde) and its psychology and, second, for the individual and his psychology upon which the group is logically dependent. In other words, the primal father's death cannot in principle be a case of bloody murder. Following the dictates of primary masochism, the father must have on the contrary *chosen* (on some level) the means for his own execution at the hands of the Others; for he alone is responsible for pursuing a path toward death that is singularly appropriate to him. In this respect I am impressed by the relatively banal fact that the choice of *being* dead is not available to the primal father who is *already alive* in Freud's fiction, already born the child of some Other(s)—some God(s), mother(s), earth, epidermis, or who knows what. In short, Freud begins his tale of the origin of civilization not with death—which, in any case, *cannot explain life*—but with the next best thing: the absolute narcissism of the fully grown super manchild.

Such, then, is the limited extent of Freud's pragmatism: like philosophers determined to prove the existence of the external world, the "getting started" problem is "solved" with a leap of faith from no-thing to some-thing, in this case, from death to narcissistic life, from metapsychological speculation to psychoanalytic observation, from instinct to society. Or as Lamarck[1] held, if evolution is always forward moving, that which was inanimate must somehow become animate—thus filling in all the evolutionary positions that were left behind during the course of evolution. Life, like flies on dung, thus appears out of nothingness, as though by magic.

The bridge between the world beyond and the material world is therefore effected by the inner world of Freud's metapsychological fiction: the superman of absolute narcissism. It is through his example that one understands life as a becoming-death. It is worth noting, though, that this "superman at the very beginning of the history of mankind," whom Freud openly contrasts with Nietzsche's *Übermensch* "from the future" (see also 18: 42), is already found on the pages of Nietzsche's first book, *The Birth of Tragedy*. It appears there as the terrible pairing of "truth and its terror" that erupt the moment one recognizes that existence is everywhere an *absurdity* (*Birth*: 51). Indeed, I would go so far as to say that Freud merely mouths the words (while purifying them in scientistic jargon) that Nietzsche gave to the demon and wood sprite Silenus who, when caught by King Midas, is compelled to speak about "man's greatest good." To the king, yet another questing Oedipus, Silenus laughs and finally utters the now famous words: "Ephemeral wretch, begotten by accident and toil, why do you force me to tell you what it would be your greatest boon to hear? What would be best for you is beyond your reach: not to have been

---

1 Jean-Baptiste Lamarck (1744-1829), French naturalist and early proponent of evolutionary theory. Lamarck hypothesized that organisms are continually driven towards increasing levels of complexity and that differences between organisms are determined, in part, by differences between the organisms' natural environments.

born, not to *be*, to be *nothing*. But the second best is to die soon" (29; original emphasis).[1]

True to form, Freud paid for this tragic truth with the "nausea" Nietzsche described in his book (52), and which Sartre popularized in his existential novel *La nausée*. Freud only added a few wrinkles to the basic program: What is best is beyond our reach, or organic death. What is good is the superman of absolute narcissism, or social death. And finally, what is worst of all is life itself, which is only a virtual or living death. It is only fitting that this lowest of the low include Freud's own psychoanalytic practice, wherein he was forced (presumably by an inner compulsion) to contend with the worst when he knew very well what is best.[2] Accordingly, Freud made of therapy a modest, somber practice of converting the patient's "[uncommon] misery into common unhappiness." True happiness, Freud teaches us, is not meant for this world, which can only dream, narcissistically, of oblivion.

In effect, Freud made of psychoanalysis nothing more than an elaborate detour on the way to what is truly meaningful: a metapsychology on the scent of death. Psychoanalysis thus becomes one way among others for coping with the world, itself a regrettable piece of sociality that plays at death even as it forestalls that end according to an inscrutable logic of conservation. In the end,

---

1   These sentiments are, however, also present in Schopenhauer, who as suggested provides a list of similar statements throughout the ages (*World* 585-88). But Nietzsche's version is as good as any, especially since it was the most current version at that time. Incidentally, it is worth noting that Rank used this citation from Nietzsche as the epigraph for *The Trauma of Birth* (Kramer 7). Rank's scepticism about analytical therapy was merely a reflection of Freud's own therapeutic pessimism: both knew that analysis had become interminable and that patients were being sacrificed to the grail of "research." But Rank, just like Ferenczi, sought to alter that theory and therapy accordingly, making it more humane and hopeful; but it was here that they betrayed Freud's dark philosophy of resignation and fell afoul of his sycophantic followers. [Dufresne's note]

2   As Freud puts it in a letter of April 21, 1918, "this has been a troubled time, marked by a growing resentment against the whole outer world, which was no doubt intensified by the necessity of being kind and tolerant every day to ten human beings [patients] who had gone off the rails" (Freud and Andreas-Salomé 77). [Dufresne's note]

in other words, psychoanalysis is just like life: terminable upon completion—which is to say, whenever one gets around to it.

25. *Paradox of the Freudian Death Drive* (2006)[1]
Slavoj Žižek

[I]n the shift from desire to drive, we pass from the *lost object* to *loss itself as an object*. That is to say: the weird movement called "drive" is not driven by the "impossible" quest for the lost object; it is *a push to enact "loss"—the gap, cut, distance—itself directly*. There is thus a *double* distinction to be drawn here: not only between *objet petit a* [object little-a, unattainable object of desire] in its fantasmatic and postfantasmatic status, but also, within this postfantasmatic domain itself, between the lost object-cause of desire and the object-loss of drive.

This is why we should not confuse the death drive with the so-called "*nirvana* principle," the thrust toward destruction or self-obliteration: the Freudian death drive has nothing whatsoever to do with the craving for self-annihilation, for the return to the inorganic absence of any life-tension; it is, on the contrary, the very opposite of dying—a name for the "undead" eternal life itself, for the horrible fate of being caught in the endless repetitive cycle of wandering around in guilt and pain. The paradox of the Freudian "death drive" is therefore that it is Freud's name for its very opposite, for the way immortality appears within psychoanalysis, for an uncanny *excess* of life, for an "undead" urge which persists beyond the (biological) cycle of life and death, of generation and corruption. The ultimate lesson of psychoanalysis is that human life is never "just life": humans are not simply alive, they are possessed by the strange drive to enjoy life in excess, passionately attached to a surplus which sticks out and derails the ordinary run of things.

This means that it is wrong to claim that the "pure" death drive would have been the impossible "total" will to (self-) destruction, the ecstatic self-annihilation in which the subject would have rejoined the fullness of the maternal Thing, but that this will is not realizable, that it gets blocked, stuck to a "partial object." Such a notion retranslates the death drive into the terms of desire and its lost object: it is in desire that the positive object is a metonymic stand-in for the Void of the impossible

---

1 From *The Parallax View*. Cambridge, MA: MIT Press, 2006.

Thing; it is in desire that the aspiration to fullness is transferred to partial objects—this is what Lacan called the metonymy of desire. We have to be very precise here if we are not to miss Lacan's point (and thereby confuse desire and drive): drive is not an infinite longing for the Thing which gets fixated onto a partial object—"drive" is this fixation itself in which resides the "death" dimension of every drive. Drive is not a universal thrust (toward the incestuous Thing) braked and broken up, it is this brake itself, a brake on instinct—its "stuckness," as Eric Santner (2001) might have put it. The elementary matrix of drive is not that of transcending all particular objects toward the void of the Thing (which is then accessible only in its metonymic stand-in), but that of our libido getting "stuck" onto a particular object, condemned to circulate around it forever.

The basic paradox here is that the specifically human dimension—drive as opposed to instinct—emerges precisely when what was originally a mere by-product is elevated into an autonomous aim: man is not more "reflexive" than an animal; on the contrary, man perceives as a direct goal what, for an animal, has no intrinsic value. In short, the zero-degree of "humanization" is not further "mediation" of animal activity, its reinscription as a subordinated moment of a higher totality (for example, we eat and procreate in order to develop a higher spiritual potential), but the radical narrowing of focus, the elevation of a minor activity into an end in itself. We become "humans" when we get caught into a closed, self-propelling loop of repeating the same gesture and finding satisfaction in it.

Select Bibliography

References: Editor's Introduction

Deleuze, Gilles. "Coldness and Cruelty." *Masochism*. New York: Zone Books, 1991.

Ellenberger, Henri. *The Discovery of the Unconscious: The History and Evolution of Dynamic Psychiatry*. New York: Basic Books, 1970.

Ferenczi, Sándor. "Stages in the Development of the Sense of Reality." *Sex in Psycho-Analysis*. Trans. E. Jones and C. Newton. New York: Dover Books, 1956 [1913].

———. *The Clinical Diary of Sándor Ferenczi*. Ed. J. Dupont. Trans. M. Balint and N.Z. Jackson. Cambridge, MA: Harvard UP, 1995 [1932].

Freud, Sigmund. *Beyond the Pleasure Principle*. Trans. G.C. Richter. 1920. (This volume, page 49.)

———. *Civilization and Its Discontents*. Trans. G.C. Richter. 1930. (This volume, page 132.)

———. "An Autobiographical Study." In *The Standard Edition of the Complete Psychological Works of Sigmund Freud*. Trans. James Strachey, 20: 3–74.

———. *New Introductory Lectures*. SE 22: 1–182.

———. *Moses and Monotheism*. SE 23: 3–137.

———. A Phylogenetic Fantasy: Overview of the Transference Neuroses. Ed. I. Grubrich-Simitis. Trans. A. Hoffer and P.T. Hoffer. Cambridge, MA: Belknap Press, 1987.

Freud, Sigmund and Lou Andreas-Salomé. *Sigmund Freud and Lou Andreas-Salomé: Letters*. Ed. E. Pfeiffer. Trans. William and Elaine Robson-Scott. London: Hogarth Press, 1966.

Freud, Sigmund and Sándor Ferenczi. *The Correspondence of Sigmund Freud and Sándor Ferenczi, 1914–1919*. Vol. 2. Ed. E. Falzeder and E. Brabant. Trans. P. Hoffer. Cambridge, MA: Belknap Press, 1996.

———. *The Correspondence of Sigmund Freud and Sándor Ferenczi, 1920–1933*. Vol. 3. Ed. E. Falzeder and E. Brabant. Trans. P. Hoffer. Cambridge, MA: Belknap Press,

Freud, Sigmund and Arnold Zweig. *The Letters of Sigmund Freud and Arnold Zweig*. Ed. E. Freud. Trans. William and Elaine Robson-Scott. London: Hogarth Press, 1970.

Jones, Ernest. *The Life and Works of Sigmund Freud: The Last Phase, 1919–1939*. Vol. 3. New York: Basic Books, 1957.

Marcuse, Herbert. *Eros and Civilization: A Philosophical Inquiry Into Freud*. 2nd edition. Boston: Beacon Books, 1966 [1955].

Nunberg, Herman and Paul Federn, eds. *Minutes of the Vienna Psychoanalytic Society*. 4 vols. Trans. M. Nunberg. New York: International Universities Press, 1962–75.

Roazen, Paul. *Freud and his Followers*. New York: Meridian, 1976 [1975].

——. "Nietzsche, Freud, and the History of Psychoanalysis." *Returns of the "French Freud": Freud, Lacan, and Beyond*. Ed. T. Dufresne. New York: Routledge, 1997.

Strachey, James. "Editor's Introduction." *The Project for a Scientific Psychology*. Sigmund Freud. *Standard Edition of the Complete Psychological Works of Sigmund Freud*. Vol. 1: 283–93.

References: Translator's Note

Dufresne, Todd. *Tales from the Freudian Crypt*. Stanford: Stanford UP, 2000.

Freud, Sigmund. "Das Unheimliche." *Imago*, 5.5-6 (1919): 297-324. [Also *Gesammelte Werke*, v. 12: 229-68. London: Imago, 1947.] [Trans. "The 'Uncanny.'" *Collected Papers*, v. 4: 368-407. Translated by Alix Strachey. London: Hogarth, 1925.] [Trans. "The 'Uncanny.'" *Standard Edition*, v. 17: 217-56. London: Hogarth, 1955.] [Trans. *The Uncanny*. Translated by David McLintock. London: Penguin, 2003.]

——. *Jenseits des Lustprinzips*. Leipzig: Internationaler Psychoanalytischer Verlag, 1920. [Also *Gesammelte Werke*, v. 13: 3-69. London: Imago, 1940.] [Trans. *Beyond the Pleasure Principle*. Translated by C.J.M. Hubback. London: International Psycho-Analytical Press, 1922.] [Trans. *Beyond the Pleasure Principle*. Translated by James Strachey. London: Hogarth, 1950.] [Also *Standard Edition*, v. 18: 3-64. London: Hogarth, 1955.] [Trans. *Beyond the Pleasure Principle*. Translated by John Reddick. London: Penguin, 2003.]

——. *Massenpsychologie und Ich-Analyse*. Leipzig: Internationaler Psychoanalytischer Verlag, 1921. [Also *Gesammelte Werke*, v. 13: 71-167. London: Imago, 1940.] [Trans. *Group Psychology and the Analysis of the Ego*. Translated by James Strachey. London and Vienna: International Psycho-Analytical Press, 1922.] [Also *Standard Edition*, v. 18: 67-143. London: Hogarth, 1955.]

——. *Das Ich und das Es.* Vienna: Internationaler Psychoanalytischer Verlag, 1923. [Also *Gesammelte Werke*, v. 13: 237-89. London: Imago, 1940.] [Trans. *The Ego and the Id.* Translated by Joan Riviere. London: Hogarth, 1927.] [Trans. *The Ego and the Id. Standard Edition*, v. 19: 3-66. London: Hogarth, 1961.] [Trans. *The Ego and the Id.* Translated by John Reddick. London: Penguin, 2003.]

——. "Das ökonomische Problem des Masochismus." *Internationale Zeitschrift für Psychoanalyse* 10.2 (1924): 121-33. [Also *Gesammelte Werke*, v. 13: 371-83. London: Imago, 1940.] [Trans. "The Economic Problem in Masochism." *Collected Papers*, v. 2: 255-68. Translated by Joan Riviere. London: Hogarth, 1925.] [Trans. "The Economic Problem of Masochism." *Standard Edition*, v. 19: 159-70. London: Hogarth, 1961.]

——. "Notiz über den Wunderblock." *Internationale Zeitschrift für Psychoanalyse* 11.1 (1925): 1-5. [Also *Gesammelte Werke*, v. 14: 1-8. London: Imago, 1928.] [Trans. "A Note Upon the 'Mystic Writing-Pad.'" *Standard Edition*, v. 19: 227-32. London: Hogarth, 1961.]

——. *Das Unbehagen in der Kultur.* Vienna: Internationaler Psychoanalytischer Verlag, 1930. [Also *Gesammelte Werke*, v. 14: 421-506. London: Imago, 1948.] [Trans. *Civilization and its Discontents.* Translated by Joan Riviere. London: Hogarth, 1930.] [Trans. *Civilization and Its Discontents. Standard Edition*, v. 21: 59-45. London: Hogarth, 1961.] [Trans. *Civilization and Its Discontents.* Translated by David McLintock. London: Penguin, 2002.]

——. "Psychoanalysis." *Gesammelte Schriften*, v. 12: 372-80. Leipzig: Internationaler Psychoanalytischer Verlag, 1934. [Also *Gesammelte Werke*, v. 14: 299-307. London: Imago, 1948.] [Trans. "Psychoanalysis: Freudian School." *Encyclopaedia Britannica*, 13th ed., v. 3: 253-55. Translated by James Strachey, 1926.] [Also *Standard Edition*, v. 20: 261-70. London: Hogarth, 1959.]

——. "Die endliche und unendliche Analyse." *Internationale Zeitschrift für Psychoanalyse* 23.2 (1937): 209-40. [Also *Gesammelte Werke*, v. 16: 59-99. London: Imago, 1950.] [Trans. "Analysis Terminable and Interminable." *Standard Edition*, v. 23: 211-53. London: Hogarth, 1964.]

Goethe, Johann Wolfgang von. *Faust: A Tragedy.* Translated by Bayard Taylor. Boston: Houghton, Mifflin, 1870.

Holder, Alex. "A Historical-Critical Edition." *Translating Freud.* Ed. Darius Ornston. New Haven: Yale UP, 1992. 75-96.

Jones, Ernst. Introduction. *Beyond the Pleasure Principle.* Translated by C.J.M. Hubback. London: International Psycho-Analytical Press, 1922.

Kiell, Norman. *Freud Without Hindsight: Reviews of his Work (1893-1939)*. Madison: International Universities Press, 1988.

King, Peter. *Multatuli*. New York: Twayne, 1972.

Mahony, Patrick. *Cries of the Wolf Man*. New York: International Universities Press, 1984.

Multatuli [Edward Douwes Dekker]. *Ideën [Ideas]*. Amsterdam: Meijer, 1862.

Ornston, Darius. "Improving Strachey's Freud." *Translating Freud*. Ed. Darius Ornston. New Haven: Yale UP, 1992. 1-23.

———. "Alternatives to a Standard Edition." *Translating Freud*. Ed. Darius Ornston. New Haven: Yale UP, 1992. 97-113.

———. "Obstacles to Improving Strachey's Freud." *Translating Freud*. Ed. Darius Ornston. New Haven: Yale UP, 1992. 191-222.

Roazen, Paul. *Meeting Freud's Family*. Amherst: U of Massachusetts P, 1993.

Spitteler, Carl. *Imago*. Jena: Diederichs, 1906.

References: *Beyond the Pleasure Principle*

Breuer, Joseph and Sigmund Freud. "Über den psychischen Mechanismus hysterischer Phänomene: Vorläufige Mitteilung." *Neurologisches Centralblatt* 12 (1893). [Trans. "On the Psychical Mechanism of Hysterical Phenomena: Preliminary Communication." *Standard Edition*, v.2: 3-17. London: Hogarth, 1955.]

———. *Studien über Hysterie*. Leipzig and Vienna: Deuticke, 1895. [Also *Gesammelte Werke*, v.1: 77-312. London: Imago, 1952.] [Trans. *Studies on Hysteria. Standard Edition*, v.2. London: Hogarth, 1955.]

Doflein, Franz. *Das Problem des Todes und der Unsterblichkeit bei den Pflanzen und Tieren* [The Problem of Death and Immortality in Plants and Animals]. Jena: Fischer, 1919.

Fechner, Gustav. *Einige Ideen zur Schöpfungs- und Entwicklungsgeschichte der Organismen* [Some Ideas on the History of the Creation and Development of Organisms]. Leipzig: Breitkopf und Härtel, 1873.

Ferenczi, Sándor. "Entwicklungsstufen des Wirklichkeits-Sinnes." [Degrees of Development of the Sense of Reality]. *Internationale Zeitschrift für Psychoanalyse* 1 (1913): 124-38.

Fliess, Wilhelm. *Der Ablauf des Lebens* [The Rhythm of Life]. Leipzig: Deuticke, 1906.

Freud, Sigmund. *Die Traumdeutung*. Leipzig and Vienna: Deuticke, 1900. [Also *Gesammelte Werke*, v.2-3. London: Imago, 1942.] [Trans. *The Interpretation of Dreams. Standard Edition*, v.4-5. London: Hogarth, 1953.]

———. *Drei Abhandlungen zur Sexualtheorie*. Leipzig and Vienna:
Deuticke, 1905. [Also *Gesammelte Werke*, v.5:29-145. London:
Imago, 1942.] [Trans. *Three Essays on the Theory of Sexuality*.
Standard Edition, v.7: 125-245. London: Hogarth, 1953.]

———. "Erinnern, Wiederholen und Durcharbeiten." *Internationale
Zeitschrift für Psychoanalyse* 2.6 (1914): 485-91. [Also *Gesammelte
Werke*, v.10: 126-36. London: Imago, 1946.] [Trans. "Remembering,
Repeating and Working-Through." *Standard Edition*, v.12: 147-56.
London: Hogarth: 1958.]

———. "Zur Einführung des Narzissmus." *Jahrbuch für Psychoanalyse* 6.1
(1914): 1-24. [Also *Gesammelte Werke*, v.10: 138-70. London: Imago,
1946.] [Trans. "On Narcissism: An Introduction." *Standard Edition*,
v.14: 69-102. London: Hogarth, 1957.]

———. "Triebe und Triebschicksale." *Internationale Zeitschrift für Psy-
chologie* 3.2 (1915): 84-100. [Also *Gesammelte Werke*, v.10: 210-32.
London: Imago, 1946.] [Trans. "Instincts and Their Vicissitudes."
Standard Edition, v.14: 111-40. London: Hogarth, 1957.]

———. "Eine Kindheitserinnerung aus *Dichtung und Wahrheit*." *Imago* 5.2
(1917): 49-57. [Also *Gesammelte Werke*, v.12: 15-26. London: Imago,
1947.] [Trans. "A Childhood Recollection from *Dichtung und Wahrheit*."
Standard Edition, v.17: 147-56. London: Hogarth, 1955.]

———. Introduction to *Zur Psychoanalyse der Kriegsneurosen*: 3-7. Leipzig
and Vienna: Internationaler Psychoanalytischer Verlag, 1919. [Also
Gesammelte Werke, v.12: 321-24. London: Imago, 1947.] [Trans.
Introduction to *Psychoanalysis and the War Neuroses. Standard Edition*,
v.17: 207-15. London: Hogarth, 1955.]

———. "Die Widerstände gegen die Psychoanalyse." *Imago* 11.3 (1925):
222-33. [Also *Gesammelte Werke*, v.14: 99-110. London: Imago,
1948.] [Trans. "The Resistance to Psycho-Analysis." *Standard
Edition*, v.19: 213-22. London: Hogarth, 1961.]

———. Sándor Ferenczi, Karl Abraham, Ernst Simmel, and Ernest
Jones. *Zur Psychoanalyse der Kriegsneurosen* [On the Psychoanalysis
of the War Neuroses]. Internationale Psychoanalytische Bibliothek,
v.1. Leipzig and Vienna: Internationaler Psychoanalytischer Verlag,
1919.

Goette, Alexander. *Über den Ursprung des Todes* [On the Origin of
Death]. Hamburg: Voss, 1883.

Hartmann, Max. *Tod und Fortpflanzung* [Death and Reproduction].
Munich: Reinhardt, 1906.

Jung, Carl. "Die Bedeutung des Vaters für das Schicksal des Einzelnen."
Jahrbuch für psychoanalytische und psychopathologische Forschung 1

(1909): 155-68. [Trans: "The Significance of the Father in the Destiny of the Individual." *Collected Papers on Analytical Psychology*. Translated by Constance E. Long. London: Baillière, Tindall, and Cox, 1916: 156-75.]

Lipschütz, Alexander. *Warum wir sterben* [Why We Die]. Stuttgart: Kosmos, 1914.

Low, Barbara. *Psycho-Analysis: A Brief Account of the Freudian Theory*. London: Allen and Unwin, 1920.

Marcinowski, Johannes. "Die erotischen Quellen der Minderwertigkeitsgefühle" [The Erotic Sources of Feelings of Inferiority]. *Zeitschrift für Sexualwissenschaft* 4 (1918): 313-21.

Müller, F. Max. *The Upanishads*. New York: Dover, 1962.

Pfeifer, Sigmund. "Äusserungen infantil-erotischer Triebe im Spiele" [Expressions of Infantile-Erotic Drives in Play]. *Imago* 5 (1919): 243 ff.

Plato. *Symposium*. Translated by C.J. Rowe. Warminster: Aris and Phillips, 1998.

Rank, Otto. *Der Künstler:Ansätze zu einer Sexual-Psychologie*. Vienna: Heller, 1907. [Trans. "The Artist." Translated by Eva Salomon with James Lieberman. *Journal of the Otto Rank Association* 15.1 (1980): 5-63.]

Schopenhauer, Arthur. "Über die anscheinende Absichtlichkeit im Schicksale des Einzelnen" [On the Apparent Intentionality in the Fate of the Individual]. *Sämtliche Werke*. Ed. Arthur Hübscher. v.5. Leipzig: Brockhaus, 1938.

Spielrein, Sabina. "Die Destruktion als Ursache des Werdens" [Destruction as the Cause of Becoming]. *Jahrbuch für Psychoanalytische und Psychopathologische Forschung* 4 (1912): 465-503.

Stärcke, August. Introduction to "Die 'kulturelle' Sexualmoral und die moderne Nervosität" ['Civilized' Sexual Morality and Modern Nervous Disorders]. Leyden: 1914.

Weismann, August. *Über die Dauer des Lebens* [On the Duration of Life]. Jena: Fischer, 1882.

——. *Über Leben und Tod* [On Life and Death]. Jena: Fischer, 1884.

——. *Das Keimplasma: Eine Theorie der Vererbung*. Jena: Fischer, 1892. [Trans. *The Germ-Plasm: A Theory of Heredity*. Translated by W. Newton Parker and Harriet Rönnfeldt. London: Scott, 1893.]

Ziegler, Konrat. "Menschen und Weltenwerden" [Cosmogony and the Origin of Man]. *Neue Jahrbücher für das Klassische Altertum* 31 (1913): 529-73.

References: Appendix A

Capelle, William. *Die Vorsokratiker* [The Pre-Socratics]. Leipzig: Kröner, 1935.

Freud, Sigmund. *Die Traumdeutung.* Leipzig and Vienna: Deuticke, 1900. [Also *Gesammelte Werke*, v.2-3. London: Imago, 1942.] [Trans. *The Interpretation of Dreams. Standard Edition*, v.4-5. London: Hogarth, 1953.]

———. *Drei Abhandlungen zur Sexualtheorie.* Leipzig and Vienna: Deuticke, 1905. [Also *Gesammelte Werke*, v.5: 29 ff. London: Imago, 1942.] [Trans. *Three Essays on the Theory of Sexuality. Standard Edition*, v.7: 125-245. London: Hogarth, 1953.]

———. *Totem und Tabu: einige Übereinstimmungen im Seelenleben der Wilden und der Neurotiker.* Leipzig: Heller, 1913. [Also *Gesammelte Werke*, v.9: 1-205. London: Imago, 1940.] [Trans. *Totem and Taboo: Some Points of Agreement Between the Mental Lives of Savages and Neurotics. Standard Edition*, v.13: 1-162. London: Hogarth, 1955.]

———. *Jenseits des Lustprinzips.* Leipzig: Internationaler Psychoanalytischer Verlag, 1920. [Also *Gesammelte Werke*, v.13: 3-69. London: Imago, 1940.] [Trans. *Beyond the Pleasure Principle.* Translated by C.J.M. Hubback. London: International Psycho-Analytical Press, 1922.] [Trans. *Beyond the Pleasure Principle.* Translated by James Strachey. London: Hogarth, 1950.] [Also *Standard Edition*, v.18: 3-64. London: Hogarth, 1955.] [Trans. *Beyond the Pleasure Principle.* Translated by John Reddick. London: Penguin, 2003.]

———. "Die infantile Genitalorganisation." *Internationale Zeitschrift für Psychoanalyse* 9.2 (1923): 168-71. [Also *Gesammelte Werke*, v.13: 291-98. London: Imago, 1940.] [Trans. "The Infantile Genital Organization." *Standard Edition*, v.19: 140-53. London: Hogarth, 1953.]

———. *Das Ich und das Es.* Vienna: Internationaler Psychoanalytischer Verlag, 1923. [Also *Gesammelte Werke*, v.13: 237-89. London: Imago, 1940.] [Trans. *The Ego and the Id.* Translated by Joan Riviere. London: Hogarth, 1927.] [Trans. *The Ego and the Id. Standard Edition*, v.19: 3-66. London: Hogarth, 1961.] [Trans. *The Ego and the Id.* Translated by John Reddick. London: Penguin, 2003.]

———. "Die endliche und unendliche Analyse." *Internationale Zeitschrift für Psychoanalyse*, 23.2 (1937): 209-40. [Also *Gesammelte Werke*, v.16: 59-99. London: Imago, 1950.] [Trans. "Analysis Terminable and Interminable." *Standard Edition*, v.23: 211-53. London: Hogarth, 1964.]

Kammerer, P. *Das Gesetz der Serie* [The Law of Series]. Stuttgart: Deutsche Verlags-Anstalt, 1919.

Multatuli [Edward Douwes Dekker]. Ideën [Ideas]. Àmsterdam: Meijer, 1862.

Rank, Otto. "Der *Familienroman* in der Psychologie des Attentäters" [The *Family Romance* in the Psychology of the Assassin]. *Internationale Zeitschrift für ärztliche Psychoanalyse* 1 (1913): 565 ff.

———. "Der Doppelgänger." *Imago* 3 (1914): 97-104. [Trans. *The Double: A Psychoanalytic Study*. Translated by Harry Tucker. Chapel Hill: U of North Carolina P, 1971.]

Twain, Mark. *A Tramp Abroad*. London: American Publishing Company, 1880.

References: Appendix B

Blanchot, Maurice. *L'espace littéraire*. Paris: Gallimard, 1955.

Céline, Louis-Ferdinand. *L'Herne*. No. 3. 1963.

Clark, Ronald. *Freud: The Man and the Cause*. New York: Granada, 1980.

Derrida, Jacques. "The Law of Genre." *Acts of Literature*. Ed. Derek Attridge. New York: Routledge, 1992.

Dufresne, Todd. *Tales From the Freudian Crypt: The Death Drive in Text and Context*. Stanford: Stanford UP, 2000.

Ferenczi, Sándor. "Stages in the Development of the Sense of Reality." *Sex in Psychoanalysis*. Trans. E. Jones and C. Newton. New York: Dover, [1913] 1956.

———. *Thalassa: A Theory of Genitality*. Trans. H. Bunker. New York: Norton, [1924] 1968.

———. "The Problem of Acceptance of Unpleasant Ideas–Advances in Knowledge of the Sense of Reality." *Theory and Technique of Psycho-Analysis*. Comp. J. Rickman, trans. J. Suttie et. al. New York: Basic Books, [1926] 1952.

———. "The Unwelcome Child and the Death Instinct." *Final Contributions to the Problems and Methods of Psychoanalysis*. Ed. M. Balint. London: Hogarth, [1929] 1955.

Freud, Sigmund. *Beyond the Pleasure Principle*. Trans. J. Strachey. London: Hogarth Press, 1950.

———. *Beyond the Pleasure Principle*. Trans J. Strachey. New York: Liveright, 1950. [Cited as "*Beyond2*"]

———. *Civilization and Its Discontents*. Trans. J. Riviere. London: Hogarth, 1930.

———. *Collected Papers*. Ed. J. Riviere and J. Strachey. 5 Vols; No. 7–10, 37. New York: The International Psycho-Analytic Press, 1933–50.

——. *The Ego and the Id.* Trans. J. Riviere. London: Hogarth Press and the Institute of Psycho-Analysis, 1927.

——. *Inhibitions, Symptoms and Anxiety.* Trans. A. Strachey. London: Hogarth Press and the Institute of Psycho-Analysis, 1936.

——. *New Introductory Lectures on Psychoanalysis.* Trans. W.J.H. Sprott. London: Hogarth Press and the Institute of Psycho-Analysis, 1933.

——. *The Origins of Psychoanalysis: Letters to Wilhelm Fliess, Drafts and Notes: 1887–1902.* Ed. Marie Bonaparte, Anna Freud and Ernst Kris. New York: Basic Books, 1954.

——. *The Standard Edition of the Complete Psychological Works of Sigmund Freud.* Ed. James Strachey. 24 Vols. London: Hogarth Press, 1953–66.

Freud, Sigmund and Lou Andreas-Salomé. *Sigmund Freud and Lou Andreas-Salomé: Letters.* Ed. E. Pfeiffer, trans. William and Elaine Robson-Scott. London: Hogarth, 1972.

Hegel, G. W. F. *Science of Logic.* Trans. W.H. Johnson and L.G. Struthers. London: G. Allen and Unwin, 1929.

Guthrie, W. K. *Early Presocratics and the Pythagoreans.* A History of Greek Philosophy, Vol. 1. New York: Cambridge UP, 1962.

Kaufmann, Walter. *The Portable Nietzsche.* New York: Viking Press, 1954.

Kerr, John. *A Most Dangerous Method: The Story of Jung, Freud, and Sabina Spielrein.* New York: Vintage, 1993.

Keynes, John Maynard. *Essays in Persuasion.* New York: Harcourt, 1932.

Kierkegaard, Søren. *Works of Love.* Trans. D.F. Swenson and L.M. Swenson. Princeton, NJ: Princeton UP, 1946.

Klein, Melanie. *The Collected Works of Melanie Klein Volume 1 – "Love, Guilt and Reparation" and Other Works.* London: Hogarth, 1975.

Klossowski, Pierre. *Un si funeste désir.* Paris: Gallamard, 1963.

——. *La révolution de l'Edit de Nantes.* Paris: Minuit, 1959.

Kofman, Sarah. "Freud and Empedocles." *Freud and Fiction.* Trans. S. Wykes. London: Northeastern UP, [1969] 1991.

Kojève, Alexandre. *Introduction á la lecture de Hegel.* Paris: Gallimard, 1947.

Kramer, Robert. "Insights and Blindness: Visions of Rank." Introduction to *A Psychology of Difference: The American Lectures*, by Otto Rank. Princeton: Princeton UP, 1996.

Kroner, Richard. "Bemerkungen zur Dialektik der Zeit." *Verhandlungen des dritten Hegelkongress.* Rome, 1934.

Laplanche, Jean. *Life and Death in Psychoanalysis*. Trans. J. Mehlman. Baltimore: Johns Hopkins UP, [1970] 1976.

Laplanche, Jean and J.B. Pontalis. "Fantasme originaire, fantasmes des origines, origine du fantasme." *Les Temps Modernes* 215 (April), 1964.

———. *The Language of Psycho-Analysis*. Trans. D. Nicholson-Smith. New York: Norton, 1973.

Lawrence, D.H. *Aaron's Rod*. New York: Penguin, 1976.

Marcuse, Herbert. *Eros and Civilization*. London: Sphere, 1970.

———. *Reason and Revolution: Hegel and the Rise of Social Theory*. New York: Oxford UP, 1941.

Miller, Henry. *Sexus*. New York: Grove Press, 1965.

Monod, Jacques. *Chance and Necessity*. Trans. A. Wainhouse. London: Collins, 1970.

Nietzsche, Friedrich. *The Philosophy of Nietzsche*. New York: Modern Library, 1927.

———. *On the Genealogy of Morals*. Trans. Walter Kaufmann. New York: Random House, 1969.

———. *The Birth of Tragedy and The Genealogy of Morals*. Trans. F. Golffing. New York: Doubleday, 1956.

Pautrat, Bernard. "Nietzsche Medused." *Looking After Nietzsche*. Ed. Laurence Rickels.
Albany: SUNY, [1973] 1990.

Plato. "Laws." *The Collected Dialogues*. Trans. A.E. Taylor. Ed. Edith Hamilton Cairns and Huntington Cairns. New York: Pantheon, 1961.

Pontalis, J.B. "L'utopie freudienne." *L'Arc* 14 (1968): 5–14.

Rehm, W. *Orpheus: Der Dichter und die Toten*. Düsseldorf: L. Schwann, 1950.

Reich, Wilhelm. *The Function of the Organism*. Paris: Editions du Seuil, 1966.

Rey, Jean-Michel. *Parcours de Freud*. Paris: Editions Galilée, 1974.

Rimbaud, Arthur. "Letter to Paul Demeny." Unpublished correspondence. May 15, 1871.

Riviere, Joan. "On the Genesis of Psychical Conflict in Early Infancy." *Developments of Psycho-Analysis*. Ed. Melanie Klein. London: Hogarth, 1952.

Róheim, Géza. *The Origin and Function of Culture*. New York: Nervous and Mental Disease Monographs, 1943.

Satner, Eric. *On the Psychotheology of Everyday Life*. Chicago: U of Chicago P, 2001.

Schopenhauer, Arthur. *The World as Will and Idea*. Trans. R.B. Haldane and J. Kemp. London: Kegan, Paul and Trübner, 1896.

Sterba, Richard. *Reminiscences of a Viennese Psychoanalyst*. Detroit: Wayne State UP, 1982.

Sulloway, Frank. *Freud, Biologist of the Mind: Beyond the Psychoanalytic Legend*. New York: Basic Books, 1979.

Valéry, Paul. "Situation de Baudelaire." *Variété II*. Paris: Gallimard, 1948.

Webster, Richard. *Why Freud Was Wrong: Sin, Science, and Psychoanalysis*. New York: Basic Books, 1995.

Index

Eryximachus, 144, 148, 319–21

evolution (biological), 17f, 41, 67, 77ff, 80, 93, 95, 373

Ewers, Hanns, 104n2

excitation, 39, 52ff, 65–74, 98f, 119–22, 129ff, 202, 221, 223, 240f, 302, 312, 357

existentialism, 304

external world, 65, 67ff, 79, 104, 108, 116, 120, 122, 125, 127, 132, 173, 178, 182, 194, 200n1, 207, 224, 225n1, 234ff, 276, 279, 367, 369, 373

Fate, 63ff, 104ff, 118, 126f, 229, 236, 291

Faust, 46, 81, 190, 236

fear, 55, 117f, 176f, 206, 224, 230f

Fechner, Gustav von, 17, 22, 52f, 92n1, 112, 119

Federn, Paul, 23

femininity, 120f, 123, 208

feminism, 140

Ferenczi, Sándor, 17f, 20, 28, 35, 37, 56, 80n1, 139f, 369, 374

Feuerback, Ludwig, 22

Fliess, Wilhelm, 31ff, 43, 83, 280, 329

fort-da, 14, 57, 200, 216, 218, 316f, 323, 326, 340–47, 356f

freedom, 250, 254, 257, 306f, 371

free will, 104, 155n3, 345

Freud, Ernst, 57n1, 338n1, 339f, 342, 344

Freudo-Marxism, 20, 26, 140f

Freund, Anton von, 24, 27n1

fright, 55f, 71, 157f, 224

Fromm, Erich, 15, 20, 27, 140f, 275

Gasché, Rodolphe, 16, 140, 283

Gerusalemme Liberata, 64

Gestalt, 162

Glaucon, 314

God, 25, 126, 133, 147, 151f, 168, 187, 228, 230n1, 259, 304, 318, 372

gods, 104, 144f, 147, 207, 228, 245, 323, 328

Goethe, Johann Wolfgang von, 46f, 81, 133, 190, 192, 195, 215, 258n1

Goette, Alexander Wilhelm von, 84

Gomperz, Heinrich, 94n2, 315f, 352

Gomperz, Theodor, 22, 31

Guattari, Félix, 20, 140, 265

guilt, 120, 124f, 127, 135, 177, 181, 200, 203, 210, 212, 230, 269, 277, 370f

Guthrie, William Keith Chambers, 283n1

Haeckel, Ernst, 17

Halberstadt, Sophie Freud, 24, 57

happiness, 144, 155, 207, 212, 225, 250, 252, 254, 258, 275f, 368f, 371, 374

Hartmann, Eduard von, 22, 84

Hartmann, Heinz, 160, 164

hate, 90f, 109f, 180ff, 205, 209, 283f, 369

Hegel, Georg Wilhelm Friedrich, 15, 20, 141, 189–93, 197, 219, 338

Heidegger, Martin, 13, 345n1, 346

Heine, Heinrich, 104, 135, 209, 228

Hephaestus, 147, 327ff

Heraclitus, 188

Hering, Ewald, 87, 106, 292f, 295f

hermeneutics, 14, 140, 198

Hoffmann, Ernst Theodor Wilhelm, 23, 102, 104
Holder, Alex, 38, 40f
Homer, 145, 323
homosexuality, 109f, 371
Horace, Quintus Horatius, 37, 368
Hubback, C.J.M., 37, 39f, 43
Hugo, Victor, 158
humanism, 275ff, 279f
Hume, David, 22, 240
Husserl, Edmund, 346, 362, 364

id, the, 15, 22, 44f, 51n1, 107, 109–12, 116, 118, 125, 135, 159, 175, 183, 185, 201, 203f, 226, 251, 253, 306
Imago, 46, 126, 204
inheritance of acquired characteristics, 17ff, 67, *see also* Lamarck, Jean-Baptiste
intentionality, 359, 363–66

Jackson, John Hughlings, 201
Jones, Ernest, 17f, 22, 24f, 37–40, 45, 57, 231
Jung, Carl Gustav, 20, 24, 33, 46, 64n1, 89, 139, 165, 186, 269

Kammerer, Paul, 106
Kant, Immanuel, 13, 16, 22, 68, 125, 152, 291n1, 340n1
Kerr, John, 139
Keynes, John Maynard, 196
Kiell, Norman, 37
Kierkegaard, Søren, 198
King, Peter, 46
Kipling, Rudyard, 46
Klein, Melanie, 14f, 101, 139f, 175, 261, 311
Klossowski, Pierre, 245f, 267
Kofman, Sarah, 284n1

Kojève, Alexandre, 15, 191, 193, 197
Kramer, Robert, 374n1
Kroner, Richard, 191
Kultur, see civilization, culture, *and* society

Lacan, Jacques, 14f, 27, 139f, 159, 166n1, 166n2, 173n1, 263n1, 311, 353, 368, 376
Lamarck, Jean-Baptiste, 17f, 373
Lamartine, Alphonse de, 158
language: figurative, 13, 42, 96, 359; dream, 103; and truth, 153; energy, 202; structure of, 293f; ambiguity in, 362
Laplanche, Jean, 140, 260, 270n1
Lawrence, David Herbert Richards, 271
Leonardo, 216, 236f
libido, 73, 87–90, 97n1, 108, 111ff, 115f, 119, 122–26, 128, 134, 162, 165, 168, 172–79, 198, 201f, 204, 206n1, 207–10, 214f, 219, 227, 236, 243, 264f, 268, 271, 275, 278, 311f, 369, 371, 376
life drive, *see* sex drive
Lipschütz, Alexander, 84f, 91f
Loeb, Jacques, 85
Logos, 227f, 237
love: group, 28; and loss, 62ff; object-, 90f, 112, 181f, 361, 364, 367, 369; self-, 103, 369ff; and hate, 109f, 283f; and the super-ego, 118; and strife, 136, 142–48; and death, 202, 205, 211, 223f; of life, 213, 238; of fate, 229, 236; and the body, 317, 319
Low, Barbara, 92, 119, 221, 307

RECYCLED
Paper made from
recycled material
FSC® C103567

Marquis Book Printing Inc.

Québec, Canada
2011

Printed on Silva Enviro 100% post-consumer EcoLogo certified paper,
processed chlorine free and manufactured using biogas energy.

100%   PERMANENT

 11 trees

 10,714 gal. US of water
116 days of water consumption

 1,354 lbs of waste
13 waste containers

 3,520 lbs CO2
6,676 miles driven

 17 MMBTU
83,493 60W light bulbs for one hour

 10 lbs NOx
emissions of one truck during 15
days